Proposer Qualifications

[ ] **Experience:** Is company experience stated and backed up by summaries of past projects? Are current and past contracts cited? Are all relevant? Are names and telephone numbers of references supplied? Are commendation letters included? Is corporate support for project shown?

Graphics

[ ] **Graphics:** Is RFP analysis charted to show proposed functional flow? To illustrate advantages of plan? Are graphics used effectively? Are they self-explanatory? Easy to follow?

Headlines

[ ] **Headlines:** Are all major topics covered? Do all headlines sell? (Are all major selling points made subject of headlines?) Does list of headlines (Table of Contents) summarize proposal's main points, especially sales arguments?

Executive summary

[ ] **Executive Summary:** Is it brief, hard-hitting, and to the point? Does it cover main points, especially reasons to buy? Does it start with strength and build to a climax?

Strengths or Weaknesses

[ ] **Strengths:** Are all strong points turned to advantage?

[ ] **Weaknesses:** Are all weak points compensated for? (Have they all been turned around to become strengths?)

Letter of Transmittal

[ ] **Letter of Transmittal:** Is it addressed to Contracting Officer? (In content as well as in form!) Does it stress items to appeal to CO, to make CO an ally? Stipulate that signer is authorized to make offer? Period of time that offer is firm? Invite inquiries? Offer presentations, supplements, discussions, negotiations?

Response Matrix

[ ] **Response matrix:** Is one offered? Is it complete? Is it effective guide for evaluators? Does it cover all evaluation criteria?

Special Items

[ ] **Proposal introduction:** Does it begin with strength—capture attention by starting with major benefit offered or other attention getter?

[ ] **Proposal, overall:** Is it "professional" looking? Has it been carefully edited and proofed? Is it neatly reproduced? Are suitable covers provided?

[ ] **Figures:** Are all figures titled with *selling* captions—pointing out benefit to customer? Are all designed to tell their own story, without heavy reliance on text to explain?

[ ] **Résumés:** Have all résumés been carefully rewritten to present maximum staff qualifications and strength for *this* project? Do they cover each individual's past *achievements and successes in relevant work?*

[ ] **Understanding:** Is understanding of customer's needs clearly shown *throughout* proposal, not merely by lip service up front? (Do all elements of proposal—discussions, staffing, management, deliverables, schedules, reflect complete understanding?)

[ ] **Proposed offer:** If appropriate, does proposal offer to go *beyond* customer's own statement, to demonstrate real effort to think out problems and needs, and to offer sound solutions?

The Winning Proposal

How to Write It

Business Communications Series

Consulting Editor
Arthur H. Kuriloff, Management Consultant

Holtz and Schmidt **The Winning Proposal . . . How to Write It**
Monroe **Effective Research and Report Writing in Government**
Monroe and Fisher **A Short Course in Effective Research and Report Writing in Government**

In memory of my parents, David and Anna Holtz, who inspired me to use whatever talents I had for worthy accomplishments.

Herman Holtz

To my parents, William and Florence Schmidt, for the understanding, patience, and support they lovingly provide.

Terry Schmidt

Contents

The Winning Proposal . . . How to Write It

567890DODO898

This book was set in Caledonia by Black Dot, Inc. (ECU). The editors were Donald W. Burden and Frances A. Neal; the design was done by Caliber Design Planning; the production supervisor was Charles Hess. The cartoons were done by Caliber Design Planning; the drawings were done by J & R Services, Inc.
R. R. Donnelley & Sons Company was printer and binder.

Library of Congress Cataloging in Publication Data

Holtz, Herman.
    The winning proposal . . . how to write it.

    (Business communications series)
    Includes index.
    1.   Proposal writing in business.   2.   Government purchasing—United States.   3.   Public contracts—United States.   I.   Schmidt, Terry, joint author.   II.   Title.
    HF5718.5.H64   808'.066658021   80-29373
    ISBN 0-07-029649-9

The Winning Proposal

How to Write It

Herman Holtz
Terry Schmidt

McGraw-Hill Book Company
New York St. Louis San Francisco Auckland Bogotá Hamburg
London Madrid Mexico Montreal New Delhi
Panama Paris São Paulo Singapore Sydney Tokyo Toronto

Foreword

As a former Commissioner of the Federal Supply Service and, currently, the president of a small consulting firm based in Washington, D.C., and oriented toward federal government marketing, I have been in a position both to review proposals in response to negotiated government procurements and to prepare and submit proposals in response to federal government requirements. Further, in my present capacity I have had firsthand experience in working with firms that were actively engaged in projects and encountered problems in the preaward phase of interpreting government requirements as well as in the offer phase of preparing technical proposals.

From the vantage point of an appointed federal government executive in charge of an agency whose responsibilities encompassed the acquisition of products and services for governmentwide use, I wholeheartedly concur with the premise, findings, and conclusions expressed in this new book, written by Herman Holtz and Terry Schmidt, *The Winning Proposal . . . How to Write It.* In the final analysis, the art of "proposalmanship," as coined by Herman Holtz, is nothing more than the skillful writing of a sales presentation. In every good sales presentation, the problem (expressed in this instance by the federal government) must be addressed, but more importantly, the problem must be addressed in a manner which convinces the government that the offeror is knowledgeable, resourceful, and innovative in terms of the techniques to be applied in solving the problem. In other words, the burden placed upon one is to submit a proposal which will convince the government that the offeror alone possesses the unique set of characteristics and traits needed to accomplish the tasks contained in the scope of the work. Acquisition of the skills to write a good proposal, therefore, marks the difference between the offeror who is successful and the offerors who "spin their wheels" through failure to recognize a proposal for what it is—the selling of one's capabilities to the federal government.

How important is this art associated with writing a good proposal? In order to provide some perspective on the importance of proposals and "proposalmanship," one need only consider the fact that the federal government is second to none in terms of its impact on the general economy. Total expenditures to acquire goods and services are well over $100 billion each year. The question then arises: How does the government contract for goods and services? Simple analysis of the contractual methods employed by the federal government discloses that approximately 85 percent of the procurement dollars spent in any fiscal year are expended through negotiated procurement.

Utilizing this method of procurement, the government will define the tasks to be accomplished and request potential offerors to submit, under separate cover, a technical proposal and a cost proposal. The design of this technical proposal and the art of writing a winning proposal are presented in *The Winning Proposal . . . How to Write It.*

The ability to sell one's capabilities through the proposal mechanism, it can readily be seen, is one of the most critical factors in successfully doing business with many of the departments and agencies comprising the federal government. As Commissioner of the Federal Supply Service, I saw many of the problems detailed in this book. I was afforded, as the head of that agency, many opportunities to review proposals supposedly addressing problems confronting not only the Federal Supply Service but the governmentwide procurement system. The primary fault found in the majority of proposals submitted by offerors was a failure to convince me and my support personnel that the offeror had the experience, knowledge, and capability to cope with the problems and the scope of work as defined in the request for proposal. Simply stated, offerors failed to sell their capabilities as being both unique and, at the same time, affordable.

In this book, the authors address the commonplace problems associated with "proposalmanship" in a manner which will assist offerors in winning government contracts. It is not an exercise in theory—it is the model of practicability drawn from Herman Holtz's long and successful winning career! This step-by-step approach to writing a winning proposal should be widely circulated and read by contracting officers as well as by executives of large and small business firms who intend to pursue federal government contracts. I congratulate Herman Holtz and Terry Schmidt on a professional effort deserving of success.

Michael J. Timbers, *President*
Washington Management Group, Inc.
Washington, D.C.

These are usually *minimum* requirements to qualify a proposer as a serious contender for the contract. Of themselves, even these are rarely sufficient to actually *win* the contract. Something more is usually needed.

It is that "something more" which is the main focus of this book.

Who Can Benefit from This Book

The major purpose of this book is to furnish guidance in techniques and methods for developing winning proposals for United States government contracts. Yet, those who compete for federal contracts are not the only ones who can benefit from this book; the information will be of great value to many other readers.

The federal government has always required formal proposals, proposals which must furnish a great deal of information about the proposer and the proposer's qualifications—formal *presentations*, in fact, which must *sell*. On the other hand, proposals to local and state governments and commercial proposals have been little more than price quotations, with specifications and contract terms.

But that is changing as greater numbers of organizations adopt the federal plan and require formal proposals. Moreover, the techniques and methods offered here have proved highly successful in responding to the "tenders" and proposal requests of foreign governments, which in turn are becoming more accustomed to receiving proposals similar to those offered the United States government.

In addition to those considerations, there is help here for anyone who wishes guidance in methods for developing a basic idea into a complete plan. A great many people are inspired with new ideas, but most are unable to carry the idea forward from its conception. This book teaches methods that will be helpful to anyone who wishes to develop creative imagination and learn how to turn basic ideas into practical plans for action.

Herman Holtz
Terry Schmidt

1

What Is a Winning Proposal?

Only a short answer is provided in this chapter. The full answer will become apparent gradually, as you read on and study the messages.

Those involved in contracting talk of "writing proposals," and many seminars in proposal writing are offered each year. The implication seems to be that writing the *winning* proposal is a matter of being the best writer. Yet the winning proposal is rarely that proposal which is the best written—at least in the sense of the greatest skill in use of the written language or style of expression. Something more than writing must be involved.

In fact, before we can answer the question "What is a winning proposal?" we have to answer the question "What is a proposal?" The answers to both these questions are far less obvious than they might appear to be. In fact, since knowing what a proposal is and knowing what a *winning* proposal is are almost tantamount to knowing how to write the winning proposal, this entire book is devoted to the purpose of answering these questions. This chapter provides some beginning answers—definitions, in fact—but a complete answer to the second question ("What is a winning proposal?") requires all the remaining chapters.

What Is a Proposal?

Until the federal government became a major buyer of almost everything the industrial, commercial, and professional portions of the private sector could provide, the term *proposal* meant little more than the word "bid." The prospective customer, seeking a contractor to build a bridge or launch a major advertising campaign, issued a set of specifications, detailing what was to be done as precisely as the customer could define the desired results, and requested proposals. The competing contractors submitted their responses. Usually, these contained an agreement to comply with all specifications, offered a price, and listed the contract terms and conditions required by the contractor. Such proposals might or might not have been accompanied by a brochure or other advertising literature of the contractor.

Some contractors made a practice of responding in this manner to a large number of solicitations, doing little else to pursue contracts. They played the percentages, on the assumption that if they won even a tiny percentage of the contracts so bid on, they would have ample business. (Mathematical probability would work for them, if they submitted enough bids.) Other contractors were much more selective in their choice of projects to bid for, (1) having their marketing representatives talk to the prospective customers, (2) doing enough research to identify those projects for which they believed their chances of success were better than average, and (3) relying on marketing effort that went beyond the bid alone—e.g., the personal sales efforts of marketing representatives.

These conditions still exist in a large proportion of what might be termed "commercial proposals." Many are little more than bids, and customers do not require more when they request proposals. However, this is not the case when submitting a proposal to a federal agency, and the practices and requirements there are gradually influencing the preparation of proposals to state and local governments and to companies in the private sector.

Proposals to federal agencies are necessarily far different and far more complicated to write because a great deal more information is required than in the case of commercial proposals. This is not arbitrary but is the result of requirements set forth in the various procurement regulations of the federal government.

The Procurement Regulations

Prior to World War II, the United States government was not an especially important customer for anything other than a relatively small quantity of military goods and office necessities. Of course, World War II mobilization of both military and civilian forces and government agencies changed that: as is the case with every war, the federal government necessarily bought huge quantities of many kinds of goods and services.

The difference between this war and others, however, was this: Despite rapid demobilization and dissolution of many wartime civilian agencies, after the war had ended, the government found it necessary to continue and even expand the research and development of modern weapons systems. Moreover, a "weapon" or "weapons system" no longer meant a gun or tank; it included such sophisticated devices as computers, missiles and their launchers, radar, communications systems, and ultimately, even space satellites and observation systems. And since a large defense budget and extensive government buying now appeared to have become permanent features of government, the first formal set of procurement regulations appeared: the Armed Services Procurement Regulations (ASPR; pronounced, commonly, "asper"). And shortly thereafter, the Federal Procurement Regulations (FPR), based on ASPR but for nonmilitary procurement, followed. (And still others, such as NASA's NASPR, have followed those.)

The expectation in writing those first sets of procurement regulations was that most procurement would be of standard commercial goods and services which could be specified in great detail, even if modified slightly to meet military conditions. Therefore, it was anticipated that the chief consideration in selecting contractors would be price—that is, the contract would usually be awarded to the lowest bidder. However, the drafters of those procurement regulations recognized that it would not always be possible to specify the desired product or service precisely, especially where research and development were required to produce the end product, such as in the case of developing a new jet fighter. Therefore, the regulations made provision for awarding contracts on some basis other than that of low bid. That is, the regulations permitted *negotiated* procurement, rather than *formally advertised* procurement, in which the government was legally authorized to select that contractor whom it thought most competent to produce the best result and negotiate an acceptable contract with that contractor.

To expand on this a bit further, let's consider a typical situation. An agency of the Department of Defense finds that its radar equipment is aging and becoming obsolete—perhaps the scientific literature indicates clearly that better radar is now possible, or the agency discovers that the Soviet Union has developed radar superior to our own. Or, as in many cases, an agency discovers that the Soviet Union has developed a new missile or aircraft against which our radar detection is now inadequate. It is essential to improve our radar, to *find* some way of improving it so that it can cope successfully with this new missile or aircraft.

Accordingly, the military agency prepares information describing what a new and improved radar set must be able to *do* to cope successfully with this new challenge, and invites private sector aerospace firms to submit proposals. A great many proposals are received, some from well-known companies, others from new or little-known companies. The agency now has the problem of trying to determine which of these is best qualified to produce what is needed. A "bad" contract—one which results in an aborted or unsuccessful effort—has far more disastrous consequences than a waste of money: it means a serious lag in time and weakness in our national defense capabilities. It is quite essential that the agency make a good selection—select a firm which can and will produce the result called for.

In such a case, price becomes a secondary consideration. Selecting a contractor because of a low bid, without regard to whether the contractor can deliver what is required, is an exercise in futility. The first consideration is to select that contractor most likely to deliver the result or most likely to deliver the best result. (Sometimes the research and development, in capable hands, produces a result far better than anyone thought possible in the beginning.)

Negotiated procurement—procurement in which judgment of the bidder's technical and professional qualifications takes precedence over price—is clearly justified, both legally and morally. But what has happened is this: Instead of being the exception to the rule, negotiated procurement *is* the rule, accounting for some 85 percent of all federal procurement dollars. Nor is this new "rule" confined to military procurement; it prevails in all federal procurement.

Keeping the Game Honest

The drafters of procurement regulations recognize that a procurement system which permits agencies to select a contractor on the basis of judgment, rather than the hard and fixed standard of low price, has within it the possibility for corruption. Therefore, there are numerous statutory controls built into the procurement regulations, and into federal policies and procedures for procurement, to minimize the possibilities for wrongdoing in making contract awards. It would be naive to believe that all federal procurement is simon-pure, with no questionable contract awards. But at the same time, there is little doubt that it is among the cleanest government procurement systems in the world, with corruption far more the exception than the rule. There are many statutory safeguards, including administrative appeals and legal processes to protest awards considered to be improper or illegal. These various safeguards will become more and more apparent as we explore the activities involved in developing the winning proposal, offering many case histories to illustrate the points clearly.

The Proliferation of Federal Procurement Methods

A number of factors have caused the gradual emulation of federal procurement methods by state and local governments, by firms in the private sector of American business, and even by foreign governments and foreign firms. One such influence has been the general effect of increasing numbers of people throughout the world becoming familiar with United States government procurement methods. (For example, United States government procurement is not confined to the United States; many contracts are awarded to foreign governments and foreign firms.)

Another has been the impact of federal requirements for subcontracting. Many federal contracts are so huge that the contractor must seek the support of a great many other firms to help do the job. For example, the first billion-dollar contract in our history was awarded to RCA to design, build, and install the Ballistic Missile Early Warning System (BMEWS) in Greenland, Alaska, and England. RCA awarded over 300 subcontracts, at a cost totaling approximately two-thirds of the dollars involved in the primary contract. When such large projects and such large sums of money are involved, the government is well aware that there will be many subcontracts awarded, and requires the prime contractor to exercise approximately the same control over subcontract awards as the government has exercised over the prime contract award. As a certain way of complying with federal regulations, therefore, major prime contractors tend simply to apply the same principles to those firms bidding for the subcontracts.

State and local governments receive a large percentage of their funds today from federal largesse, in the form of revenue sharing and grants of many kinds. Each of these programs of aid to state and local governments has its own set of regulations, according to the federal statutes authorizing and establishing the program. In some cases, there are virtually no strings attached, and the recipients are free to spend the money as they will; in others, there are stringent requirements governing how the funds may be spent. Therefore, many state and local governments are emulating the federal systems of procurement.

And finally, many contractors already familiar with the United States government procurement system find it effective to use the same proposal-writing practices with foreign governments, with state and local governments, and with private firms, whether such elaborate proposals are required or not. The examples set by these firms have tended to influence the requirements of these other buyers in the solicitation of proposals.

The General Application of the Methods Presented Here

As a result of all these factors, there is much to be gained by using the methods required by federal agencies in preparing proposals to all other prospective customers, despite the fact that such proposal responses exceed the requirements of many of these other customers; in virtually no case will a proposal so prepared fall short of anyone's requirement. Therefore, while this book is written with proposals to the United States government in mind, everything advocated will apply well to any proposal-writing requirement.

The Major Difference

Aside from what the customer has requested that a proposer supply in a proposal response, the sole major difference between procurement by a government agency and a private sector firm is this: the government agency is required by statute to request certain things and pursue certain procedures in selecting a winning proposal and making a contract award. The private sector firm has no such statutory requirements, but is free to award a contract to anyone desired for any reason. And, of course, a foreign government is controlled in its procurement by its own laws and procurement regulations, whatever they may be. Therefore, in proposing to any government, the proposer ought to be well acquainted with the laws governing the procurement and proposal presentation; in proposing to a firm in the private sector, the proposer ought to bring to bear all the marketing and sales skills it is able to muster.

Let's translate this difference into the more practical aspects of proposal writing—what it means in *required* proposal content. The sole justification for negotiated procurement by federal agencies is that price is of secondary importance in many cases, while technical or professional competence and record of accomplishment are of primary importance. This, of course, makes it essential that those who review and judge the proposals submitted have some objective means for evaluating the proposer's competence and track record.

And to be truly objective, the customer must not be unduly influenced by such factors as the general reputation or size of the company. It becomes necessary then to require that the proposer explain the qualifications of the organization—that the proposer present credentials.

Commercial customers, under no legal obligation to decide which proposer is most competent, have not in the past ordinarily required such evidence or information. Instead, they *assume* that anyone proposing or bidding for the project is capable. Obviously, while such credentials are not always required by firms requesting proposals, it can do no harm and may help materially to include those credentials in any proposal submitted.

Therefore, throughout this book, discussions, explanations, and methods will be offered with specific reference to proposals to the federal government. However, everything said will apply with equal validity to proposals submitted to any other customer: state, local, or foreign government; domestic or foreign firm; and domestic or foreign association or organization of any kind, for-profit or not-for-profit.

Once Again, What Is a Proposal?

Lecturers at proposal-writing seminars have been heard to define the proposal as "a contractual document." That is meant to be cautionary, a reminder to the listener that the proposer is firmly bound contractually by what has been written in the proposal. It's a warning to be careful of what is promised, for fear that promises made to get the contract will result in problems later. In one sense, this is more true for commercial proposals than it is for government proposals for this reason: A no-nonsense, profit-oriented customer (i.e., a business firm) is likely to hold you to the exact letter of the contract, making no allowances whatsoever for any carelessness on your part. A government official is, in many cases, far more lenient and tolerant in accommodating your mistakes, especially if you are new to government contracting or have an excellent record of past performance and good contract administration. Of course, you should not be careless in stating your terms and defining exactly what you propose to do and what it will cost, but for this reason you should be especially careful in proposing to private sector firms. Relatively few government contractors wind up in federal courts suing or being sued by the federal government, although suits between customers and contractors in the private sector are relatively common.

At the same time, there is a special factor bearing on this truth: most contracts with the federal government follow well-established procedures and fall into standard patterns, with only minor differences among them. Contracting with the federal government continually, one learns soon enough what to expect in most cases. That itself, however, can lead to careless, sometimes costly, mistakes. Some federal contracting officials can be as tough as private sector executives are when it comes to enforcing contracts to the letter.

There are those who hold that most, if not all, proposals are pro forma documents, serving merely to satisfy the law by going through the motions of compliance with procurement regulations, but actually having little effect on the award decision. There are, for example, those marketing representatives—the sales employees of the companies—who insist that 99 percent of the credit for winning a contract is due to their efforts alone, rather than the excellence of the proposal.

The attitude is understandable: everyone wishes to believe that his or her own work and effort is the most important and most essential to the company. Marketing representatives, therefore, have little difficulty persuading themselves that personal charm and salesmanship are the true decisive factors. At least one such marketing representative in Washington, D.C., insists that the customer specify what to write in the proposal. In fact, this representative goes even further, refusing flatly to write or request the writing of a proposal *until* the customer has prescribed exactly what is to be said in the proposal! But this is not unique: the same thing has been said many times in many ways by others.

Another cause of such beliefs is the rationalization of those who are uncommonly unsuccessful in preparing proposals that win contracts. Either unable to write winning proposals or unwilling to make the effort required to do so, and equally reluctant or unable to face the facts of their own proposal-writing shortcomings, they rely on such a myth to help them explain away their failures.

As in the case of most myths, there is a modicum of truth in this one. There are indeed some isolated cases where a firm is "wired in" for a contract, which means that it is so highly favored that no other firm has a very good chance of competing successfully. However, such cases are much more the exception than the rule. Moreover, even in such cases, the favored firm must submit a proposal, and the proposal must be at least as good as the best of the others submitted. In more than one case, a favored firm in these circumstances has become overconfident and careless, ultimately losing the contract it was so sure of getting to a competitor that had submitted a superior proposal.

Even in the case of unsolicited proposals and sole-source awards, where there are no competitors, an acceptable proposal is required.

In short, there is no escaping the fact that proposals are a key element in winning contracts, despite any differences of opinion over *how* important a role the proposal plays in any contract-award decision.

To provide a short answer to the question of what a proposal is, then, we can say the following:

• It is a *bid* for a contract, supported by an array of credentials which attempt to convince the customer that the proposer is the best qualified bidder or proposer to achieve the results the customer wants to achieve.

- It is an *offer* to provide some specified goods or services, explaining the terms, the costs, and the suitability to satisfy the customer's needs.
- It is an attempt, in writing, to *persuade* the customer to select the proposer for the award—a *sales presentation.*

It is *not* a "contractual document." Here is why:

In most cases, the successful proposal *becomes* a contractual document, included in the contract by reference—that is, those portions of the proposal which make specific promises to perform certain functions, provide services, or deliver end products and state prices are incorporated in the contract when and if the customer *accepts* the offer and issues a contract *based* on the offer. But at that point, the proposal ceases to *be* a proposal! It has now become part of a contract. While it is being developed, reviewed, evaluated, and discussed, it is by definition still a proposal.

Is this a nit-picking distinction? Does it make any real difference? Are we playing games with semantics? Our answer to those questions is *no.* The distinction is important because we must bear in mind at all times in developing a proposal that it is essentially a sales presentation or there would be no purpose in developing and offering it. This doesn't detract from the caution to specify and promise only what the proposer wishes to incorporate in a firm contract; that's sound advice. But it does tend to make you "take your eye off the ball" if you concentrate on a contractual document, rather than on a sales presentation.

You read earlier about why the procurement regulations authorize a method called negotiated procurement. Proposals are requested in order to initiate and implement this process of negotiating a contract with whoever appears to be the best prospective contractor. But to gain a better understanding of all the causes behind and conditions underlying the whole system of procurement, let's have a look at the federal establishment and the conditions under which it operates the giant bureaucracy that it has become. And bear in mind, as we do this, that "the government" is people—*them,* not *it*—from the Chief Executive down to the rank-and-file office workers, technicians, and other federal employees—some 2.8 million of *them.* It is *people* with whom you have to deal, to whom you must sell, and with whom you must finally negotiate.

Why Do Federal Agencies Request Proposals?

Every government agency—and there are thousands of federal organizations that have buying power (procurement authority)—has its own mission and sets of objectives. The Office of Personnel Management (OPM), formerly the Civil Service Commission, has a training department with six branches. Each of these branches develops and presents training programs within its own purview—data processing, office procedures, management, and others. The Department of Transportation (DOT) includes the National Highway Transportation Safety Administration, the Federal Railroad Administration, the Urban Mass Transit Administration, and other such bureaus within the Department. The Department of Defense (DOD) includes all the military services and all the branches of each military service. Most of these agencies need help from private sector contractors to carry out their missions. They need this help for at least three reasons:

1. Federal agencies rarely have enough staff of their own to operate their computers, conduct all their own studies, develop all their publications, and carry out all the other functions and duties required of them.
2. Federal agencies rarely have enough physical facilities to do all their own work. Those with computers often find that they have overloads of work, more than they can handle in house. The military need private sector help to develop new equipment, despite the arsenals and laboratories operated by the services.
3. Federal agencies often do not have the specific knowledge required to complete their missions. Out of the mainstream of developing technology and social programs themselves, they necessarily turn to those who are engaged daily in the art.

There are two circumstances under which such needs arise in federal agencies:

1. The needs are ongoing, with the needs of the agency perpetually exceeding in-house capability.
2. The needs are temporarily in excess of in-house capacity, as a result of new programs, reorganization, or other special circumstances.

To illustrate the first case, take the example of the dozens of in-house computers in federal agencies, especially in Washington, D.C. The majority of such installations require permanent *facilities management* contractors, whose staffs work directly on government premises, operating and programming the computers.

As another example of such needs, we could turn to the Minority Business Development Agency of the Commerce Department (formerly the Office of Minority Business Enterprise in Commerce). The central office of this agency merely administers the $50 million program, which is actually implemented and carried out by some 300 contracting organizations throughout the United States.

On the other hand, when Congress created the Pension Benefit Guaranty Corporation, that organization had to start from the ground up, with temporary staff borrowed from various other agencies, and, initially, with contractor help.

In all cases, the agency has a problem to solve, and is forced to turn to "contracting out" for a solution. The success of the agency in meeting objectives and carrying out its mission depends on getting a satisfactory contractor. The request for proposals (RFP) may be regarded as an offer to award a profitable contract, when the contract is for some fairly routine set of services, such as computer operation. However, in a great many cases, the RFP is actually a *plea for help* by an agency with pressing problems and great need for assistance.

This is the point that so often escapes proposal writers. Take the case of a Job Corps executive a few years ago, as an example. This individual had the idea of utilizing mobile training facilities in such skills as welding. His idea was to have such training facilities tour the Job Corps centers, rather than transferring the Job Corps members to the centers offering the training that they had opted for. He had studied the proposition and was convinced that it was well worth trying. He had placed his request for approximately $1 million to install such a system experimentally.

His superior was not hostile to the idea, but he said that he had to have some kind of backup—documentation to support the expenditure of $1 million. The executive's hunch was not enough to justify the approval of $1 million.

Thereupon, the executive set about finding a contractor who could conduct the necessary study within 30 days or so. It was a difficult assignment, and he had a great deal of trouble finding a contractor to accept the challenge. He needed—badly—a contractor who was both qualified to carry out the study and willing to undertake a crash program to do it. Nothing in the proposal he requested was quite so important as the assurance that the job would be completed in time.

So the reason an agency issues an RFP, seeking proposals, is always because *they need help*. They may not be unduly concerned about the urgency or difficulty of the project, for it may be a routine kind of project. Or they may be quite concerned, for it may be a most difficult project. But in both cases, the purpose of the RFP is to get help. And the proposals must, of course, offer help, of the right kind and on a timely basis.

What the Agency Expects (Wants) to Find in the Proposal

The nightmare of a purchasing agent in industry is that some supplier— probably the one supplying the most critical item—will fail to deliver or will deliver unacceptable items. Hardly anything could represent a greater catastrophe or a greater failure of the purchasing function. Price is suddenly relatively unimportant. The experienced commercial buyer is well aware that few characteristics of suppliers are more important than dependability and is therefore somewhat inclined to buy from known suppliers—suppliers of demonstrated dependability—even when a new supplier offers lower prices.

Government procurement people are not different in that respect. They, too, want the peace of mind that comes of contracting with suppliers of known dependability. Or of known competence, when that is the prime consideration.

One contracting officer puts it thus: "My job is to get the best results possible, in the shortest time possible, at the best price possible." Note the sequence of priorities, price being the last.

Those issuing an RFP and evaluating proposals received in response to the RFP want to have a sense of security in their selection of a winner. They want to feel confidence in the proposer's ability and sincerity. And they want to feel that they have paid a *reasonable* price—that the contract represents good value.

There are four major factors involved in most proposal evaluations. First, the three areas of concern about the technical proposal, then the cost considerations:

1. The proposer fully *understands* the customer's needs and problems.
2. The proposer *knows how* to satisfy the needs or solve the problems and *offers a suitable plan or program* for the purpose.
3. The proposer is *well qualified,* by virtue of experience and resources— *including qualified personnel—to carry out the proposed plan or program.*
4. The price asked is reasonable for the program and results promised, and is entirely compatible with the program described—overall, the proposal represents a good value and is within the agency's budget.

These are the things the agency wants to find in proposals. The agency ordinarily intends to select that proposal which best meets these objectives and award the contract to that proposer.

The agency is not playing guessing games. Not ordinarily. It is true—let us not be so naive as to pretend that it is not—that some contracts are wired. Sometimes an agency deliberately withholds critically important information to give some favored contractor an edge. (The favored contractor is one who knows more than the others, and so is not impoverished by having some information withheld from the RFP.) But this is the exceptional case, not the general one. And even in such cases, wiring cannot be 100 percent effective: even wired contracts often go to others than those for whom they were intended, to the dismay of the agency.

In the usual case, the RFP has provided all the information the agency has on the subject. If it is sparse in details, it may be because of poor writing by the agency staff, but it is more often a reflection of what the agency knows about its own needs and problems. In fact, it illustrates why the agency needs help.

Can the agency tell you what to put in your proposal—write it for you, in effect? Hardly. Giving any proposer information not provided to all is a most dangerous game for government officials, and extremely few would attempt to play it. Later, we will discuss how to get more information without tipping off the competition. But rest assured that most agencies are entirely circumspect in honoring the obligation to treat all proposers equally in the matter of information they need to prepare their proposals. You will see the evidence for this.

staffs of specialists in proposal writing. Smaller organizations are compelled to rely on improvised proposal teams, assembled when a proposal is to be written and usually consisting of those who can be freed from regular duties without regard to proposal-writing experience or special qualifications. It is, therefore, no wonder that about two-thirds of all proposals written do not survive even preliminary evaluations by the federal agencies.

The Art of Writing Proposals

Proposal writing is something of an art, admittedly. But even art is based in methodology, and there are methods which are used successfully by many companies, large and small, to develop successful—winning—proposals. Relying on pure instinct in proposal writing is the fatal error for many. And it is this failure to write proposals that win contracts which has given rise to many of the myths—for example, the claim that most contracts are "arranged" between the agency and the contractor rather than won competitively as a result of writing a superior proposal.

There are three main phases in proposal development:

1. Analysis of the customer's stated requirements to gain full understanding of the need and the problems.
2. Formulation of an approach or preliminary program design and strategies for capturing the contract.
3. Implementation of the approach or design—actual writing of the proposal.

Proposal writing is actually only one part of the function. The writing itself is the final act in a process which includes numerous other functions. That is, what is referred to here and elsewhere as "proposal writing" incorporates several sets of methodologies and functions. Failure to recognize this probably accounts for many of the unsuccessful proposal efforts. Far too many proposal writers plunge directly and abruptly into writing with only a single, often cursory, reading of the solicitation and instructions.

Study of how federal agencies generally evaluate proposals to select the best one and negotiate contracts points to these factors as critical in most such evaluations:

1. Clear evidence that the proposer fully understands the requirements of the customer.
2. An approach which appears technically sound, achievable within the constraints explained by the customer, and offered in enough detail to provide convincing evidence of these characteristics.
3. Clear evidence that the proposer can carry out the proposed program effectively—qualified staff, capable management, and experienced organization.

Preface

The Need for Writing Proposals

Incredibly, no one knows just how much the United States government spends for goods and services every year. Budget figures are published for such items as interest on public debt, Social Security payments, and many other fixed expenses and long-term commitments. But the thousands of government offices go into the public marketplace every year to buy an unlimited variety of goods and services to meet spontaneous wants—from go-go dancing to rental of mules, from bumper stickers to high-speed aircraft, from grocery bagging to aerial scattering of sterilized screwworm flies, from computer programming to census taking. How much goes for such procurements? Official estimates vary as widely as do estimates from private sources, but all agree that the figure has now reached at least $100 billion annually, and it is almost certainly far in excess of that. In all probability, such spontaneous buying represents at least 25 percent of the budget. Government "buyers"—contracting officials and their staffs—currently number over 130,000. That is, about 5 out of every 100 federal employees are engaged full-time in making and managing procurements—government contracts. But several times that number of federal employees are "program people," who conceive and request the procurements and who manage the work done under those contracts.

In short, government contracting is big business, representing a significant portion of the gross national product. Some 250,000 of America's 13 million businesses—roughly 2 percent—do at least part of their business with federal agencies, and many do all their business with those agencies.

Some federal buying is done through competitive bidding, seeking the lowest price, but that amounts to only about 15 percent of government buying. About 85 percent of all federal procurement is accomplished via "negotiated procurement." In practical terms, this means that firms will be invited to write and submit proposals, the agency will evaluate those proposals, and the agency will conduct negotiations with one or a few of those selected as a result of proposal evaluation.

In short, proposal writing is an essential art for those pursuing government business seriously. It is, in fact, survival for those firms which do little else than government contracting.

The very large corporations which do a great deal of government contracting—often multimillion-dollar projects—usually maintain permanent

What Makes a Proposal a Winner?

The principles laid down in this introduction furnish the entire reference framework for this book. There is recognition that no system is perfect: even this system has its inequalities and irregularities. But, for the most part, it is honest and efficient, giving all an equal opportunity, based on merit. And that is the real point: Most contract awards do go to those offering the most meritorious proposals.

Note that carefully: "to those offering the most meritorious *proposals,*" not necessarily to the most meritorious companies. Those companies which lead the field in winning government contracts may or may not be the most capable companies in their technical or professional fields, but they are among the most capable companies in writing proposals. Case histories to be presented in these pages will illustrate this most clearly.

The overall goal of this book is, therefore, to present information which will help you to write the *winning* proposal—not just any proposal, but the winning one. And that means that the winning proposal must have this one distinguishing characteristic: It must persuade the reader that it is the best proposal, offered by the best organization for the job.

The chief editor on the RCA BMEWS project used to admonish the technical writers that it is not enough to write so that you can be understood; you must write so that you cannot be *mis*understood. Adapting this principle to proposal writing, the message is that it is not enough to prove that your organization can do the job; you must prove that your organization can do the job better than anyone else.

If there is one most common mistake that newcomers to the proposal-writing field make, it is the mistake of showing that their organizations can do the proposed job well, but failing to make a *better showing* than competitors do.

And that is, to a large extent, the essence of successful proposal writing; proposals must present, describe, communicate, and explain, but, above all, they must *persuade.* The best of plans and programs must be *sold;* they do not sell themselves.

This does not mean that a good proposal is an exercise in making a high-pressure sales pitch. Not for a moment. The customers are intelligent and perceptive. They know, at least generally, what they want, and they will usually detect and be "turned off" by pomposity, obfuscation, superlatives, and grand but unsupported promises. They will generally detect and swiftly reject hastily assembled plans and programs which do not go to the heart of their problems and demonstrate effectiveness in satisfying their needs. You must therefore do a serious study of the customer's needs, as explained in the RFP, and develop well-thought-out plans and programs that will do the job. But you must also *provide the evidence* that these are the best plans and programs, and that you are the best organization to implement them. *That* is what proposal writing is all about.

What Is to Come

In the pages to follow, there will be presented a great deal of information and many suggestions for ways to accomplish these two ends—developing the best plans and programs and selling them to the customer. One key topic is going to be that of strategy—the capture strategy upon which your entire proposal ought to be based, including technical or program strategies, cost strategies, and presentation strategies. You'll also learn many successful techniques for turning liabilities into assets, avoiding the most common proposal faults, protecting your own proprietary ideas, getting special attention, ensuring a high technical score, using the Freedom of Information Act effectively, combating competition, and getting the contracting officer's support for your proposal, as well as many other tips and ideas gained through experience.

More and more you will come to understand that there are several specific skills involved in writing any proposal, but especially in writing the winning proposal. And it will occur to you, if it has not already, that there is no special mystique in proposal writing. Writing winning proposals is the application of these certain skills:

Painstaking and thoughtful analysis
Efficient and effective design
Salesmanship
Skill in writing persuasively

You may already have all these skills. If so, it is our intention to show you how to bring them all to bear, in a concerted and integrated effort, to create winning proposals. If you lack one or more of them, we hope to make you aware of your need for them and to help you begin to develop them. They're useful in most other callings as well as in proposal writing.

Some Main Points to Remember

1. A proposal is a sales presentation. Its sole purpose is to make the customer an offer and to sell it to the customer to win the contract.
2. Federal agencies, and other customers, ask for proposals because they need help. But they need properly qualified help, and what you offer—propose— and what you present as your credentials are weighed carefully to judge your qualifications for the job.

3. No matter what you may have heard elsewhere, the proposal is a most important element in winning the contract. No federal agency executives are going to risk the success of their programs by accepting a poor proposal.

4. There is more—far more—to writing the winning proposal than writing itself. Writing is the last act of a three-act process, in which the first act is to take steps to ensure that you know what the customer wants. In fact, one of the prime concerns is just that, and the customer specifically reviews your proposal to determine whether you do indeed understand the need.

2

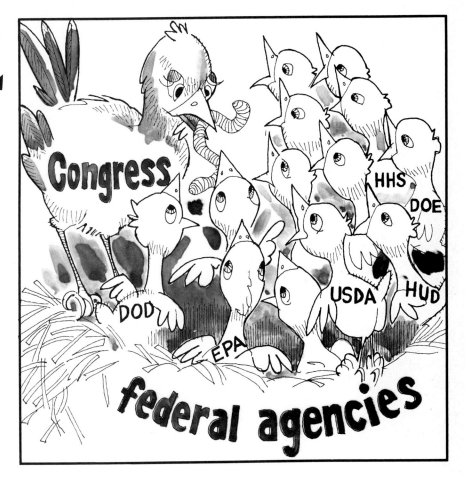

Where and How It Begins

Procurements are born as "wants" or "needs," but the causes for wants or needs are many.

The Problem of the Budget

Overall, the United States government spends money as though there were a bottomless pot of it. Or so it appears. The late Senator Everett Dirksen of Illinois was reported frequently to have observed, "A billion here and a billion there, and pretty soon we're talking about real money!"

The United States government, however, is divided into thirteen departments, over sixty independent agencies, and a number of quasi-official organizations. Most of these have regional offices, one in each of the ten federal regions, and many of them have far more than ten other offices scattered around the United States.

However, many of these agencies are subdivided into numerous bureaus, and these have other offices.

In addition to that, there are numerous military bases and military facilities in the United States, as well as Coast Guard stations, training institutions, and various other facilities.

That huge, multibillion-dollar budget that Congress appropriates each year filters down ultimately to these thousands of federal bureaus, each with its own budget. Each executive in the government must fight a personal, internal battle of the budget.

Each year, those thousands of offices and bureaus prepare their own budget requests to be compiled by major entities (departments and independent agencies) and presented to Congress in their various budget hearings. And when the major entity finally gets its money authorized—sometimes by October 1, the date it should be approved, but often much later than that—it distributes the funds among the various bureaus which make it up. Each such bureau or office may therefore wind up with what it asked for or it may wind up with less. And sometimes it winds up with more and has an embarrassment of riches.

This can lead to a wide variety of procurement situations. Any given agency (using the term generically, to apply to any federal entity of any size) may find itself in one of the following situations:

- Forced to cancel some or all of its planned procurements
- Trying to get an unusually low price for a program for which it is insufficiently funded
- Trying to spend more money than it had originally planned to
- Trying desperately to find worthy programs to fund, to get rid of sudden riches it has been ordered to spend (frequently with too little time left in which to spend it)

The latter case is not at all unusual. It comes about, usually, in this manner: Congress often is late in approving at least some of the agency budgets, so that it may be quite late in the year or even in the early months of the new year before the agency knows how much money it will have to spend. The money must be spent by the end of the fiscal year, September 30. The agency may therefore have only six or eight months in which to make all its procurements. As the last quarter of the fiscal year (July, August, September) approaches, it sometimes becomes apparent that there is going to be a good bit of money left over by September 30 unless draconian measures are taken. The head of the agency thereupon begins to dispense money lavishly to various offices in the agency, with orders to spend it by September 30!

However, given the typical case of a well-planned budget for which authorization has been received by October 1, each agency can plan its annual procurements. The preliminary plans upon which the original budget estimates and budget requests were based are probably going to be changed to adjust to the realities of the actual budget approved. Programs planned may be dropped or scaled down in scope if the approved budget is less than requested, or they may be expanded if the budget was increased.

The fact that the agency got the budget it requested does not mean, however, that each office in the agency is going to get the budget *it* requested. Except for programs specifically mandated by Congress, the head of the agency has the authority to distribute and use the budget and may make other allocations within the agency than those used to prepare the original budget request. One office may lose some of the money it thought it had, while another may get more money. Final procurement plans are therefore often changed once the budget allocations are announced. And even these may be changed before the year is over.

And, to complicate the matter further, a given office may have been allocated funds for specific programs only, or it may have discretionary funds, to be used as the head of the office sees fit, throughout the year.

On the other hand, the executive who has no money to spend, but has an urgent need, may be able to persuade agency officials that this need merits taking away money from another office. Office heads may therefore suddenly find that they do not have the money they thought they had!

Such things lead to a sudden drying up of a formerly lucrative source of contracts. For example, the Postal Service spent a great deal of money on training programs and materials for several years, but increasing deficits resulted in a sharp curtailment of such expenditures. Many suppliers who had lived on Postal Service business and failed to cultivate other sources were forced to the wall as a result of this.

Because of such circumstances, government markets change a good bit, and they change more radically and less rationally than do commercial markets. Sharp reductions and even virtual disappearance of some government markets may be quite abrupt. Their reappearance or the appearance of new government markets can be just as sudden and abrupt. The increasing energy problems brought about swift creation of several new federal agencies, and a great many contracts from these agencies, as one example of this.

Initiating a Procurement

Given all the factors described, executives who have survived all the contingencies and have some money to fund their projects may now begin to implement their plans. Aside from having gotten general approval and having some money in their budgets, they must do several other things first:

- Prepare an estimate of what the project will cost. (Proposers are bidding against an in-house estimate, the tentative budget for the job, whether they realize it or not.)
- Prepare a formal requisition to the budget office of the agency (which keeps track of various funds and budgets within the agency), to get verification of the availability of the funds and approval for their dedication to the proposed project.
- Advise the contracting officer, probably discussing it with the latter, to establish type of contract anticipated, type of solicitation, and other important administrative details.

The budget office will advise the office on the proper appropriation numbers to use and reserve the funds now authorized. The contracting officer must have that information to go forward with the procurement. Given the assurance that the procurement has been authorized by the proper officials and that the budget office has verified the availability of the funds and has issued the proper identifying appropriation numbers, the contracting officer is ready to discuss the procurement with the requesting official.

Among other things, the contracting officer is the authority on the legality of the proposed procurement. (Most senior contracting officials are either accountants or lawyers and are frequently both.) Characteristically, most contracting officials would prefer a formally advertised procurement, in which sealed bids are solicited. The advantages, nominally, are many. Among them are that it is easy to determine who the winner is (the low bidder), the paperwork is far simpler, the time required to consummate the procurement is much shorter, there is far less probability of a protest (appeal) by those who have lost, and the entire procurement is therefore far cleaner. However, the contracting officials can usually recognize the need for a negotiated procurement—usually, but not always. There are exceptions.

In one such case, the U.S. Forest Service was seeking a contractor to prepare a training program for its own personnel. The contracting official persuaded the office requesting the procurement that it was a suitable subject for an advertised procurement. An information for bid (IFB) was therefore issued. However, because it was a custom project, a prebid conference to answer questions and clarify the requirement was held.

The large number of questions asked at the prebid conference swiftly made it clear that the explanation of the requirement (the statement of work, or

SOW, in the jargon) which accompanied the solicitation was not interpreted by all parties in the same light. Nevertheless, the Forest Service proceeded with its IFB procurement.

A fair price for that particular project would probably have been on the order of $10,000 to $12,000. Bids received, however, ranged from under $6,000 to over $80,000! The award went to the low bidder, of course, who was not necessarily the best-qualified bidder. But the enormous disparity in bid prices was clear evidence that the bidders had widely varying views of what was required, despite the prebid conference, which was supposed to clarify the requirement.

In other cases in which the agency perceives that a mistake has been made in choosing formal advertising as the procurement method, the agency has canceled the solicitation and reissued it as an RFP.

In any case, the contracting officer will generally discuss with the requestor the type of solicitation, the type of contract, and other details. The contracting official is normally thoroughly familiar with the law—the federal procurement regulations which apply to the case—and is, of course, concerned with conformance with the regulations. In that and other respects, the contracting officer acts as an advisor to the requestor. However, the contracting officer is also a watchdog, ensuring legality and controlling the procurement process.

The contracting office maintains various bidder lists, according to the types of procurements the agency normally makes. For example, there may be a list of engineering firms, another list of advertising agencies, another of training developers, and so forth. Frequently, however, the contracting officer will invite the requestor to furnish names of firms the requestor would like to have invited to bid or propose. (In at least one case, however, the contracting officer will not permit the requestor to furnish such names, and the requestor then calls the firms he believes should be invited to bid and advises them of the solicitation; the firms may then request copies.)

Types of Contracts

While there are only two *basic* types of contracts—fixed-price and cost-reimbursement—there are many variants of each. A fixed-price contract calls for a firm, fixed price to be paid for the job, as the name suggests. A cost-reimbursement contract calls for paying the contractor all direct and indirect costs, as defined and specified in the contract, plus some fee or profit percentage. The final amount is estimated, but is not known because the specific amount of work to be done is not specifically known. The well-known cost-plus contract is the most famous variant of this class. But each has its own set of variants, and there are even some contract forms which must be considered hybrids of the two basic types. Here is a brief description of each of the more common variants:

Cost-Plus–Fixed-Fee

In this most famous version, the government will pay all direct and indirect costs (general and administrative, or G&A, and overhead) plus a specific fee. The direct and indirect costs may vary within a specified range, but the fee will remain the same unless the contract is later amended.

Cost-Plus–Award-Fee

This is the same as the above, but the fee is not fixed. Rather, it is determined by a rating board and is based upon the rated quality of the contractor's performance. In some cases—NASA, especially—the two types are hybridized, with the fee including both a fixed fee and an award fee.

Time and Material (T&M)

In this type of contract, the contractor has listed his various labor costs by category (for example, engineer, writer, and illustrator) and will be paid those rates. (Usually, in this type of contract, the various labor rates are presented as *billing* rates, which include the overhead and profit percentages.) Again, the total amount of the contract must be estimated, since the volume of work cannot be predetermined accurately.

Basic Ordering Agreement

This is somewhat similar to the T&M contract, but may be for supplies, rather than labor, as the T&M usually is. (In the T&M, materials are usually not too significant; the contract is issued primarily to obtain labor services in various specialized categories.)

A firm fixed-price contract, then, specifies exactly what is to be done, both qualitatively and quantitatively. A cost-reimbursement contract merely estimates the quantitative—and sometimes the qualitative—results required and establishes *rates* of payment based on what is, finally, furnished. It is not, however, a blank check. In most cases, firm ceilings are set on all rates and quantities, although practices have varied widely in this respect too. That is, the above are several broad types of variants, but each contract is drawn up individually and may vary widely in details concerning how the concept is implemented.

The contracting official again acts as both an advisor and a watchdog in the selection of contract type and the determination of contract details. The type of contract selected must be appropriate to the need, of course, but must also be so written as to conform with legal requirements. In this respect, most contracting officials would prefer a firm fixed-price contract, if possible. Again, it is a cleaner procurement, with far less probability of disputes later. (Cost-reimbursement contracting often leads to disputes between the contractor and the government over what are allowable costs, what justifies cost overruns, and other sensitive areas which are endemic to projects of indeterminable exact requirements. In many cases, the requestor must argue for a chosen preference in contracting, and does not necessarily win the argument!)

Another matter which may be taken up during these preliminary preparations is that of the need for a preproposal conference. In some cases, the need for such a conference is apparent early in the proceedings. In others, the need becomes apparent only after the solicitation has been issued. (More on this later.)

Before going on to the next step, one item should be noted. (Its importance to the proposal writer will be apparent later, if it is not already.) In some cases the contracting official tends to stress the role of advisor, whereas in other cases the contracting official tends to stress the role of watchdog. This can have a profound effect on evaluation of proposals and selection of a winner.

Some Main Points to Remember

1. There are many hundreds of federal operating units—agencies—and each has its own programs or missions. Consequently, each has distinctive needs.
2. Despite the lengthy budget process, agencies often have unexpected excess funds or suddenly lack funds previously thought to be available. Consequently, markets change, markets dry up, contracting opportunities often become suddenly and unexpectedly available, and frequently contract procurement is on an urgent schedule, trying to beat some deadline or other. This is so common as almost to be the norm.
3. An executive responsible for managing an office or program within the agency requests a contract procurement if the money is available, but the legal and administrative authority for translating the request into a competition and contract award rests with the contracting officer of the agency. The contracting officer is both an advisor, helping the program executives make the needed contract procurements, and a watchdog, seeing to it that procurement regulations—the laws—are complied with. In most cases one of these two roles dominates, depending on the nature of the contracting officer and which role the officer perceives as the more important.
4. There are two basic types of contract, firm fixed-price and cost-reimbursement, although there are variants of each and even hybrids of both.

3

The Customer Writes the Statement of Work

The government explains what it wants—sometimes.

The Problem May Begin with the Statement of Work

Like a customer asking for automobile service, the government may need a service it can specify exactly (an oil change), or it may need help in solving a problem (a funny, grinding noise in the engine). A solicitation to bid for moving household goods or supplying a maintenance crew does not require much detail to explain. But a requirement to design and develop a new type of radar or determine the best means for combatting drug abuse requires a great deal of explanation. Every government solicitation, therefore, must include an SOW (which, in the simpler cases, may merely be a set of specifications).

In practice, the requestor has probably already prepared the SOW before initiating the procurement. Chronologically, however, it is more convenient to think of it as being written after all the preliminaries have been attended to. We shall assume that the solicitation request has been cleared and discussed with the contracting officer, and the SOW must now be provided to the contracting office.

What Should Be in a Statement of Work?

Putting it as briefly as possible, an SOW should tell the proposer what the government wants. But while it's simple enough to request prices for delivery of 100 gross of no. 2 black lead pencils within 30 days, it's not so simple to explain that the government has need for an answer to an urban-blight problem or for a training program to increase office efficiency. These require a great deal of background information to explain the problem, the need, the surrounding circumstances, and other pertinent—and necessary—details if proposers are to respond intelligently. But even within this reference framework, a great deal of variation occurs for a variety of reasons.

Ideally, an SOW for a custom service project which requires creative effort by the contractor should be specific enough to give the proposers a clear idea of what is needed and the constraints within which the project must function yet permit the proposers to offer their own ideas for getting the best results. Unfortunately, few SOWs actually fall in this range. Most tend toward one of two extremes. At the one extreme is the SOW which explains the problem and specifies the required work in such detail that the proposer is not permitted to do very much more than echo the customer's words and agree with them. At the other extreme is the SOW which is so vague and general that the proposer is not at all sure what is wanted and is stabbing blindly in the dark to respond at all.

This leads to the suspicions cited earlier—either that the procurement is wired or that the government is playing games to see who can guess what is really wanted. But in most cases, poor SOWs are either the result of poor writing or an indication that the agency understands little of its own problem beyond recognition of symptoms that spell trouble.

For Instance   In one case the Environmental Protection Agency (EPA) issued a solicitation which requested the development of a written training course for a target population (intended audience) that was functionally illiterate—at least, in English. Embarrassed when the anomaly was pointed out by proposers, the agency withdrew the RFP.

Another EPA SOW described a number of tasks to be performed in connection with and in support of its pesticide registration program. But each task was described as an entity with no apparent relationship to the other tasks. It required a team of experts, working for hours in a conference room and diagramming the tasks in a series of flowcharts, to work out the interrelationships among the various tasks—for they were all related to the pesticide registration program (ergo, related to each other). The writers of the SOW themselves probably did not understand the interrelationships.

The U.S. Navy was equally superficial in its study of what it wanted when it decided to begin to "go operational" with job performance aids, otherwise known as "JPAs." JPA technology had been developed under both Air Force and Navy contracts, and a number of experimental or demonstration projects had been carried out. The Navy had decided, finally, that enough developmental work had been done and that enough knowledge of the technology now existed to organize such work on a regular basis. Therefore it issued an RFP stating these assumptions and calling for a contractor to carry out a series of tasks:

1. Research all prior work on JPAs, compile the materials, study and analyze them, and reduce them to a firm set of known principles.
2. Using these principles, develop several sets of programs (JPAs), along with suitable developmental test procedures, conforming with all known and accepted technology relating to JPAs and training practice.
3. Test the programs thus developed, in actual use, and from this formulate a set of standards and specifications to be used for future JPA development.

The SOW referred to these tasks as Phases 1, 2, and 3, discussing them in detail. It suggested that the Navy had not yet decided whether to award a single contract for all or three contracts, one for each phase.

In general, the SOW was rather rambling and repetitious. It appeared to have been a paste-up, an indication that the individual(s) responsible for preparing it had either not fully understood the entire need or had simply assembled the SOW in great haste, without regard to its total usefulness.

Again, lengthy and careful study was necessary to pin down specifics. It soon developed that the three phases were, indeed, phases—sequential events—but it would be folly indeed to issue three separate contracts. That is, such a set of contracts would be all but impossible to coordinate and manage efficiently.

Classifying SOWs

Aside from falling into the black and white classes of extremely vague and exceptionally detailed, plus all the shades of gray between those extremes, there is at least one other basis for distinguishing an SOW by general type. Most occur in one of the two categories below:

1. Describe requirements for standard services which can be defined rather well—computer programming, engineering, drafting, illustrating, writing, research, surveys, conference organization, or other clear-cut needs.
2. Require creative—and sometimes even innovative—effort to solve a problem or furnish a service which is not too well defined—design something new, make a study and design a program dictated by the study, research a subject about which little is known or can be predicted, or other difficult-to-nail-down functions.

In the first case the customer can furnish specifications of some sort—required qualifications of personnel to be supplied, time limits, characteristics of deliverable end products, schedules, and many other such elements. In the second case specifications are rather general and often even the end product cannot be well identified.

So it becomes understandable, for at least some cases, that the customer can not always supply a highly detailed SOW. In some cases the customer is forced to contract on a more or less open-ended basis. In such cases the customer may prepare an SOW which provides mechanisms to monitor progress and make operating decisions as the work progresses. (That's one consideration which sometimes leads to cost-reimbursement contracting.)

Suppose, for example, that the customer finds that all the computer-generated reports are full of error, but is unable to learn more about the problem without calling in a contractor. The real problem—erroneous reports are a symptom, not the problem—may be any of the following, or even due to other factors:

- Poorly designed data forms
- A poor computer program
- Inaccurate inputting of data
- Inaccurate data provided for inputting
- Functional (electrical) computer problems

The customer can furnish proposers information about the equipment, sample reports, sample data forms, and other materials, if able to perceive the usefulness of such information. Beyond that the customer cannot do very much, not knowing very much more about the problem.

In some cases the requestor is expert in the subject in which contractor services are desired—the requestor with the inaccurate reports may be thoroughly knowledgeable about computers, for example. In that case the requestor will provide the information items mentioned and probably much other information. But the customer may be an engineer, psychologist, or any other kind of specialist and know little of computer technology. In this case, the customer doesn't really know what the proposer needs to know and may, in fact, be naive enough to believe that the circumstance of inaccurate reports generated by his computer is itself the problem, which (the requestor believes) any computer expert can solve, given a bit of time and money. So an SOW may well reflect the writer's lack of knowledge about the field in which services are needed.

Many times an SOW is written—perhaps "assembled" is a more accurate word—by a team of people, rather than by an individual. And that may mean that each has written an assigned portion, or it may mean that each has gathered some raw materials somewhere and pasted up his assigned portion. This is what often leads to the repetitious meandering of some SOWs.

In some cases, the requestor will dig out of the files an old RFP which somehow resembles the one now contemplated, and borrow heavily from the old one. And requestors have been known to borrow old RFPs from other agencies, leading sometimes to the Air Force issuing an RFP which makes reference to the Army, rather than to the Air Force!

Marrying the old and the new—old, borrowed RFPs and new material intended to adapt the old RFP to the present problem or need—then leads to some of the anomalies found in many SOWs.

Theoretically, all material forming the solicitation package, including and even especially the SOW, should have been reviewed and approved. Technical experts should see to it that the technical content is accurate, and the contracting officer should see to it that it is intelligible and has enough information and instructions to permit proposers to respond effectively. Unfortunately, it is not always possible to get suitable technical review, and contracting officers are usually not technically suited to pass judgment on the content of the SOW (although many contracting officers recognize in principle that SOWs are rarely written well enough).

The Importance of Recognizing Such Problems and Characteristics

Why is it important that you, the proposal writer, be concerned over the customer's problems and failings in writing an SOW? The importance is this: As a proposal writer, you must respond to what the SOW calls for—or *what you think it calls for.* Your analysis of the requirement is the principal consideration in the design of your proposal. That is, you must *analyze* the SOW. Recognizing such faults and failings as we have been discussing here adds to your understanding of the requirement, of course. Later, when we get into *how* to respond, you will see even more clearly how important it is to be able to recognize those problems which are inherent in the SOW, as distinct from the problems which are inherent in the requirement itself. Such understanding will have a great influence on the *strategies* you elect to use in pursuing the contract.

It may occur to you that you should call or write the customer when you uncover such problems as anomalies and ask for clarification. That's the *obvious* course of action and, strategically, it's the wrong course of action. Again, that's a subject we'll discuss at greater length in a later chapter.

Are These Typical Problems in SOWs?

It may appear from what has been said here that all or nearly all SOWs are characterized by these kinds of problems. Not so. The problems are typical and common, but most SOWs do not exhibit such problems to an extreme degree. In the vast majority of cases the SOW falls somewhere in midrange, between these extremes.

Some Main Points to Remember

1. The statement of work (SOW) should specify exactly what is wanted by the requesting agency. Unfortunately, for many reasons SOWs are considerably less than completely lucid, and the proposer must make a strenuous effort to determine what the customer really needs. In short, it's all too often up to the proposer to interpret the SOW.
2. There are exceptions, cases in which the services or products required are well known and perhaps commonplace. But these are more often the exception than the rule.
3. The customer's description of a problem actually indicates only the symptoms rather than the problem itself. That's one of the many things you, as the expert, must determine from your study of the RFP and SOW.

4

The Rest of the Package

It's called a "solicitation package" because there is far more to it than a mere description of what the government wants done or delivered.

The earlier chapters have tended to focus on problems and difficulties. They may have given the impression that those in government who buy services and products are incompetents. Such a meaning is not intended. By its very nature, bureaucracy creates such problems. For example, when Congress enacts legislation mandating a new program, it is usually assigned to an existing agency, which may or may not be well suited to handling it. Or a new agency may be created, leading to even greater problems of finding a beginning cadre of qualified individuals able to handle the new hot potato.

There are, in fact, a large number of highly competent and dedicated individuals serving in government positions who do understand the complexities of procurement and do the best they can, under the difficult circumstances in which many government agencies operate. In fact, to the discerning eye, many RFPs and their accompanying SOWs signal quite strongly, "Help! Please help!"

In some cases the requestor in the government has previously served in private industry, working for contractors. Having been on the other side of the fence, the requestor understands the contractor's problems quite well. In those cases you will usually find the SOWs quite well written. In fact, the agency staff who work together to produce the RFP and the SOW may be junior, with little experience. In other cases the staff are well experienced, with much tenure in their jobs and expert in the work to be done. That may lead to an excessively detailed—hence, excessively restrictive—SOW. But even when the staff are quite expert, they do not always have a good appreciation of the problem—they may even be aware only of the symptoms—and that can lead to poor SOWs too, if the writers are unaware of their own lack of understanding.

Aside from that, some people in government who write SOWs are simply poor at explaining themselves in writing, some are simply careless, and some are just guilty of bad thinking and really do not understand their own problem. Nevertheless, it's the only game in town, and if you want to pursue government contracts, you have to tolerate the problems. Besides, in many cases, a poorly written SOW is an asset to a resourceful proposer, as you will eventually discover in these pages.

The SOW Is the Heart of the Bid Set

The SOW is of primary importance, of course. Until you read it, you can't be sure you even want to propose for the job. And even after reading it, you may still be uncertain until you gather up some information you didn't get in that SOW. But it's certainly not the only consideration, nor is it the only part of the solicitation package you must study carefully before making your bid/no–bid decision.

By now, having read the chapters that preceded this chapter, you are aware that preparing the bid set is not the sole responsibility of the contracting official. In fact, the role is somewhat like that of the buyer or purchasing agent in private industry: to buy that which is requested. But the requestor must specify what is to be bought; write a purchase description, if necessary; and otherwise participate in the purchase.

The Role of the Contracting Officer

Most contracting officers are either lawyers or accountants, and many are both. The role they play in government procurement entails both accounting and legal considerations. For one, the contracting officer must determine which of the procurement regulations apply to the procurement; whether indeed everything about the procurement, as requested, is according to regulations and has all the proper approvals; and whether the proposers have complied with all legal requirements. (Later, during the course of contract performance, there will be another important role, but that is beyond the scope of this discussion.)

Accordingly, the contracting officer will add these items to the descriptive material provided by the "program" people:

- Statements of which federal regulations govern the proposed procurement and resulting contract. Sometimes copies of the regulations are enclosed, while in other cases, the regulations are included "by reference."
- What are commonly referred to as *checkoff forms* or *offeror representations* customarily appear on the reverse of various forms such as the request for quotations (Figure 4.1*a* and *b*). These are forms, most of which require placing check marks in various boxes, certifying the proposer's compliance with a variety of laws and regulations concerning the legal entity the organization represents, minority enterprises, equal opportunity, environmental considerations, small business status, and other such matters. Year by year, the number of these forms grows.
- A form, usually Standard Form 33 (Figure 4.2), which is in fact a contract should both the contracting officer and the proposer sign it. The proposer is supposed to sign it when the proposal is submitted, and, technically, the proposer automatically has a contract if the contracting officer signs it for the government. Strictly speaking, this can be done with no further communication with the proposer, although it is not normal practice.
- A letter presenting the solicitation package (Figure 4.3) with general instructions, such as the date and time proposals are due; where to deliver or mail them; who to call if there are questions; and information concerning a preproposal conference, if one is planned; along with some general boilerplate information.
- In many cases a specimen formal contract called the "schedule." This does not refer to the schedule for deliveries and milestones, which are part of the SOW, but is a legal term for the specific clauses and paragraphs of the formal contract (see Figure 4.4).

STANDARD FORM 18, MARCH 1971 GENERAL SERVICES ADMINISTRATION FED. PROC. REG. (41 CFR) 1-16.201	REQUEST FOR QUOTATIONS *(THIS IS NOT AN ORDER)*	PAGE OF 1

1. REQUEST NO.	2. DATE ISSUED	3. REQUISITION/PURCHASE REQUEST NO.	4. CERTIFIED FOR NATIONAL DEFENSE UNDER DPS REG. 1 AND/OR DMS REG. 1 RATING:

5. ISSUED BY	6. DELIVER BY *(Date)*

7. DELIVERY

☐ FOB DESTINATION   ☐ OTHER (See Schedule)

FOR INFORMATION CALL   *(Name, area code and tel. no.) (No collect calls)*

8. TO NAME AND ADDRESS *(Street, city, state, and ZIP code)*

9. DESTINATION *(Consignee and address including ZIP code)*

10. Please furnish quotations to the issuing office on or before close of business (date) _____. Supplies are of domestic origin unless otherwise indicated by quoter. This is a request for information, and quotations furnished are not offers. If you are unable to quote, please so indicate on this form and return it. This request does not commit the government to pay any costs incurred in the preparation or the submission of this quotation, or to procure or contract for supplies or services.

SCHEDULE

11. ITEM NO.	12. SUPPLIES/SERVICES	13. QUANTITY	14. UNIT	15. UNIT PRICE	16. AMOUNT

17. PRICES QUOTED INCLUDE APPLICABLE FEDERAL, STATE, AND LOCAL TAXES.

DISCOUNT FOR PROMPT PAYMENT _____ %10 CALENDAR DAYS; _____ % 20 CALENDAR DAYS; _____ % 30 CALENDAR DAYS; _____ % _____ CALENDAR DAYS.

NOTE: Reverse must also be completed by the quoter.

18. NAME AND ADDRESS OF QUOTER *(Street, city, county, State, including ZIP Code)*	19. SIGNATURE OF PERSON AUTHORIZED TO SIGN QUOTATION	20. DATE OF QUOTATION
	21. SIGNER'S NAME AND TITLE *(Type or print)*	22. TELEPHONE NO. *(Include area code)*

18-112

FIGURE 4.1a
Standard Form 18, sometimes used to request proposals.

REPRESENTATIONS AND CERTIFICATIONS

The Quoter represents and certifies as part of his quotation that: (Check or complete all applicable boxes or blocks.)

1. SMALL BUSINESS

He ☐ is, ☐ is not, a small business concern. A small business concern for the purpose of Government procurement is a concern, including its affiliates, which is independently owned and operated, is not dominant in the field of operation in which it is quoting on Government contracts, and can further qualify under the criteria concerning number of employees, average annual receipts, or other criteria, as prescribed by the Small Business Administration. (See Code of Federal Regulations, Title 13, Part 121, as amended, which contains detailed industry definitions and related procedures.) If the quoter is a small business concern and is not the manufacturer of the supplies offered, he also represents that all supplies to be furnished hereunder ☐ will, ☐ will not, be manufactured or produced by a small business concern in the United States, its possessions, or Puerto Rico.

2. REGULAR DEALER-MANUFACTURER (Applicable only to supply contracts exceeding $10,000.)

He is a ☐ regular dealer in, ☐ manufacturer of, the supplies offered.

3. CERTIFICATION OF INDEPENDENT PRICE DETERMINATION (Applicable only to quotations in excess of $2,500.)

(a) By submission of this quotation, the quoter certifies, and in the case of a joint quotation, each party thereto certifies as to its own organization, that in connection with this procurement:

(1) the prices in this quotation have been arrived at independently, without consultation, communication, or agreement, for the purpose of restricting competition, as to any matter relating to such prices with any other quoter or with any competitor;

(2) unless otherwise required by law, the prices which have been quoted in this quotation have not been knowingly disclosed by the quoter and will not knowingly be disclosed by the quoter prior to opening in the case of an advertised procurement or prior to award in the case of a negotiated procurement, directly or indirectly, to any other quoter or to any competitor; and

(3) no attempt has been made or will be made by the quoter to induce any other person or firm to submit or not to submit a quotation for the purpose of restricting competition.

(b) Each person signing this quotation certifies that:

(1) he is the person in the quoter's organization responsible within that organization for the decision as to the prices being quoted herein and that he has not participated, and will not participate, in any action contrary to (a)(1) through (a)(3) above; or

(2)(i) He is not the person in the quoter's organization responsible within that organization for the decision as to the prices being quoted herein but that he has been authorized in writing to act as agent for the persons responsible for such decision in certifying that such persons have not participated, and will not participate, in any action contrary to (a)(1) through (a)(3) above, and as their agent does hereby so certify; and (ii) he has not participated, and will not participate, in any action contrary to (a)(1) through (a)(3) above.

(c) This certification is not applicable to a foreign quoter submitting a quotation for a contract which requires performance or delivery outside the United States, its possessions, and Puerto Rico.

(d) A quotation will not be considered for award where (a)(1), (a)(3), or (b) above has been deleted or modified. Where (a)(2) above has been deleted or modified, the quotation will not be considered for award unless the quoter furnishes with his quotation a signed statement which sets forth in detail the circumstances of the disclosure and the head of the Agency, or his designee, determines that such disclosure was not made for the purpose of restricting competition.

REVERSE OF SF-18 (3-71)

☆ U. S. GOVERNMENT PRINTING OFFICE: 1974 O - 553-722

FIGURE 4.1b
Reverse of Form 18 with checkoff items.

SOLICITATION, OFFER AND AWARD

| | 3. CERTIFIED FOR NATIONAL DEFENSE UNDER BDSA REG. 2 AND/OR DMS REG. 1
RATING: | 4. PAGE
1 | OF |

1. CONTRACT (Proc. Inst. Ident.) NO.	2. SOLICITATION NO.	5. DATE ISSUED	6. REQUISITION/PURCHASE REQUEST NO.
	☐ ADVERTISED (IFR) ☐ NEGOTIATED (RFB)		

7. ISSUED BY	CODE	8. ADDRESS OFFER TO (If other than block 7)

In advertised procurement "offer" and "offeror" shall be construed to mean "bid" and "bidder"

SOLICITATION

9. Sealed offers in original and _____ copies for furnishing the supplies or services in the Schedule will be received at the place specified in block 8, **or**
if handcarried, in the depository located in _____ until _____ local time _____.

                                                                           (Hour)   *(Date)*

If this is an advertised solicitation, offers will be publicly opened at that time.

CAUTION — LATE OFFERS: See pars. 7 and 8 of Solicitation Instructions and Conditions.

All offers are subject to the following:

1. The Solicitation Instructions and Conditions, SF 33-A, _____
edition which is attached or incorporated herein by reference.

2. The General Provisions, SF 32, _____ edition, which is
attached or incorporated herein by reference.

3. The Schedule included herein and/or attached hereto.

4. Such other provisions, representations, certifications, and specifications
as are attached or incorporated herein by reference.
(Attachments are listed in schedule.)

FOR INFORMATION CALL (Name & telephone no.) (No collect calls) ▶

SCHEDULE

10. ITEM NO.	11. SUPPLIES/SERVICES	12. QUANTITY	13. UNIT	14. UNIT PRICE	15. AMOUNT

See continuation of schedule on page 4

OFFER (pages 2 and 3 must also be fully completed by offeror)

In compliance with the above, the undersigned agrees, if this offer is accepted within _____ calendar days *(60 calendar days unless a different period is inserted by the offeror)* from the date for receipt of offers specified above, to furnish any or all items upon which prices are offered at the price set opposite each item, delivered at the designated point(s), within the time specified in the schedule.

16. DISCOUNT FOR PROMPT PAYMENT (See par. 9, SF 33-A)

_____ % 10 CALENDAR DAYS;   _____ % 20 CALENDAR DAYS;   _____ % 30 CALENDAR DAYS;   _____ %   CALENDAR DAYS

17. OFFEROR	CODE	FACILITY CODE	18. NAME AND TITLE OF PERSON AUTHORIZED TO SIGN OFFER (Type or print)
NAME AND ADDRESS (Street, city, county, State and ZIP code)			
AREA CODE AND TELEPHONE NO. ▶		19. SIGNATURE	20. OFFER DATE
☐ Check if remittance address is different from above — enter such address in Schedule.			

AWARD (To be completed by Government)

21. ACCEPTED AS TO ITEMS NUMBERED	22. AMOUNT	23. ACCOUNTING AND APPROPRIATION DATA

24. SUBMIT INVOICES (4 copies unless otherwise specified) TO ADDRESS SHOWN IN BLOCK _____	25. NEGOTIATED PURSUANT TO	10 U.S.C. 2304(a) ( ) 41 U.S.C. 252(c) ( )
26. ADMINISTERED BY (If other than block 7) CODE	27. PAYMENT WILL BE MADE BY CODE	

28. NAME OF CONTRACTING OFFICER (Type or print)	29. UNITED STATES OF AMERICA BY *(Signature of contracting officer)*	30. AWARD DATE

Award will be made on this form, or on Standard Form 26, or by other official written notice

33-130

Standard Form 33 Page 1 (REV. 3-77)
Prescribed by GSA, FPR (41 CFR) 1-16.101

FIGURE 4.2a

Standard Form 33, Request for Proposals.

REPRESENTATIONS, CERTIFICATIONS AND ACKNOWLEDGMENTS

REPRESENTATIONS *(Check or complete all applicable boxes or blocks.)*
The offeror represents as part of his offer that:

1. SMALL BUSINESS *(See par. 14 on SF 33-A.)*

He ☐ is, ☐ is not, a small business concern. If offeror is a small business concern and is not the manufacturer of the supplies offered, he also represents that all supplies to be furnished hereunder ☐ will, ☐ will not, be manufacturered or produced by a small business concern in the United States, its possessions, or Puerto Rico.

2. MINORITY BUSINESS ENTERPRISE

He ☐ is, ☐ is not, a minority business enterprise. A minority business enterprise is defined as a "business, at least 50 percent of which is owned by minority group members or, in case of publicly owned businesses, at least 51 percent of the stock of which is owned by minority group members." For the purpose of this definition, minority group members are Negroes, Spanish-speaking American persons, American-Orientals, American-Indians, American Eskimos, and American-Aleuts.

3. REGULAR DEALER — MANUFACTURER *(Applicable only to supply contracts exceeding $10,000.)*

He is a ☐ regular dealer in ☐ manufacturer of, the supplies offered.

4. CONTINGENT FEE *(See par. 15 on SF 33-A.)*

(a) He ☐ has, ☐ has not, employed or retained any company or persons *(other than a full-time bona fide employee working solely for the offeror)* to solicit or secure this contract, and (b) he ☐ has, ☐ has not, paid or agreed to pay any company or person *(other than a full-time bona fide employee working solely for the offeror)* any fee, commission, percentage, or brokerage fee contingent upon or resulting from the award of this contract; and agrees to furnish information relating to (a) and (b) above, as requested by the Contracting Officer. *(Interpretation of the representation, including the term "bona fide employee," see Code of Federal Regulations, Title 41, Subpart 1-1.5.)*

5. TYPE OF BUSINESS ORGANIZATION

He operates as ☐ an individual, ☐ a partnership, ☐ a nonprofit organization, ☐ a corporation, incorporated under the laws of the State of _____ .

6. AFFILIATION AND IDENTIFYING DATA *(Applicable only to advertised solicitations.)*
Each offeror shall complete (a) and (b) if applicable, and (c) below:

(a) He ☐ is, ☐ is not, owned or controlled by a parent company. *(See par. 16 on SF 33-A.)*

(b) If the offeror is owned or controlled by a parent company, he shall enter in the blocks below the name and main office address of the parent company:

NAME OF PARENT COMPANY AND MAIN OFFICE ADDRESS *(Include ZIP code)* ▶		
(C) EMPLOYER'S IDENTIFICATION NUMBER *(SEE PAR. 17 on SF 33-A)*	OFFEROR'S E.I. NO.	PARENT COMPANY'S E.I. NO.

7. EQUAL OPPORTUNITY

(a) He ☐ has, ☐ has not, participated in a previous contract or subcontract subject either to the Equal Opportunity clause herein or the clause originally contained in section 301 of Executive Order No. 10925, or the clause contained in Section 201 of Executive Order No. 11114; that he ☐ has, ☐ has not, filed all required compliance reports; and that representations indicating submission of required compliance reports, signed by proposed subcontractors, will be obtained prior to subcontract awards. (The above representation need not be submitted in connection with contracts or subcontracts which are exempt from the equal opportunity clause.)

(b) The bidder (or offeror) represents that (1) he ☐ has developed and has on file, ☐ has not developed and does not have on file, at each establishment affirmative action programs as required by the rules and regulations of the Secretary of Labor (41 CFR 60-1 and 60-2) or (2) he ☐ has not previously had contracts subject to the written affirmative action programs requirement of the rules and regulations of the Secretary of Labor. *(The above representation shall be completed by each bidder (or offeror) whose bid (offer) is $50,000 or more and who has 50 or more employees.)*

CERTIFICATIONS *(Check or complete all applicable boxes or blocks)*

1. BUY AMERICAN CERTIFICATE

The offeror certifies as part of his offer, that: each end product, except the end products listed below, is a domestic end product (as defined in the *clause* entitled "Buy American Act"); and that components of unknown origin have been considered to have been mined, produced, or manufactured outside the United States.

EXCLUDED END PRODUCTS	COUNTRY OF ORIGIN

FIGURE 4.2b
Reverse of Standard Form 33 with checkoff items.

DEPARTMENT OF HEALTH, EDUCATION, AND WELFARE
PUBLIC HEALTH SERVICE
NATIONAL INSTITUTES OF HEALTH
BETHESDA, MARYLAND 20014

April 7, 1980   NATIONAL LIBRARY OF MEDICINE

Refer to RFP Number NLM- <u>80-107/507</u>

Ladies and Gentlemen:

The National Library of Medicine, NIH, invites you to submit a contract
proposal in accordance with the requirements of this Request for Proposal
(RFP) for:

<u>Technical Services for the Local Area</u>
<u>Network System and the Data Communications</u>
<u>Activities of the National Library of Medicine</u>

<u>Seven</u> (<u>7</u>) copies of your technical proposal and <u>Seven</u> (<u>7</u>)
copies of your business proposal must be received at the Contracts Office
no later than 4:00 p.m., local time, on <u>Tuesday, May 6, 1980</u>
addressed to:

National Library of Medicine
Office of Contracts Management
Bethesda, Maryland   20209
Attn: <u>Jane P. Sturgis</u>

The attachments listed below are also to be completed and returned with
your proposal in the quantities specified:

Representations and Certifications: one (1) each
<u>Contract Pricing Proposal</u>, Optional Form 60: <u>Seven</u>
(<u>7</u>) each

Your outside envelope should be clearly marked with the RFP number shown
above for proper identification. The package should also be marked:
"NOT TO BE OPENED BY THE MAIL ROOM."

Your proposal must be prepared in accordance with the attached "Instructions to Offerors," (Sections I, II, and III). A copy of the draft
contract provisions, including the full Statement of Work and Delivery
Schedule anticipated to be incorporated in the finalized contract
document, will be found in Attachment A to this RFP. Please review it
carefully.

FIGURE 4.3
Typical letter transmitting bid set (first page).

ARTICLE II
PERIOD OF PERFORMANCE

Performance of the contract shall begin on   ; and shall not
extend beyond   , unless the period is extended by amend-
ment of the contract.

ARTICLE III
CONSIDERATION

A. Estimated Cost and Fixed Fee

1. The presently estimated cost of the work under this contract is
    $_____.

2. The fixed fee is $_____.

3. The Government's obligation, represented by the sum of the estimated
    cost plus the fixed fee, is $_____. This fee shall be subject
    to equitable reduction in the event that the actual effort expended
    with respect to any specified direct labor category is substantially
    less than stipulated in Article I.

B. Indirect Costs

Indirect costs under this contract shall be reimbursed in an amount
developed by using a rate in accordance with Clause #5, "Negotiated
Overhead Rates," of the HEW General Provisions.

ARTICLE IV
WITHHOLDING OF CONTRACT PAYMENTS

Notwithstanding any other payment provisions of this contract, failure of
the contractor to submit required reports when due, or failure to perform
or deliver required work supplies, or services, will result in the withholding of payments under this contract unless such failure arises out of
causes beyond the control, and without the fault or negligence of the
contractor as defined by the clauses entitled "Excusable Delays," "Default,"
"Termination," or "Termination for Default" as applicable. The Government
shall promptly notify the contractor of its intention to withhold payment
of any invoice or voucher submitted.

FIGURE 4.4
Typical schedule included in bid set.

It is the contracting officer's normal responsibility to ensure that the program people have provided all the materials they are required to prepare; that the procurement office has provided all those items that it must provide; that the *Commerce Business Daily* has been notified so that an announcement of the solicitation can be published (Figure 4.5); that complete packages are made ready to distribute to any requestors; and, in most cases, that those on the bidders list are sent copies of the package—that is, those on the bidders list who appear to be the right recipients of the given solicitation. (An office with diverse needs normally keeps many bidders lists for the various types of procurements.)

The program office will have to provide, along with the SOW, at least two other items:

- An indication of the criteria to be used for evaluating the technical proposals. This should include how cost is taken into account in reaching award decisions.
- Instructions to proposers on what information is required in the proposal. This may include some mandated format for the proposal (Figure 4.6), although the format is usually left to the proposer.
- Any cautions which the program office deems appropriate, such as an admonition to respond to all requirements listed and a warning that failure to do so may cause the proposal to be disqualified immediately.

Exchanges between Program and Contract People

It would be an unusual case in which the contracting officer did not have some questions for the program office after examining the material sent down. The officer may, for example, question whether the contract form asked for by the program office is really the best-suited form for the requirement.

Contracting officers tend to be the watchdogs by virtue of their role and responsibility. They make all efforts to get the best price, for example, and will raise objections should anything cause them to suspect that the program people are about to approve a price which appears to be exorbitant. And some will even make strenuous objections to selecting any but the lowest bidder whose technical proposal makes him an acceptable contractor. So the importance of price as a factor in selecting the winning proposal is often a reflection of the contracting policy.

Contracting officers tend strongly to dislike cost-plus or other types of cost-reimbursement and task-type contracts (e.g., time and material contracts). They would usually prefer a firmly quantified and specifically characterized product or service, at a firm fixed price. And they would far prefer that a procurement be made via formal advertising than via negotiated procurement.

U. S. GOVERNMENT PROCUREMENTS

Services

A Experimental, Developmental, Test and Research Work (includes both basic and applied research).

A - - DEVELOPMENT OF AN EARLY TRAINING ESTIMATION SYS-TEM. The objective of this research is to provide the Army training and hardware development community with an advanced technology for early generation of improved system descriptions suitable for input into emerging automatic training and hardware development aids. Offerors should be prepared to demonstrate a reasonable strategy for meeting the research problems, particularly the design communication language and the evaluative simulation methodology. Offerors should also have a research team that has prior experience with hardware and training system development. The period of contract performance is twelve months with possible follow-on research. Copies of the solicitation will be available only upon written request. Attn: Mr. Clyde Williams. Telephone requests will not be honored. Availability of the solicitation is limited and will be furnished on a first-received, first-served basis until the supply is exhausted. RFP: MDA903-80-R-0036.

★ **A - - COMMAND/CONTROL SYSTEM DEVELOPMENT.** Negotiations are being conducted with Computer Systems Management, Inc., based on an unsolicited proposal. See Notes 40 and 46. R. Cooper.

★ **A - - TEST BED DESIGN AND IMPLEMENTATION FOR THE TRAIN-ING AND INFORMATION SYSTEM FACILITY.** Negotiations are being conducted with Planning Systems Incorporated, 7900 Westpark Drive, McLean, VA 22102 on a sole source basis. See note 46. (312)

  Defense Supply Service - Washington, Room 1D245, The Pentagon Washington, DC 20310

A - - CENTER FOR THE CLINICAL TESTING OF BACTERIAL VAC-CINES RESPIRATORY VIRUS VACCINES, AND ANTIVIRALS. Conducting studies of vaccines and antivirals under development. These studies will require healthy subjects and subjects at high-risk to influenza, respiratory syncytial and parainfluenza viruses. Closed as well as open-field vaccine trials will be necessary. Additionally, the offeror should have demonstrated expertise in working with respiratory viruses, as well as, experience in vaccine studies under the conditions and in the population groups cited above. Any contract awarded will be subject to HEW regulations regarding the use of human subjects in experimentation. The work advertised in this RFP is a continuation of work currently

H Expert and Consultant Services.

H - - CONSULTATION ON INTERNATIONAL TELECOMMUNICATIONS AND DATA TRANSMISSION. The Agency may need consulting services in the area of international telecommunications, particulary in the transmission of data over voice-grade, dial-up international telephone lines. Any contract awarded for these services is subject to the availability of FY 80 funds and approval by the Director. Offerors must demonstrate expertise and experience in dealing with regulatory and technical issues in the following areas: 1) U.S. and foreign government telecommunications; 2) Low data rate reliable data transmission; 3) data encryption; 4) certification of telecommunications equipment for export from various countries for use in other countries; 5) knowledge of regulations covering international dial-up telephone links of various countries; and 6) knowledge of planned upgrading of international dial-up telephone systems and current estimates of availability and reliability of telephone communications between Austria and other countries. It is estimated that the work will require one man year of effort through December 1980. Firms with the above demonstrated capabilities and expertise are invited to submit a written response in two copies within 15 days of date of publication. Respondents will not be notified of the results of the review but sources deemed fully qualified will be considered when proposals are solicited. This notice is not an RFP. Responses should reference Synopsis 76 and attention ACDA/GC/C. Telephone inquiries wil not be honored. This notice does not commit the Government to award a contract. (312)

  The U.S. Arms Control and Disarmament Agency, 21st and Virginia Ave., N.W., Washington, D.C. 20451

H - - ACTUARIAL ASSISTANCE to effect close-out of terminated private pension plans which have filed notice with the Pension Benefit Guaranty Corporation pursuant to Section 4043 of Title IV. A request for copies for the proposal (RFP-80-6) should be received by issuing office NLT ten days from the date of listing of this synopsis in the CBD. RFP availability is limited and will be furnished to the requestor on a first received, first served basis until the supply is exhausted. Telephone requests will not be honored. (312)

  Division of Procurement, Pension Benefit Guaranty Corporation, 2020 K Street, N.W., Washington, DC 20006

★ **H - - ENGINEERING AND TECHNICAL SERVICES** furnish support in the Operation Maintenance and Condition Assessment of selected General Electric Co. Equipment and Systems. Indefinite quantity, time and material type contract. Period of performance 27 months amounting to approximately 16,000 man hours. Negotiations will be conducted with General Electric Company. RFP N00140-80-R-0134. See Note 46.

★ **H - - ENGINEERING AND TECHNICAL SERVICES** furnish support in the Operation Maintenance and Condition Assessment of selected General Electric Co. Equipment and Systems. Indefinite quantity, time and material type contract. Period of performance 27 months amounting to approx. 16,000 man hours. Negotiations conducted with General Electric Company. RFP N00140-80-R-0134. See Note 46. (312)

  Naval Regional Contracting Office, U.S. Naval Base Phila., PA 19112

★ **H - - CALIFORNIA STATE/LOCAL COMMUNITY SUPPORT SYS-TEM** demonstration and program development project for severely mental disabled adults in California. Sol. 2-6-78-0006 - Mod. #5. Negotiations will be held with the State of California Department of Mental Health, Sacramento, California, for services necessary to continue the implementation of a plan for state-wide development of a community support system to meet the needs of California adults with severe mental health or emotional disabilities. This organ-

FIGURE 4.5a

Examples of notices published in *Commerce Business Daily.*

K Modification, Alteration, and Rebuilding of Equipment.

K - - MODIFY A TRACK VEHICLE (MODIFIED M109SPH) STRUC-TURE to accommodate a new weapon system. Services will include machining existing aluminum plates and attaching newly designed structural members by fastening or welding. Material: 5052 H34 and 6061T6 Aluminum Plates; 5083 H112 and 5456 H321 Aluminum Forgings; and Armor Plate per Mil 46027. Welding IAW MIL 45207 using 6061 and 5083 weld rod. It is planned to furnish Vehicle (containing no armament) as GFM. Dimensions: W - 10 ft; L - 12 ft; H - 9½ ft; weight - 50,000llbs. Contractor must have facilities to house vehicle while designated work is performed and to insure against theft and vandalism. No security clearance required to obtain APPI. Firms interested in obtaining complete APPI should contact Mr. E. M. Smith, AIMILO. Tel 201/328-4104/4106 or address below. (311)

Commanding General, ARRADCOM, ATTN: DRDAR-SB, Bldg. 10, Dover, NJ 07801

K - - INSPECTION, REPAIR, MAINTENANCE, MODIFICATION, and Installation of Avionics Equipment in Government-owned aircraft. The Forest Service intends to negotiate a 1-year multiple service contract with a full service FAA-approved facility capable of performing all of the needed services at one location. Criteria for evaluation of facilities will include the following: 1. Technical qualifications, experience, and training of the Contractor's personnel who will do the avionics work. 2. Equipment and facilities owned or leased by the Contractor which will be available for the avionics work. This criteria includes both conditions and appropriateness of the Contractor's equipment and facilility location. 3. Bid price for hourly work with straight time constituting 70 percent, overtime 20 percent, and Sundays and Holidays 10 percent. 4. Discount from list prices. Requests for Proposals R-80-04 due Dec. 12, 1979 (312)

Contracting Officer USDA - Forest Service, 324 25th Street, Ogden, UT 84401

★ **K - - REPAIR/REFURBISHMENT OF ACTIVE EMISSION RECEIVER PROCESSOR (AERP)** IAW the specifications in the schedule. Negotiations for a Basic Ordering Agreement will be conducted iwth Norden Systems Inc., 100 Norden Place, Norwalk, CT as this firm is the sole manufacturer of the AERP and uniquely possesses the technical familiarity necessary to provide this effort in a timely manner. See note 46. (312)

Commander, Naval Sea Systems Command, Washington, DC 20362

★ **K - - MODIFY MINIRANGER III POSITIONING SYSTEM** to a 16 code option. Solicitation NASO-80-00052 is currently being negotiated on a sole source basis with Motorola, Inc., 7402 S. Price Road, Tempe, AZ 85283. (312)

NOAA, Northwest Administrative Service Office, 1700 Westlake Avenue North, Seattle, WA 98109

R Architect - Engineer Services.

R - - FACILITIES PLANNING AND ENGINEERING SERVICES to perform two major services. The first is to develop a permanent security and safety lighting system for the Smithsonian Buildings on the Mall (The Museum of History and Technology, The Museum of Natural History, The Freer Gallery of Art, The Smithsonian Castle Building, The Arts and Industries Building, The Hirshhorn Museum and Sculpture Garden, and The National Air and Space Museum) at a conceptual/planning level which over a period of years could be designed in detail and then implemented when funds are available. This service will require this firm to work with the various Smithsonian Bureaus in developing the project's conceptual study. This study shall take into consideration the types of lighting to satisfy the requirements for safety and security with consideration for aesthetics needed for these Smithsonian Buildings. The product of this study shall be a report which defines the problems, criteria and options and then a specific solution in terms of a general lighting systems approach which will meet the more specific criteria of each building or complex of buildings on the mall as well as the overall requirements for illumination. The second service shall be to analyze, design and provide contract documents for a permanent lighting security system for the Freer Gallery of Art, The Smithsonian Building, The Arts and Industries Building, and the gounds immediate to these structures, including parking and garden areas, hereafter called the South Mall Group. The system, based on the accepted conceptual plan, shall be so designed to provide lighting where and when needed, at the levels required, by the use of additional fixtures, discreetly installed and/or modification of existing fixtures to provide those required increases in intensity. Fixture selection or modification and replacement shall be done to harmonize with the architecture of each building and the existing decorative and/or service lighting for each building and the immediate grounds. The system shall be zoned appropriately with each zone being controlled from pre-selected locations. The work under this service includes the following tasks: 1. The firm shall again work with various concerned Smithsonian Bureaus to establish and verify specific program requirements for security and safety lighting, energy consumption of such a system and its aesthetic impact for the South Mall group. This task shall use the general criteria and concepts established in the previous service to start development of this specific design problem. 2. Survey each building of the South Mall group and its adjacent grounds for existing lighting system (their condition and effectiveness), power sources, and effective yet unobtrusive locations for lighting. 3. Develop a design and contract documents for bidding purposes for the system by two methods. (A) Individual buildings, phased over several years, or (B) one lump sum contract for the South Mall group. 4. Cost estimated for both methods shall reflect incremental adjustments for inflation. Time frames: 1980, 1981, 1982. The purpose of this will be the submission to appropriate agencies and/or bureaus for funding. 5. Provide those services needed for shop drawing review. The firm shall have as part of its staff or retained as consultants all those consultants licensed and experienced in those disciplines required to perform the work. It is imperative that all consultants and individuals involved in this project be thoroughly described in the 254 and

FIGURE 4.5*b*

Examples of notices published in *Commerce Business Daily*.

<u>INSTRUCTIONS TO OFFERORS</u>

<u>SECTION I</u>

<u>GENERAL INSTRUCTIONS</u>

<u>INTRODUCTION</u>

The following instructions will establish the acceptable minimum requirements for the format and contents of proposals. Special attention is
directed to the requirements for technical and business proposals to be
submitted in accordance with these instructions.

1. <u>Contract Type and General Provisions</u>
   It is contemplated that a <u>cost-plus-fixed-fee</u> type contract
   will be awarded. Any resultant contract will include the general
   provisions applicable to the selected offeror's organization and to the
   type of contract awarded. Any additional clauses required by Public
   Law, Executive Order, or procurement regulations, in effect at the time
   of execution of the proposed contract, will be included. Anticipated
   period of performance is from <u>September 1, 1980</u> through
   August 31, <u>1981</u>.

2. <u>Authorized Official and Submission of Proposal</u>
   The proposal shall be signed by an official authorized to bind your
   organization. The proposal shall be typewritten and reproduced on
   letter- size paper. All required copies must be legible. To expedite
   the proposal evaluation, all documents required for responding to the
   RFP should be placed in the following order:

   I. <u>COVER PAGE</u>
       Include RFP title and number, name of organization and typed
       name and signature of official authorized to bind your organiza-
       tion; and distinguish, by hand stamp or other appropriate method,
       the original from copies.

   II. <u>TECHNICAL PROPOSAL</u>
       See Technical Proposal Instructions for recommended format.

   III. <u>BUSINESS PROPOSAL</u>
        See Business Proposal Instructions for recommended format.

FIGURE 4.6
"Information Required" (excerpt from first page of bid set).

(In the formally advertised procurement, sealed bids with public bid openings are used, the contract going to the lowest bidder.) However, about 85 percent of all procurement is made via negotiated procurement because the low-bid method is so often simply not adequate for selection of the best bidder. But contracting officers may question the program office in the interests of providing the best service possible, for procurement is a service to the program departments of the agency.

In some cases, but not all, the contracting officer may ask the program office to suggest suitable bidders, or at least ask if the program office has some well-qualified organizations they'd like to see proposals from.

In any case, the contracting office records each requestor of a solicitation package so that it may send out modifications or any notices which may become necessary.

Once a solicitation has been issued, answering questions asked by requestors of the bid sets becomes a sensitive matter, for it is taboo that any proposer shall have gotten information which was not made available to everyone else. Therefore, contracting officers normally request that all questions be addressed to them. They then transmit the question to the program office, and if the answer includes information which was not in the original bid set or readily available to everyone, they will probably write up a modification which transmits that same information to all requestors. This is to prevent anyone from having an unfair advantage over anyone else in the competition. But it is also to prevent the release of information whose release would be either illegal—contrary to procurement regulations—or contrary to agency policy.

For that reason, some RFPs will actually tell the reader how much money is available or estimated by the program office, while in others there is not the slightest hint. That is, some agencies permit such information to be included in the solicitation package, while others have a strict policy against it.

Contracting officers are, of course, just humans. Therefore, what has been said here about their policies and practices is general and not always true: There are contracting officers who will fight tooth and nail in favor of the lowest-cost proposer who submits a technically acceptable proposal, but there are others who will give the program office entirely free rein to select whom they will, regardless of price (as long as the price is within the budget). There are contracting officers who accept whatever the program office sends down, as long as it meets all legal requirements, while there are others who will question and challenge everything they do not like. There are contracting officers who will leave almost all the details to their junior staffs, while there are others who will personally monitor every move. But all contracting officers will check, or cause to be checked, the mathematics in the cost estimates, signatures, and other such details. That's part of their basic job.

But that is beginning to get us into the subject of the next chapter.

SOME MAIN POINTS TO REMEMBER **45**

Some Main Points to Remember

1. The solicitation package, or "bid set," as it is often called, contains a number of documents in addition to the SOW. It is wise to study all of the package. However, you must be alert for anomalies and other errata in solicitation packages, for they are prepared by humans, often in great haste and under great pressure, with resulting slipups.

2. Do not be deceived by this into believing that the government is staffed totally with incompetents. Quite the contrary, many government executives have served their time in private industry, and have an excellent understanding of the procurement process from your viewpoint, as well as theirs. However, many agencies have problems which have been visited on them by outside forces, and are doing the best they can. In fact, that is exactly why they so often need help from the private sector!

3. The SOW merits your most scrupulous attention, for that is where the agency has described its view of what it needs, whether an accurate description or not.

4. Among the more important items in the bid set is the list of "evaluation criteria," those specific benchmarks the agency will use to measure your proposal and compare it with others for quality.

5. The contracting officer may well become your ally if you submit an acceptable technical proposal and are the low bidder, for most contracting officers are eager to get the best price possible for the government. But you can't count on it if you don't know the contracting officer because not all contracting officers will actually fight for the low bidder. That means that it is a wise move to try to learn all you can about the contracting officers and what policies they pursue and impose on their agencies.

5

The Customer
Evaluates Proposals

The evaluation process is the heart of the matter.
This is where you win—or lose—the competition.

The Customer's Work Is Still Not Done

We're going to take a long skip forward in the proposal process to the customer's next chore—evaluating your proposal. We've had a nickel tour of all the preparatory headaches and problems, going through all the steps to get the bid set out on the street and into your hands. We're going to skip over your headaches and problems in writing your proposal, for the moment, and have a look at what the customer must do after receiving your proposal.

You'll remember that those who evaluate your technical proposal are not to know your cost estimates until after they have completed the technical evaluation and committed themselves to final scores for each proposal. So evaluation is divided into two parts: technical and cost evaluations. Really, it's three parts, for following these two evaluations a final decision must be made about which proposal to select.

What Is Evaluated?

The typical customer would probably rather select a firm arbitrarily to do the job. The temptation, of course, is to select a large, prestigious firm in order to provide some sense of security. But there would be misgivings too, especially if the contract were not a particularly large one; the customer would wonder whether the large firm would tend to treat the project as a small job, to be put on the back burner and done at the firm's convenience. Undoubtedly, such thoughts will have some influence—no evaluation process can be made completely objective—but the law is the law, and the evaluators must at least attempt an objective evaluation.

In issuing the RFP, the agency has already given the proposers some idea of what it will look for and how it will score various aspects and portions of the proposals. These evaluation criteria and the evaluation plan overall can vary widely from one agency to another and even from one procurement to another in the same agency. At one extreme, the criteria may number twenty or more separate items—usually several major items, each subdivided—with detailed commitment to a given minimum-maximum point range for each. At the other extreme, little more than lip service may be paid to the requirement that the agency furnish such criteria, and there may be only two or three items, with no quantitative information provided on how they will be scored.

A Typical Detailed List of Criteria

Here is how an RFP might set forth the evaluation criteria in a well-detailed plan:

Evaluation Criteria	Points
Understanding of the requirement	15
Approach:	
Analysis of the problems	5
Practicality of approach	5
Probability of success	10
Qualifications of offeror:	
Proposed-staff qualifications (résumés)	15
Experience and resources of organization	10
Project planning:	
Project organization	5
Specificity of deliverables	10
Management plans and procedures	10
Costs	15
Total:	100

This is not an all-or-nothing score for each item; any given item may be assigned from zero to the maximum number of points listed for that item. Nor is the scoring on an absolute scale, although the implication is that it is. That is, customers have some internal scoring criteria, which they do not reveal, to guide them in making these evaluations and awarding point scores—e.g., costs may be evaluated on the basis of overall economy and reality—but they could not define for you exactly what would constitute a perfect score for any one item. Lacking such absolute standards, customers are inevitably forced to evaluate much of the content of your proposal on the basis of *comparative* evaluation—your proposal versus others. In fact, they are likely to select what they judge to be the best proposal overall and evaluate all others against the standard of that "best" proposal.

This was borne out rather clearly in a debriefing recently when the offeror who had lost at the last moment, after having been given strong indications of being the winner of the contest, pressed the evaluations team for enlightenment on what each criterion item really meant in relation to some standard or definition of what would merit a perfect score. Pressed hard to define exactly what they had in mind as "perfect" for each item, or even to furnish a precise definition of such things as the relevance of experience, the team was finally forced to confess that it had used comparative evaluation—had used what it regarded as the best proposal to become the standard for judging all others!

A clue to this is furnished by the very specificity—detail—of the advertised criteria. The more precisely detailed the criteria advertised in the RFP, the less likely that the customer will have to rely on the proposals themselves to furnish the standards.

A Typical List of Vague Criteria

All too often, offerors are faced with something like the following to guide them in writing proposals:

> Proposals will be evaluated on the basis of the following items:
>
> 1. Approach
> 2. Quality of staff proposed
> 3. Qualifications of offeror as an organization
>
> Item (2) will have twice the weight of item (1), and item (3) will have one-half the weight of item (1).
> Awards will be made as it appears to be in the best interests of the government, costs and other factors considered.

With such criteria—and assuming that the customers do have some better-detailed guidelines to be used internally in the evaluation—it is rather obvious that the customers are permitting themselves the widest possible latitude in making an "objective" evaluation of each proposal. They are virtually confessing that they have no hard, fixed standards for judgment, but will call them as they see them.

Clues to Evaluation Standards

The RFP is not entirely without other clues to what the customer would like to see. In most cases, the RFP will have given some indication of what kinds of experience and what other factors are desired. In some cases these are so detailed and specialized as to lead directly to the suspicion that the whole thing is wired—designed for some specific contractor, with little chance that it will go to anyone else. But in any case the evaluation criteria may be studied and analyzed with respect to these expressed preferences.

On the other hand, sometimes the criteria are stated as virtual requirements and appear to be warning those not meeting the standards of offeror qualifications that it would be wasteful of their time and money to even consider making a proposal! In one such case—which was rather obviously wired—the RFP expressed certain explicit desires concerning contractor qualifications, then reversed field and confessed that the government (meaning the agency, of course) had no real expectation of finding a contractor who matched these characteristics exactly. The RFP then set forth a list of evaluation criteria which made clear provision for awarding fewer points than the maximum! Obviously, someone wrote up a set of idealized qualifications, but someone else in the organization with a more realistic view of the world, wrote the evaluation criteria.

How Much Reliance Should You Put in These Criteria?

It would be most unwise to completely ignore the evaluation criteria: someone in the agency has written them and has had them approved by management. But usually an RFP is the product of several people's work, with relatively little coordination, plus paste-ups of material borrowed from earlier RFPs, and it has all been put together in haste and under great pressure. Ergo, many RFPs do not "hang together" very well, but contain many anomalies and paradoxes. You may even find that the listed evaluation criteria and other elements of the RFP directly contradict one another!

Evaluation Is by Committee

In an effort to attain the greatest degree of objectivity, proposal evaluations are normally made by a team with an odd number of members—three, five, seven, etc. In some cases it is named *source evaluation board,* or some equivalent title. Each member of the team makes an independent evaluation (in theory). However, there are many variations here, as there are in all things governmental. (By now, you may have begun to suspect that there is little that is uniform throughout the government establishment.) Different conditions call for different measures.

For one thing, the size of the procurement governs the method or at least the size of the team. A small procurement ("small" in government terms, that is!) calls for a small team, frequently even a single evaluator, whereas a large procurement requires a large selection panel or board. But that does make sense, too, for this reason: For a small procurement, in most cases each evaluator reads the entire proposal and each scores the entire proposal. But in a large procurement this is not practical for at least two reasons:

1. The size of each proposal, and often the large number of proposals submitted, mean that it is not possible for everyone to read every proposal and evaluate each in any reasonable length of time: evaluation would "take forever."
2. It would be nearly impossible to find a number of government staff who are qualified to judge *all* elements of a large proposal—technical discussions and plans, management proposed, quality control, publications aspects, etc. Large projects require not only large proposals—some run to literally thousands of pages—but large programs, involving a wide variety of technical and professional skills and special abilities.

The only practical thing to do in such cases is to set up a rather large source selection board, with different members of the board assigned to read and evaluate different portions of each proposal. Some evaluators are therefore technical experts and study technical sections, while others are management experts and evaluate the proposers' management plans.

It's quite easy to get an indication of how many people are going to evaluate your proposal: the number of copies requested indicates that. You may in the case of small jobs be required to furnish only one to three copies of your proposal. But in the case of large procurements as many as thirty to fifty may be required!

What Does the Customer Generally Look for?

If the stated criteria are not absolutely reliable as indicators of evaluation, what then *does* the typical government customer look for? That's a fair question and merits consideration here.

To answer it, let's consider the problems of those concerned with making purchases for their organizations. Anyone charged with selecting a source or making any kind of buying decision is immediately "exposed," in the sense that any kind of bad result is an immediate condemnation of the buyer's judgment (although a good result is not usually recognized as deserving plaudits!).

Therefore, anyone involved in selecting a source for goods or services must be concerned with success—delivery and performance by the contractor. It is in the interests of those making evaluations to select that proposal which they truly believe to be in the best interests of the government, at least as far as their objectivity permits them to make judgments on that basis.

Therefore, evaluators usually take their own interests into account by minimizing the risks of failed deliveries or failed performances by the contractors. In general, they will try to select those best qualified and showing greatest promise of delivering the promised results.

The criteria usually reflect this concern. They address such important questions as these:

Do you (the potential contractor) fully understand our problems and needs?
Are you expert enough at whatever skills and technologies are needed to furnish the planning and performance to satisfy our needs and solve our problems?
Will you provide fully qualified staff people to do the work?
Have you done such work successfully before?
What, *specifically*, do you promise to deliver?
Do you have a track record to prove that you can and will deliver?
Can you prove your abilities at all the above?

That last question—proof—is key to the whole evaluation process. The proofs of the offeror's abilities can be partly verified if inquiries are made of the offeror's other customers—preferably other federal agencies—but much of the proof lies in what the proposal says. Evaluation points are awarded on what the proposal *says*, not on information the evaluators may gather by other means. Information from other sources—e.g., calls to other customers of the offeror or the evaluator's own knowledge of the offeror—inevitably have some influence on the evaluator's judgment, but awarding points on that basis is strictly taboo. The evaluator could not defend that action.

Overall, the evaluator's chief concern might be summed up in a word: confidence. Confidence in the offeror and in everything stated in the proposal. Confidence that the contract will be fulfilled in every respect, with complete satisfaction to everyone concerned. In a large sense the whole art of proposal writing is aimed at that one goal: creating confidence.

Who Are the Evaluators?

Generally speaking, the evaluators are selected from among the staff of the agency for which the work is to be done. And in most cases the team is led by some senior staff member whose judgment is likely to be final and may even override the judgment of the team.

However, here again, there is no single practice which is universal. There are many cases in which an agency will cast about in its parent organization for those who can serve as evaluators, particularly if the proposal is technical and its evaluation requires technical knowledge.

Then again, there are cases where outside consultants are paid to assist the agency in evaluating proposals. This appears to be practiced fairly widely in the agencies dealing with social programs and grants, but it is possible that any agency, faced with a highly technical requirement, may hire consultants to assist in evaluation.

In fact, it is not unusual for agencies to have hired consultants (both individual consultants and consulting companies) develop the RFP and the SOW. Sometimes the RFP results from a study performed by a consulting firm under contract. But there are cases (such as that cited earlier as an example of debriefing) in which the SOW is actually written by an outside consultant (who is thus automatically disqualified from bidding for the contract, of course).

In some agencies, the agency head reserves the right to review all proposal evaluations and award decisions, and no awards may be made without the approval of the agency head. In many cases, that agency head also reserves the right to reverse the evaluators' work and arbitrarily choose a contractor from among those proposals submitted. (This is subject to a challenge in the form of a "protest" action, by those who have not won, should they choose to lodge an appeal or even file suit. This will be taken up in more detail later.)

Because there is a protest process by which an unsuccessful proposer may challenge and contest the agency's decision, the evaluators necessarily show at least some regard for what they represented as being the criteria for evaluation, if only to be able to defend their decisions. The existence of such a process offers at least some recourse from faulty judgment or open bias in evaluation.

The Critical Factor(s)

There is usually at least one highly critical factor, sometimes more than one. This can be *the* decisive factor, other considerations being equal or roughly equal. And this paramount consideration, which may be regarded as "the critical factor," may or may not be apparent—i.e., the proposer may have to read between the lines of the RFP to detect it.

For example, let us suppose that the agency is in something of a money squeeze and has been forced by the strictures of available budget to make their in-house estimate wishfully—hoping that at least one of the offerors can do the job they want done for the money available. If the proposer detects that factor successfully—and that is one factor which is rarely, if ever, actually specified—and is able to design a program which will do the job for the money available, that alone will probably be adequate to win the contract. But it depends on the proposer's ability to detect that factor between the lines of the RFP.

The RFP will probably furnish clues, although these may be quite subtle. For example, the evaluation criteria may offer to give heavy weight to low price to encourage a great deal of energetic "pencil sharpening" by the proposer in writing the cost proposal. The RFP may state flatly that a "firm fixed-price contract is anticipated," but invite the proposer to propose other types of contract, with (of course) a rationale for so doing. The evaluation criteria may stress "evidence of cost consciousness" on the part of the proposer, offering substantial points for that. These or many other clues—including other intelligence gathered by the proposer—can point to cost as a critical factor.

The opposite is sometimes the case: The agency, especially as year-end approaches (September 30), may prefer a relatively elaborate program, at a high price, and actually give low ratings to proposals offering great economies! Or the agency may truly feel that the proposer who appears to be offering a bargain basement price is actually guilty of not understanding the agency's needs fully and hence underestimating the scope and cost of the project.

The agency may be seeking a conservative, play-it-safe approach, or it may prefer some higher-risk, innovative ideas. Management may be considered to be the most critically important item, or staff qualifications may take precedence. The critical items are usually reflected somewhere in the listed evaluation criteria, but are not necessarily in plain sight: they may well be concealed and expressed or indicated in rather subtle terms. Finding and responding effectively to such critical factor(s) strikes a nerve in the customer's organization: it is likely to make up for any deficiencies (as long as none of those are fatal).

Evaluators are *people,* it must be remembered, and respond to different appeals as individuals, as well as representatives of the government. The sales appeal of a proposal depends at least partially on how it appeals to the individuals in the agency. The problems of the agency are the problems of the senior staff: solving problems for the agency is solving problems for the staff, and they are quite conscious of that in evaluating the offers represented by the proposals.

Clues may be afforded by the very nature of the project called for. The project may be quite complex, calling for the coordination and integration of a great many difficult and highly technical tasks, and perhaps even require a large amount of subcontracting. In such case it should be readily apparent that the project will require rather sophisticated management, with well-designed procedures and checks. The SOW must inevitably somehow reflect the customer's awareness of this and concerns about the proposer's capabilities for managing large and complex projects. The proposal should therefore devote an adequate amount of coverage to consideration of management problems and the provision of an adequate management system. Quality control may be a factor; it is often overlooked by both customer and proposer. But in a great many cases it is a distinct subject which ought to be addressed separately.

Does the Customer Recognize Critical Factors?

The fact that a customer has failed to specify in the evaluation criteria or elsewhere concern for some aspect of the proposed project is not a certain sign that it will not be considered in the actual evaluation.

- The customer may not have thought of it specifically when writing the RFP, but may recall it later, during study and review of the proposals.
- The customer may have overlooked it, but be prompted to recognize it by an astute proposal writer who has made a point of it.
- The customer may have thought the point implicit in one of the general evaluation criteria, although the implication may not have registered with everyone responding to the RFP.

Let's take quality control as a case in point. It is not at all common to make a specific point of quality control in RFPs and work statements. Frequently, the customer has simply overlooked the matter, but in many cases simply expects to find quality control discussed as a responsibility of project management.

In the first case—where the matter has been simply overlooked—any proposer who makes the point that although quality control was not mentioned in the RFP, it is an important matter, and then proceeds to discuss it *and provide for it,* is going to earn a good many extra points—the proposal will be charitably treated in all listed evaluation criteria because the customer has been subtly influenced to favor the proposal. (Remember, the criteria per se may be "objective," but human *judgment* assigns *values* to each criterion item in each proposal.)

At the same time, the customer is now motivated and alerted to search out quality-control coverage in every other proposal. If there is none, that is, of course, to the detriment of the technical score awarded each other proposal. Therefore, you have not only raised yourself in the customer's eyes, but you have also inflicted a wound or two on your competitors!

It is essential to interpret those evaluation criteria for yourself and to try to "psych out" what factors the customer is likely to consider in analyzing your performance in each of the areas so specified. But in so doing, *assume* that the customer has been completely alert and sophisticated enough to have overlooked nothing in setting standards for evaluating your performance in your proposal, or, at least, that competitors will be sharp enough to do so and will not permit the customer to overlook any point which should be made in a proposal.

This in itself may prove to be the key to the winning strategy. Having found what appears to be critically important to success in the project, but appears to have been overlooked by the customer (at least not specified in the RFP), you can often build your entire proposal around this as the single point where you can show up the competition and shine brightly yourself.

Sometimes, however, this strategy backfires. Here's a case in point, which also demonstrates that the customer is not always completely alert and has not always thought out the problems thoroughly:

The EPA issued an RFP some years ago for a written text to train building superintendents (janitors, in fact!) in New York City in methods for firing their furnaces so as to minimize air pollution. The SOW went on to describe the target population (those to be trained): they were described as "functionally illiterate," at least in English, although some of them might be literate in Spanish. That is, to put it plainly, they could not read English effectively!

The irony was not lost on the proposers. Almost unanimously, they stressed the problems of using a printed text to train people who could not read. Of course, no one proposing could afford to ignore such an obvious difficulty. At the same time, no one wanted to ruin their chances for winning a contract. So everyone offered a way out of the dilemma by proposing some sort of "nonverbal" training program.

The EPA people felt compelled to withdraw the requirement entirely until they could take the problem into account in describing what they wanted. They really had little choice. The difficulty was so plain and struck so directly at the heart of the proposed project that they had to fall back and rethink their need.

This kind of thing is not uncommon. However, the problems overlooked at the time of developing the work statement and RFP are usually far less obvious and farther removed from the heart of the project. There was the case, for example, of the Postal Service, which was seeking programs to train technicians in the maintenance of the complex equipment in its new bulk mail centers. Among the many problems of the Postal Service is one similar to that experienced by the military services: it takes in new workers who have no skills and spends a great deal of money providing technical training only to lose the people to industry, where they can get more money once they are armed with technical skills.

The Postal Service mentioned this in passing, without giving a great deal of weight to it. But the alert organization that won the contract proposed a training program which would consider this specific problem, among others, and provide at least some preventive measures to safeguard the Postal Service's investment in training the technicians.

It is therefore entirely legitimate and even good practice to suggest some of the evaluation criteria (indirectly, of course) in your proposal. A single such item, properly selected and handled, may win the contract.

Sins of Omission

If you skimmed over the earlier observation that the evaluator cannot give you points for information derived from any other source than your proposal, here's an illustration of how that can happen. The Office of Minority Business Enterprise (OMBE, now renamed Minority Business Development Agency) supports some 300 organizations throughout the United States for the purpose of aiding minority entrepreneurs in gaining a place in business. These organizations, many of which exist solely to do this work and have no other source of funds, are funded at various annual amounts, ranging up to several hundred thousand dollars each, and even more in a few cases.

These are not grants but contracts won competitively, and they expire each year—i.e., each organization must respond to an RFP and submit a new proposal each year for renewal (actually, a new contract). Of course, the possibility exists for each that it might lose the contract. On the other hand, the incumbents obviously have great advantages in the bidding, and most win new contracts every year.

One, funded at approximately $375,000, had had the contract in Phoenix for several years, winning renewal each year. After several years of success, the organization grew a bit careless, and in that section of the proposal where it was to describe its qualifications for the job, it did a rather hasty and careless job, supplying few details. Its rationale was, "OMBE knows us; we've done the job for them for years. We don't need to waste time giving them a lot of information they already have."

But that year, the organization had a competitor—this lean and hungry new contender for the job wrote a good proposal and priced the job at $10,000 less than the incumbent asked.

Now $10,000 in $375,000 is not very much money—it's less than 3 percent. But the technical proposal was weak in that it provided virtually no information about the proposer's technical and professional qualifications for the job. The contract was awarded to the new contender and in obvious dismay the incumbent promptly protested.

The OMBE evaluator had great difficulty in making the incumbent understand why it had lost many technical points—had come up virtually zero in the qualifications section. But that, combined with its second place in cost, offset the advantages it had long enjoyed as an incumbent contractor.

The evaluator could have done nothing else. A protest by the incumbent could be defended against successfully. A protest by the new contender, under the conditions as stated, could hardly have been defended against very effectively.

Whether OMBE was pleased with the performance of the incumbent organization and wanted to reaward the contract to it, or whether OMBE was displeased and glad to have solid grounds for replacing it, is not known. But even if OMBE had been pleased and wanted to award a new contract to the incumbent—an assumption one always makes in the lack of any contrary evidence—it would have had great difficulty in doing so, and even greater difficulty in making that decision stick. The incumbent defeated itself through ignorance or carelessness, or both.

In proposing to the government, you must bear in mind that unlike the situation with private concerns, the award decisions are based in statutory requirements—the law states rather plainly what the main considerations must be and what rules must prevail. The evaluators have some discretionary powers in the judgments they make, but these are limited. Certainly, in the absolute absence of required information they cannot stretch discretion far enough to award you points for what is not in your proposal!

Costs are another matter, and there are many ways to take costs into account. Let's have a look at a few of them.

What about Evaluating Costs?

While the customer has been studying your technical proposal and judging its merits, your cost proposal has been locked away by the contracting officer, probably after a quick scan of your costs. The contracting officer may also have looked at your indirect rates—overhead and G&A costs—and your labor rates, and decided whether they appear to be reasonable or not. But that's about all the contracting officer can do now; full evaluation must wait until the evaluation of your technical proposal is complete and the scores officially recorded.

That done, the contracting officer may now release the cost proposals to the evaluators and work with them to judge the merit of your cost projections.

Indirect Costs

Most government contractors offer two kinds of indirect costs: that which is classed as overhead and that which is classed as G&A. (These will be discussed in detail later.) Some companies break their overhead costs down into two classes, overhead and fringe benefits. But it all adds up to some "burden" rate added to your direct costs.

The principal element of indirect or burden rates, for most organizations, is that called overhead, and contracting officers generally study overhead rates—or, at least, note them—carefully. There are no real standards for overhead rates—i.e., no one can tell you just what your overhead rate ought to be—but there are general levels for various kinds of organizations. The general fact is this: An organization with a great deal of costly equipment—e.g., a capital intensive company—is likely to have a rather large overhead rate, even as much as 400 percent in some cases. This is because it has a heavy depreciation rate on equipment each year. On the other hand, companies that do not require a great deal of equipment for their operations and hence do not have such heavy capital investments are labor intensive, and should have relatively low overhead rates, ranging from as low as 35 percent to somewhat in excess of 100 percent.

Hence, an overhead rate of, say, 150 percent for a service company is likely to raise a disapproving eyebrow on the countenance of a contracting officer. In fact, any overhead rate in excess of 100 percent for a service company is likely to invite closer scrutiny. The contracting officer may well consider this to be an indication of a lack of cost consciousness, of an inefficiently run organization, or even of a possibly inflated figure which could not be supported under audit.

The same may be true of G&A rates, but to a lesser extent, since G&A rates usually run to much smaller figures—3 to 15 percent—and have less overall significance, consequently, in determining final costs ("the bottom line").

These considerations are, of course, on an absolute scale, without respect to the given project proposed.

Direct Costs

Direct costs—primarily labor rates, for these are usually the bulk of the direct costs—draw the same attention. A claim to pay a secretary $20,000 a year is likely to draw attention and be met with some skepticism. Or, if true, to reinforce the suspicion that the contractor is neither cost conscious nor realistic in controlling costs. In any case, the contracting officer is going to gain some general impression of the cost reality from a scan of labor rates, again on the absolute scale, and not with regard to the project under consideration.

The contracting officer has some standards by which to judge these rates, as well as by which to judge indirect rates: general knowledge of approximately how such rates run at the time and knowledge of the rates other contractors have bid, enabling comparison to competitive rates for similar job responsibilities.

Evaluating the Costs for the Given Project: The Cost Proposal

Once the technical proposal evaluation is complete and the contracting officer is free to confer with the evaluators on the cost proposals, it becomes possible to evaluate the cost proposal in terms of the technical proposal and the project per se. By this time, the contracting officer has had time and opportunity to rank-order the cost proposals and determine who is lowest in cost, who is second lowest, and so forth, down to the highest-cost proposal.

Now at this point, there are several evaluation methods possible, according to what was decided earlier. For one, if specific points were to be awarded for costs—e.g., if costs were rated 15 points—the lowest-cost proposal would normally receive 15 points—possibly, but not necessarily, as we shall soon see. The other cost proposals would each be graded at some lesser point score, according to the internal standards for making the judgments.

Presetting specific point scores for cost proposals is sometimes done, but not too frequently. More often, costs do not get specific rating, but are "taken into consideration." In a fair number of cases a formula is worked out which consider costs and technical merit, which results in determining a cost per technical point. A typical such plan works along these lines:

1. The proposal scoring the highest number of technical points is selected.
2. The costs accompanying that proposal are divided by the number of technical points to arrive at a cost per technical point—e.g., a $500,000 proposal which has scored 92 technical points would have a cost per technical point of $5,434.78: $500,000÷92 = $5,434.78 per technical point.
3. The process is repeated with all other proposals which have been judged to be technically acceptable.
4. That proposal with the lowest cost per technical point is selected.

There are several variations on this, but all follow the general principle of (1) screening out all unacceptable proposals, (2) setting a cost per point for each remaining (acceptable) proposal, and (3) awarding to the one with the lowest cost per point.

The basis for selection among the remaining methods—those which are so general and undefined as to permit the agency to select almost any proposal it chooses to—may be (1) selecting the lowest bidder among those whose proposals are judged technically acceptable (regardless of cost per point, that is), (2) selecting that proposal which appears to be realistic in costing, vis-à-vis the technical proposal, and (3) selecting the highest-scoring (technically) whose cost is within the budget—that is, selecting the most attractive proposal the agency can afford!

But even these do not cover every situation; there are many other factors which enter into final judging.

Fighting for the Low Bidder

Take the case of the tough-minded contracting officer who wants to award the contract to the lowest bidder who has submitted an acceptable technical proposal. There are such contracting officers, and sometimes it's virtually a policy that the lowest qualified bidder will get the contract.

But suppose the program people want to fight for someone who is not the low bidder, but for one reason or another, is favored for the contract. They have at least two courses of action open:

1. They can have "best and final" sessions and possibly negotiate their favored contractor down to a low bid, or at least one which meets the low bid.
2. They can write a "justification" for the contracting officer (some contracting officers would simply call for such a justification, as a matter of course), which if effectively written, would probably win approval of their choice.

Comparing the Cost Proposal with the Technical Proposal

One thing that will be done during this final processing is to evaluate the costs against the program proposed in order to verify their compatibility or detect any incompatibility. For example, if the technical proposal has shown the project leader putting 40 weeks of his time into the project, the cost proposal must show that 40 weeks. Obviously, if it shows 48 weeks or some other incompatible number, the cost proposal immediately becomes somewhat disreputable.

Or suppose that the technical proposal shows a staff of twelve people, but the cost proposal reflects a staff of fourteen people.

In general then, the cost proposal must "track" the technical proposal.

Cost proposals are generally evaluated according to the following considerations:

1. The contracting officer's general scrutiny of rates
2. The stated evaluation criteria
3. How it tracks with the technical proposal

Final Acts of Evaluation

Although RFPs normally caution the reader that the government reserves the right to make the award without further discussion—i.e., entirely and solely on the basis of the proposals submitted and the evaluation of said proposals—that proves to be true only in relatively small procurements. For any procurement running to, let us say, $100,000 or more (and frequently even for smaller procurements), such precipitate action would be the exception rather than the rule. Here are several things which the government is likely to do, once it has completed the evaluations of both cost and technical proposals:

1. At a minimum, call the successful offeror and ask for verification of prices quoted and check willingness to enter into contract on the terms stated.
2. Ask the successful offeror to come in to discuss the proposal, answer questions, explain anything not clear, and possibly even to amend the price asked. This is known as asking for a best and final offer and is part of the negotiation.
3. Extend this best and final invitation to several offerors, usually the top-ranked few, but sometimes to everyone who has delivered a technically acceptable proposal.
4. Enter into actual across-the-table negotiations.

Which of these or similar actions an agency opts for depends on the size of the procurement, the time constraints, formal agency procurement policy, and the specific circumstances surrounding the procurement. A small procurement for something on the order of $25,000 to $50,000 is unlikely to draw more than a telephone call or letter requesting verification as in (1) above. But the best and final process is quite commonly practiced. However, some contracting officers feel that everyone who prepared a decent proposal—i.e., one which was not disqualified technically—should be entitled to at least the courtesy of being asked for a best and final offer, as well as the courtesy of discussing the proposal. (Some agencies are motivated in this by the fear of being accused of not giving every bidder a fair and equal opportunity.)

On the other hand, there is in many agencies a belief that it's a total waste of time to talk further with any proposer whose price is way out of the ball park—"out of the competitive range," as contracting officers are wont to express it. That is, if the in-house estimate is $300,000, and the majority of acceptable proposals range from $250,000 to $350,000, it seems futile to hope that someone with a bid price of $475,000 is going to be able to come down within that competitive range. Ergo, why waste time talking to this one?

But there are really no hard-and-fast rules. Here is an incident to illustrate this:

The Job Corps, when it was still part of the Office of Economic

Opportunity, issued an RFP for a small job, estimated to run to something like $50,000 to $60,000. A large number of proposals were received.

The lowest bid was approximately $40,000. The highest bid was $78,000. However, the proposal asking for that highest price was judged to be outstanding in quality, and the evaluators were eager to have that proposer do the job, if possible. Usually (in other circumstances) that proposer would have heard no more until being notified that the bid was outside the competitive range and the job had therefore been awarded to someone else. But in these unusual circumstances, the technical evaluators asked the contracting officer to try to negotiate an acceptable price with that proposer. The contracting officer therefore called the proposer up and said something such as this:

"We like your technical proposal. In fact, we agree that it's outstanding. But your price is out of sight. We simply can't go for it. Do you think that there is any possibility we can negotiate something acceptable, without compromising the quality of the program you offer?"

Ultimately, the two parties reached agreement for $63,000. And that's the real meaning of negotiated procurement. The government must judge which proposal is in the best interests of the government rather than which is lowest in price.

One other factor can enter into the government's decision about best and final or other negotiations: time. There are some circumstances, such as the approach of September 30th, which place great pressure on the agency to consummate the process and award a contract or—at the least—to obligate the funds for the program. And those funds cannot be obligated unless the contract is firmly identified, and the exact amount of money committed. So, near the end of the fiscal year every effort is made to accelerate all the steps of the process, and that itself may lead to a swift award after proposal evaluations, with no other actions.

Some Main Points to Remember

1. While there is a strong temptation for the government agency to select a large and well-known firm as the successful proposer, there is also the understandable fear that the large firm will regard a few hundred thousand dollars as a small contract and not give it priority treatment. Large firms don't always have a built-in advantage in competing for contracts.
2. Aside from the above, there are certain statutory protections for all proposers: the agency is not entirely free to choose a contractor arbitrarily, but must conform with the regulations, which require that all proposals be evaluated by some set of objective criteria.
3. Inevitably, most evaluations of proposals come down, finally, to using

whichever technical proposal is considered the best as something of a standard against which to measure the others. You are therefore not judged entirely on how good, in an absolute sense, your own proposal is, but largely on how your proposal compares with the one considered best. This means, of course, that you must try to make yours the one that is used as the standard—the one that is considered best.

4. Sometimes the evaluation criteria are quite specific and clearly stated—but not always. Frequently they are rather vague, perhaps deliberately so, but in any event, they permit the agency maximum latitude in making its judgments of comparative quality.

5. Frequently the clues to what the customer is really concerned about—what evaluation criteria, in the final analysis, are truly most influential—must be divined by the proposer, for they are not plainly stated. This does not necessarily mean that the job is wired, although it may indeed mean that. Still, even when evaluation criteria appear to be unreasonably restrictive, they may be contradicted elsewhere in the RFP. (Such an anomaly may furnish excellent grounds for a subsequent protest.)

6. The number of copies of your proposal required is an excellent clue to the number of people who will read and evaluate your proposal. Large proposals, for large projects, are usually evaluated by different teams for different elements or sections of your proposal.

7. Sometimes you can add evaluation criteria yourself by pointing out important factors the customer may not have identified in writing the RFP. Such actions often have a salutary effect on passing your competitors by.

8. Don't expect to get credit for anything which is not explicitly presented in your proposal, no matter how well known or prestigious your firm may be. Legally, the agency cannot give you credit for anything you have not included in your proposal. "What they know about you" doesn't count.

9. Costs are not necessarily critically important, but they are never unimportant, especially to contracting officers. Keep your costs as low as possible and you may make an ally of the contracting officer.

10. Be sure you understand how costs are scored, if they are scored at all. Costs may be the critical key to success.

6

Common Faults and Failures

"Don'ts" can be as important as "dos."

The Meaning of *Responsiveness*

Somewhere in all or almost all solicitation packages is a notation that the proposer is required to furnish such information as requested, and that failure to do so "may be construed as nonresponsiveness." The implication is that nonresponsiveness is the kiss of death, and it often is. On the average, about two out of three proposals are classed as nonresponsive and disqualified from further consideration for that reason.

The terms *responsive* and, especially, *nonresponsive* are rather general terms, open to many interpretations. That is probably one reason that so many proposals go down to sudden death under the latter label: it's a convenient means for dealing a fatal thrust to a proposal which is generally weak or sadly deficient in one respect or another. However, the term may also, on occasion, be used as an excuse for knocking out a proposer the evaluators do not favor—or perhaps to clear a lane for a proposer the evaluators do especially favor! In any case, the proposer is well advised to take any and all steps available to ensure that his proposal is responsive and can be defended against any charges to the contrary. But first we must examine more closely those specific examples of nonresponsiveness commonly found among proposals.

In the most general of terms, being responsive means offering the customer a proposal that meets—responds to—the stated requirement. Suppose the customer has expressed a need for a custom program of some sort and the proposer offers to provide an off-the-shelf program which almost, but not quite, meets the stated needs. The proposal is clearly not responsive: it hasn't offered what the customer asked for.

Usually, the case of a nonresponsive proposal isn't as clear-cut as this. Most nonresponsive proposals are not so *grossly* nonresponsive as this. It is more common for the proposer either to have overlooked some of the customer's requirements or to have tried to get around them. Here are a number of typical ways in which proposals are nonresponsive:

Staffing

Most RFPs specify fairly clearly what the staffing qualifications are to be—that is, they describe the qualifications of the principal staff members: education and experience. Proposers often offer résumés of proposed staff which do not conform with the customer's stated requirements.

Another such fault is that many RFPs specify that at least some of the key staff members proposed must be permanent employees of the proposer at the time of proposal submittal. Proposers often ignore this requirement, usually because they cannot meet it.

Company Qualifications

Most RFPs stipulate that the organization offering the proposal must demonstrate certain experience and other qualifications *as an organization,* in addition to the *individual* qualifications of staff members. Again, often because they cannot meet the requirement readily, proposers tend to ignore the requirement.

Schedule

While the RFP may invite the proposer to offer a schedule, it also usually furnishes either a complete schedule or at least a tentative deadline for completion. Proposers sometimes ignore the customer's statements in proposing a schedule.

Specifications

A most common kind of nonresponsiveness is simply neglecting to respond specifically to each and every specification listed.

General

In general, failing to furnish *any* item of information requested—even a complete listing of past and present contracts—is, at least technically, being nonresponsive and may be pronounced so. However, of all kinds of nonresponsiveness, none is quite so common or quite so deadly in its effects as that which causes the customer to comment that the proposer "just doesn't seem to understand the problem." And that is far more common than you might suppose.

Understanding the Problem—But Failing to Prove It

One of the customer's chief concerns is that the proposer understand the requirement. And again and again, proposals fail to demonstrate that understanding. That is, while the proposer may truly understand the customer's problems or needs, that understanding is often not *demonstrated* clearly in the proposal. One extremely common mistake, in spite of RFP admonitions to avoid it, is using the customer's own words in describing the problem or requirement that the proposal purports to respond to. Obviously, repeating the customer's own words is not proof of understanding!

Of course, the proposal itself demonstrates—or fails to demonstrate—understanding. But should the proposal get off to a bad start by making the error of quoting the customer's own words as an indication of understanding, the damage would be done; and once the customer has been so prejudiced against the proposal, the damage might never be undone.

There is a humorous cliché about people offering solutions to which there are no problems. Some proposals do appear to do this. At least, they appear to offer solutions to other problems than that which the customer has described in the RFP!

Perhaps the most grotesque kind of nonresponsiveness is that in which the proposer demonstrates no comprehension of what the customer wants when asking that understanding of the problem be demonstrated. In one case, to illustrate this, the U.S. Postal Service Training and Development Institute issued a solicitation for a training program. The basic problem was one of training supervisors of mail handlers—clearly a management problem.

At least one proposer worked hard at misunderstanding what the RFP was referring to when it asked the proposer to demonstrate understanding of the problem, for the proposal opened with a "statement of the problem" that might have been copied from the facade of the main Post Office building in downtown New York City—that dramatic statement about "rain and snow and gloom of night" not "staying these couriers from the swift completion of their appointed rounds"! Rather than address the problem of training managers, he chose to try to curry favor—obviously—by paying lip service to the overblown phrases of years ago, which are often the butt of humor by postal employees!

"The problem" of course, refers to the immediate problem to which the RFP is addressed, not the overall problem of the agency's mission as a federal agency. It certainly does no harm to reveal an understanding of the agency and what its various major goals and objectives are, but those must not be confused with the immediate problem which caused issuance of the solicitation. Nor should a proposal be corny enough to echo those pompous statements made by politicians and bureaucrats of many years ago. Not if you wish your proposal to be taken seriously.

Despite years of struggle to do so, the government as a whole has failed to make any real progress in eradicating bureaucratic language. There are counterforces in government determinedly resisting such efforts. At the same time, this is not a license or an invitation to write proposals in this style. Quite the contrary, evaluating proposals is difficult enough when they are written clearly, and evaluators do not appreciate having additional difficulties placed in their paths.

Using Buzzwords and Other Clichés

If you could look over the shoulders of some proposal evaluators while they are puzzling over the documents, you might see such marginal notations as these:

Madison Avenue!
???
What does this mean?
Are they kidding?
Snow job!

Trying to snow evaluators by pompous (and often meaningless) phrases and "64-dollar words" is usually a self-defeating game. Evaluators are not impressed by language which conveys nothing.

One executive in the Department of Energy states flatly that there are occasions when page 2 of a proposal is never seen because page 1 has been written so badly as to convince one of the futility of reading further. Another executive, in the Labor Department, who seeks contracts with organizations that will provide competent professional personnel, finds a badly written proposal not "professional"—immediately prejudicial to the organization. Still another executive, in the Treasury Department, expressing a similar view, believes that writing is a projection of thinking. Unclear writing reflects unclear thinking, and who would care to contract with people who can't think clearly!

Here are some examples of bad writing which, although amusing, are pretty deadly in their effects when you are trying to impress a customer with your planning and presentation.

One proposal, explaining how a piece of equipment was to be designed, described how terminal numbers would be designated by referring to the "assignation" of the terminals, which led the evaluator to comment on "electronic porno."

Another proposal, explaining that all key circuits would be "backed up" by reserve units which would automatically be switched into place should the primary circuit fall, made reference to the "duplicity" of the circuits in the proposed equipment. The evaluator responded that there was no need for treachery in these circuits!

A common failing—what we might call the "Madison Avenue syndrome"—is to offer *claims*, instead of *facts*. Typically, such proposals are heavily larded with superlatives. Every noun is qualified as "superior" or "most efficient" or otherwise categorized by an adjective as the very best. This practice almost invariably wearies the evaluator quickly and raises the suspicion that the proposer "doth protest too much."

In short, such proposals are long on claims and short on proof—or even evidence. But here is another escape route often overused.

The Authority Syndrome

Someone has made the jest that to borrow language from two or three sources is plagiarism, but to use fifty or more is research! Obviously, some proposal writers allow themselves to be heavily influenced by that idea.

Such proposals are characterized by an excessive amount of footnoting—hardly a page appears without several footnotes, with their typical "op. cit." and "ibid." appearing in monotonous procession.

The underlying philosophy, evidently, is to "prove" everything by citing "authorities"—other authors. There are many citations—from published books, from professional papers, and from articles which have appeared in journals. The idea is that the information is unassailable, since it was respectably published; hence, the footnotes are automatically convincing evidence—the proposer hopes.

This is not to say that footnotes and citations should never be used. Far from it; used properly such citations are quite helpful. It's the enormous overuse that causes the problem: each page appears to have measles, and the evaluator struggles mightily to maintain some consciousness of the continuity of the proposal, despite being distracted by the footnotes.

Moreover, it is a confession of weakness, when overdone, suggesting that the proposal contains *no* original work but is simply a rehash of what has already appeared in the literature. One effect is to convey, at least to some evaluators, that the proposer lacks self-confidence and leans too heavily on others for substance.

The Rambling Wreck

One in-house proposal guide compares many proposals to river rafts floating along with the current and going where the current takes them rather than being steered on a straight course toward a known objective. It's an apt metaphor for many proposals. Many do just that—ramble along, apparently aimlessly, making many vague generalizations and promises, but offering little evidence of a thought-out *plan of action*.

The customer plans to spend money—often a large sum—to fund a project. It is not likely that the money will be entrusted to anyone who has not revealed rather clear plans for effective spending—that is, who appears not to have a specific plan of attack on the problem. A proposal that fails to tell the customer just what you plan to do with the money you are asking for is not likely to get serious consideration.

More Specific Weaknesses

Most of the weaknesses described so far are of a general nature—fuzzy language, clichés, vague generalizations, unsupported promises, and the like. But proposals also commonly contain such other specific weaknesses as the following:

Weak Management Plans

In many cases, the customer believes that the project will be a complex and difficult one, and requires sophisticated, firm management planning. The proposal is expected to furnish some detailed information on management plans—project organization, staff assignments, procedures, processes, controls, and other matters of direct concern in management. Failing to find these, the customer concludes that the proposer, whether technically competent or not, has shown no evidence of being able to *manage* the project.

Poor Liaison with the Agency

One matter which is almost always of great concern to the customer is that of liaison and communication between the contractor and the government—specifically, between the contractor's project manager and the agency's project manager. Typically, the government's project manager wants a direct line of communication with the decision maker who runs the project. Customers find underwhelming those proposals which offer project management via committees or panels. They look for plans providing such direct communication that a telephone call will produce immediate action, should immediate action be deemed necessary.

Very much along the same line of reasoning, the customer is likely to regard the provision of a low-level manager as conducive to poor control—that is, the customer wishes to see proposed as a contractor's project manager an individual with ample authority to make and execute decisions promptly, who is able to respond directly to customer requests.

The government's control of a contracted project is necessarily through the contractor's manager. It is a common mistake to overlook this obvious fact and to fail to provide the customer with means for effective control of his project.

In some cases, while the government may not dictate to the contractor precisely who shall be the manager of a given project, agencies often do give indications of which individual they would regard with favor—or disfavor—as a proposed manager. In one such case the customer sent what it thought were clear signals to the proposer that the proposer was out in front of all competitors—except for a proposed project manager who was unacceptable to the government's project manager. The contractor ignored the signals, and the agency turned to the proposer with the next-highest rating and negotiated a contract with that firm, to the shock and dismay of the former firm.

Making Unwarranted Assumptions

The case described in the previous paragraph is one of making an unwarranted assumption. The contractor who proposed the unacceptable project manager had been doing work for the agency for some years. Therefore, the contractor assumed that it was in a strong enough position to compel—or at least to persuade—the customer to accept its proposed manager. It was unthinkable to the contractor that the customer would turn to anyone else. Such cases of contractors becoming "fat, dumb, and happy" are not uncommon. Here is a typical case.

One firm had supported NASA's Goddard Space Flight Center for 6 consecutive years. Proposing for a third 3-year contract, the company decided that it was regarded highly enough by the customer to raise the price considerably above that justified by inflationary pressures. Despite more-than-broad hints from the customer that the price was too high, the company persisted in its refusal to reduce its price significantly. It even ignored the fact that there were at least five other contenders for the contract who had been invited to submit best-and-final offers. Of course, it lost the contract as a result of its extreme overconfidence.

Failing to Specify the Deliverable(s)

Often enough, the SOW is something less than clear, and fails to specify exactly what is to be delivered. This circumstance, however, does not justify allowing the proposal to be unclear on what is to be delivered. Quite the contrary, the writer of the SOW has some justification for being less than crystal clear—the writer is asking the proposer to propose a project and deliverable items. It is just as incumbent upon the proposer to propose *specific* deliverable items as it is for the proposer to explain the proposed project in detail. In fact, one experienced proposal writer has said that a large part of the art is "comprehending the deliverable." (The author of that exceptionally clear insight is unknown to us, so we must salute an anonymous sage with our thanks.)

A Few of the Difficulties Normally Encountered

Why do so many proposers make these and other mistakes? There are many possible explanations. For one, consider the incredible pressures under which proposals are usually written. In most cases the writers have only a few weeks—rarely more than 60 days and frequently not more than 30 days—in which to generate a document which is equal to a good-sized book. However, proposal writing rarely starts immediately, because days and even weeks are consumed in studying the solicitation and deciding whether to submit a proposal, often leaving the writers only about 2 weeks in which to get things together and produce a winning proposal.

But the mistake, overall, is often one of general approach to the whole problem of proposal writing, even to making decisions as to what to bid. In a few cases, especially for very large procurements, 3 months or even more may be allowed. But these are the exceptions, rather than the rule. As a result, most proposals begin at a somewhat leisurely pace, which begins to accelerate as the due date approaches and the team of writers begins to realize that there is not enough time. Many—perhaps most—proposal efforts are therefore finished in a blaze of frenzied activity: all-night sessions, and, at the end, ruthless cutting of sections which should go into the proposal but must now be excluded if the proposal is to be submitted at all.

In a few cases of founder-led companies the marketing success of the company is due to the proposal-writing talents of the leader, who does most of the writing and personally directs the rest of it. But in most other cases companies do one of the following:

1. They bid for everything under the sun, writing "quick and dirty" proposals, and striking pay dirt once in a while by pure chance. They play a numbers game, never turning out a really good proposal, but making probability statistics work for them.
2. They bid very selectively, market most aggressively, write proposals for contracts only where they have made themselves well-known and well-liked, are thoroughly familiar with the customer's situation, and virtually have an understanding with the customer that they are the heavy favorite for the job. (They will not propose for *anything* without these factors working for them.)
3. They write fairly decent proposals, turn out a fairly large number of them, and win often enough because the competition, too, rarely writes really good proposals.

4. They have a thorough and complete system and methods for doing some combination of the other methods. They do their field marketing and information-gathering; they are fairly selective, but write a goodly number of proposals every year; and they turn out consistently good proposals, using a well-organized and competent proposal-writing staff.

Unless the last description fits your own organization, you are playing Russian roulette with your business, restricting your growth severely—possibly even losing a great many contracts you should have won. And, in addition to that, you are probably running a much higher overhead expense than necessary, since so much of your proposal-writing expense is a waste.

The Typical Proposal-Writing Environment

Although the United States government periodically announces plans to smooth out the peaks and valleys of bidding and proposal-writing requirements, there are inevitable, usually predictable, peaks and valleys of proposal-writing activity. The most pronounced peak occurs around June, July, and August, immediately preceding the end of the fiscal year (September 30). Since any money unspent at that time must be returned to the Treasury, and since returning money to the Treasury is a bureaucratic sin, the agencies are almost frantic in these final months of the fiscal year to award contracts and "obligate" whatever money they have left. There are also valleys—December, for example, and the month or two immediately following the end of the fiscal year.

For some companies, the peaks and valleys have a different pattern than they do for others because peaks and valleys of procurement are not the same for all federal agencies. Some of them tend to get their budgets approved and appropriated by Congress promptly, as the new fiscal year begins, while others often have their annual budgets held up for months, while Congress wrangles over legislative programs (e.g., the abortion issue held up HEW's funds for months, one year). Too, some agencies will make the vast bulk of their year's awards during a single period, while others spread their contract awards over the year.

In any case, this makes it somewhat difficult to maintain a permanent crew of proposal writers in an organization, unless they double in brass as functionaries for other duties when they have no proposals to write. But even then, writing proposals involves different technical and professional specialists for different requirements, unless the company is highly specialized and restricts itself to a narrow arena of activity.

The typical large company, then, is likely to have a proposal department consisting of writers who write reports and manuals when they have no proposals to write, and who are supported by the technical and professional experts of the company, selected for each given proposal effort when there is a proposal to do. (Or perhaps it is the technical and professional experts who are being supported!)

The smaller company usually has no fixed proposal-writing function, but assembles an ad hoc team for each proposal effort, usually the technical and professional experts, with or without support from writing and editorial specialists.

In either case, a proposal-writing team almost invariably has the following general characteristics:

1. It's an improvisation, usually including either those people who otherwise have little of importance to do, or those people who give a few grudging hours of their time now and then.
2. It almost always lacks the most important and most useful staff member—probably the most knowledgeable and able professional—because he or she is tied up on a critically important project or is out of town.
3. The leadership of the team is rather vague and ill-defined.
4. No specific procedure, format, design, or approach to proposal writing is established, but it is expected to somehow fall out of this group (is it really a *team?*) of experienced and competent individuals.

The typical results of this effort are these:

1. Immediate arguments as to what's most important in the RFP and the proposal which is to be written, how the proposal should be organized and formatted (each individual has a pet format or organization, usually based on one learned in some previous company), and how the work should begin
2. Endless meetings, while time flies, with no resolutions, often turning into pure "bull sessions"
3. Grudging volunteering for writing assignments, with only vague agreements on what is to be written

And, typically, some individuals write at great length, while others dispose of their assignments in an hour or two with two or three sheets of double-spaced handwriting; many points are missed entirely; illustrations are an afterthought; and 70 percent of the way into the job, nothing resembling a proposal has yet emerged.

It is a literal truth that many proposals are finally abandoned after a great expenditure of time and effort (money, that is!) because it has become obvious that there is no possibility of assembling a decent proposal in the remaining few days. Of course, that's because so many days were wasted.

And it is true, too, of course, that many proposals submitted should have been abandoned because of this, but weren't, resulting in a pro forma submittal which has no possibility of success at all and does nothing but injury to the professional image of the organization and its staff.

Every Rule Has Exceptions

There are exceptions to this. There are organizations, both large and small, that understand the problem of creating a good proposal in a short time with an ad hoc team and that cope ably with the problem, turning out proposals of which they need never be ashamed, often quite superior proposals.

These are organizations that have instituted and follow a carefully planned set of procedures and methods designed specifically to cope with these problems and make the miracle of a good proposal in a few weeks happen consistently. They do not gamble, depending on chance or solitary genius, but utilize and exploit the great potential of many minds harnessed to work together and pull together.

They recognize that proposal writing per se—the crowning achievement—is only part of the proposal-development process, that much work precedes the actual writing and that the writing itself is not—and should not be—even undertaken until preliminary work is complete.

They recognize that proposal development involves several phases (and sub-phases) of activity, including at least these major ones:

1. Analysis of the requirement and critical factors
2. Synthesis of approaches and major strategy
3. Planning, outlining, designing, and drafting proposal
4. Low-level review, troubleshooting, revision, finalizing
5. Management review
6. Final revision and production

To present these in some logical order and progression, they are shown as though they were sequential. However, in practice some of these are iterative processes, as Figure 6.1 shows.

The figure is a preview of things to come in the remaining chapters of this book. It is not by chance that nearly one-half of the figure is devoted to preparatory tasks, those which precede the actual writing. Most badly written proposals are badly written in the sense that the writing is a direct result and reflection of poor thinking. And the poor thinking, in turn, is the result of not having enough information, of not having completed research and planning, and of lunging forward into writing before you are ready to write, before you have decided *what* you are going to write.

That's the first problem we need to solve.

FIGURE 6.1
Major phases
and functions in
proposal devel-
opment.

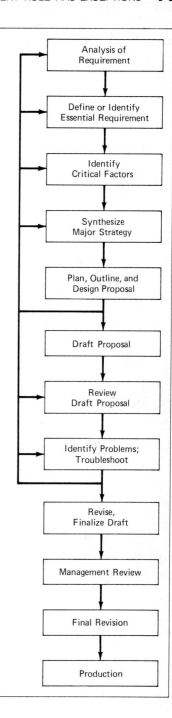

Some Main Points to Remember

1. The most common faults and failures of proposal writers are lumped under a general heading of *nonresponsiveness*. This refers to anything which somehow fails to address the customer's stated needs and problems. Failure to demonstrate understanding, proffering a solution which does not address the requirement directly, neglecting to provide all the information requested, and taking issue with the RFP are all examples of nonresponsiveness which may result in immediate disqualification or rejection of your technical proposal.

2. Another most common fault that costs proposers serious consideration is pompous, inflated prose that really conveys no useful information, but is a clear attempt to overpower the reader with superlatives and hyperbole. Such an approach is rarely well received. And quite frequently, the writer of such rhetoric is not really skilled enough to do even that skillfully, resulting in a ludicrously inept presentation, to the detriment of any future submittals by that proposer.

3. Rambling presentations, wandering hither and yon and rarely making major points clearly, even at random, are also condemned to failure. Faced with such a proposal, the reader is hard put to pin down precisely what is being offered or promised, much less what the justification is for the positions taken by the proposer.

4. There are two extremes in the approach to proposals: the company that proposes only on sure things (therefore writing very few proposals and missing many opportunities) and the company that proposes on almost everything, with hastily improvised proposals depending on boilerplate materials (thereby rarely, if ever, writing a really good proposal, but always hoping that lightning will strike occasionally). The right approach is somewhere between the extremes: Be selective in pursuing projects, but take the time and make the effort to write a good proposal *every* time.

5. The ultimate mistake, perhaps, is to begin writing too soon—before you have made a thorough analysis of the requirement and are sure you know where you are going with your proposal. Writing itself is only part of proposal development. What you write cannot be better than the information on which you base your writing. There is no time to do it over—rarely does a proposal effort permit you the luxury of a leisurely schedule. You have to get it right the first time, and you can do that only when you have spent enough time preparing to write—gathering and organizing the information.

The First Requirement

If you don't know where you're going, how can you tell whether you've arrived at the right place?

It may appear that undue emphasis has been given in these pages to understanding of, and responsiveness to, the customer's wants. That emphasis is deliberate. It is in developing that understanding that most unsuccessful proposals find their waterloo. Most of those common mistakes and faults described in the previous chapter stem from faulty understanding and result in a lack of responsiveness.

Someone with a wry sense of humor has observed that to train a dog, the trainer must be smarter than the dog. Similarly, to sell a customer a program responsive to the customer's wants, you must know at least as much about those wants as the customer does. In fact, you will often find that you must know more about the wants than the customer does if you are to write the winning proposal!

Make no mistake about this: In many, many cases, the customer does not have a completely clear or accurate idea of what the agency needs or even exactly what the major problem is. Many RFPs and their SOWs describe *symptoms* only; it's your job to determine what the *problem* is.

Defining the Problem

Defining or identifying a problem is usually a matter of discriminating between the symptoms and the problem itself. Let's take, as an example to illustrate this principle, a case in which a customer calls for services to straighten out the in-house computer system because it delivers faulty reports. The customer believes that the computer software (program material) is at fault, and therefore calls for the services of specialists in software—systems analysis, programming, and whatever else the proposer's diagnosis indicates it necessary.

In actuality, the faulty reports are symptomatic. The cause(s)—the real problem(s)—may be any or all of the following:

Faulty software
Faulty equipment
Poorly designed data-collection forms
Poor input information
Inaccurate recording of input data

That is, the true problem may have nothing to do with the computer at all!

Here is an actual case that illustrates the value of effective analysis and definition of the customer's wants:

The division of the Postal Service which handles computer data issued an RFP soliciting a contractor to negotiate a Basic Ordering Agreement (BOA) type of services contract. That is, the Postal Service would issue task orders, as needs arose, and the contractor would satisfy the requirements under the conditions and set rates established by the contract.

Since the Postal Service could not predict exactly what tasks would need to be done and what specialists would be needed—its reason for selecting a BOA type of contract—the statement of work listed a wide variety of specialists who might be needed at any time:

Systems designers
Computer systems engineers
Systems analysts
Senior programmers
Midlevel programmers
Junior programmers
Computer operators

Moreover, since the Postal Service had several different types of computers and used programs written in several different computer languages, the statement of work went on to specify a list of computers—IBM, Honeywell, Sperry Rand, and Control Data Corporation models—and a list of languages—FORTRAN, COBOL, PL/1, BASIC, and others.

The requirement stipulated was that the contractor must have on staff and be able to produce on demand any combination of specialists, with capabilities in any combination of machines and languages!

The permutations possible under this requirement are quite staggering. An enormous staff of specialists would be required, for example, if the contractor were indeed required to have permanently on staff a systems analyst experienced in each machine and each language. That is, it would probably require a large number of systems analysts, since it is quite unlikely that any single individual would know all machines and all languages.

The winning proposal described these difficulties and "took an exception"—announced that it offered a plan which deviated from the stated requirement—because there was probably no single organization which could literally meet that requirement. It then went on to define the true need or problem—to *produce* (not necessarily to already have on staff) any specialist or combination of specialists, on demand. The proposal went on to demonstrate the unusual recruiting abilities of the organization submitting it. (The firm specialized in producing technical specialists for short-term assignments.)

Fully conscious that the customer might regard this as a nonresponsive proposal, the writers were at great pains to lay claim to responsiveness, making their case thus: *Responsiveness* is producing the required service or result, although the methods employed might be different from those suggested in the SOW. In short, the proposal tactfully suggested that it was unfair and unrealistic to dictate the manner of satisfying needs as long as the proposing firm could demonstrate that they would meet the needs by whatever legitimate means. Obviously, the Postal Service evaluators agreed with the arguments, for the proposal won a contract.

In this case, the Postal Service started with the assumption that the problem was to find a firm that had all the required specialists on staff. (Possibly it was unaware that there are a number of firms whose business is recruiting technical and professional specialists on short notice for temporary assignments.) The successful proposer, thinking clearly, changed the customer's thinking and made the customer understand that the true problem was to *produce* those specialists on short notice for temporary assignments.

A Test for Problem Definition

There is a simple test to determine whether you are dealing with a problem or its symptoms. A proper problem definition contains within it the seeds of the solution—virtually dictates the solution, in fact, or at least suggests it strongly. If the problem statement does not suggest a solution, there is a large possibility that it is dealing with the symptoms rather than the problem.

Take this case of the Postal Service needs, for example. Once the problem is clearly understood to be the ability to *produce* a variety of computer experts on demand, the solution is obviously effective and rapid recruiting. And had the Postal Service so defined the problem before it issued the solicitation, it would have been at pains to solicit firms whose specialty is such recruiting (of which there are a large number). Instead, it was compelled to read and discard a large number of proposals from small software firms that could not possibly meet the requirement, but that hoped for the best and submitted proposals anyhow!

One excellent way to begin is to assume that what you are studying *is* a symptom and ask yourself (or your team), "What are the possible *causes* of this symptom?" If you find a number of possible causes, there is a large probability that you are indeed dealing with a symptom rather than the problem itself.

Take the case of the new manager who assumes command of an ailing organization. Having been hired to make the organization healthy again, the manager's first objective is to find out exactly what does ail it. The manager confronts the assistant manager who has been inherited along with the job and asks for a definition of the main problem.

The assistant manager reports that the organization, which produces training programs of various kinds, has almost invariably failed to produce an end product on schedule or within budget, and that that is the main problem of the organization. "No," the new manager demurs, "that can't be the problem; that must be two symptoms. But what's the problem? What causes these two symptoms? *Why* is this group of people unable to produce, as planned and scheduled?"

The assistant manager insists that the problem has been defined. But the new manager reasons that these are possible causes:

Poor estimating and planning
Unqualified or poorly qualified staff
Poor management and supervision
Poor management systems

Each of these possible *causes* suggests its own solutions: improve estimating and planning, hire more qualified staff or train incumbent staff, strengthen management through better procedures or hiring more experienced managers and supervisors. But even these are possibly *direct* causes, which are symptoms of other problems. In the actual case from which this example is drawn *all* the possible causes proved to be existent, but some of them were the result of other problems. For example, archaic hiring practices and inadequate salaries automatically excluded the firm from getting good staff. And this applied to midlevel managers and supervisors, too, resulting in poor management! So some of the causes were related to each other.

And there was still another cause which the new manager could not have anticipated but which became apparent later: Because of a large turnover of help and faulty record keeping, when a new contract was awarded to the organization, the proposer of the project was usually already employed elsewhere. Since the firm did not save all the "backup paper" generated to cost the project, the new manager was stuck with a project that had been planned and costed by someone else. The manager had to struggle to deliver what had been promised without knowing how the previous manager had planned to perform and deliver. So even some of the causes of the main symptoms were themselves symptoms of underlying problems.

This failure to have recorded somewhere—preferably in the proposal itself—precise, *quantified* information frequently has other consequences. Not only is the proposal less credible and persuasive than it ought to be, the failure to quantify has within it the seeds for disputes and losses. That is, the risks under the contract are greatly increased for two reasons:

1. If the proposal originator is no longer available, as in the case reported, the project manager is at a great disadvantage.
2. If the customer demands more than the contractor has planned to deliver, it is difficult to resolve the dispute and the contractor is almost certain to lose the argument.

In one such case the customer (the U.S. Navy) contracted for a training manual, but did not suggest a number of pages, illustrations, or other specifics except results desired and source information to be used. The contractor proposed 600 pages of text and illustrations, estimating the number of illustrations, all of which were to be line drawings. A dispute did develop later, the customer deciding that more pages were needed. However, the contract was based on the proposal (included in the contract by reference), and the contractor had no trouble defending its position. (This point will come up again later, in discussions of strategies and other elements of proposal planning and development.)

Part of the problem to be faced in designing and writing a proposal is, often, *how much,* as well as *what.* The customer does not necessarily have an idea of "how much" of whatever is to be supplied is needed; the proposer is expected to estimate "how much."

Strategy and Its Development

Strategy is the principle underlying a plan which is expected to produce success. And success is the achievement of a goal or objective. Tactics are the means of implementation. Strategy is a concept, an idea. Tactics are procedures, methods.

In the proposal field, we must consider at least four kinds of strategy:

Technical or program strategy—the concept or approach which is expected to achieve success in gaining the objectives of the program
Cost or pricing strategy—the concept or approach which will make some economy possible, perhaps to make the proposer a low bidder
Capture strategy—the concept which is expected to make the proposal the winner and gain a contract award
Presentation strategy—the concept of designing the presentation (proposal) to make its contribution to successful capture strategy

Ordinarily, the capture strategy will be one or more of the other three strategies—that is, the plan for success may be based on offering the lowest price, the best program, the most dependable program, or some other such characteristic. If, for example, the proposer becomes convinced that low bid is going to be the most influential factor in the selection, achieving the position of low bidder, without serious compromise to the customer's program goals, should be the main avenue of attack in designing the proposal.

To a large degree, it always comes down to the program—how to offer the most dependable plan, the lowest price, the shortest schedule, the best management, or whatever seem to be the customer's most worrisome concerns.

If strategy is the key to success and success is achieving one or more given objectives, it is fairly obvious that one must first set the objectives—not that obvious objective of winning the contract, but that objective which we think will warm the customer's heart in reading and evaluating our proposal!

The purposes in analysis are, in addition to gaining complete understanding, these:

1. Identify the customer's concerns and rank-order them, trying particularly to identify one main concern—that critical item which is likely to be the most influential factor in selecting a winner.
2. Identify in the SOW all anomalies, if any, and all probable problems in carrying out the project and satisfying the customer's wants.
3. Consider the competition and estimate what competitors are likely to offer and their strengths, relative to your own.
4. Consider all possible approaches to doing the work and meeting the customer's wants (especially that most critical item), and select an approach.

At this point, you are leaving the analytical phase and actually beginning synthesis—synthesis of strategy, approach, and program. Having decided what is that most critical item—the customer's principal "worry item"—you have really set yourself an objective: to steer toward that item, whether it is low price, accelerated schedule, outstanding staff, sophisticated management, ultra-high dependability, or whatever. You are necessarily now considering program approaches and designs which will achieve that objective and persuade the customer to award that contract to you.

But suppose the customer does not have—or is at least not conscious of—any particular facet of the project which worries him especially? Suppose, for example, that the customer assumes that there are no real problems involved in the project and that a competent contractor will be able to carry out the work as a routine? If that is the case, and it often is, your job is to decide for the customer what the principal worry item *ought* to be, and then *sell* that to the customer! That is the fruit of item 2, just listed, suggesting that your analysis must search for and identify anomalies and potential problems.

In short, you must give the customer some *reason*—some *clear-cut, specific* reason—to buy from you, rather than from one of your competitors. And that is another definition of capture strategy: the reason you furnish for buying what you propose.

In some off-the-cuff research carried out in connection with this book, a colleague who queried a number of people in government and private firms gathered a distinct impression that the respondents were pretty much in agreement on three characteristics of successful proposals:

1. They are extremely specific in what they propose.
2. They define clearly the bounds of the project proposed.
3. They are highly credible.

A complete understanding, one which may require you to delve far beyond the surface impressions imparted by the text of an SOW, is indispensable to achieving the above three characteristics. And only a thorough analysis can bring you that kind of understanding.

Some Main Points to Remember

1. Analysis is the key to understanding the requirement. You cannot hope to solve a problem without knowing what the problem is.
2. It's easy to confuse a problem with its symptoms. One way to check is to ask yourself, when studying a statement that purports to describe a problem, "What are the possible causes of this?" If there are a variety of plausible possible causes, with no clear indication of which is the most probable, you are very likely studying a symptom, rather than a problem.
3. One way to decide that you have identified or defined the problem is this: An accurate and precise problem definition usually points directly to the solution—or at least strongly suggests one or two solutions. That is, the problem definition suggests the probable cause, which in turn suggests the solution.
4. Never assume that the customer knows more about the problem than you do. With thorough analysis, you are quite likely to become far more expert than anyone—even more than the customer—in what the customer needs.
5. By the time you have completed the analyses of the requirement, your feet are usually already on the road toward the approach and strategy you will employ.

8

Analytical Methods

There are numerous analytical methods available,
but they all require you to *think*.

The poorly written proposal usually suffers from the same basic defects that other poor writing exhibits: incoherent organization, rambling trains of thought, incomplete ideas, and other such faults—faults of *content*, rather than of style. It is not skill in handling language that is the distinguishing asset of the skilled professional writer nearly so much as it is skill in gathering, sorting out, and organizing information. And that is as true for the writing of proposals as it is for the writing of anything else.

In the case of proposals, such faults are especially prevalent because most proposals are written hurriedly. In a matter of weeks, at most, the proposal team must create a document that would in other circumstances be the subject of perhaps a full year's work. Yet there are organizations that regularly and consistently manage this feat several times a year to win their share of contracts. They do so not through genius but through hard work and methodical discipline. Without that concentrated effort to gather, sort out, and organize the needed information, a competent proposal is almost impossible, and a winning proposal is an accident. But the methods can be learned.

Typically, in organizations not geared to proposal writing—that is, in organizations that improvise a proposal team when the occasion requires one—the effort begins with a meeting that quickly becomes a bull session and accomplishes little except to reveal that no one in the meeting really knows where or how to begin. Even where there is a leader who makes writing assignments, little happens except for scheduling a second meeting, at which no one can boast of having made very much progress in writing.

Ultimately, someone produces a tentative outline or plan with enough copies for everyone. Immediately, the atmosphere changes. Each attendee begins to react to the material offered, usually by "throwing rocks" at the author of the plan. But the meeting now begins to address the problems and results in the formulation of a working plan and rough outline born out of the one originally offered.

Such a rough plan or outline is sometimes referred to as "talking paper" because it gives the attendees something concrete to focus on and react to in order to get their minds working, to make them *think*.

What Is *Thinking*?

Most people, prefacing a remark with something such as, "I think. . . ," probably ought to be saying, "I have the impression, gained somewhere. . . ." The fact is that few of us do a great deal of real *thinking*—truly independent, objective analysis and reflection. Instead, most of us substitute prejudice and other preconceived ideas for thinking. We tend to rely on what appears to us to be secure: what we read in the literature, what we have done in the past, what we have observed being done elsewhere, and other ideas which are at least relatively familiar and which we *can justify*.

Offering a really new or different idea is frightening. It represents risk—the risk of failure, the risk of ridicule, the risk of being held in contempt. Conceiving and offering new ideas requires courage. It required a great deal of courage for Governor Earle to authorize the Pennsylvania Turnpike, the first high-speed highway, in the face of ridicule from experts. The experts regarded the project as Earle's folly. They "knew" that automobile tires could not withstand sustained speeds of more than 35 miles per hour, the speed limit of that day.

Experts derided the building of the first skyscraper buildings. They would sway in the wind and crack. Architects and builders with greater confidence had the courage to go on.

The first steamboat was known as Fulton's Folly. When he demonstrated it, the crowds shouted, "It won't start!" And when he came back to the pier, they shouted, "It won't stop!"

Edison was likewise advised by experts that the electric light was an illusion, a thoroughly impractical idea that only a fool would pursue.

As Don Dible, author of *Up Your OWN Organization* (Entrepreneur Press, Fairfield, Calif. 1971) remarks at his seminars, "Pioneers are people who get arrows in their backs, and missionaries are people who wind up in the pot."

Thinking requires the courage to try something new and different and the intellectual honesty to recognize that the ideas you are putting forth do not represent true thinking. Winston Churchill observed once that "people would rather die than think."

Yet, some people do think. Some have the courage to do so or we would not have the automobile self-starter, the laser, the airplane, or any other fruit of human thinking. Unfortunately, those who do are very much in the minority in our general population—those, that is, who do so of their own volition, spontaneously.

What we need, then, to avoid the waste of aimless meetings and meet the tough schedules of proposal writing is some organized method for getting the effort going without delay. We need to gather information but in most proposals we also need to *create* information—project designs, approaches, procedures, management schemes. We need, therefore, some mechanism for inducing people to really think. Fortunately, such mechanisms exist and can be adapted to the needs of a proposal effort.

First, let's talk about gathering the *available* information.

When All Else Fails, Read the Instructions

A proposal is the result of several decisions. But the quality of any decision is directly dependent on the quality of the information upon which the decision is based. One main purpose of analysis is to refine and add to the raw information represented by the solicitation. And in most cases, the solicitation is the main source of information. It must be read most carefully and many times, both *on* and *between* the lines.

Again and again, proposal writers waste hours in discussions, telephone calls, and other research, seeking answers which are found, eventually, in the RFP itself. Here are two cases to illustrate this.

A NASA installation issued a solicitation for cataloging work to be done on site—in the government's facility, that is. The SOW was brief and almost cryptic, describing the volume of cataloging to be done and requiring the proposer to list the staff proposed and the costs. It was clear that there was an incumbent contractor doing the work at present, but the solicitation did not specify how many people were presently engaged in the work.

One proposer went to great lengths to inquire about how many people the project employed, meeting frustration at every turn. Analysis of the volume of work suggested that only two people were required. Yet it was by no means certain that only two were, in fact, presently employed in the work. It seemed absolutely necessary to find out what the present staffing was.

The proposer was at the point of calling the contracting officer for permission to visit the site—which, in itself, would not necessarily supply the answer wanted. But, for fear of triggering information which would be sent to all proposers, he decided instead to devote more time to study and analysis of the slender SOW.

Although the writer of the SOW had consciously avoided stating how many were already employed on the job, the information was plainly in the statement; indirect references were made to four individuals by functional titles—secretary, senior cataloger, junior cataloger, and parts lister.

Convinced that two could handle the work, the proposer suggested employing three (instead of the four apparently now doing the job) and demonstrated that three would be an ample staff. The contracting officer decided that this proposal could not be denied the contract.

In another case, which involved publications support to a division of the Department of Agriculture, the solicitation called for a variety of publications services under a BOA. One proposer, invoking the Freedom of Information Act, asked for a list of prices currently charged by the incumbent contractor. Studying the list, he found that it was going to be most difficult to be the low bidder, which he thought he had to be to win the contract.

He was almost at the point of submitting a "no bid," when he decided to study the solicitation package more closely in one final effort to find a strategy for being the low bidder. Concealed (virtually) in a thick appendix of specifications he found his answer.

One of the many items to be priced for the contract was typing double-spaced pages of manuscript. Using the then-standard $8 \times 10\frac{1}{2}$ inch paper (now $8\frac{1}{2} \times 11$ inches, as in commercial practice), a typical typing area would normally be about 7×9 inches, at the largest. And using the more popular elite or 10-point type this would amount to 27 lines of 84 characters and spaces each, or a grand total of 2,268 keystrokes. The price currently being paid by the Department of Agriculture seemed about right for such a page of draft typing, but it didn't seem possible to cut that.

However, buried among that stack of specifications, this proposer found the customer's own specification for a "page" of typing. It specified a page as 55 characters wide and 18 lines deep, a total of 990 characters and spaces! That was less than one-half the number he had assumed would represent a typical typed page. The price now being paid for *that* page of typing was quite high. He had little difficulty now in cutting the price and winning the contract.

The first step in analysis is, then, careful and thorough reading of the solicitation. That can rarely be done in a single reading. It usually requires several, and the readings should be done with a large writing pad, making up a checklist.

Why a Checklist?

It is said about those who slaughter and process hogs that "they use everything but the squeal." The checklist you should make as you begin reading the solicitation may not be quite that useful, but it comes close. If you follow the plans suggested in this book, the checklist will serve a number of purposes and wind up as part of your proposal.

One immediate purpose in making the checklist is to set down every item you should consider and respond to in your proposal, so that nothing "falls between the cracks" and furnishes grounds to tag your proposal as nonresponsive. It's quite easy to miss important items. Or miss items which do not appear to *you* to be important, but which the *customer* thinks important.

Specifically, there are three types of information which are required on the checklist:

1. The listing of information required in your proposal. Some of these items may be in the SOW, but many will be found elsewhere—in the customer's cover letter, in the *schedule*, when one is included (a specimen of the anticipated contract with some of the entries necessarily blank), and even elsewhere in the solicitation package.
2. The specifications. These are usually entirely in the SOW, but be alert for any which may appear elsewhere in the package. For a hardware procurement or the purchase of any commodity, these are likely to be a lengthy and well-defined listing of required features and characteristics. But for a custom-services contract, the "specifications" are often anything but specific. Still, they are there, implied, at least, and they include such things as reports required, due dates, and whatever else the customer has provided to convey the expected results.
3. The evaluation criteria. These should, of course, be given prominence in your checklist.

The best way to proceed with this is to record each item as you encounter it in your reading and make whatever notes appear to be pertinent. It might begin to shape up somewhat as in Figure 8.1.

Almost invariably you will begin to find anomalies or apparent anomalies, redundancies, and provisions which are either lacking in detail or are simply unclear about what the author intended to say. There is no better time than now to surface problems which are inherent in the solicitation or requirement itself. And as you progress through your checklist, you will find that many of these questions will send you back to the beginning to start reading again. Or you may find answers to some of the questions which plagued you in an earlier portion of the solicitation.

Once you have completed your draft list—and it usually takes more than one reading to do this—you may find it expedient to rewrite the list, organizing it according to the following categories:

Project specifications
Proposal requirements
Evaluation items

At the same time, you will want to group all the redundancies as a single item with all the citations of that item listed opposite it. For example, if the

ITEM	PAGE	NOTES
CPFF anticipated	Cover letter	Will consider alternates proposed.
Proposal due 11/17/80, COB	Cover letter	
Monthly progress reports	4 of SOW	
3-phase program	8 of SOW	1st phase task analysis? Required results each phase not specified. Be sure to cover and specify in proposal.
1-year schedule projected; accelerated schedules invited.	22 of SOW	
Staff qualifications specified. 2 Ph.D.s, several M.A.s, all college grads.	31 of SOW	Screen résumés carefully against specs. Also, against evaluation criteria. *Anomaly*: Specs for 2d Investigator greater than those for Principal Investigator. Resolve.
1st phase to be 13 weeks.	33 of SOW	
1st phase to be 17 weeks?	Schedule 35 of SOW	Resolve length of 1st phase.

FIGURE 8.1
Typical entries on a draft checklist.

solicitation has called for progress reports at four different points, list progress reports, but also list all the pages demanding them. These redundancies sometimes contain within them their own anomalies, which must somehow be resolved. (It often becomes apparent that several people contributed to the solicitation and that there was little central editing and control.)

Sometimes you will find that suspected anomalies are not really that at all, but stem from semantic differences. For example, one writer may have referred to a "task analysis," another may have called it the "needs analysis," and still another may have called it the "front-end analysis," although all refer to the same function. This can be confusing, of course, and it is necessary to establish that all the terms refer to the same process.

As you can see, there have been a number of immediate benefits from drafting the checklist, in surfacing and drawing your attention to incipient problems, as well as clarifying what you must now do, both in writing the proposal and in designing the program and costing it later. But there are other uses for the checklist as the analysis and proposal development progress.

The first information resource is, then, the solicitation itself, and the checklist is the first step in squeezing the maximum of information from it.

Searching for the Deliverable

A second use of the checklist, even before the concentrated analysis which is usually necessary, is to search out and identify or define as clearly as possible the deliverable item. That is what the project is all about, what the customer is willing to commit all the dollars for.

In some cases, the deliverable is quite clearly defined. An R&D contract to develop a new aircraft usually calls for a test prototype (often several such prototypes) and a complete set of drawings and reports. But the most important end item is that prototype and its drawings. The same is usually true for any hardware R&D project.

This is also true even in software, where the entire project is geared to developing an end item—a training program, a manual, a movie, a management plan, a computer program, or other such easily identifiable products. But it's less true where the project is designed either to deliver a service to a third party—treat alcoholics, for example—or to perform studies and researches to gain new information.

Where a tangible product is required, whether hardware or software, it is usually defined by the specifications. These define the various characteristics the item must have to be acceptable to the customer. But in those cases where the customer does not truly know what the end result of the project will or must be, the proposer finds it necessary to aid the customer in projecting the deliverable item(s). Many proposers shrink from this problem for fear of offering something not acceptable to the customer. But the evasive tactics such proposers use are simply whistling in the dark. The customer will be persuaded by some other proposer, who has had the courage and wisdom to make the projection.

One recent RFP, for example, issued by the EPA, called for the contractor to perform literature searches and gather up all the state-of-the-art information on methods for coping with chlorine pollution in water. The contractor was then to translate this information into a manual, incorporating into that same manual materials developed elsewhere by the EPA or EPA contractors.

But there were other provisos. The contractor had also to convene a conference of qualified authorities in the field to review the draft manuscript and make suitable comments and criticisms, after which the customer would review the marked-up manuscript, and ultimately issue authority for the contractor to complete the project—convert the now-approved manuscript into a manual.

Superficially, that seems straightforward enough: the end product is to be an instruction manual. But the manual is not the only deliverable item. The customer obviously attaches a great deal of importance to the review conference required. And it is the contractor who must not only organize and conduct the conference, but also identify suitable, qualified technical authorities and persuade them to give their time for the conference. So although the conference is not a "deliverable," in the strictest technical sense of the word, the contractor is nevertheless required to deliver those technical authorities. These should be regarded as an interim deliverable.

An adjunct to the checklist should be an identification or definition of the deliverable item(s), drawn as clearly as is possible at this early stage, although this is subject to refinement as the analysis proceeds.

In study projects the deliverable item is generally a final report, although interim progress reports, meetings, and even presentations are often required. But in the end the final report is essentially all the customer has in hand for the money, and a stack of pages stapled together may represent millions of dollars. Of course, the money went to pay for all the effort, for gathering the information that is contained in that stack of pages. But the pages—that report—is *the* deliverable.

The provision of services to a third party is another kind of proposition, and the deliverable is less tangible than in most other cases. The Minority Business Development Agency (formerly Office of Minority Business Enterprise) spends some $50 million annually to fund about 300 organizations to provide free services to minority entrepreneurs. The deliverable here is the service itself, and the only tangible product is the reports. But the true deliverable, as the customer wishes it to materialize, is *success* in providing the services. Such success is commonly measured by the number of dollars in loans the organization has been able to help minority entrepreneurs get, by agreements with large firms to provide work for the minority "clients," and by other measures of helpful services actually provided. The services themselves are of little value unless they help accomplish the customer's *mission*—in this case, actually *helping* the minority entrepreneurs in some way which can be measured and made a matter of record. (Documentation is never unimportant in government circles and is especially important where the deliverable item is somewhat intangible.)

So things are not always what they appear to be in RFPs, and you must sometimes distinguish between the apparent or nominal deliverable and the true deliverable. That true deliverable is the *result* the customer is pursuing with the contract.

At this point, you have collected a number of sets or items of information:

1. The definition of the deliverable—*what the customer wants to buy*
2. The specifications which, presumably, describe that deliverable in some detail
3. The list of items the customer needs to know about in order to choose the best contractor—what it will take to sell the customer
4. The measures the customer says will be applied in judging those last-named items

You have these items pretty much in the customer's own language, perhaps modified slightly as you have interpreted them in drafting the checklist, often laden with redundancies, anomalies, uncertainties, and even gaps. But if you have done this job thoroughly, you have as much raw data as is available from the RFP, and you are ready to begin serious analysis. In this next phase of analysis you will explore these lists and develop premises to form the basis of your proposal.

Analysis by Group Methods

It is rather well accepted that, properly coordinated, a group of people can produce better information than can an individual. In the Army, for example, when it is necessary to estimate the range to a target, an accepted method is to have individuals estimate independently, and then average the individual estimates. This provides surprisingly accurate results in most cases.

Unless you are writing the proposal alone, you are well-advised to gather together the entire proposal team to analyze the requirement and devise your proposal strategies and approaches. But it is necessary to *manage* this group, according to some preset method or procedure, to avoid a babel and make progress. And there are several methods which have been proved in practice to work. All resemble each other to some extent.

Brainstorming

Brainstorming, the invention of advertising executive Alex Osborne, is one widely used method for achieving a synergy of ideas. Briefly, it consists of gathering a group of individuals, selecting a single question or topic, and inviting a free flow of ideas. The work is done in phases. In the first phase, the basic rule is that no judgments are made. That is, all ideas and idea fragments are invited; all are accepted, for the moment, and recorded. None are jeered at, sneered at, laughed at, or applauded. They are simply entered into the record for consideration. Anyone may "piggyback" an idea on one previously uttered.

When the outpouring of ideas has finally ceased, the first phase is over and the second phase begins. In this phase, the ideas are evaluated. Many are discarded; others are considered in their original form or, possibly, with modifications or in combination with other ideas. Finally, whichever are considered best are adopted. A third phase, which may or may not include full group participation, is implementation of the adopted ideas.

The method requires a leader, of course, who must pose the question, lead the session, and maintain discipline. The leader will also have to be the final arbiter in making any final choices and selections, or in settling disputes should any arise.

Value Analysis

Value analysis—also called value engineering and value management—is a method developed by a General Electric Company engineer, Larry Miles, after World War II. During that war the United States found itself facing many shortages of needed materials, as warring nations usually do, and was compelled to utilize many substitute materials (such as plastics for metals) in production processes. A GE executive discovered something curious: sometimes the substitute material proved better in practice than did the original material for which it was a substitute. And he found this to be true fairly often. He assigned Miles to investigate this.

Out of Miles's work finally emerged the overall discipline he developed, which is an organized, procedural attack on products and processes, seeking more efficient design and methods.

The basis of value analysis is *function:* a first objective is to determine what something *does*, rather than what it *is*. A distinguishing feature is that the discipline differentiates between a *basic* or *primary* function—the chief objective of the device or process—and *secondary* or *supporting* functions, which may or may not be necessary to the basic function.

Deciding what the basic function is is probably the most critical and important element of the entire discipline. It is on this basis that the team—value analysis is based on a team effort, with brainstorming an important method—is able to determine several key facts:

Which, if any, secondary functions are necessary to the basic function
What other ways the basic function can be accomplished
What the basic function costs
What other ways to accomplish the basic function cost

On this basis, unnecessary secondary functions can be stripped away, saving time or money, and sometimes a totally different way of accomplishing the basic function can be uncovered. Moreover, each secondary function which is deemed to be necessary may itself become the subject of value analysis, to find better ways to accomplish it.

Value analysis depends heavily on certain rules, which all but compel the analysis to be conducted on an objective basis. One rule is that a function must be expressed simply, as a verb and noun. A tie clip's basic function might be expressed as "fastens tie." A secondary function might be "is decorative." Being decorative is not supportive of the basic function. However, here the team will recognize that being decorative has certain value and is necessary for other reasons. No one, for example, would suggest that a paper clip be used as a tie clip! On the other hand, if a strictly utilitarian object, such as an electrical junction box, has a decorative rim which adds to manufacturing cost, the team will advocate its elimination.

Value analysis may be applied to any aspect of work efficiency. Although used most frequently to minimize cost, value analysis may also be used to minimize time required—that is, to seek faster ways to accomplish a basic function, rather than less costly ways—or to minimize materials required (or a specific material, for that matter). If tin were in short supply, value analysis might be used to find substitutes that would work as well or better. The interesting feature of value analysis is that while reducing costs, the studies often result in improvement as well.

Applying the basic methods to RFP analysis may reduce costs, and thus these basic methods should probably be used to address each cost center individually: time, labor-hours, overhead, outside costs, materials, or whatever other centers of major cost are anticipated. However, the study would begin by seeking to determine the basic function of the overall project—the end result sought by the customer.

Systems Analysis

The term *systems analysis* has been used widely, without firm definition. It has become almost a generic term, rather than the identifying name of a given methodology. It is applied to any study of what a system is, is not, or should be. The chief feature of system analysis is that it examines an entire system, rather than the components. That is, it *focuses* on the system.

Inevitably, systems analysis closely resembles value analysis, although it is not bound firmly to a prescribed set of rules and procedures as value analysis is. But the basis of systems analysis is also *function*—what the system is supposed to *do* as a system and the subordinate functions in the system necessary to the main function.

Systems analysts tend strongly to rely upon graphics—charting—which proves to be an effective approach. This underlies much of the method advocated here.

Why It Can't Be Done

Some organizations favor a why-it-can't-be-done method of RFP analysis. In this method, a brainstorming session addresses the question of why it can't be done. All possible obstacles to successful accomplishment are suggested—it's never been done before; it's almost impossible to find enough qualified staff; it requires quantum leaps in the state of the art; not enough time is allowed;

excessive development work is required; and so forth. And, as in brainstorming, when the flood of reasons has subsided, a second-phase session examines all the recorded reasons for the impossibility and throws out those which are frivolous or can't be logically supported.

The purpose of this kind of session is to surface all the problems, rather than to prove that the project should not be undertaken. This offers at least two major benefits: it provides the proposer a data bank with which the project can be planned thoroughly and designed realistically, and it furnishes a basis for powerful arguments to be included in the proposal. (Later, we shall discuss how these are to be used effectively.)

This is not a complete analysis in itself and should be used *in addition to, but not in place of,* a general analysis. This analysis may contribute to, but will not serve in place of, an analysis to identify the requirement or to answer several other important questions. On the other hand, it can contribute materially to the program design and to technical arguments in your proposal.

There are a number of other analytical methods recognized academically, but the most potent ones, for proposal purposes, are those revolving around the concept of function. However, one which has proved its merits many times over is a combination of functional analysis and the use of charts. We refer to it here as the *graphics* method of analysis.

Graphic Analysis

The use of graphics in analysis, like the use of a checklist, has by-products beyond the immediate one of furnishing an analytical tool. Ultimately, the charts developed will find their way into the proposal itself to explain the approach and support the arguments. And in so doing, they will be far more useful than are charts developed as an afterthought to explain the text. (Later, we shall see that the whole idea of using graphics to support text is a logical reversal.)

The simple fact is that a first reading of many RFPs may confuse, rather than illuminate—only rarely are an RFP and work statement so well organized and well written that a reader can grasp the entire need and concept in a first reading. Preparing a checklist, therefore, as a first step, is not necessarily directly helpful, nor is it always possible to determine on first reading just what should and should not be entered into that list—that is, what is important and what is trivial. Preparing a rough flowchart, setting down graphically what the customer has stated textually, is often an aid to grasping the customer's overall idea. In fact, and contrary to the suggestion that preparing a checklist is a good first step, in some cases it is better to sketch out a rough flowchart first.

As in the case of the checklist, only far more effectively in most cases, the flowchart begins to show up anomalies, redundancies, and gaps in the need or project, as described in the work statement.

The Agenda

The leader needs to have an agenda of some sort—at least a list of questions to be addressed. Here are a number of items you would ordinarily seek answers to, although a given case may require many more questions and answers:

1. What is the *stated* need or problem?
2. Is this the *real* need or problem (if not same as above)?
3. What appears to be the customer's chief *concern* (e.g., cost, time, dependability, innovation, etc)?
4. What approach best meets the answers to above questions?
5. What general or capture strategy does this suggest?
6. What is to be the theme of our proposal?

Each of these is a broad question which merits more detailed examination.

Stated Need Versus Real Need   Even when the customer has stated the need or problem accurately, the SOW often includes so much information about the need that much of the information supplied is extraneous, dealing with trivia rather than the *essential* need. Because of this, the essence of the need is not always obvious, but must be distilled from the statement of need, stripping away the distractions to reveal it. Let's use the example of the EPA solicitation cited earlier.

Despite the fact that the solicitation package is about one inch thick, the SOW is only slightly over three pages of text, plus a schedule of events and dates which must be met. The opening paragraph of the SOW, which ostensibly defines the overall requirement, reads as follows:

> **General Discussion**
> The goal of this proposed study is to derive from the published scientific literature a detailed and comprehensive data base regarding certain classes of chemicals. The information compiled will serve two distinct purposes: 1) to establish a core information base concerning the health and ecological effects of the compounds present in all environmental media (food, water, air, soil, etc.) and 2) to compile the recommendations for ambient water quality criteria for the Office of Water Planning and Standards for the compounds listed. The environmental quality and health effect documents for a given pollutant(s) must accurately reflect the latest scientific knowledge useful in indicating the kind and extent of all identifiable effects on public health or welfare which may be expected from the presence of such pollutant(s), in varying quantities and differing averaging times, through various media.

The next paragraph goes on to cite the EPA publications manual as the source of specifications for "successive and final draft of the documents," although "the documents" were not specified or referred to earlier! (Except, perhaps, by implication.)

The third paragraph specifies that the contractor will provide the usual range of publication skills and functions and states that the product must be reviewed by the peer review (not yet explained!) and EPA authorities.

It is then made clear that this study and writing will cover chlorine only, although the end product, a manual, will cover other pollutants. But the contractor will be furnished draft materials from other sources to incorporate, along with his own material on chlorine, in the final manual.

It is quite obvious that this first page of the statement was written and typed at a different time than were the second and third pages. In fact, the second and third pages are quite obviously taken from some earlier RFP and are copies of copies!

This probably caused what appears to be excessive stress on publications skills and experience, rather than on technical or professional knowledge of the biochemical fields involved. A firm of writers and editors might easily be misled into thinking that they would qualify for the contract, whereas it is most unlikely that the contract will go to anyone other than a staff of biochemists. Studying the requirement even briefly suggests rather strongly that the project will demand a great deal of knowledge of the field in order to recognize what literature to review, what to abstract information from, and what information is new or at least up to date.

So whereas the *stated* need is made to appear to be for publications skills and effort, the real need is almost certainly for relevant technical and professional skills and effort, with publications know-how important, but almost surely of secondary importance.

The evaluation criteria tend to support this, again stressing publications experience relevant to criteria documents in the health and ecological assessment field, but pointing also to "scientific and support staff required" for the job.

Elsewhere, in the description of what the customer wants to find in the proposal, the revelation finally comes: the customer wishes to know about your technical approach, anticipated problems, methods, and procedures. The SOW then continues to discuss the need for technical management. Here, much more stress is laid on technical matters related to content than on technical matters related to producing a publication.

The stated need is, in this case, for a contractor to prepare a criteria document. But the real need is for a contractor to gather, assess, and compile the information for the document. There is no doubt that the latter set of skills will weigh more heavily in the evaluation than will the publications skills. And even that is not all of it: The contractor must handle just about all the work required to organize and conduct the peer-review conference, including identifying qualified individuals and persuading them to participate. It is likely that the capability for doing this will be weighted heavily in evaluation.

In a formal analysis, conducted by a staff of people who are knowledgeable in the relevant technical and professional fields of environmental health hazards and biochemistry, the staff should be able to evaluate the real problems to be anticipated in carrying this project out to a successful conclusion. In fact, the success of the analysis depends heavily on the knowledge of those specialists. The individual responsible for leading the proposal effort and directing the team may or may not be expert in the subject matter of the proposal and is likely not to be, in many cases. The systems employed, therefore, must be such that the leader can utilize the technical and professional capabilities and experience of the proposal staff as if they were his or her own. That is one major consideration in using the overall analytical system we advocate here. It does accomplish just that. Whatever preliminary work has been done by the leader to prepare checklists and drawings, and to formulate preliminary estimates of critical factors, produces "talking paper"—guidelines which set the experts' feet on the road. But it should be considered to be a rough draft, requiring much work before final revisions are made.

The Basic Analytical Method: The Chief Advantage of Using Graphics

The recommended method—the system of analysis using graphics as a tool—is based on the principles of value analysis (functional analysis), using brainstorming methods as a medium and flow charting as an aid. (Value analysis has a specialized flow diagramming method called "FAST," for Functional Analysis Systems Technique, which is beyond the scope of our discussion here.) Functional analysis enables the team to be thoroughly objective, with a criterion for gauging their objectivity. The flow charting aids communication among the team but, even more helpfully, it exposes gaps, anomalies, and other problems. But it has as its most important attribute the capability of enabling a nonexpert to lead the team in making expert analyses and expert synthesis of a program.

Let's take the case of a proposal to the U.S. Corps of Engineers, for logistics support of construction work the Corps does in Saudi Arabia. The basic need was for a United States contractor to receive supplies and construction materials at some central point in the United States and ship them to Saudi Arabia, to the various construction contractors. The logistics contractor was to receive the shipments in Saudi Arabia also.

The leader of the proposal team was not a logistics expert and had no special technical qualifications in any area except that of proposal writing. Prior to the first meeting with the proposer's staff of experts, the leader studied the work statement and prepared a checklist and simple block diagram:

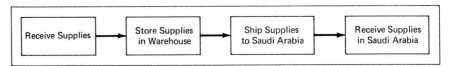

The leader assembled the team of experts in a large conference room, before a blackboard that ran the length of the room. After distributing copies of the checklist—everyone already had a copy of the work statement, which they had read before the meeting—the leader drew the simple block diagram on the blackboard, saying with a gesture toward the diagram, "Here is the job."

The experts snorted and chuckled at the gross oversimplification. The leader agreed that the job entailed a bit more than was shown in the diagram, but admitted not being an expert in such systems. It was up to the experts to expand that block diagram into something more representative of the project.

It took all of that day and several subsequent meetings to develop that diagram into a true flow diagram. Supplies of many kinds had to be received and stored in a warehouse. But the shipments had to be inspected and accepted, with deficiencies noted on DD 250 forms. Some items had to be repaired, some had to receive regular maintenance (tractors, for example). Warehouse records had to be made up and kept. Lost shipments had to be traced. Ships had to be loaded. A safety program had to be developed. A computer system had to be maintained. A site had to be selected and proposed. And on the Saudi end, construction companies had to pick up their supplies at the warehouse there. But if they failed to, the logistics contractor had to deliver the supplies!

Before the proposal was finished, that simple block diagram had expanded into a 6-foot flowchart. And ultimately, it had to be married to two other flowcharts, one showing the EDP (electronic data processing) system, and the other showing the creation and flow of reports and records.

The design problems were fought out in that conference room during those meetings. Problems were anticipated and solutions developed. And during the course of all this work, it became apparent which individual had the greatest competence in or best grasp of each area of work. This led to the best decisions on writing assignments, another "bonus" result of the method.

This is one way to use the graphics method; others are possible. In some cases a practical method is for the individual making the initial study of the RFP and work statement to translate the work statement into a flowchart, charting the work as the customer has described it. This usually results in a draft flowchart, as described earlier, which is probably a far cry from how you will ultimately propose to handle the project, but it's an excellent beginning, despite the many faults it will contain. (The faults, usually readily discernible, are likely to be the greatest asset of the draft flowchart.)

A useful variation of this idea is to have each individual assigned to study the RFP prepare a draft flowchart, and compare the different flow charts at a later meeting. This method begins to approach brainstorming itself, in that a variety of individual interpretations of what the work statement says are documented for comparison.

The choice of method depends primarily on the nature of the RFP and work statement. If a work statement does, in fact, describe a project in some detail, suggesting steps, phases, procedures, and the like, it lends itself well to being flow charted directly from the statement. However, if the statement is somewhat general or vague, identifying little beyond the end result required, the burden of project design is entirely on the proposer.

A Few Tips on Flow Charting

Somehow flowcharts appear mysterious and cabalistic to many who have never worked with them before. Possibly this is because many such charts use boxes of various shapes to suggest the functions described. (In computer programming, for example, there are standard shapes for boxes describing most major functions in data processing, just as there are such standard shapes in construction drawings and other specialized fields.) Using boxes of special shapes is a help, to the initiated, because the shapes help the reader of such a chart recognize a type of function at a glance. Moreover, a "busy" chart—one having a great many boxes—can become quite confusing; here, the different shapes help the user find his or her way through the maze of boxes and lines.

There is no good reason for not using simple square or rectangular boxes, however; they are perfectly acceptable, especially in proposals. (The customer may not be too familiar with flowcharts and therefore may be less confused or less intimidated by rectangular boxes than by specially shaped ones!)

The basic idea in a flowchart is to show, graphically, the sequence of events or phases of a process—how the end result is achieved or the end product developed. Take the simple case of preparing a technical manual for an agency. The most *basic functions* are these:

Gathering the data (research, which is really part of writing)
Organizing and outlining
Writing
Editing
Typing
Proofreading
Illustrating
Production (master copy for printing, usually

The simplest presentation would be as follows:

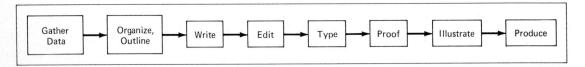

This is oversimplified in that it presents the *logical* sequence of events, but not necessarily the actual or chronological sequence. That is, for example, illustrating work does not usually wait for the completion of typing and proofreading, but is generally concurrent. Too, this simplified presentation does not reflect the manuscript reviews and revisions and the several draft stages usually part of such a project. The chart is, then, a rough draft that can be used to identify the main functions and steps, but requires a bit of sophistication before it can be regarded as an accurate representation. For one thing, in many such projects the contractor is required to first prepare an outline or "book plan" and submit it to the customer for review and approval before beginning a serious writing effort. This would be represented in the following manner:

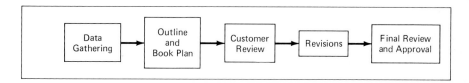

Another way to represent this, one which actually conveys more information, is this:

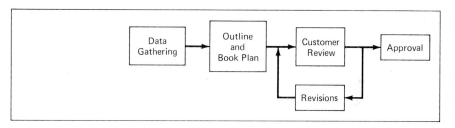

The advantage of this latter representation is that it shows a *feedback loop*, which represents as many reviews and revisions as necessary to gain final approval, rather than the single draft review shown in the first representation.

Flowcharts can also distinguish concurrent events from consecutive events, as do PERT (program evaluation and review technique) diagrams, which are frequently used for that purpose. Here is an example of how that may be accomplished graphically:

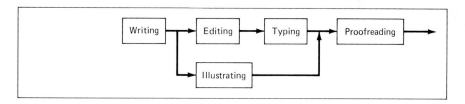

This shows writer-generated sketches going to an art department to be drawn into illustrations, which are developed as writing and editing progresses. The illustrations go to proofreading also to check the words used in the illustration.

Each block of the original, simplified chart may be developed into a series of blocks which are either consecutive or concurrent. Data gathering or writer research, for example, may entail all of the following source materials:

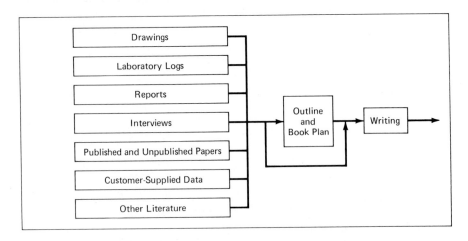

Developing your flowchart in this detail enables you to begin getting a true appreciation of the magnitude of your task and the potential problems. But it may also help you find new ideas, shortcuts, and other aids to both designing the project and preparing an effective presentation—proposal, that is.

Just presenting the above to a customer who has given you only a rather general idea of where to find source materials helps convey some idea of your own knowledge and competence in your field; the ability to plan in detail is rather good evidence that you (1) understand the need and (2) know your business. But that comes later. At this moment we are using graphic techniques to assist us in analyzing the requirement and gaining a full perspective on the size and scope of the work required, as well as potential problems. In fact, it all but compels you to go from generalizations to details, and details are essential to winning.

By this time you have made a progression from that first, general chart that was based almost entirely on what the customer said in the work statement, to a more detailed chart that shows the step-by-step functions and phases *you know are necessary.*

The act of deliberately expanding each block of the draft chart is a key device in forcing yourself to think out the project in detail. You may not wish to present all the finite detail in your final charts, which are going to be incorporated in the proposal itself. But whether you do or do not use the fully detailed charts, it is good analytical technique to develop them for the purpose of surfacing every task and subtask. Only on the basis of this knowledge of the project will you be able to propose proper staffing and estimate costs with a fair degree of accuracy.

There are cases, of course, where you have little to start with except some idea, whether clear or detailed, of the end result or end product required. Such cases require a somewhat different technique to prepare a first-draft flowchart. Let's take a case where the customer has not been especially clear about anything except the fact that the agency has a problem. Let us suppose that the task is to prepare or revise (update) engineering drawings from the actual equipment model, a process often referred to as *reverse engineering.* You know that the end product is to be one or more drawings that depict the equipment as it actually exists. Since you know little more than what the end product is to be, that is probably the best place to begin your chart:

Working backward, you first ask what is necessary—specifically, that is, not generally—to preparing that new drawing? The proper answer to that question furnishes the blocks leading to the last one. You do know, however, that the customer will have to furnish the equipment itself—or access to it, if it is impractical to move the equipment to your own facility. You know that you will have to examine the equipment for all materials and dimensions, inquire as to manufacturing processes or specify from your own knowledge what they should be (for example, stamping, milling, punching, extruding, and so forth), and determine what the assembly and disassembly procedures are. (Most sets of engineering drawings must include all this information.)

You know, then, that you will have to disassemble the equipment, make measurements, decide on all processes for manufacturing and assembly procedures, and translate all this information into drawings. In fact, the final block will be, in most cases, not *a* drawing, but a *set* of drawings:

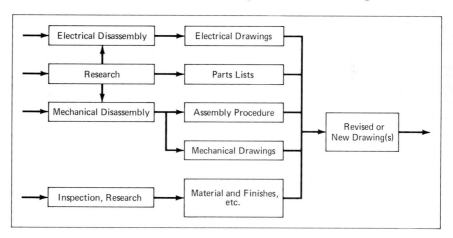

Regardless of whether this is a single end drawing or a set (for simple equipment and simple drawings, all the information could be on a single drawing), all the above and possibly other information will be required before the final drawing or drawing package can be prepared. As a next step, then, you must work back from each of the four items shown, to determine what is necessary to achieve that item. And then you must work backward again, and again, until you reach the starting point, which is, probably, examination and disassembly of the prototype equipment supplied.

In the actual case, you are likely to have at least a reasonable presumption of the starting point, as well as of the end result or end product required:

The problem is to get from one end to the other—to fill in the functions, phases, and processes indicated by the broken line. Obviously, people who are expert in the art of reverse engineering must do this, drawing upon their own experience and knowledge of typical problems and typical needs for the work. But, at the same time, they must fit their knowledge and experience into the situation presented by the work statement. This may introduce unusual problems or difficulties. Or it may introduce unusual opportunities to do the work more efficiently or more economically than usual!

Problems May Be Your Most Important Opportunity

A vice president of U.S. Industries with an unusual penchant for incisive thinking was fond of observing that "there are no problems—only opportunities." His thinking was sound enough. He meant to dramatize the proposition that anyone can do a job when no problems are involved, but solving problems to get a job done was the way to demonstrate your own worth, whether as an employee or as a contractor. Ergo, problems represented opportunities.

The concept fits well here. In many cases, an RFP will specifically instruct proposers to delineate in their proposals all problems they anticipate, along with information on how the proposer plans to cope with the problem. Often enough, this is the subject of evaluation criteria. But even when the customer has not thought to request such data, smart proposers make an effort to furnish it anyhow. It may be the key to winning the contract, particularly if no competitor has been thoughtful enough or honest enough to discuss anticipated problems and the means for successfully coping with them.

Therefore, a major focus during analysis ought to be on discovering the problems which should be anticipated. And the more probable the problem or the more serious the problem, the more important it is to point it out and discuss it.

For example, our experience in preparing technical manuals tells us that one problem which occurs frequently is that promised data fails to appear: the engineers are not available for interview, the logbooks cannot be located, the reports contain little useful information, and other promised or typical avenues of information peter out into near nothingness.

The government agency invariably requires one or more reviews of draft manuscripts and even of final camera-ready masters. The RFP will stipulate that the government will take x number of working days to complete review and furnish either approval or suggestions for revision. But almost invariably, the government will take several times the stipulated number of days to perform the review. Or the project will require more than the usual number of revisions. If the end date stated in the RFP is of some critical importance, such delays become serious problems. The proposal should recognize the hazard and offer contingency plans to cope successfully with the problem.

This is where the "why it can't be done" type of analysis is most useful: it focuses directly on problems. This is where to invoke Murphy's law, which says that if anything can go wrong it will go wrong. Each necessary step in the project, but especially those steps which are not fully under the contractor's direct control, should be examined with a "what if" question. ("What if" the government takes two extra weeks in review? What if the printer fails to deliver on time? What if we can't get the laboratory logs? What if we can't get access to the equipment?)

The less obvious the potential problem, the more likely it is to be helpful as part of your proposal strategy, because competitors are likely to overlook it or think it too unimportant to mention. However, don't confuse "less obvious" with "trivial." Do not concentrate on trivial problems, those which should be handled as a routine and should cause you no trouble. Making an issue of trivial problems in your proposal would have an adverse effect, causing the customer to wonder whether you are competent enough for the job. If your proposal mentions these at all, it should be in passing, with the notation that your normal working procedures handle such minor problems routinely.

Graphics often furnish solutions to problems. If the schedule—time—is a problem, finding those concurrent paths, the functions that can be performed concurrently, furnishes an immediate means for shortening the schedule. The charts may also reveal tasks which may be combined to save time.

Value analysis, for example, was used by a New England engineering firm to assist the EPA in accelerating the processing of grants for wastewater-treatment plants. Using the FAST diagraming method referred to earlier, a specialized variant of the flowchart, it did not take long to discover that the chief time consumer in the overall process was the writing of technical reports on the required tests and studies. Once the analysis demonstrated that these reports were taking many months to write, it was obvious to all that this process could be readily speeded up, and all effort was then focused on doing so.

The graphic method can help determine not only *where* the problem lies, but exactly *what* it is. Value analysis and similar methods have been and are used often to improve existing products and processes. But the methods can and should be used to improve original design, as in the case of designing a project to be proposed.

The Logic of a Functional Flowchart

Functional analysis is a *logical* method. There is a logic to the analysis, and there is a logic to the graphic presentation of a functional flowchart. The basic logic of such a chart is that it relates *why*, reading from the starting point toward the end, and *how*, reading in reverse. For example:

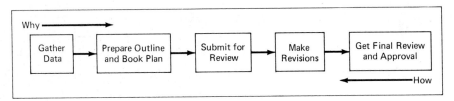

WHY:

WHY GATHER DATA? TO PREPARE OUTLINE & BOOK PLAN.

WHY PREPARE OUTLINE & BOOK PLAN? TO SUBMIT FOR REVIEW.

WHY SUBMIT FOR REVIEW? TO GET CUSTOMER COMMENTS FOR REVISION.

WHY MAKE REVISIONS? TO GET FINAL APPROVAL.

HOW:

HOW TO GET FINAL REVIEW AND APPROVAL? BY MAKING REVISIONS.

HOW TO MAKE REVISIONS? BY GETTING CUSTOMER COMMENTS (SUBMIT FOR REVIEW).

HOW TO SUBMIT FOR REVIEW? BY PREPARING OUTLINE & BOOK PLAN.

HOW TO PREPARE OUTLINE & BOOK PLAN? BY GATHERING DATA.

Checking your charts for "why" and "how" serves more than one useful purpose. It provides an indication of whether the chart is clear, or whether it explains the process. It helps you identify any missing steps. And it helps you identify problems, if any.

Of course, it is also true that asking "Why?" or "How?" is the key to developing the chart in the first place. That is, if you are working forward from the beginning, for each block you draw ask yourself "Why?" The answer should be in the next block—implicit there, at least. And if you are working from the end result backward toward the beginning, for each block ask "How?" for the same reasons.

In the case above, it is assumed that the reader of the chart understands that "Submit for Review" includes "Get Customer Comments for Revision." However, if you think that an unwarranted assumption (that possibly the reader will not understand the full functional message abbreviated in the telegraphic wording normally used in such charts), then you must either spell it out in its entirety or add a block.

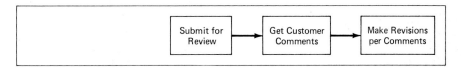

In any event, reading a functional flowchart in the forward direction should tell you why each function or step is planned, and reading it in reverse should tell you how each function or step is to be accomplished.

A good plan is to include all functions and steps, even the most trivial and obvious ones, in the first draft of the chart. This is recommended as a sort of insurance against missing something. (It's quite easy to take things for granted when you are familiar with the process, but the customer may not be so familiar with it.) In later revisions of the chart you can readily eliminate the unnecessary blocks or combine blocks, as each case suggests.

One large advantage of working from the end result or end product toward the beginning of the process is that you are actually designing the project as you go. And you are designing it on a sound basis of *how* and *why*. This lends itself well to group or team methods. For each step you may ask yourselves what else would do the job or serve the purpose and what the pros and cons (in terms of this requirement, that is) of each alternative are.

Even after you have finished the process, the chart serves as an excellent review medium. Others—your own management, presumably, or perhaps an editor—ought to scan the chart now and furnish (1) an opinion about whether the chart is self-explanatory and (2) devil's advocate comments, attempting to tear down your structure. If the structure is sound, you can defend it. If you can't defend it, it is wise to study it for possible change.

Must This Be a Team Method?

The methods suggested here are based on the assumption that a team has been assembled for developing and writing a proposal. This is the usual case for all except small proposals. Part of the consideration in choosing these methods is their suitability for coordinating and unifying the work of a team of people who have never worked with each other before. Yet the methods generally work well for the individual writing a proposal all alone, as is quite often the way it is done in small companies. Using the checklist, the functional analysis, the functional flowchart, and the "why" and "how" techniques, an individual can achieve a large degree of objectivity, too.

The methods, then, are suitable to three basic situations:

The improvised proposal team, working together for the first time and, possibly, not at all familiar with, or experienced in, proposal development.

The individual, working alone, striving to be objective and creative, while pursuing all details.

The individual leading or directing a proposal effort in a technical or professional field with which he or she is not particularly expert—that is, to make effective use of other's expert knowledge as though it were your own.

But there are also some special cases, where some of the methods have proved to have great value to the users.

One Special Application of the Method   Several years ago, the Consumer Product Safety Commission (CPSC) issued a solicitation inviting proposers to compete for the development of an "educational" program. This term has a somewhat special meaning in this case: in federal agency terminology, *training* is what you do to employees to improve their knowledge and performance, whereas *education* is what you do to improve the general public's knowledge and performance. In this case, the CPSC wished to catalyze a movement to inform the public about fire hazards.

The solicitation called for the development of various products to be used in public schools and by community groups, suggesting such items as a speaker's guide and wall posters. They were to inform people about the hazards of charcoal starter fluid, cigarette lighters, stoves, electric heaters, and other potential sources of fire. However, the work statement stated plainly that these were only starter ideas, and it was expected that the proposer would offer many more.

One proposer—the one who was finally awarded the contract—conducted an in-house brainstorming session to develop new ideas for suitable educational products, since that seemed to be the key to winning the contract. The session did produce a number of good, new ideas, but it also produced the key contract-winning idea: propose a *joint* brainstorming session with the CPSC staff, as a first step in the project, to finalize all ideas and also give the CPSC staff the opportunity to develop ideas. The CPSC staff obviously were intrigued very much with the concept, for they promptly awarded the contract to the proposer!

Other Useful Applications   It should not be supposed that everything must be analyzed, solved, and settled in a single session, nor that the method is used solely for analysis of the RFP, although that is its first and principal use. Large projects require several sessions. These may be concurrent, held periodically as the work progresses, or they can be decentralized, with task teams working on different aspects of the proposal and conducting their own analytical sessions in their areas of responsibility. But the method may be used also for review of the draft proposal, analyzing what has been written, how it has been written, and how the presentation has or should be organized.

The primary purpose of the analyses discussed here is to gain insights—insights into the nature of the customer's problems and true desires, insights into the necessary project design, insights into problems, and—far from the least—insights into strategic approaches which will result in a *winning* proposal.

Strategy is the key to winning. Although its development is really a part of analysis in general, its role is decisive, and therefore strategy merits its own chapter.

One final word: For large and complex projects, you may find it advisable to conduct a series of analyses; that is, conducting only one analysis to examine the need and plan the entire project may be an impractical approach. In such case, you can conduct separate analyses for each area of interest, such as the following:

The customer need (stated versus actual, as perceived)
The technical plan (technical requirements)
The management plan (management requirements)
The production plan (production requirements)
Qualifying and quantifying the deliverable item(s)
Necessary facilities (what the contractor must provide)
Necessary qualifications (contractor experience and track record)
Schedule (especially when schedule is difficult to meet)

Any one of the above may be a decisive consideration—that "critical item"—and so merit special analysis and study.

Some Main Points to Remember

1. Proposals are written under difficult circumstances—with far too little time. Only a careful plan and methodical approach makes it possible to produce *good* proposals under these circumstances.
2. Initial floundering can be avoided, and the project begun more efficiently, by advance work to produce draft materials—a checklist and rough flowchart are excellent beginning tools.
3. The prime, and most often overlooked, place to get information is in the RFP and SOW. Take the time to read these carefully several times. And then read them again. Study them. Many of the answers to your most perplexing questions are buried in that stack of paper.
4. The checklist serves several functions. Two of the most important are these: it helps you avoid missing items, which could lead to a nonresponsive proposal, and it helps you search out the items of greatest importance.
5. The draft flowchart is equally valuable. It helps you utilize the special skills of the technical and professional specialists on the proposal team, but it also helps them coordinate their thinking and their efforts.
6. One ball you must never take your eye off is the deliverable item or items. It (they) is (are) what the contract is all about—what the customer expects to get for the money. If the RFP is not entirely clear about what that deliverable is to be, you tell the customer what you think it ought to be, and then show why you propose this.
7. There are a number of good analytical techniques you can use. Three which have proved valuable for proposal work are brainstorming, value analysis (which uses brainstorming), and "why it can't be done."
8. Just as you may have to help the customer identify the proper deliverable item, you may find that you have to discriminate between what the customer has described as the need and what you find the true need to be. Again, you have to prove your case. But if you can, you have gained an important advantage over your competitors.
9. The *graphics method* of analysis has been advocated here. In fact, this method is a variant of brainstorming and value analysis, utilizing the functional flowchart as the focus of the effort and a means for clarifying functions and relationships on the systems level.
10. You can develop a flowchart from either end—from the deliverable end product, working backward to a beginning; from a known starting point, working forward to a conclusion and deliverable end product; or from both ends, depending on what you have as "knowns" when you start. Let the circumstances dictate which method you use for any given case.

9

The Evolution
of Strategies

Whatever else strategy is, it is a main sales argument.

What is *Strategy?*

Strategy is an abstraction, almost defying precise definition. It is the grand plan by means of which you anticipate success in an undertaking. It is ordinarily the result of long and thoughtful study, seeking out the soft spots (of the enemy, in military operations; of competitors and, sometimes, of the prospective customer, in marketing).

Strategy is not, however, confined to a single aspect of competition for a contract, nor a single aspect of a proposal. The concerted effort to seek out the customer's needs, both stated and real, must ordinarily focus on those major areas discussed in the previous chapter:

Cost
Technical considerations
Management considerations
Staffing considerations
Contractor qualifications
Schedule considerations
Innovation (technical or of project design)
Reliability (of project design)

Because any one, or any combination, of these considerations can be the critical factor(s) in the contract-award decision, a large part of the analysis and study of the RFP is aimed at determining which factor(s) is (are) decisive. And the capture strategy is necessarily geared to that determination. The capture strategy is therefore largely synonomous with the strategy(ies) for achieving customer goals in any or all of these considerations. That is to say, there are possible strategies for achieving a low price (cost strategies), strategies for accelerating a schedule (technical strategies), strategies for outstanding management plans (program strategies), and so forth.

There is at least one other kind of strategy to be discussed here: presentation strategy. The proposal is a presentation—a *sales* presentation—and there are strategies capable of adding great impact to that presentation.

So if your capture strategy is to offer a highly reliable program at an extraordinarily low cost, it will involve both cost strategies and technical or program strategies.

In this chapter we'll discuss various approaches which might be considered "standard" strategies in that they have been used successfully in a number of cases, and "special" strategies in that they are custom-designed for the given case. You'll read a number of case histories here, too. But first let us talk about marketing and salesmanship, or advertising, which is essentially the same thing as salesmanship. (For in the end, it all comes down to salesmanship.)

What Is *Marketing?* What Is *Sales?*

There are those who do not know the difference between marketing and sales. (And there are those who do not suspect that there *is* a difference.) *Sales*, to put it as succinctly as possible, is the business of getting orders. *Marketing* is the business of deciding what orders to pursue. That is to say, marketing involves a great deal more than the sales function itself—it includes such things as market surveys and studies, product and packaging research, projection of future needs, positioning, and a great many other items which are a logical prelude to mounting the sales campaign and pursuing the orders—or contracts, in this case.

This book, in discussing proposal writing for government contracts, addresses sales, rather than marketing, on the assumption that the marketing has been done and that the decision has been made to compete for a given contract. So while you may consider proposal writing a marketing activity, in a general sense, it is really specifically a sales effort.

The Principles of Salesmanship and Advertising

The commonly accepted principles of salesmanship and advertising are so similar as to be virtually identical. Hence, whatever is said about selling technique is equally valid for advertising or sales presentations. That is, since the proposal is a sales presentation, proposal writers should know what advertising and sales experts believe are the fundamentals of advertising and selling:

Get attention
Arouse interest
Generate desire
Close

The logic is that (1) you have to have the prospect's attention, if you are to deliver the sales message, (2) you must arouse the prospect's interest to hold attention, (3) you must persuade the prospect to desire what you are offering, and (4) you must stimulate the customer to give you the order.

The last principle is of lesser interest to us in writing a proposal because it is almost irrelevant. It refers to the situation in which the customer has not yet decided to buy, and the salesperson is laying on efforts to help the customer decide. In the case of proposals, the customer has announced (usually) an intention to buy: the proposal is an effort to persuade the customer to buy from you—buy *your* offer, rather than someone else's.

For the moment, we'll pass up discussion of how to get attention, although it is not unimportant, even in proposals. But the heart of selling, especially in the case of proposals, is in arousing interest and desire to buy. Let's examine what this means and how to accomplish it.

Felt Needs Versus Created Needs

The term *felt need* refers to a need the customer feels even before being exposed to the sales presentation and arguments. A hungry person does not usually have to be persuaded to eat. In January the householder orders oil or whatever fuel the house uses because the need for heat is undeniable. The customer entering a store to buy toothpaste or shoes has already felt the need and was thus motivated to go to the store.

On the other hand, the prospect browsing through an automobile showroom, "just looking," may not intend to buy—may not feel a need for a new car. The salesperson tries to generate buying desire by changing the prospect's mind—by persuading her that a new car is a need. Or when the prospect has asked for Zilch's toothpaste, the salesperson may try to change that felt need to a need for Jones's toothpaste. That is, the salesperson attempts to present sales arguments which will persuade the prospect to modify his viewpoint on what his need is. That's known as "creating" a need.

In either case, without a need felt by the customer, no sale can be made. People buy only what they feel a need for or can be made to feel a need for. Otherwise, the prospect would rather keep the money!

In the case of proposal writing, the customer has already expressed a need for something. Your job is to adjust the customer's perception of the need to match what you are offering—to persuade the customer that your offer comes closest to satisfying the real need. That, in simple terms, is why it is so vitally important that you arrive at an accurate estimate of the customer's need, whether that need has been accurately expressed by the RFP or not.

For example, when the Postal Service expressed a felt need for a company with an enormous number and variety of computer specialists instantly available for tasks, the winning proposal persuaded the Postal Service to agree that the true need was for a company that could *produce* those specialists on demand, whether on staff or not. The writers of that winning proposal perceived quite accurately that the customer's *true* need was for the services of those specialists when needed, however those services were made available. Whether the winning proposal created a need or clarified the customer's mind about the felt need is moot and not important, except as an outstanding example of creative salesmanship.

Frequently, and especially in cases of proposals competing for a contract, the customer has an incorrect perception of the need, confusing the means with the end. This comes about because the customer, like the rest of us, makes those unwarranted assumptions about the nature and cause of the problem. This is thinking that is chained to the past, operating on the premise that we must continue to do things the way we have done them in the past, locking out the possibility of new and better ways. In such cases it is necessary to wean the customer away tactfully, to *educate* the customer to new and better ways.

New Ideas Create New Needs

The "need" for television could not have existed before the consumer knew that television was possible—was, in fact, available. The same may be said for jet airplanes, electric ranges, investment clubs, and anything else which was invented and introduced to the market. Yet, some of these new ideas and new products took off (won wide acceptance) immediately, while others had to be sold vigorously for a long time to gain wide acceptance, and still others languished and perished. Why?

In most cases where a new idea was accepted immediately and was successful from the beginning, it was because the customer immediately recognized that the new idea satisfied a felt need, but satisfied that need in a better, more convenient, or less-expensive way than did the older method or product. Radio swiftly replaced the stereopticon and player piano, and TV quickly replaced radio as the main source of at-home entertainment. That was because each was readily recognized as satisfying the need for at-home entertainment in a better way. That is, the need was not for radio or TV, but for *home entertainment.*

Gail Borden had a much more difficult time persuading the public to accept his condensed, preserved milk because it was a bit different from the adulterated milk sold to consumers of that day; the public was not at all sure that it was *better*. He succeeded only after a great deal of advertising to *educate* the consumer and prove that his product was better.

The great problem many proposals face is that people characteristically resist change, unless they can perceive its benefits readily. Then they accept change eagerly.

Military history is full of such examples. Many experienced cavalry officers of the U.S. Army had to be retired during World War II because they could not accept the replacement of their horses with armored vehicles. And it was only near the end of the war that ordnance officers were finally persuaded to try out muzzle brakes on their guns, a device used by just about every other army in the world for many years.

There are two things to be learned from this:

1. "Need" refers to the *basic* need—not oil furnaces versus gas furnaces, but *heat.* Not staff employees versus consultants, but *specialist services.*
2. Customers often need to be *educated* to new ideas. This means actually shown that the new idea satisfies the basic need in a better way, such as at lower cost, more reliably, in a shorter time, or with some combination of added benefits.

It can never be assumed that the customer sees or appreciates the advantages. It must always be assumed that the advantages—and, in fact, that the new idea does satisfy a basic need—must be *sold*.

New ideas therefore create "new" needs only in the sense that they create a demand for the new product or process—the true need is itself not new, but the method or product for *satisfying* the need is new. The key to selling the new idea, then, is not to sell the idea itself, but rather the conviction that the new idea is an improved method or product—that is, linking it clearly to a felt need.

For example, let us suppose that the customer has a need to save money and you have a new idea which will save the customer money, although your new idea also offers several other benefits. The proper strategy is to *concentrate on the money-saving aspects* of the new idea, rather than on other virtues. The other benefits are secondary, and should be relegated to a secondary place in your sales arguments. Your task is to convince the customer that the new idea will indeed save money without sacrificing quality or other essential characteristics. It is primarily that characteristic, and perhaps only that characteristic, of the new idea which will arouse the customer's interest and desire to buy.

Despite its great cost, the electronic computer won success swiftly because it delivered two benefits—satisfied two common needs:

1. It speeded up enormously the processing of large volumes of data, reducing labor costs proportionately.
2. It made possible the processing of data which was otherwise impracticable, if not impossible.

Without the modern computer, it would probably have been impossible to carry out the space program and many other sophisticated projects. It made many things possible for the first time. It satisfied needs not only in a better manner than ever before, but it satisfied needs which could not be satisfied before.

Frank Bettger, author of the perennial best-seller *How I Raised Myself From Failure to Success in Selling*, reported that one of his most successful sales devices (he sold insurance) was this: He would make an appointment with his busy executive prospect, show up at the appointed time, and announce: "Mr.———, I can do something for you this morning that no one else in the world can do."

Mr.———'s attention was gained and his interest immediately aroused by that announcement, of course, and he automatically demanded to know what it was that Frank Bettger could do for him.

"Have you completely covered within the next hour," explained Bettger. "I've already arranged for your medical examination this morning. If you'll get your hat and come with me, we can take care of this immediately."

A unique capability which addresses a real need—especially one which makes the impossible suddenly possible—is bound to attract a bit of attention and arouse some interest. There is no felt need for that which is impossible, of course. A need, to be useful in selling something, can only be useful if there is some means for satisfying it. Making the impossible possible is creating a new need. Offering such a breakthrough, or anything approaching it, in a proposal is almost a guarantee of arousing interest, at the least. And of making the sale, if the new capability addresses a felt need and does so persuasively.

Benefits Versus Needs

Conventional wisdom in advertising and selling dictates that a prospect's interest is aroused when the advertising copy or sales presentation focuses on benefits promised the prospect—what the service or product will *do* for the customer. It is for that reason that professional advertising concentrates on what the offered service or product will do for the customer. TV commercials offer excellent examples of the technique at work.

The late Elmer Wheeler, often acclaimed as America's greatest salesman, coined the now famous admonition to all salespeople, "Sell the sizzle, not the steak." He meant, of course, appeal to the emotions, not to logic or reason. Or, to put it another way, explain the benefit to the prospective customer—make the customer's mouth water with the suggestive "sizzle."

TV commercials offer excellent examples of how to do this: Sell beer by linking beer-drinking to good times at the beach and at the corner tavern. Sell insurance by offering security—protection against disaster. Sell deodorants by promising freedom from embarrassment.

Of course, no single appeal works equally well for everyone. There are some who simply don't like beer or care for the beach. And some who already have all the insurance they can afford. So when one *positions* an offer—that is, decides who the best prospects are and designs the appeal to offer attractive benefits to those prospects—one must recognize that it is simply not possible to position an offer for everyone. Ergo, advertising and selling via general media, such as newspapers and TV, is directed to some segment of the readers or viewers. (The advertiser hopes that the segment is adequately large!)

In proposal writing, the situation is different: the presentation is not being made to the world at large, in hope of capturing the interest of some portion of that audience; rather it is directed to a selected prospect. Just as an automobile dealer must talk to an individual prospect and try to identify what benefits will motivate that prospect to buy, the proposal writer must appeal to the individual customer to whom the proposal is directed, and try to identify whatever need that prospective customer feels. The principle is the same, however, in all cases: The appeal must be to a need; only that which satisfies a need will be accepted as a benefit.

Generating Desire to Buy

Arousing interest is not enough to win the contract. Its chief function is to persuade the customer to listen (read, in the case of a proposal) to what you have to say. At this point you have made a promise: you have promised that whatever it is you are proposing will deliver some specific benefit(s)—the satisfying of need(s). The customer is interested. But it's still a promise, lacking proofs—evidence, at any rate—that you can and will deliver. That evidence is required before you can turn interest into desire.

It's as though someone has approached you and offered you an investment opportunity that promises a 25 percent return on investment within one year, with exceedingly little risk. If you have some money to invest and are looking for an investment—if you have the need—you are sure to become interested. But before you actually entrust your money to the proposition, you'll want to know a great deal more; you'll want some convincing evidence that the return will be as great and the risk as small as promised.

In the typical proposal case, there are actually two kinds of evidence required of you:

1. The technical evidence—the evidence that the plan, program, product, or service that you propose will do what you promise: produce the benefit, satisfying the need.
2. The evidence that you are a reliable and competent contractor, capable of carrying out the program proposed and being thoroughly conscientious and dependable as a contractor

Only if you succeed in presenting convincing evidence of these will your prospect want to buy from you, to accept your proposal.

This is the basic strategy of all sales presentations, the mechanism that begins with getting a prospect's attention and progresses from attention to interest, from interest to desire, and from desire to actual order or contract. But there are an almost limitless number and variety of possible strategic ideas for bringing this about, for making it *possible* to offer those benefits which will satisfy the prospect's needs. Let's survey a few of these.

Procurement, Proposals, and the Law

One major difference between marketing to the federal government and marketing to firms in the private sector is that federal procurement is subject to certain statutes. That is, the private-sector organization is free to select any proposer or bidder it wants to, based on whim or caprice. The federal agency is not free to do so, but must follow the dictates of procurement regulations—the law. Obviously, it follows that the proposer is well-advised to be familiar with the laws governing procurement. You already know from having read this far, if you didn't know before, that the federal agency must have an in-house estimate of the contract cost, must have an objective rating scheme by which to evaluate proposals, and must award technical points to each proposal on a competitive basis. Ergo, it is, at the least, somewhat difficult for a federal agency to make contract awards arbitrarily.

You know, or should know, that the law provides an appeals process, called a *protest*. Should you feel that the evaluation, the award, or any other facet of the procurement process was "defective"—not in strict accordance with the law or not affording you fair and equal treatment—you have the right to make that appeal. The agency staff handling the procurement will then be required to defend and justify their evaluation and award decisions.

You may protest any element of the procurement at any time. Perhaps you consider the solicitation to be defective. Or the evaluation criteria. Or the work statement. Or the evaluation itself. Or anything else. You are free to lodge your protest. And even having lost your protest, you are still free to take the matter into federal court and sue for what you believe are your rights.

All of this should enter into your thinking, into your strategy development and general planning. Several case histories you will read in these pages will illustrate the impact such matters may have on the procurement.

There is one other way in which the law affects—should affect—your programming and strategy. The laws define the proper relationship between agency personnel—federal employees—and contractor personnel—private employees. The law provides that contractor personnel may not direct civil service employees, nor can civil service employees issue direct orders to or supervise contractor personnel—not even when the contractor personnel are working on site. The government's project officer (also often called contracting officer's representative, contracting officer's technical representative, government project manager, and other such titles) is responsible for giving the contractor "technical direction." This specifically excludes supervision of the contractor.

The law also forbids "personal services" contracts, except as specifically excepted in a few cases. That is, the solicitation may not specify the assignment of some particular individual who is required to provide any or all of the services contracted for: the contractor may assign any qualified individual to the project.

As an extension of these provisions, the federal agency and its staff may not dictate to the contractor how the contractor shall manage the job once the contract is awarded. That is, the contractor is free to get the job done by whatever means the contractor deems best, as long as specific contract terms are not violated and a satisfactory result is delivered within the schedule and budget agreed upon.

Moreover, the contractor is always advised that only the contracting officer can agree to and authorize a change in the contract affecting the cost—authorize an increase in costs, in the practical case. That is, should a project officer request an expansion of the effort or any work not covered by the contract, the contract must be amended and the additional cost authorized by the contracting official. Otherwise—should the contractor do additional work on the basis of a request by the project officer, without the contracting official's approval—the contractor runs a serious risk of not being paid for the additional work. However, should the work turn out to be other than as originally represented in the work statement and to require services or materials other than those agreed upon, the contractor has the right to claim a change in scope of the contract and to demand additional payment.

What has all this to do with proposal strategies? Just this: It is the knowledge of these legal considerations and how they apply in practice which underlies a number of strategies used successfully by veterans of government contracting. For example, many proposers will deliberately bid a job at the estimated breakeven point or even at a loss, if it appears certain that there will be changes in scope. It is in negotiating the price for the changes that the contractor makes up any losses or lack of profit in the original bid or proposal.

There are many other tactics, equally sharp, but entirely legal. Many proposers will find these tactics more than sharp; they will find them offensive—unethical and bordering on the unscrupulous. Yet, for certain types of contracts, one may expect to find the experienced competitors so bidding, and only a complete understanding of the strategy involved in this type of bid will help one cope successfully.

To set the record straight on this, consider the following case. A Washington-area construction firm contracted for the building of an entire new wing of the Walter Reed Army Hospital in Washington, not very long ago. By the time the work was completed, the costs had increased to several millions more than the original bid, as a result of changes. (Changes are almost inevitable in construction projects.) *The Washington Post*, in a series on government procurement and irregularities found in GSA procurement, interviewed Arthur Sampson, former GSA administrator. (The General Services Administration includes the Public Buildings Service.) The interviewer wanted to know what Sampson thought of the Walter Reed Hospital cost overruns. Sampson responded that the contractors were simply applying the rules set by the government and could hardly be blamed for taking advantage of all such rules!

Among the many myths about federal procurement is one that it costs the contractor money to do business with the government—that the contractor is likely to lose money on the job, that is. Like most myths, this one has a modicum of truth in it: those contractors who are not familiar with the regulations and the practices in federal procurement and managing government contracts *can* get hurt. But that is the result of naiveté. *Experienced* government contractors usually do not get hurt. Quite the contrary, the experienced contractor knows how to take advantage of every legal provision and government policy concerning procurement and contract administration.

The impact of procurement regulations and practices on strategy formulations will become more apparent as we consider various strategies which have been used successfully.

Technical or Program Strategies

All strategy stems from an analysis and understanding of the customer's wants—those he has expressed, those he has implied, and those you have inferred. Let's take a typical case in which it is apparent that the customer is concerned primarily with the technical plausibility of your proposed program— for example, a project to increase radar capability.

Originally, all radar antennas were mechanically rotated on a pedestal, sweeping the horizon several times a minute. The chief limitation on speed has been the mechanical consideration of inertia, complicated by other mechanical considerations, such as the increase in centripetal force with increases in rotational speed. As in most things, the final design was a compromise, utilizing the highest speed which was a *practical* reality. Increasing the speed would involve a large number of new problems, some of which would be likely to cancel out any benefits that might derive from an increase in speed.

It must be assumed that the customer is aware of these basic facts. Hence, should a customer solicit ideas from you for increasing radar operating speed and overall capacity, it would be unlikely that schemes for higher-speed motors and lighter antenna structures would be viewed with any great favor or that your plans would be assigned much in the way of credibility factors. What the customer wants is an entirely new and different approach that avoids the mechanical problems just referred to.

This is a rather clear case of the need for some kind of innovation, something new and different, yet plausible; "far out" schemes are not likely to carry the day.

An objective analysis will tell you rather quickly what you must have already suspected: the successful design will not use mechanical rotation at all—no moving parts, probably, but an entirely electronic switching system. The limitation in radar operating speeds is entirely a mechanical limitation, of course; some means must be found for electrical or electronic "rotation," rather than mechanical rotation.

The chief problem you are going to face in selling whatever design you come up with is plausibility—credibility of your plan, that is. You are going to have to somehow demonstrate to your customer's satisfaction that your design approach is not far out, but has a sound enough basis to be successful.

Such plans—all innovation proposed, especially for large projects—must conform to the basic engineering principle of *evolution*, not *revolution*. (Remember what happens to pioneers and missionaries!)

Your basic technical or program strategy must be, then, not an innovative design, for everyone proposing must produce an innovative design, but a *plausible* innovative design. You must prove that your design approach has a high probability of success.

There are a number of ways to accomplish this. One is by showing that your design is not so radical as it may at first appear. You can do this by relating other programs in which designs of a similar type were used successfully. (In the actual case, a switching device using a Luneberg lens was used, and the soundness of the device was shown in the proposal.) Another is by relating your company's history of success in developing advanced radar designs or advanced high-speed switching circuits which are readily adaptable to the problem.

This latter approach asks the customer to have faith in your organization's technical abilities, whereas the first method asks the customer to rely on the soundly based principles of your proposed design. It's a weaker argument, for although the customer may have faith in your company, your proposal is likely to win more technical points for its design approach than for the company's qualifications. It's far more effective, usually, to "prove" your design, rather than prove your organization's capability.

In one such case, where the solicitation required the development of a maintenance-training approach, the successful proposer built the technical argument around making a *failure-probability analysis*, to determine just what should be taught and what topics should have priority in the training program. *Failure probability* was a new concept, which the proposer had invented on the spot—although not without study and careful thought—for proposal purposes. The proposal offered a description of how the study would be carried out, and on what basis the various failure probabilities would be estimated. However, because the idea was radically new and different, the proposer realized that it had to be made "respectable"—given some basis for plausibility. The proposal therefore pointed out that the engineering discipline known as *reliability analysis* is well-founded, has been in use for some time, and is thoroughly accepted. Failure probability was really the inverse of reliability analysis. Hence, it was not really a radical idea, but simply a logical extension—evolution, rather than revolution.

Not all projects require innovation, nor do all customers welcome it. Innovation means change, and change means some increase of risk. Many customers prefer to "play it safe" by adopting a conservative approach—doing it the way it's "always been done." In general, unless the nature of the project clearly mandates an innovative approach, innovation should be considered with great caution: a conservative approach is more likely to be welcomed.

Consider, in devising your general approach and your technical or program design, the following *probabilities:*

1. The customer prefers to minimize the risk of failure, in most cases.
2. The customer is always concerned with credibility—plausibility—of your approach, and often awards points on the estimated probability of success. (Some solicitations promise to evaluate the "practicality" of your approach.)
3. An innovative design—something "different"—requires a great deal more persuasion to sell than does a conservative, easily recognized approach.
4. The more innovative or more radical your approach, the more persuasion required to win customer acceptance—that is, the more difficult it becomes to sell to the customer.
5. If you must propose something new and different, or feel that it is to your advantage to do so, you must plan backups for contingencies—explain how you will prepare alternatives to handle unanticipated problems or design ideas which do not work out in practice.

Cost Strategies

It rarely occurs to proposal writers that there is such a thing as a cost strategy. In fact, that is where many proposals go wrong: those who design the program and write the technical proposal lose sight of the fact that they, the designers, are establishing the chief cost center of the proposed project. And since they are concentrating on technical excellence, without thought to costs, all too often they develop a marvelous technical plan which fails to win the contract because it costs too much!

On the other hand, where the proposal team has established cost as a critical factor, a "design to cost" approach may be used: the program may be designed specifically to minimize costs. In such case, cost strategies and technical or program strategies are intermingled and must be considered together.

A great many programs are open-ended, in that the program can be designed for any preconceived cost. This is often the case when the customer has provided little information that would aid the proposal writers in estimating the proper scope of the project. For example, a solicitation may request a poll or survey to determine public attitudes on some topic, but provide no clues regarding the required size and scope of the survey. It is, of course, possible to stand on a downtown street corner and question strollers all day. That would indeed be a survey or poll, and it would be quite an inexpensive one. Or one could conduct extensive telephone, personal, and mail-questionnaire interviews with hundreds of thousands of people. That would be a survey, too, and a costly one. Yet, government solicitations often leave the scope of a project open in that manner, relying on the proposers to recommend what they think to be the proper scope.

On the other hand, there are solicitations which are most difficult to price because the customer is not familiar enough with the work required to know what must be specified to the proposer. The Federal Aviation Administration, seeking a contractor to prepare—write, illustrate, and print—one of their annual reports (federal agencies often issue such annual reports to Congress), failed to specify type, paper, covers, and many other details necessary to estimate the cost.

In such cases, one is immediately tempted to call the contracting official and complain or request more information. And such a request will usually bring the desired information. But it will bring it in the form of a modification to the RFP, which will be sent out to everyone who has requested a copy of the RFP. Therefore, your question will bring benefit to your competitors—possibly more benefit to them than it does to you! Asking questions is always hazardous in that manner. Too, it may provoke a change in the RFP, and the change may be detrimental to you, rather than beneficial. There are other, better methods for the proposer with imagination. In fact, it is almost always a mistake to ask questions directly of the contracting official or the program staff in such cases.

Cost strategy does not necessarily refer to being the low bidder. There are at least two other cases where the term does not suggest that you should attempt to be, or even appear to be, the low bidder:

1. There are some cases in which the agency has some fixed amount of money it wishes to spend on the program, and will not be hospitable to cost-cutting suggestions. (In fact, it is embarrassing to the agency, frequently, to come in substantially under the budget.) And there are cases where no matter how you explain it in your technical proposal, costs well under those of the competitors signify to the agency that you either do not really understand the need or are trying to do a "quick and dirty" job. (Some people always judge quality by cost only!)
2. Contracting officials usually have an especially warm place in their hearts for contractors offering low overhead rates, no matter what "the bottom line" is. Accounting systems that ensure a low overhead rate are always to be desired in government contracting, and are well worth the extra time and trouble it takes to gather the necessary figures for such systems.

Where the customer has left the solicitation open-ended or otherwise failed to provide the information necessary to make a proper cost estimate, you are left with two immediate alternatives, other than asking for clarification. The first and more obvious one is to make your own best estimate of what is a proper scope for the project or try to guess what the customer has established as a budget for the project. This is somewhat hazardous, and can easily lead to overestimating or underestimating.

There is, however, an alternative that reduces the hazard and, in fact, increases your probability of success. That is, in effect, allowing the customer to select the price by offering several options or alternatives!

The Federal Aviation Administration solicitation referred to above offers a good case study of the method at work successfully. The successful proposer pointed out in the technical proposal that certain specifications had not been provided, and that in some instances specifications that were provided were not quantified.

Both defects made it almost impossible to estimate costs and furnish a firm price, the proposal went on. The proposal then discussed the needs of the customer in some detail, offering suggestions—recommendations, really—for the deliverable end item. *That is, the proposer furnished the specifications as proposed ones.*

The basic strategy here was to offer the *minimum configuration* that the proposer thought would meet the customer's needs, resulting, of course, in a low bid. However, the proposer realized that the customer might wish a bit "fancier" product and might well have more money to spend. Therefore, having proposed the minimum configuration and lowest cost considered feasible, the proposal went on to offer several options, for more money.

The technical proposal described the basic configuration, with the proposed specifications, and the options, with their improved specifications. The cost proposal costed out each proposed configuration separately, each with its own cost form.

This enabled the proposer to be both competitive in terms of cost and competitive in terms of product quality, while avoiding asking the questions! It also all but ensured that the customer would call the proposer in for discussion.

Many RFPs offer the opportunity to propose such alternatives or options. In fact, many RFPs all but *demand* such an approach and strategy.

The other problem, that of achieving a low overhead rate, is a matter of good accounting practice, primarily. It requires a bit more work in collecting and establishing a "paper trail" or "audit trail," as some accountants refer to it, but it does result in the lowest overhead rate possible without actually cutting costs in the contractor's operations. Understanding it requires a bit of basic explanation, first, of costs in general.

Costs and Overhead Rates   In any business, everything you spend or pay out is cost. All costs must be recovered, somehow, in your pricing, along with a bit of profit, if you are to stay in business. However, for all except perhaps the smallest, one-person enterprise, it is necessary to segregate costs by categories. The minimum number of categories feasible is two: *direct costs* and *indirect costs.*

For some reason, this concept of direct costs versus indirect costs appears to confuse many people, but the distinction is simple enough: Those costs which you incur only because of a given sale or contract and which are directly traceable (accountable) to that sale or contract, are direct costs. That is, your accounting records will prove that those costs were incurred for that contract and for that contract only.

First, you have *direct labor*—the salaries paid those individuals who work on the contract. (If they work on more than one contract, you must keep track of their time through contract charge numbers, so the accountant knows which contract to charge.)

Then you have *other direct costs*. These might be printing, postage, toll calls, travel, and any other expense you incur solely for that contract—provided that you can prove its linkage solely to that project. This means keeping a telephone log and otherwise establishing and keeping records of expenses.

But there are costs you can't really assign to a given contract or project. If you have many projects in house, it is all but impossible to assign (with any accuracy) portions of such general costs as rent, heat, light, furniture and equipment depreciation, taxes, insurance, basic telephone service, and many other costs of doing business. Nor can you accurately assign portions of *indirect labor*—accountants, truck drivers, secretaries, receptionists, and others whose work is general to the entire facility, rather than to any single contract.

Ignoring G&A costs, which are a separate category of indirect costs, all your indirect costs constitute *overhead*. (Some companies break this down further, separating *fringe benefits* as a special category of indirect costs.)

You can tell, by examining your ledgers and reading your financial statements and other products of the accounting function, how many dollars your total overhead represents. But how do you know how much of that overhead expense is chargeable to any given sale or contract? This is where the concept of an overhead *rate* enters the picture, so that the overhead dollars may be prorated fairly—that is, so that each customer pays a *fair share* of the overhead.

The accepted practice in establishing an overhead rate is to find the ratio between the direct labor dollars and the overhead dollars. That is, if your direct labor costs for a given year came to $500,000, and your overhead dollars for that year totaled $465,000, your overhead *rate* was $465{,}000 \div 500{,}000 = 0.93$. To get the percentage rate, multiply 0.93 by 100: $0.93 \times 100 = 93\%$.

What this means is simply this: For every $1 you paid out in salaries to staff people working directly on contracts, you paid out 93¢ to other employees and for other indirect costs. Consequently, you must charge your customers $1.93 plus some profit markup for every direct labor dollar, if you are to stay in business.

You must then begin your estimates by estimating the amount of direct labor you expect to need on a project, multiply that direct labor dollar total by 0.93 and add it to the direct labor dollars, then add whatever you have estimated for other direct costs, and finally add your profit figure, to arrive at a final selling price.

The most direct way to reduce this overhead *rate* is to refine your recordkeeping system so that every possible dollar spent on a contract is traced to that contract—*charged* to that contract. If your secretaries spend some of their time working on contracts—typing, for example—have them keep track of their time and charge that contract when they work on it. Keep a telephone log and charge all calls made for that contract to that contract. Do the same for all travel, printing, and any other item of expense which can be charged to the contract.

If you do this for every contract, you will reduce your overhead *rate* because you will reduce the total number of dollars charged to that "overhead expense pool." You won't reduce the cost of the contract itself—the dollars will show up elsewhere—but you will reduce the ratio or rate, while increasing the other direct costs by the same amount of dollars.

The benefits of doing this go beyond making the contracting official have a better opinion of your operating efficiency. When you charge what ought to be other direct costs to your general overhead, you are falsely inflating the overhead and *burdening other bids and proposals* unfairly. That is, your overhead rate of record is a false one because it includes items of expense which are not part of your general cost of doing business, but are misplaced other direct costs. The overhead rate should reflect the cost of doing business generally, at whatever volume you do business, and not the costs or any part of the cost of handling some particular project or sale.

There is one other way of reducing the overhead rate, in some circumstances. Consider where and how an overhead rate is established: ordinarily, it is the "historical rate." That is, it is determined by auditing your books at the end of the year, when you total your costs in their various categories. You *assume* that that is the rate at which you are doing business at the moment, but you don't really *know* that. You won't know until you do your year-end audit, and it will probably have changed somewhat because not all your costs are fixed; many are variable. Moreover, if you have a great increase in the amount of direct labor you experience and pay for, you will have (in all probability) some increase in overhead *dollars*, but not in proportion to the increase in direct labor dollars. Let's be sure we understand why this is so.

Most contractors can accommodate at least some increase in the size of their staffs without expanding their physical facilities except, perhaps, for adding a few chairs and desks and perhaps another telephone or two. Therefore, the rent, heat, light, telephone, insurance, and other such items won't increase appreciably. If the increase in overhead dollars is proportionately smaller than the increase in direct labor dollars, the rate will decrease.

Let's suppose, to illustrate this, that the $500,000 of direct labor mentioned in our example increases to $700,000 (40%), while the increase in indirect or overhead costs is only 15% (or $69,750), for a total overhead now of $534,750 (originally $465,000). The new rate would be $534,750 \div 700,000 = 0.76 = 76\%$.

If, in proposing for a new contract, you anticipate the new contract will be *in addition to* an existing, long-term direct labor base, you should recalculate your *anticipated new* overhead rate, should you be awarded the contract. That is, no matter what your *historical* overhead rate is, you may always propose a *provisional*, or estimated, overhead rate on the assumption that you will receive the contract. (If you do not, you have lost nothing, for this does not affect your established overhead rate for other contracts you have either under bid or actually in work.)

You may always bid a provisional overhead rate, especially when you are proposing to lower your historical rate. It is likely to be subject to audit unless the contract is relatively small, but almost all contracts over $100,000 are subject to audit, in any case.

There are some other tactics or strategies possible. One is to put some items below the line—take no profit markup on them (although you are entitled to take G&A, as part of your cost). Some solicitations will specify that certain items, such as materials in a contract for a project which is principally services, must go below the line. But you may propose to do so of your own volition, to keep the costs down.

In some contracts, especially those of the cost-plus variety, the contractor buys items "for the government's account." That is, the items merely pass through the contractor, to the federal agency. One such case, to illustrate this, was in a NASA contract which required the contractor to subscribe to foreign technical journals and pass them on to the NASA library. Items bought in this manner are usually priced below the line, since they are usually minor items in the contract, and the contractor is really acting as the government's agent in the purchase.

Presentation Strategies

"Getting attention" can be as important in a competitive proposal situation as it is in running a TV commercial or a large print advertisement. The customer faced with dozens of voluminous proposals can easily read your proposal as a mechanical routine, after being anesthetized earlier by poring over thousands of pages, hence paying little attention. This has actually happened in one case known personally to the authors. The customer admitted that at least one of the passed-over proposals was as good as, if not better than, the one accepted. The customer confessed, however, to not paying a great deal of attention anymore, after reading proposals all day long for several days. It was only the first few proposals read which caught attention and were remembered.

In this manner, a quite good proposal can be relegated to the pile of those which are "possibles," but not especially noteworthy. It is often quite important to be noteworthy, therefore the consideration of *presentation strategy*, with the emphasis on getting attention.

This is not to say—not for a moment—that attention-getting gimmicks are going to influence the outcome, *on their own merits*. But they can give the customer who evaluates your proposal something to remember you by and some special reason to pay close attention to what your proposal says—*offers*, that is.

There are several approaches to this. One is graphics or "cosmetics." That is, the physical appearance of the proposal, perhaps using an unusual color, such as gold or Day-Glo tints. Some proposers copy the agency's seal or logo, and reproduce it on the cover of the proposal to the agency. In one case, the very complex work required was reduced to a rather simple chart, after an intensive effort to bring some order out of a thick, but not well thought out, work statement. The proposer thought it would be helpful to reproduce this simplified chart on the cover of the proposal, but the chart proved to be just a bit too large for the purpose, and reducing it to fit would have rendered it all but illegible. The proposer therefore invented a foldout cover! (The proposal proved to be a winner, producing a 4-year, $12 million contract.)

In another case, the proposer had prepared a milestone chart, showing the proposed project with all its main phases, functions, and significant milestones, which was then reduced photographically for printing as a page of the proposal. (Professional illustrators prefer to prepare oversized art originals and have them reduced for printing, a method which makes the work easier and produces more-professional finals.) The proposal manager had an idea. Reluctant to discard the now apparently useless original chart, he decided to cover it with a transparent acetate sheet and send it along with the proposal as an "exhibit." This not only drew the attention of all concerned with evaluating the proposal and selecting a contractor, but the government's program manager got the message: the acetate-covered chart would be ideal as a project-management aid! A contract resulted.

Graphics are not the only way to draw attention. Language—the opening statements in the proposal—may impel the reader to sit up and take notice. For that reason, introductory material can be of enormous importance. And for that reason, too, it is especially important that the introduction be written as the last writing job, so that you may select the most attention-getting statements from your proposal and introduce them immediately. If, for example, you propose some startling new process or some unusually well-qualified authority—preferably, a well-known figure—that should be almost the first thing your proposal states.

Later in these pages, when we discuss the art of persuasive writing, there will be some more to say on the subject. Moreover, getting attention is only one facet of your possible presentation strategy; there are numerous other considerations. If you bear in mind that a proposal is a sales presentation, you can appreciate that the proposal should be so organized, written, and presented as to employ all known sales psychology.

Consider this: The customer is judging the proposal entirely on what the presentation itself offers—words and illustrations. The customer is asked to buy your *promise*. Credibility is almost everything after you have assembled an attractive program design; the customer is asked to *believe* in you, to trust you to tell the truth in your proposal and to carry out the proposed program and produce the promised results. All this on the strength of what your proposal *presents*. Therefore the need for presentation strategy. Or strategies.

When we discuss the art of persuasive writing later, we shall return to this subject. But it might be helpful to point out that hardly anyone writing a proposal ever fully utilizes all the many opportunities in a proposal to *sell*. Far too many proposal writers concentrate on communications only, with no thought to selling—they assume that if the customer *understands* what the proposal offers, that is sufficient: the customer will appreciate the fine program and the fine organization offering it.

The trouble with that notion is that it is utterly false. For one thing, the customer may not be capable of appreciating the quality of the program offered without help from the offeror, without "education," that is. For another thing, translating the presentation into a set of beneficial results is work, and it is futile to expect the customer to make the effort to do what *you* should have done. It won't happen.

And for still another thing, it is hopelessly optimistic to expect the customer to digest, consider, and remember everything you say. Important points must be stressed and repeated. If you have spent several paragraphs explaining your very clever project organization and how you have designed it for efficiency, why not repeat the essence of that message in your illustration title? And again in the Executive Summary (an abstract; see Chapter 10) and a few other places that ordinarily do get special attention?

But let us defer further discussion of these important matters until we arrive at the material on how to write persuasively, as well as communicate effectively.

Capture Strategy

The capture strategy—that strategy which you expect to be decisive in persuading the customer to award the contract to you—is not necessarily a single concept. In fact, it would probably be dangerous to trust all to one central strategy. You must utilize every weapon you can, to develop all the possible strategies. Yet, you must not confuse the customer or yourself about this: your proposal must have been based on some idea for a master stroke of strategy, a decisive point.

We've talked about several different kinds of strategy, which may or may not be related to each other. In the same philosophy, your capture strategy may or may not be related to other, subordinate strategies. It ought to be based on whatever you have decided, as a result of analysis, is the most important or most critical concern of the customer—cost, reliability, innovation, technical approach, management approach, or whatever. If innovation or some innovative concepts constitute your capture strategy, cost strategy is probably unrelated, and management strategy may or may not be related. But if cost is a capture strategy, the probability is that your entire program is designed to keep costs low, and your technical or program strategies are the underpinning for your capture strategy—they should prove to the customer that you can and will keep costs within the budget.

One thing you do have to do is *have* a capture strategy. It cannot be allowed to just "happen" all by itself. It must be carefully thought out and planned in advance, as inspired by whatever your analyses have indicated to you is the customer's major concern—what factor(s) will have the greatest influence on the customer's final decision.

Your capture strategy is the *reason* you provide the customer for deciding to buy from you—because you offer the lowest cost, the best technical plan, the best management plan, the most reliable team, the greatest amount of experience, or whatever you think will be that compelling argument. But, if you expect your customer to agree with you that you have offered a convincing reason for buying your proposal, your customer must certainly have a full and complete awareness of that reason. And you must plant that awareness carefully and deliberately in your presentation. You can hardly do that if you have not thought out your capture strategy in advance, and fully understand it yourself.

Consider your proposal as an argument for selecting a highway to some destination. The main argument is that the highway you recommend goes to where the customer wants to go by the fastest, most direct, and most reliable means. Oh, there are other considerations—the dining facilities and comfort facilities along the way, the gasoline and service station facilities, the availability of hotels for overnight stops. Each of these may be a subject for discussion as secondary considerations. But never lose sight of where you are going, in the main, and never permit the customer to lose sight of it either.

Let's consider a few examples:

1 The Navy wanted to develop a training manual to train junior officers in Naval security regulations. The main concern was not that the officers should be able to cite the regulations or quote from the official manual documenting them, but that the officer should be able to "secure" any given area, and should be able to inspect for and recognize any security violations.

Such training is almost reflex training: the trainee must be drilled in what to examine and what to look for until such inspection and recognition becomes virtually a reflex act. One proposer—the successful one, as it turned out—decided that somehow the printed manual that was to result from the project ought to provide such drill. And since such inspection is normally visual, the manual would have to rely heavily on graphic illustrations of relevant scenes, with emphasis on not-too-obvious violations. Reaching back in memory to a favorite puzzle game of years past, the proposer adapted the idea, offering a manual which would have a great many scenes of security violations, with the challenge to the student: "What's wrong with this picture?" In this case, the rationale was that conditioning drills were an essential chief element of the program, and "What's wrong with this picture?" an effective way of providing the drills. In the writing of the proposal, the argument was fleshed out with appropriate citations of the need for "relevant behaviors" and other technical considerations to prove the validity of the proposer's concept.

2 In the case of the TFX-111 airplane project, it was quite obvious that cost was not a major consideration. Secretary of Defense Robert McNamara wanted an airplane that both the Navy and the Air Force could use. He was convinced that the idea was both feasible and sensible, and was worth almost any cost to bring to reality.

One of the two leading contenders for the project focused the proposal sharply on the technical problems and devoted the entire proposal to proving the superiority of the design offered. The other focused all arguments on design features to make the airplane truly common to both military services. To put this another way, one proposer based capture strategy on claimed superiority of aerodynamic design, while the other based strategy on evidence that the product would meet the goal of serving both services.

McNamara opted for the second proposal, against the unanimous recommendations of all his advisers, which says something for promising the customer what he wants to hear. (This is not to say that the first proposal would not have been for a program that would have produced a common-use airplane, but the proposer did not *focus on and emphasize promises to meet the customer's stated goal.*)

3 In proposing a roster of engineering services to the U.S. Army Night Vision Laboratory at Fort Belvoir, Virginia, the successful proposer based capture strategy entirely on price. In fact, the plan offered reflected a rather sharp, perhaps unethical (but entirely legal) practice, which took advantage of technicalities. (This will be explained later, in an appropriate chapter.) The result was so low a price as to constitute "an offer" the customer "couldn't refuse." It all but ensured the award, *provided the offer could be made credible.* That is to say, the proposer, in offering an extraordinarily low price, had created a credibility problem. The customer would now require some strong evidence that the proposer (*a*) fully understood what was entailed and what would be required (that is, that the low price was not the blunder of someone who hadn't thought out the job), (*b*) was experienced and technically capable of doing the work required (that is, had not blundered out of ignorance of the nature of the work), and (*c*) was financially stable and responsible—could be counted on to make good, even if financial losses were involved. The successful capture strategy therefore compelled the proposer to work hard at demonstrating these things.

This latter case demonstrates clearly that while your capture strategy may be a simple one, it always entails some evidence that you can deliver on what you have promised. But in some cases, if your promise is revolutionary enough, it may create unusual burdens of proof, without which the strategy cannot succeed. Therefore, you must always consider, when you decide on a strategy, what the consequences of your decision may be: What will you be compelled to prove? What evidence can you offer? This of itself may mandate—force upon you—some of your other, subordinate strategies, as it did in the above case.

There is another aspect to the question of credibility. On the one hand, the customer will want evidence that the plan you propose is *technically* feasible—that it will result in the benefits predicted. But the customer will also be concerned with (1) evidence of your *technical capabilities and competence*, as the implementers of the plan proposed, and (2) evidence of your *dependability* as a contractor. As a *minimum*, to even get serious consideration, let alone selection as the winner, you will have to show these elements:

1. Understanding of the customer's need
2. A practical technical plan or program for satisfying the need
3. The means to carry out the program proposed—qualified staff, facilities, experience, and any other resources required
4. A "track record" as a contractor for similar programs

It is the latter two, items 3 and 4, which are the other elements of credibility. In some cases, these alone are the most important elements of the proposal. In many cases, what is required is more or less routine—no real technical or management problems involved. In such cases, the customer may well be concerned primarily with the qualifications of the organization and the staff proposed, far beyond other considerations. In fact, even when there are technical or management problems to be solved by your proposed approach, the quality of the individual staff members you propose and the quality of your organization's experience and past accomplishments are often the decisive factors. In no case should this be underestimated or treated casually.

You will be required to furnish names and résumés of all key staff proposed. A common mistake made by many proposers is to use boiler-plate résumés. That is, a standard résumé is maintained in the files for each senior staff member, and the same résumé is used for all proposals. But most individuals have different sets of qualifications, and no résumé can focus with equal intensity on all. That is, an electronics engineer may have extensive experience with various types of equipment or systems, but the customer is interested in only the one which is the subject of the solicitation. A customer who wishes to have an improved digital encoder will not be satisfied with a résumé in which digital encoder experience is shown as secondary to digital computer experience: the résumé will have to be rewritten to lay primary stress on the individual's digital encoder experience.

Make it a flat rule that all résumés will be written on a custom basis for the proposal at hand. It's well worth the time and trouble.

The organization's experience and qualifications are very much the same thing. The past projects most closely resembling the one being proposed should be given prominence, with other, less-relevant experience subordinated or not mentioned, if there is enough directly relevant experience to cite.

As a basic strategic approach, do not make either the individual or the organization appear to be a generalist, despite the fact that either may be. Most customers seeking custom services of any kind, and especially those with problems requiring technical solutions, prefer to deal with specialists. Always make your staff and your organization appear to specialize in the field of interest.

Many solicitations will call on you to provide specific information about past and current government contracts. Usually, you will be asked to list each contract or project, describe it briefly, and furnish the dollar amount, the agency, and the contracting official's name and telephone number. In some cases even more information is called for. But whether the solicitation requests such information or not, it is a good idea to provide it, as evidence of the organization's technical capability, competence, and dependability—its track record. It is also desirable that you furnish the names and telephone numbers of the program staff member responsible for providing technical direction, since it is that individual (not the contracting official) who can provide information on your technical capabilities, technical performance, and responsiveness.

A tabular presentation is suggested by the number and uniformity of information items to be provided, perhaps in a form somewhat as follows:

Contract No. and Agency	$ Amount	General Description of Project	Contract Official	Government Program Manager	Remarks

This format has the advantage that it is an efficient way to present the information, and it can be scanned and digested rather easily. On the other hand, it is somewhat inflexible, in that it has to be completely restructured for each proposal, to give prominence to the most-relevant projects. For that reason, some proposers use an independent paragraph to describe each past project, enabling them to cut up and paste the standard paragraphs in any order desired.

Here again, however, it is worth the extra trouble to use whatever presentation is most effective, and the tabular format is recommended. Consider, too, that even the standard-paragraph idea does not afford complete flexibility because many projects have such diverse functions required as to make it possible to rewrite each project description to stress what is most relevant to the proposal.

Consider, for example, a past project in which the organization set up and operated a Job Corps center. In describing this project to a new customer, the description could be written to provide evidence of the organization's ability to organize a new start, to undertake a diverse program, to provide job training, to conduct a socioeconomic program, or to stress any other aspect of relevant experience. Therefore, even if you use the paragraph format, it is worthwhile strategically to consider rewriting at least some of the paragraphs for the proposal at hand.

As in the case of any other capture strategy, if your company or staff qualifications are the pivot upon which your strategy and customer approval turn, you want to introduce this as early in the proposal as possible; the earlier you can focus the customer's attention on that which is of greatest concern, the greater the interest with which the customer will read your entire proposal. It is that item of greatest concern which is the most effective at arousing interest, and the objective is to arouse that interest as rapidly as possible. If you use the chart or tabular format to present your credentials, it is entirely appropriate to use it twice: once in the chapter or section devoted to the subject of your organization's experience and qualifications, and once at the beginning of your proposal, with a brief reference to it, as you highlight your organization's most-relevant qualifications in the introduction.

A General Strategic Approach

There are many different classes and kinds of strategy possible and necessary, as described. In general, however, it is all presentation or *sales* strategy. The cleverest technical and cost strategies are of no value if the sales strategy fails to carry the day. While the basics of sales presentation are to get attention, arouse interest, and generate desire to buy, sales strategy for proposals is perhaps more understandable when expressed in this manner:

1. Show accurate and complete understanding of the customer's *need*, and especially on whatever is of greatest concern to the customer.
2. Present a practical plan which will satisfy that need and be responsive to that greatest concern.
3. Prove—provide strong evidence—that the plan will work, that it is the *best* plan possible, that it is entirely feasible, and that it entails little, if any, risk of failure. Provide a maximum amount of specific detail in the plan, to make it highly credible.
4. Prove—provide strong evidence—that you can be depended on to carry out the plan, as a competent and reliable contractor with competent and reliable staff members.

Some Influences on Strategies

"The government" is people, individuals. An understanding of the individuals and internal agency policies may greatly influence strategic development. For example, there are some contracting officials who exercise all their prerogatives and responsibilities, and insist on trying to swing the contract award to the lowest qualified bidder. There are others who will permit the technical evaluators to award to anyone they choose. If you know that the contracting official, in your case, is one of those who tries energetically to find the lowest qualified bidder, keeping your costs low is likely to get the contracting official on your side—create an ally.

There are some agencies that invariably conduct negotiations with several of the most highly rated proposers. But some start with the most highly rated proposer, and only negotiate with others if they fail to reach a contract agreement with the number one contender.

A large contract is almost certain to call for proposers to submit their best and final offers, whereas smaller contracts are often awarded without discussion or proposal follow-up of any kind, depending on the agency and its policy.

Some agencies have fixed policies on the maximum fees or profit margins they will allow—and sometimes even on the maximum overhead rates they will agree to. It is futile and may harm your proposal to ask for more.

In some cases, the customer is well-disposed toward small companies, whereas in others the opposite is true.

Bear in mind that the customer is often perplexed, having a difficult time making a choice between two or more well-qualified proposers, all of whom have submitted good proposals with acceptable prices. As far as proposal evaluation reveals, there is little difference between these offerors.

In such cases as these, success may hinge on a single factor which otherwise may not have been of great importance. In one case, a single paragraph concerning a past project made the difference, for example, enabling the customer to single out a proposer from a large field and yet feel satisfied that the final evaluation was fair and objective. In one, slightly different, situation, an Army team visited the facilities of five minority-owned data-processing firms for the purpose of selecting qualified 8(a) bidders (minority-owned firms that qualify for noncompetitive awards under the Small Business Administration's 8(a) program). All were invited to submit informal proposals, and all were judged to be capable of handling the contract. Only one firm, however, followed up its submittal with an inquiry, a visit, and the offer of a formal presentation. Due to the special interest shown, and due to that alone, the Army selected that firm for the contract.

Summary of Strategies

The basic strategy of a proposal is always a presentation or sales strategy, for the proposal is a sales presentation. It must follow the soundly established sales principles of getting attention, arousing interest, and generating buying desire. To do so, the proposer must arrive at a good understanding of the customer's need—perhaps distinguishing between the customer's *stated* need and the *true* need. That is, if the customer has not understood the need clearly, and the proposer does arrive at a better understanding of that need, it is necessary to explain this to the customer in some convincing manner.

Usually, the customer has some primary concern, which may or may not be made clear in the RFP. It is necessary to make the best estimate possible of what that concern is, for that is likely to be the most decisive factor in selecting the successful proposer. And it is usually around that matter of greatest concern that the main strategy—the capture strategy—is built. At the same time, there are many areas and aspects of the proposal which must be sold and which can be based on specific strategies supporting the capture strategy—cost strategy, technical strategy, presentation strategy, management strategy, and others.

It is critically important that the major strategy be decided upon in advance, after analyzing the RFP and deciding what the customer's needs and concerns are. Only by fixing a specific strategy in advance can the proposal writers know where they are going—have a specific objective to reach.

The number of possible strategies and their variants is almost beyond counting. However, it is possible to state a general strategic approach, somewhat along the following lines:

1 The capture strategy is based on a promise to satisfy the customer's main or critical need. This may be the stated need, or it may be something else—a *true* need, which the customer either has not articulated or has failed to make clear in the work statement. If your strategy addresses a need other than the stated one, you will almost certainly have to do a selling job, or educate the customer, to prove your premise as to what the true need is.

The effectiveness of your capture strategy is based on your accuracy in identifying the need to be satisfied and on the credibility of your plans to satisfy it. You *must*, therefore, be deeply concerned with credibility. And the more revolutionary, startling, or extravagant the promise, the more essential is the need for evidence to establish credibility.

2 Other, subordinate strategies may be either simply in addition to the main, capture strategy, to strengthen the proposal overall, or in direct support of the capture strategy. That is, the capture strategy may well require such support, to be credible: technical innovation is likely to require proof of feasibility, cost-cutting promises must be shown to have a rational basis, etc. Generally speaking, a presentation is far more effective when all strategic ideas are clearly linked, all supporting the capture strategy and making the basic promise(s) of , the proposal highly credible.

3 The basic plan or approach and the benefits promised must be credible technically—that is, appear to be highly practical and with an excellent prospect for complete success. But the credibility of the proposer as a capable and dependable contractor must also be proven. Strategically, the proposal must provide clear evidence that the organization and the key project staff offered have all the necessary experience and technical capability required to carry out the plan that has been proposed. Further, the proposal must also demonstrate that the organization has delivered reliably in the past, that it is a highly *responsible* contractor.

4 Philosophical discussions and generalized observations, of themselves, are not plans and do not inspire confidence. Neither do general promises to produce good results. Confidence is established and credibility achieved only when the proposal offers *specific detail*—specific *commitment* to provide defined goods or services and deliver defined results. It is possible to provide a

great deal more detail than is required; however, you do not lose points for too much or unnecessary detail, but you do lose them for insufficient detail or missing items of information which the customer believes should be in your proposal. Beyond the question of score keeping, however, a wealth of detail is always impressive, demonstrates that you know what you are doing, and shows that you are prepared to be firmly committed to the project and promised results.

Some Main Points to Remember

1. Strategies are a must, as in any sales or marketing effort. Your main, or capture, strategy is aimed at providing the customer one or more compelling reasons for selecting your proposal as the one to be favored with a contract award—that reason or those reasons which are intended to convince the customer that the agency *needs* your service.
2. Without a specific strategy, your proposal doesn't *go* anywhere. A clearly formulated strategy is equivalent to an objective, giving purpose and unity to your proposal.
3. What is true for your capture strategy is equally true for any subordinate strategies you should employ—strategies to get attention, strategies to reduce costs, strategies to produce attractive and innovative ideas. Each gives that section or element of your proposal a focal point.
4. The overall strategy is inevitably one that is calculated to *create* a need for what you offer. That can be done successfully only by persuading the customer that your offer will satisfy the *felt* need—that basic need of which the customer is already aware—in some superior manner or with added benefits. The strategy is therefore based on your identification of the customer's true need, which may or may not be as the RFP has stated it—that is, you may have to help the customer gain a better insight into the true need.
5. For your strategies to be effective, especially your capture strategy, you must persuade the customer that you will indeed produce the results promised, the satisfying of the need as you have described it. Two kinds of proof are required: proof that your proposed plan is logically sound and should produce the promised results, and proof that you can carry out the plan successfully—have all the required technical qualifications and resources—and are a thoroughly dependable contractor.
6. Beware of being *too* innovative or different. The more revolutionary a program or product you offer, the greater the apparent risk. Therefore, to a large degree, the amount of evidence you must present to make your proposal and your qualifications credible is directly related to the degree of

innovation or the magnitude of the benefits you promise. Big promises require big proofs.

7. All sections of your proposal or all proposal elements ought to be based on individual strategies. However, they are not a loose assortment of ideas, but should be linked logically, all part of some master plan, and the customer should be able to see the linkages. If promised economies are a main thrust of strategy, for example, the proposal should clearly show how these are to result from some aspects of technical design, project management, proprietary resources, or other elements presented in your proposal. That is, there must be a *logical* linkage of all elements, particularly of those that constitute the cause-and-effect rationale of your promised principal benefit.

10

Proposal Elements and Formats

One cardinal principle of selling is to make it easy for the customer. This applies to proposals too.

Customers often have great difficulty evaluating proposals because of the wide variety of formats and treatments. Inevitably, despite preestablished evaluation criteria and guidelines, the evaluation must be on a comparative basis. The number one technical plan, for example, is whichever is selected as the best of the lot; the others are then stacked up against it. But with varying formats and schemes of presentation, it isn't always easy to make accurate comparisons.

Occasionally a customer attempts to solve this problem by mandating a format, describing it in the solicitation. In practice this turns out to be the exception rather than the rule; either customers are not entirely sure of what constitutes the best format or they are reluctant to restrict the proposer from offering what the proposer believes to be the most effective and easy-to-follow presentation. Therefore most solicitations prescribe the kinds of information to be included, but not the order or manner of presentation.

In those few cases where a specific format is prescribed, the obvious thing to do is respect the customer's wishes and follow that format as nearly as possible. In all other cases we recommend the format and design described in this chapter.

Format Logic as a Technical Argument

The three major phases in proposal development are these:

1. Analyses (identifying the true need)
2. Approach and design development, strategy formulation
3. Writing the proposal

These steps are chronological (although there may be iteration); each step is a prerequisite to the following step—this is the basic logic of proposal *development*. (Note that "proposal writing" is not the whole process, but the final step in the process.)

There is also logic in the format recommended here. Let's look at how you would conduct a sales call if a customer had called your firm about a problem or need and asked that the firm send out a representative. After seeking out the buyer who had called, you would approach him with your hand extended and say something like this:

"Hello, Mr. Jones. I'm Ann Smith from Action Electronics. You called and asked, according to the information I've got here, about having some special coils designed for your new squelch circuits. If we can talk about your problem for a few minutes, I think I can help you."

Having introduced yourself properly and established firmly why you are calling on Jones, you're ready to show him what your firm can do. And once you are sure that you have a firm grasp on Jones's need you can go ahead and make your oral proposal with some confidence.

Proposal procedure is not much different, except that you are not face-to-face with the customer, but with the customer's surrogate—a solicitation and its SOW, which attempt to describe the customer's need. Circumstances surrounding most proposal requests do not permit you to conduct an interview with the customer to query each point; instead, you have "queried" the solicitation and gathered your detailed information by reading between the lines, by analyses, and by any other means open to you. However, the same basics apply as in the personal call:

1. Introduce yourself
2. Identify your reason for being there
3. Review, discuss the customer's need
4. Make your offer

(There are, in the case of a proposal, a number of special considerations also, due to the special circumstances of this type of selling. We'll discuss these later, after we have settled on the basic format and design.)

In one sense, the proposal is a classic presentation of logic—a syllogism:

Major Premise (general statement or understanding of the need)
Minor Premise(s) (analyses and points made about the need and means for satisfying it)
Conclusion (specific offer made in proposal)

In fact, there is still another syllogism embodied in the proposal:

Major Premise (our understanding of the need)
Minor Premise(s) (our analyses, approach, specific offer, and qualifications)
Conclusion (award should be made to us)

This, then, is the basic logic of the proposal format: first, based on the premises of the needs as stated and as explored and expanded on in our technical discussions, the plan we offer is the best plan; second, based on the premises of our plan being the right plan, our technical and professional capabilities and specific resources being right, and our track record being excellent, we are the logical awardee or contractor for the project. This logic underlies the basic, four-section format recommended here:

I. INTRODUCTION
Who we are (briefly and with reference to more details later in the proposal); why we are here (citation of the solicitation and our suitability as a contender ofor the contract); and a brief statement demonstrating our understanding of the requirement in general

II. DISCUSSION
Expansion of the last part of the first section (understanding of the requirement), exploring the requirement in depth, guiding the reader through our analyses and conclusions, culminating (logically) in the approach(es) we recommend and propose

III. PROPOSED PROGRAM

How the approach is to be implemented, as a logical extension of the second section, making specific pledges, promises, and commitments—that detailed program, in short, for which we propose to sign or negotiate a contract

IV. OUR QUALIFICATIONS AS AN ORGANIZATION

Our available resources—personnel, facilities, and financial resources—our past achievements, and any other available evidence demonstrating our desirability as a contractor

This is a basic format which, along with some miscellaneous front matter yet to be discussed, fits most proposal requirements. There are occasional special instances, in addition to the case in which the customer specifies a format, where this basic design should be modified. These will be discussed later, after we have explored all the implications of the basic design and how it can best be implemented. (Even in customer-mandated formats the general presentation philosophy of this format can usually be followed. It makes sense as a *technical* argument, but does it make equal sense as sales logic—that is, is it the right format for a *sales* argument?

Format Logic as a Sales Argument

In sales and advertising it is generally considered essential to capture the prospective customer's interest by the promise of certain, desirable results (benefits), and then to generate a desire to buy by providing evidence that proves or at least persuades the prospective customer that those benefits will indeed result from the purchase—that is, the offeror must establish *credibility*.

In the format recommended here the introductory section addresses the customer's needs in some succinct manner. The purpose of the brief subsection in which an understanding of the need is demonstrated is to strip away all the trivia and nonessential detail which is customarily found in the customer's SOW, thus highlighting the essence of the need. In the event that the customer has failed to accurately identify the need or has confused the problem with its symptoms, this subsection would be the place to make that point tactfully and set the stage for the discussion which follows.

In that discussion the proposal must explore the customer's requirements thoroughly, demonstrating valid analyses and conclusions and stressing the results to be achieved and the best manner in which to achieve them. And in this process a key issue is that of addressing that (those) critical point(s) which are of concern to the customer, whether the customer has highlighted or confessed them or not. That is, the discussion must pursue the perceived critical benefit of low cost, great dependability, innovative solution, most

highly qualified staff, most sophisticated management, or whatever the proposer has decided will most influence the customer.

In short, the discussion—which, remember, is merely a logical extension of the statement of understanding made in the introduction—focuses on benefits or desirable results. (In practice, the discussion is usually written first and the introductory statement of understanding is virtually an abstract of the discussion.)

Therefore, Sections I and II, if properly developed, meet the requirements of arousing interest.

Now the proposal must go on to establish credibility—"prove" that the promised results will follow an award to the proposer. And that proof or evidence consists of three elements:

1. The apparent *validity*, or logic, of the analysis of the requirements, the approach taken, and the proposed program in all its detail
2. The proposer's technical and professional credentials—qualifications of proposed staff members, physical and financial resources, and qualifying past experience of the organization itself
3. The proposer's record as a responsible and dependable contractor— evidence that the proposer has performed well in past projects

The first element is actually begun during the discussions, where the validity of the analyses and the proposed approach are shown. The analyses must be persuasive, and the approach must be the logical outgrowth or conclusion of those analyses. The program itself, presented in Section III of the proposal, is the logical outgrowth of the approach, the approach implemented.

It is desirable to include *all* details of the proposed project in the third section. The existence of these details, presenting a complete plan, is itself highly persuasive, suggesting strongly that the proposer has done all the necessary homework and is indeed prepared to conduct a successful project. And it is in this section, preferably, that the qualifications of the proposed key project staff—résumés—be presented as part of the necessary detail.

Finally, in Section IV the proposer presents the technical and professional qualifications of the company and its record as a contractor. And it must not be presumed, as so many proposers have done to their ultimate dismay, that this section is simply pro forma; it is often even more important than the earlier sections. In many cases, the reliability of the contractor is of the utmost concern to the customer.

This format, then, does satisfy the requirements of a sales presentation, as well as those of a sound technical argument. But there are other elements, some mandated by the solicitation, some required by generally accepted conventions in proposals and publications, and some necessary to meet other requirements. *All of these, regardless of the original reason for their inclusion, may be turned to advantage as sales influences.* Let this be a basic philosophy in writing proposals:

A proposal is a sales presentation. Therefore, miss no opportunity to sell throughout the proposal. Design every section, element, page, paragraph, illustration, and headline for maximum sales impact.

We'll be looking at some of these possibilities as we discuss the proposal elements in greater detail. First we'll talk about the proposal itself and then about the front matter and other elements. But even before we do that, let's consider an element of selling which we have neglected: getting attention.

The Importance of Getting Attention

It is said in Tennessee and a few neighboring states that before you can train a mule you must smite the mule between the eyes with the largest club you can handle. That is to get the mule's attention.

There are a few cases in government marketing where your competition is limited to only two or three other proposers. Most of the time the competition is considerably greater. You may very well find yourself competing for the prize with as many as twenty, thirty, or even forty competitive proposals. And many of your competitors may be well-known corporations whose names are immediately known to the customer. Despite the mandate to evaluate all proposals objectively and on the basis of what each proposal actually presents, evaluators cannot help being at least subtly influenced by the name and reputation of a prominent corporation. And even if you are writing a proposal for one of those prominent corporations, you are likely to be competing with others as well known as your own.

When a large number of competitors submit proposals, it is often of supreme importance to get attention, especially if your own organization is not a very prominent one. You will have difficulty in getting your messages across—arousing the customer's interest and generating desire to buy—if you fail to capture attention swiftly. A case history clearly illustrates this.

A consultant was retained by a bureau within the Department of Labor for several months to assist the bureau in producing a training program. During that time the consultant became well acquainted with a young executive there who was responsible for the work being done by the consultant and who was also managing several contracts. One day, the consultant listened quietly as the executive grumbled aloud about the problems he was having with one of the contractors, in trying to get the results he wanted from the contract.

After a while the consultant said, "Bill, I know the job you refer to. As a matter of fact, I submitted a proposal on that one, and I thought it was a fair enough proposal at a fair enough price, but I never heard again. I've always wondered why I wasn't at least invited to submit a best and final offer."

Bill shrugged and replied, "I can't say. But I'll look up your proposal in my files and let you know whatever I can about it."

Several days later, Bill told the consultant: "I reviewed your proposal for that job, and I must say it was at least as good a proposal as the one I got from the————Corporation" (naming the contractor). "I don't know why I didn't ask you in to talk. I probably should have. But I remember that there were a lot of responses and that by the end of the day I hardly knew what I was reading anymore. You were probably unlucky enough to have me read yours at four in the afternoon, rather than nine in the morning when I was still awake and alert."

On the other side of the coin, let's consider this true story.

The Educational Science Division of U.S. Industries prepared a proposal in response to a Job Corps requirement for a training program in electrical appliance repair. Among the specifics proposed was an offer to prepare a large number of multicolored posters as training aids. Samples were included in the proposal, although the samples were in black and white. Since the organization had a full-scale art department, the illustrators did the work as professional illustrators ordinarily prefer; originals were created oversize—about 3 × 5 feet, in this case—and reduced photographically for printing in the proposal. The originals, moreover, were in full color.

After the proposal had been completed and was being prepared for final production—printing, binding, and delivery—the head of the art department asked the manager of the proposal team if he had any need for the original illustrations. The proposal manager was about to shrug them off and advise the chief illustrator to dispose of them as the illustrator saw fit when he was suddenly struck with a thought.

"Yes, certainly," he said. "Bring them over. I want them."

His first idea was to send the posters down as life-sized examples which would also show the colors not shown in the page-size reproductions. But he instantly realized that this was an excellent opportunity to gain some attention.

He packaged the proposal copies together with the posters and delivered a 3 × 5 foot package labeled "Proposal!" And he deliberately delivered the package several days before the due date so that it would stand in a corner of the procurement office (it wouldn't fit on a shelf!) arousing curiosity.

The strategy was spectacularly successful; the package aroused speculation and comment which lasted for days. And when it was finally opened and the contents revealed, the story circulated throughout the building for days and became something of a minor classic.

To further dramatize the situation, the proposal manager had also enclosed a notice saying that the posters would become government property if the proposer was awarded the contract; requesting the posters' return otherwise, stressing that they had been developed at great expense and effort (they were highly professional and the claim was both true and credible); and saying that the proposer would have other uses for the posters if they were not used in the proposed project.

Of course, such a strategy works only if the proposal is itself a sound one; getting attention does not win the contract, but it ensures that your proposal will be read carefully and with awareness of who submitted the proposal. In the case cited here the technical proposal received high marks; the cost proposal was another story. The contracting official called the company and said that while the Job Corps liked the technical proposal, the price asked was "out of sight." He had called, he said, to inquire whether there was any possibility of negotiating a more modest price. Assured that the proposer would welcome an opportunity to discuss costs, the Job Corps agreed to negotiations and a contract was ultimately agreed upon—still at a higher price than most of the other proposals, although about 20 percent lower than the original "asking" price.

It is doubtful that the Job Corps would have attempted to negotiate a contract with the company had their enthusiasm not been thoroughly aroused and their imagination stimulated by the proposer's ploy.

When and *Why* of Getting Attention

It should hardly need to be pointed out that a proposal needs to command attention as early as possible, just as a commercial on TV or a print advertisement tries to command immediate attention. In the case history just related, it would not have been possible to get so much attention any earlier—several days before the proposals were even opened! Of course, it is not often possible to bring off such a coup as that, and if it were, everyone would be doing it and the impact would soon be lost. Yet you cannot wait too long or you will never get that attention at all. The fact is that many proposals are never read all the way through—an evaluator may become convinced after only a few pages that the proposal does not qualify. Or, if the content is stultifying enough, the evaluator may read through the proposal, stifling yawns continuously. Getting attention, therefore, must be accomplished reasonably early and must progress swiftly into "arousing interest," or the effect will be lost.

The points at which an attention-getting element may be introduced effectively are therefore these:

Prior to actual opening of proposal packages, as in the case history described here. Opportunities for this are relatively rare, but this is highly effective, if you can devise a method.

By accompanying items, such as the posters called "exhibits" in the case history. Other devices used successfully have included tape recordings

and, in at least one case, a photo blowup illustrating the chosen site proposed for a project in which site selection was a major consideration. Some other ideas will be suggested later, offering information on presentation strategies and techniques.

The cover of the proposal may offer some opportunities to command attention. In one case the project was so complex that perhaps even the customer did not quite grasp the involved relationships among the various discrete tasks required of the contractor. The successful proposer worked hard at an all-day brainstorming and analytical conference to translate the SOW into a coherent flowchart. The proposer then reduced that flowchart, which was still fairly complex, into a simplified flow diagram in which each major task was identified by a symbol or block, showing the basic relationships among the tasks and functions. This was then printed on the cover of the proposal, as well as on one of the proposal pages, with an explanatory figure title. In this case, rather than using the conventional flowchart, the proposer used a pictorial type of flowchart in which line drawings of the items—reports, tapes, cards, and others—were used. This is frequently a more suitable kind of illustration for a proposal cover than the cabalistic symbols of the technical flow diagram.

In the front matter of the proposal—the Letter of Transmittal, the Executive Summary, or other material appearing before page one of the proposal proper. The Response Matrix, which will be described later, may itself command a certain measure of attention, if properly presented. Another item of front matter which may be used to some effect is a frontispiece— an illustration which appears even before the title page and reflects some central idea or theme. In fact, a well-thought-out frontispiece can be highly effective as a sales aid. If getting attention is to depend on the Letter of Transmittal or the Executive Summary, it will have to command attention by what is *said*—text, that is.

The same consideration obtains if the opening paragraphs are to command attention. At this point you are quite close to the point of diminishing returns. That is, you have already bypassed several opportunities to get attention, and if you fail to capture it in the first page or two of the body of the proposal, it is futile to try further; you will simply have to hope that the reader is dogged enough to work through the entire proposal and become persuaded that you have offered a sound plan and acceptable set of credentials. You can assume that the customer will indeed read at least the first few pages—at least your introductory section. But if you have something attention-commanding to say there (for example, if you have a startling offer to make or have retained the world's foremost authority on something relevant to the project), you could have and should have said it in abstract at least in the Letter of Transmittal or Executive Summary.

Later, in discussing the art of persuasive writing, we'll talk about some methods for luring a reader on, page after page. But first we have to persuade the reader to turn to the second page; at least one government executive has assured these authors that he sometimes does not turn to the second page, having already become convinced on the first page that further consideration is a waste of time!

Section I: Introductory Gambits

Chess players know what a gambit it. It's giving away or sacrificing a piece, usually a pawn, to gain some advantage. Usually it's offered as a lure to attract an opponent into a predictable move—to *control* an opponent's next action.

Skilled negotiators often use conversational gambits, turning the negotiation into a desired channel or drawing attention away from the direction in which it appears to be headed.

In the general proposal strategy offered here, the introductory section offers conversational gambits to the reader. There are several purposes in so doing:

To create a favorable initial impression by spotlighting the proposer's greatest strengths for the project and contract under discussion

To command attention or (if that has already been accomplished) to begin generating interest as quickly as possible

To lure the reader into a desired channel or train of thought

To set the stage for what is to follow

To arouse *curiosity*, if not interest, and so lure the reader into turning to the second page—and keep on turning the pages

Let us consider three possible attitudes with which an evaluator—customer—may approach your proposal and open to the first page (neglecting the possible effect of the front matter, for the moment):

With great anticipation, expecting great things

With great skepticism, expecting a me-too offer

With determined objectivity, maintaining an open mind

If yours is the first case, you are already at a great disadvantage; the proposal may be excellent, but the reader has expected too much and is therefore disappointed.

If yours is the second case, a strong opening is an absolute must to overcome the obvious disadvantage of reader bias.

If yours is the third case, the situation is much like the second case; you still need a strong opening, but the need is not quite as great. The reader is likely to read carefully and judge as objectively as possible.

One problem is that a reader may begin reading the first of a large stack of proposals with determined objectivity, but soon begin to approach each succeeding proposal with great skepticism, having read several poor proposals in the meanwhile. This is not uncommon. You have no control over the sequence, of course, and so you must assume the worst in planning and writing your proposal.

Even if you are fortunate enough to have your proposal evaluated by readers who are conscientious enough to read every proposal through from cover to cover and make scrupulously honest evaluations, you are still competing with the reader's own fatigue and boredom in reading so many versions of the same thing. Anything you can do to reduce the fatigue and boredom is going to be a welcome change to the reader and will result in a more thoughtful contemplation of what you offer. (More of this in the chapter on persuasive writing.)

Remember the admonition to make things as easy as possible for the customer? It applies in many ways. The magazine advertisement which has a coupon or, even better, a separate order card you can tear out easily is one way. Look at one of these carefully. Many require you to do nothing more than fill in your name and address, and check off "bill me" or write in a credit card number, and drop it in the mail box. (It has prepaid mailing permit indicia.) Or the mail solicitation that arrives in your morning mail is another way. It usually has a prepaid envelope for sending in your order.

How does this apply to proposal writing? Make it as easy as possible for your customer to understand what you are saying and to follow your line of argument—not because your reader can't grasp those 64-dollar words and convoluted sentences, but because your reader just won't be troubled to struggle with your verbiage and will go on to spend time with an easier-to-read proposal. Of course, while this should be a general rule for the entire proposal, it is especially important at the outset. One thing you certainly wish to avoid is having the reader mumble softly after the first paragraph or two, "Uh-oh, this is going to be one of *those*."

An executive in the Department of Labor who reads a great many proposals puts it this way: He contracts for professional services, to be performed by professional people. He does not expect proposals to be written in the exquisite style of Henry James, but he does expect them to be clear, intelligible, and easy to follow. The use of unnecessarily complex ideas, obscure and rare terms, and other such obfuscation he considers to be firm evidence of an attempt to snow him. He thinks that is highly unprofessional, and while he will read the proposal through because he wants to be scrupulously fair, he is already strongly prejudiced against it. Even worse, to him, is the ludicrous misuse of terms which he also encounters. It's amusing, he says, but it does not inspire his confidence in the proposer.

One key aspect of the gambit, then, is to make the opening page the harbinger of an easy-to-read proposal, which is likely to be a refreshing change!

A number of thoughts on how to do this will be offered later, in Chapter 13 on writing. However, one reliable way of accomplishing this is by the simple discipline of keeping sentences short and direct, restricting each to a single thought. The use of the simplest synonym helps also. (It is not absolutely necessary to use short sentences to achieve easy readability, but it's the most direct route for the individual who is not a professional writer.)

The introduction (first section or chapter) need contain only two elements:

1. A brief introduction to the proposer—identify yourself and your basic interest in and qualifications for the project
2. A summary statement of the requirement, as you understand it, getting to the essence and laying the foundation for the discussion to follow

Introduction to the Proposer

Here you should identify your organization—the organization which is actually responding to the RFP; if it is a division or subsidiary of a larger organization, make that clear. Identify the solicitation to which you are responding unless you have chosen to do so in "head data," which makes it unnecessary to do so in the text. Sketch in your overall qualifications briefly, with the promise of furnishing the details in a later section. And if you have something special to offer, say so briefly here as a teaser or attention-getter. Consider the example in Figure 10.1.

The terms "Introduction" and "About the Offeror" are generic and not the best ones to get attention and arouse interest, but we'll cover that topic later. Head data is used here to minimize the tiresome detail which would otherwise have to be reported in the opening sentences. The sentences have been kept as short and direct as possible. The proposer has summarized both organization and individual qualifications briefly and has explained that the details of such qualifications will appear later in the proposal.

All of this represents the minimum information that should appear here. Of itself, it is enough to at least assure the reader that the proposal has been prepared by an organization qualified in the field of interest and is therefore probably worth studying seriously.

The reason for concern with demonstrating basic qualifying credentials immediately is this: An amazingly large number of proposals are submitted by firms seeking to enter new fields for which they are totally unqualified. The result is sometimes a competent proposal—where the proposer has taken the time and trouble to study the requirement and research the field. But quite often the proposals submitted are totally inept and so much so that the customer wonders if the proposer has even read the RFP! It is therefore advisable to establish your qualifications as soon as possible and provide some

TECHNICAL PROPOSAL in response to
RFP DE-80-A-10-0009 for a study of
the economic impact of wind energy
conversion systems.

SECTION I

INTRODUCTION

ABOUT THE OFFEROR

The Systems Division of Syzygy Technical Corporation is
pleased to be able to offer the Department of Energy a unique
resource, in response to the solicitation referenced above.
The Systems Division has been actively engaged in studies of
wind energy conversion systems since 1975. In that time, we
have carried out studies and development programs for the
Department of Energy, the National Science Foundation, and
the Department of Agriculture. We offer an organization and
staff of professionals highly experienced in the field.
(Fuller details of organization and staff qualifications
appear in later sections of this proposal.) However, we are
privileged to offer the Energy Department a special and unique
resource: The staff we shall propose to carry out the study
will be headed and directed by none other than Dr. Gottfried
Heimische, who is widely acknowledged as the leading authority
in this field.

FIGURE 10.1
Example of opening statement of proposal.

sort of assurance that your proposal is a serious response to the requirement and is worth reading.

In the sample shown here, the proposer has gone a giant step further: the proposer has introduced a *compelling* reason to read the proposal with an attention-getting offer to provide the services of an outstanding technical or professional authority as the key figure in the project. Of course, if you utilize such a strategy, you must be offering the services of someone who is truly well known as an authority by others (including the customer, of course) in that field.

Anything that is special about your proposal ought to be introduced here. If you have some unusual (and relevant) resource, such as an electron microscope or remarkable proprietary process, use it to command attention here, at the beginning of your proposal. Use *anything* here which can command immediate attention and cause the customer to read more eagerly—to turn to the second page with anticipation. Here are a few suggestions for such items:

- Any unusual and impressive resource—a prominent technical or professional authority, an unusual research library, proprietary processes, equipment.
- Unusual qualifying experience or accomplishments which have direct relevance.
- A subcontractor who is especially well qualified or can offer any other special resource.
- A special insight into the requirement or problem, which is so remarkable or important that you feel it useful to introduce it here, rather than a few paragraphs later when you will be discussing the requirement itself.
- A special promise or pledge you can make as to results or effort—for example, an absolute guarantee that you can carry out the entire project in significantly less time than projected in the work statement or with substantially greater results. This may be, in fact, an attention-getting lead on your main strategy, if your strategy is such that it represents a dramatic offer.

A number of prominent authorities on advertising and sales presentations are in agreement that advertising is most effective when the selling is done in the headline—that is, when the headline is used not only to command attention, but to launch the sales argument and, in fact, to present as much of the sales argument as possible. That is essentially the philosophy behind the introduction of such ideas into the opening paragraph of a proposal—get to at least one major point or strategy of your proposal as quickly as possible and as dramatically as possible. It must be done briefly, however, almost as a teaser to draw the reader on, for that is part of its purpose. If, for example, you are able to offer ironclad guarantees of early delivery of results, offer the promise—*what* you pledge to accomplish or predict as an outcome. But don't tell all here; don't tell *how* you will accomplish this. Instead, make it clear that the entire plan or methodology is to be revealed in the pages to come.

Whether you do this here in the first subsection of the first section of your proposal or in the second subsection, where you discuss the requirement to summarize it and demonstrate understanding, is a matter of judgment. It depends primarily on where it can be presented with greatest impact. As a basic rule of thumb, however, consider this: If the idea can be dropped in summarily, with little or no preparatory discussion, you can use it in the first paragraph; if it requires some discussion as groundwork, it will probably be more effective in the second subsection (although a hint may be used in the first paragraph).

Understanding of the Requirement

The second element of the first section may actually begin on the first page of your proposal if the proposal is fairly short, but it will directly follow the introductory teaser. Again, the sidehead "Understanding of the Requirement" (or "Problem") is generic; a suitable sidehead should be devised to match the individual case and to support the persuasive aspect of the presentation.

This subsection has two major purposes:

1. To demonstrate immediately that you do have a firm grasp on the requirement, problem, customer's needs, and so forth.
2. To set the stage for the discussion to follow and, especially, for your major strategy.

If you have given some hint of your strategy in the opening statements, this is also the place to begin following up. But even here, you shouldn't fire both barrels; an extended discussion will follow, and that is where you should explore the strategy in detail. In this subsection, as in every portion of your proposal, you would be well advised to plant some inkling of additional revelations yet to come so as to persuade—motivate—your reader to keep turning pages in anticipation, eager to learn more of what you propose.

For example, in bidding to the Job Corps for a lecture-based training program in a trade which requires access to service literature, the point was made strongly in the Understanding of the Requirement that the whole project involved the problem of training semiliterate individuals for a trade which required at least a fair proficiency in basic academic subjects. Having introduced the problem clearly, the subsection promised to reveal a number of techniques for dealing with it successfully.

Ideally, a writer wants to keep the reader turning pages, and in many if not most cases it is the writer's responsibility to make the reader *want* to keep turning pages—to *motivate* the reader to do so. Bear in mind as you write that you are always *competing* for the reader's attention; there are many other proposals waiting to be read.

However, the stated purpose of this subsection is to demonstrate your complete and accurate understanding of the need or problem to be solved. This is the main function of the paragraphs which make up the remainder of the first section of your proposal. And this matter of your complete and accurate understanding is of great importance to the customer, who has almost certainly muttered "they just don't seem to understand the problem," after reading many proposals. (The authors have seen just such notations made in the margins of proposals, after evaluation.)

The neophyte proposal writer is sorely tempted to echo the words of the work statement here, and many do. It's a disastrous mistake, one which many RFPs actually caution against. Repeating the customer's own words does not demonstrate your understanding. Quite the contrary, it suggests that you have not taken the time or do not have the background to grasp what the customer needs or has said in the work statement. At the absolute minimum, you must express the customer's description of need in your own language. And even that is usually not quite enough. It proves only that you understand the customer's *words,* but not necessarily the *need* or *problem!*

Probably the most effective way to demonstrate complete and accurate understanding is to identify the *essence* of the customer's need or problem— that is, strip away the miscellaneous trivia usually found in work statements and focus on the core. But make it clear in so doing that you are not neglecting the less important matters, which probably must have your attention too, but that you are clarifying the *essential* need or problem by setting the distractions aside for the moment. The ability to do this is pretty sound evidence of true understanding.

If in so doing you are able to uncover hidden or not-obvious problems (or needs), so much the better. This is even better evidence of your understanding, and it may be that the customer has completely overlooked these problems. Therefore, if you make the customer aware of needs or problems for the first time—and if you convince the customer that these are true needs or problems and are important to the success of the project—you are certain to have an interested reader who is now aware that you have done a competent analysis. You will have scored a bull's-eye!

The Job Corps example just described is such a case. The customer, who was not familiar with the needs of the trade to be taught (electrical appliance repair), was probably not conscious of the academic requirements to master that trade. Pointing such things out and promising satisfactory solutions has at least three effects:

1. It's highly persuasive evidence that the proposer knows the field of interest and has done the homework—studied the need thoroughly.
2. It commands attention and interest; the reader is compelled to read on to discover the methodologies and solutions to be employed.
3. It is a devastating blow to competitors, if they have failed to demonstrate equal insights and knowledge—that is, if they have not even identified or discussed the problem.

In this particular case, failure to recognize and cope successfully with this problem would seriously threaten the success of the project. If this is so, that point should be made quite clearly. Motivation—sales argument—can be based on rewards, as we have discussed, but it can also be based on fear—avoidance of failure, in this case. And frequently the fear motivation is even stronger than the reward motivation because it focuses on that bit of insecurity which almost all of us have!

Bear in mind that the customer is a government executive who is "on the spot" with this project, especially if a large sum of money is involved. It is on this executive's judgment that a contractor will be selected, that a large sum of money will be obligated, and that success or failure of the project will ultimately depend. A major consideration is confidence in what the proposer has to say and how competent the proposer appears to be.

In fact, you will find that many RFPs state specifically, as part of the evaluation criteria, that the proposal will be judged partially on how well it appears to identify problems and the solutions it offers to cope with anticipated problems. But whether the RFP says so or not, it is always advisable to make an honest appraisal of the project and its probable problems. Deliberately ignoring probable problems or making a hasty analysis which fails to consider probable problems may make you one of those competitors who has failed to make the right points and has suffered by comparison with other proposals. In short, you must assume that your competitors have done a thorough analysis, know their business, and have reported their analytical results honestly in their proposals.

Length or Size of the First Section

A frequent question at proposal-writing seminars is "How long should this first section or chapter be?"

Abraham Lincoln is reported to have answered the question "How long should a man's legs be?" with the answer "Long enough to reach the ground." Facetious though it may be, it's a good answer to our question. The first section of the proposal should be long enough to do the job of introducing yourself, presenting your basic qualifications as a serious contender for the job and your basic understanding of the requirement, and whatever you can come up with as motivation for reading on. Or perhaps we should say "short enough" to do the job, for this first section is introductory and should be as short as it can reasonably be made.

The actual length in pages will depend on the overall size of the proposal, which in turn depends on the amount of information required. An RFP for a large project is usually far larger than one for a small job and requires a great deal more information. Consequently, some formal proposals may be only 25–50 pages in total length, whereas there are some which have run into thousands of pages and several volumes. In the latter case, an entire volume of perhaps 200 pages may have been devoted to introductory information and front matter. On the other hand, for a small-to medium-sized proposal two or three pages may suffice as an adequate first chapter. Again, individual judgment is required. But remember that the first chapter or section is introductory and should be no longer than absolutely necessary to set the stage.

Section II: Technical Arguments

Whereas the first section ordinarily has only two subsections, the second section can vary widely in the number of subsections it may contain. There were only three main objectives in the first section: introducing yourself and your basic qualifications for being a contender for the job; hooking the reader with some gambits, usually indicative of your basic strategy; and immediately demonstrating an understanding of the requirement while laying the foundation for your proposal. The goal of the second section is to sell your proposal through logic, to persuade the customer of the rightness of your proposed program. But depending on the nature of the requirement and its size, you may have to establish a number of objectives to achieve this goal.

In all cases this is where you must present your technical arguments to prove either that yours is the best approach or that you are the best-qualified contractor for the job, according to the nature of the requirement. If, for example, what you are proposing for is an R&D job in a sophisticated technological area ("high technology," as some refer to it), you will have to devote most of your technical arguments to your proposed methods and what is possible today in the field (the state-of-the-art arguments). That is, for such a requirement you focus on the *technology* you are about to propose. But if the requirement is for something not involving the uncertainties and risks of development in a sophisticated technological field, then your discussion must center on whatever is required to meet that requirement. For example, if the customer merely needs more "hands and feet," to meet a need you must emphasize your ability to provide a dependable supply of the right, qualified hands and feet.

Therefore, in one case you might be concentrating a great deal of your discussion and technical arguments on the state of the art, to demonstrate that one approach is "pushing" the state of the art and is technically risky, whereas another approach is along well-established lines and known feasibility and is therefore almost certain to be successful. But in another case, you might be concentrating on matters of project management, rather than technical development. So "technical argument" may not be truly very technical at all.

Consider the varying degrees of technical capability needed for the following typical kinds of requirements:

Research and develop a new high-speed aircraft.
Conduct a survey among low-income apartment dwellers.
Write a technical manual.
Update a large set of engineering drawings.
Research the best method for coping with railroad grade crossings in small
 cities.
Develop a computerized management information system.
Manage a computer installation in a government building.
Supply a large number of engineering personnel to a NASA facility.
Develop procedures for designing better roofing quality in federal buildings.
Prepare an environmental impact statement.
Develop a training program in occupational safety and health.
Write and produce TV and radio spot announcements.

You can easily imagine that your discussions and technical arguments would vary widely were you to bid all of these requirements. The main focus of your technical discussions might center on a wide number of factors, such as the following:

Technology or state of the art
Recruiting capabilities
Statistical competence
Knowledge and experience in demographic factors
Drafting facilities and competence
Computer programming or systems analysis (might be state of the art, however)
Training technology
Editorial considerations

Then again, there may be more than one major consideration. A large R&D effort might have to consider many separate areas with extended discussions. For example, a proposal to develop a radically new fighter aircraft with all its weapons and related systems would have to consider and discuss at least these areas:

Airframe
Weapons systems
Navigational aids
Defensive systems
Power plant
Basing and supply requirements
Technical management of an extensive and complex program
General, administrative management of a complex project
Documentation of a complex project
Training follow-up
Testing
Quality control

In short, one major objective of the second section is to present your technical arguments. These arguments may be several in number or singular, and even if singular, they may be along different lines.

The Minimal Objectives

Whatever the case, the following is the minimum you wish to accomplish in the second section:

- Elaborate on your understanding to demonstrate it beyond any reasonable doubt and to persuade the customer that you have identified or defined the true need.
- Explore the requirement(s) in regard to what the contractor must do or provide to achieve successful results.
- Identify all problems which can and should be anticipated; discuss them, especially for their potential to endanger ultimate success; suggest solutions, measures to avoid, or contingent plans to cope with.
- Make comparative analyses of all possible alternatives, pointing out pros and cons of each.
- Present logical conclusions, which represent proposed approach.

This is the logical flow of the discussion section. It should recapitulate your own initial analyses of the requirement and the best approach to a project design.

Relative Importance of the Various Elements

It is hazardous to say that any one of these elements is more important than another. All are important in accomplishing the goal. However, there is one element which is strategically most important in sales persuasion, but which many proposal writers tend to overlook. That is the identification of potential problems.

There are two general kinds of motivators: rewards and penalties. Or, in this case, perhaps it is more appropriate to say hopes and fears. A customer is motivated to buy primarily in the hope and expectation of deriving some desirable result, or benefit, as a result of the purchase. But many purchases are made to avoid an undesirable result—out of fear. Insurance, for example, is almost always sold by the specter of leaving a family unprotected, failing in one's responsibilities, being without income during illness, being faced with a disastrous lawsuit or devastating hospital bills, or similar catastrophes. In this case the fear is a far more powerful motivator than would be any hope of gain.

But fear as a motivator is not confined to the selling of insurance. Political candidates are sold to the voters by the fear of what the other candidate is likely to do, as well as by the great rewards promised by the candidate making the speech. Financial advice publications are sold to investors by the promise of helping them avoid such financial disaster as poor investments, as well as by the promise of great gains. Antiperspirant and deodorant preparations are sold primarily on the fear basis, as are burglar alarms, security locks, fire extinguishers, and many other devices.

It would be a rare project which was conducted without a serious problem arising. The customer is well aware of that, as are your competitors. To gloss over potential problems or to ignore them is to risk losing credibility and to suffer badly by comparison with other proposers who have introduced the potential problems and discussed them frankly. Even worse, it is to neglect a powerful selling opportunity. Problems must be anticipated and discussed frankly to achieve all the following:

- To reflect your own expert knowledge and experience, furthering your demonstration of complete understanding and complete capability
- To demonstrate that you have indeed made a serious study of the requirement and have planned most carefully
- To rise above your competitors, who may not have been as thorough or as honest in preparing their proposals
- To exploit fully the benefits of the fear motivation in selling your approach

What the Contractor Must Do or Be

In the RFP the customer has presented a set of attributes and functions considered necessary to get the job done successfully. These are usually listed as evaluation criteria and often as mandatory minimum qualifications. In the course of discussing the requirement in some depth, contractor functions and qualifications become apparent. Frequently, the customer has not even considered some of these functions or qualifications. In such cases it is often persuasive to point these out in the discussions. The objective is, of course, to persuade the customer that these are important considerations, that you measure up to all of them well, and perhaps, that a number of your competitors do not measure up too well. Therefore, it is not amiss to have a subsection entitled something like "Necessary Contractor Functions" or "Necessary Contractor Qualifications." Here you paint a profile of such functions or characteristics as your discussions have demonstrated are necessary or highly desirable (at least, for the project as you propose to carry it out!).

The Extent of the Coverage

There is a tendency on the part of many proposal writers, especially those who are highly skilled professionals, to condense the technical discussions, presenting little more than the recommended approach(es). A frequently employed rationale is that the customer is as technically knowledgeable as are the proposal writers and will therefore be wearied and bored by technical detail.

However, this is often not the case at all. It is an assumption, and one not often justified for at least three reasons:

1. The customer may very well not be as experienced or as technically knowledgeable as the proposer. This is particularly true for some professionals who have spent many years in government service and have not had the opportunity or the motivation to keep up with a fast-growing technology.
2. The customer may be quite up to date technically, but not as highly specialized in experience as the proposer. This is often true in today's environment of extreme technological specialization.
3. The customer may simply be unwilling to accept your word for it that you have explored all the byways of the various approaches and selected the best one—and completely unwilling to think the technical problems out.

In all cases, even at the risk of wearying or boring a customer, it is important to "educate" the customer. It is risky to assume that after exhaustive analysis the customer will perceive or agree with you that your approach represents the best possible. The finest plan in the world must still be explained and sold. The customer is entitled to know *why* you deem your proposal to be the right way or the best way to satisfy the need. *Why* is probably at least as important as are *what* and *how*.

The Focal Point of the Discussion

In conventional engineering the engineer designs a device on paper—makes up engineering drawings—and then builds the device to the design as drawn. In practice this is often not the case. Frequently, the engineer takes an existing model, modifies it to meet the current need, and then makes up the drawings to reflect the actual working model. This is known as "reverse engineering."

In writing a proposal, you have usually designed the program you wish to propose first. Then you prepare a proposal to sell the program. That is, when you write those discussions and descriptions of what you propose to do, you are working from the paper model you have already constructed. You are really *reporting* your analyses and design considerations rather than developing them, although the manner in which you present them makes it *appear* that you are developing them as you go.

Since you know where you are headed—you know the logical conclusions of your discussions and arguments and what the working model is—your discussion does not include *all* the exploratory discussions that took place during the analytical phase, but only those which advanced the analysis toward the conclusions—approach and model—you finally reached. Therefore, your discussion should be the *logical* proof of your approach and design. And, of course, it is also the embodiment of your main strategy, which is either the same as your project design or closely related to it.

The technical discussion is therefore an exercise in reverse engineering. You have the starting point—your understanding of the requirement or

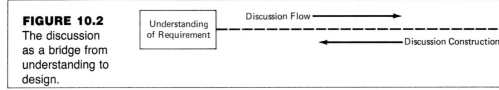

FIGURE 10.2
The discussion as a bridge from understanding to design.

need—and the finishing point—your project model (see Figure 10.2). Your discussion section must bridge the gap: get you from the starting point to the model, but constructed in reverse (see Figure 10.3). You have an approach which is dictated by the model you have decided upon. This is, in turn, the result of the logical conclusions of your analyses and explorations of alternatives. In creating the discussion section, then, you are really proving your design—proving its validity, that is. And since you know in advance what you are trying to prove, you can construct your arguments accordingly.

This does not mean that your logic ought to be distorted or your arguments specious. Presumably you did do an honest and effective job in your original analysis. But it does mean that your arguments should be directed to *what the customer wants*, rather than to any prejudices of your own.

This is where it is easy to go astray, to take your eye off the ball. For example, you may feel that there are far more effective ways to get the desired results than the one your strategy dictates to you as being *right for this proposal*. This may be the best solution possible within whatever you have concluded is the customer's budgetary limit. But to argue that this is the best compromise possible between the ideal project and the limits imposed by a presumed budget is to defeat yourself by raising doubts in the customer's mind. That is, the point that this *is* a compromise solution is generally to be avoided. Instead, simply accept the limitation, whatever it is, and propose the best project you can conceive under that condition. Then be totally enthusiastic in presenting that as the very best plan to meet the need.

Again and again, proposal writers mumble to themselves, while writing, that the customer ought to be doing something differently than the RFP specifies, that the customer's approach is all wrong. This is, of course, negative thinking, and it inevitably finds itself reflected in the proposal. But it can be avoided by using the method presented here:

1. Develop the approach and the proposed project according to your adopted strategy and whatever constraints you find specified or clearly implied by the RFP and whatever other intelligence gathering you have done.

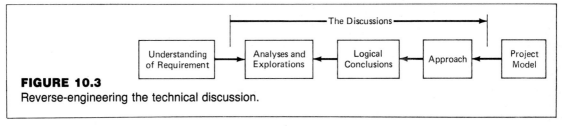

FIGURE 10.3
Reverse-engineering the technical discussion.

2. Accept that proposed design or plan as the best one, the right one for this set of circumstances.

3. Having accepted the proposed design or plan as the best one, develop the logical arguments to prove that it is indeed the best. Forget whatever doubts or misgivings you have about the wisdom or desirability of the program overall. They're totally irrelevant and self-defeating. Your concern is to satisfy a customer, not to indulge your own notions.

This is not a contradiction of earlier advice to aid the customer in identifying true needs and problems. Those are still valid ideas. But the final determinants are (1) those results the customer must have to satisfy the basic need, (2) those constraints or limitations under which those results must be achieved, and (3) that strategy you have adopted. You must remain true to these, but within this set of bounds, you must be totally dedicated to the rightness of your proposal, and that conviction must come through in everything you write.

One final note on this subject: Don't lose sight of your main strategy. If the project design *is* the strategy, then obviously that is what you must focus the customer's attention on. But if there is some particular aspect of the design which you believe is going to be most influential in gaining the customer's endorsement, then your discussions must highlight that.

Take, for example, the supplying of computer software experts in large number. Does your strategy depend on your already having a large staff of specialists? Or is it based on your recruiting plan? Or on a large roster of consultants or contract workers? It is that aspect of your project design which is paramount in importance, regardless of how cleverly you may have designed other aspects of the project.

Bear in mind that the customer's perspective is quite different from yours. Let us suppose that you are planning a project which requires extensive library research as a first step. And let us suppose further that you have that entire library in your own office and that you can complete the research in not more than one day because the literature is at your hand and you are thoroughly familiar with it. Does that make it an insignificant task?

The answer is *no*. Examine that task from the perspective of your probable competitors, who may be far less expert and well equipped than you, and from the perspective of the customer, who probably perceives it as a fairly extensive and arduous effort. Never mind the fact that *for you* it happens to be an easy task. Be objective about it and give it its proper weight and prominence in your discussion. And if it merits a more portentous name, such as "Task Analysis," assign it that name in your charts and text. Otherwise, you (1) may lose an important advantage and (2) may lead the customer to believe that you have underestimated the importance of some major element in the project. You may defeat you own strategy by having lost sight of it or having failed to implement it properly.

Even if your strategy is based on the fact that you have certain special facilities or capabilities to get the job done less expensively or more rapidly than anyone else, you must not take that capability for granted nor minimize its importance in your discussion. Quite the contrary, make a great deal of it, emphasizing how much better equipped you are for the job than anyone else. Highlight the problems anyone else is likely to have with the task. Use the facilities as part of those contractor's capabilities mentioned a few paragraphs ago. Thread the idea throughout the discussion, with frequent reminders that you offer special advantages as a contractor for the project. But be sure that it is something important to the project and is likely to influence the customer.

Section III: Program Proposed

Section II made certain commitments, ending in a clearly delineated approach shown by logical argument to be the best way to do the job. Section III is the logical next step in the proposal: exactly how you now propose to put that approach and those technical arguments to work, how you propose to implement them. Where Section II labored to explain what *should be* done, Section III explains what you *will do* after being awarded the contract. Section II *is*, in fact, your proposal. What has gone before is scene-setting, preparing the reader to see the *rightness* of what you propose to do.

Section III is likely to be the largest section of your entire proposal, for it should cover many things, and do so in specific detail. No matter what the first two sections have said, this section must provide the final proof that you do have a satisfactory understanding of the customer's need, that you are a competent contractor who can plan an adequate program, that you can deliver on the general promises made in the discussions and pledges, that you can plan to cope with all problems, and that you do understand clearly what must be delivered to the customer as end results or end products. If your specific plan fails to demonstrate these things to the customer's satisfaction, earlier promises made are of little help: this is the acid test.

The Elements of Section III

As in Section II, the number of separate elements or topics to be discussed in depth in this section can vary widely according to the nature of the requirement and the proposal. As a minimum, however, you should address these specific items for even the smallest project and proposal:

- Proposed project staff and organization, with résumés of key staff
- Main tasks, subtasks, allocation of hours to staff vis-à-vis tasks and subtasks
- Schedule of performance promised
- Specification of all deliverable items and services

For some small proposals, at least some of these items may be presented as simple charts, tables, or listings, with little text explanation required. In other, usually larger, proposals, a great deal of text may be required and some of these topic areas may have to be broken into several separate discussions. For example, if the project is fairly large and complex, it will probably be necessary to have a separate discussion of project management, and that may have to include a complete treatment of management philosophy, controls, and procedures. In some cases, it is even necessary to present forms, copies of purchasing procedures, personnel policies, and sundry other details. And where appropriate, it is often necessary to provide complete descriptions of such items as quality control procedures and estimating procedures.

Treatment of Section III Presentations

Section II was discursive. It examined, weighed, argued, reasoned, perhaps even pleaded. Section III takes an entirely different tone. Section II argued *to* a conclusion; Section III proceeds directly *from* that conclusion. It flatly and unequivocally states what the proposer will do. Section II was largely *qualitative;* Section III is *quantitative.*

That last point is important. Section III must quantify all quantifiable items: labor hours, pages, reports, pounds, feet, meetings, days, months, and so forth. These are what you are willing to contract for and promise to provide or deliver. And these are what the customer is going to use as a yardstick by which to estimate the reasonableness of your costs, presented separately in a cost proposal.

Pitfalls of Failure to Quantify

Failure to quantify here has at least two undesirable results: the failure may be construed as evasion or a lack of true competence on your part, and failure to quantify may lead to later contract disputes which you are almost certain to lose. That first hazard is self-evident; the second requires some explanation.

Quite often the customer has no clear idea of how many labor hours a job is likely to require or how many pages an end product ought to contain. It is left to the proposer to make estimates. But quite often the proposer also fails to specify an estimated quantity, and a contract is signed without such specification.

Ultimately this is likely to lead to a dispute. In an actual case calling for the development of a training manual, the proposer expected to produce a manual of about 300 pages. But the government's program manager and staff made continual requests for more pages, more illustrations, and more of everything. The project finally reached a point where the contractor saw clearly that the contract would now run at a financial loss, and he appealed to government's project manager. That individual saw no reason to reduce the government's demands, and the matter finally wound up in the hands of the contracting officer.

The outcome? A compromise. The government reduced its demands somewhat, but the contractor was unable to get any more money because there was no proof that the government's demands exceeded that which was contracted for! The contractor therefore lost money and had no legal recourse.

The problem is not uncommon. Make it a rule to *specify* quantities for everything quantifiable even if the customer has failed to offer specifications. There is no need to point out that the government has not specified quantities, but only to list your own estimates in Section III. If the proposal is accepted, it becomes part of the contract—what you have agreed to supply and what the customer has agreed to accept. Should a dispute arise later, legally you have a place to stand.

It's not unreasonable to expect the proposer to furnish such estimates or specifications. The customer, in issuing the RFP, has issued a call for help. The premise is that the proposer is the expert and can advise the customer what is needed and in what quantity. Be sure that Section III is a *complete specification* of the job, regardless of who has supplied those specifications. (If you *are* that expert the customer expects you to be, you should be able to write the specifications when necessary!)

That specificity applies across all elements of the section—to the deliverable items; to the phases, tasks, subtasks, or other functional items in the proposed program; to the management plans and procedures; to staffing and organization details; to quality control provisions; to purchasing or subcontracting; and to staff résumés and any other items covered in the section. The time for philosophizing and making general observations was in the previous section, if at all. However, in providing the specifics, bear in mind that you have at least two purposes:

1. To demonstrate your capability for precise planning and to support your contention that the program proposed is viable—to prove your case.
2. To cover all the bases and protect yourself against such contingencies as might result in disputes and problems later on—disputes you are likely to lose and problems you can do without. Hence, a few admonitions and precautionary notes may help.

Schedule Promises

In most cases the RFP has furnished a required schedule. You usually have some end date or period of performance to advise you as to how much time is to be allowed for the entire project, and you usually have at least a few intermediate dates referenced to customer-perceived milestones.

It is a mistake to simply acknowledge and promise to adhere to the schedule provided, for at least these reasons:

1. You should provide the evidence that you have done meticulous study and planning. Providing your own schedule supports this idea and adds to your credibility.
2. Your schedule must be entirely compatible with your own program, with all its plans, procedures, and perceived tasks and subtasks. Build your schedule around these while checking to ensure that you have not violated any of the customer's important required deliveries—for example, do not seize additional months of time arbitrarily. But do not make the mistake of destroying credibility by offering a schedule which does not match your proposed program.
3. The customer often provides a description of schedule requirements which either is not truly specific or includes potential problems. This is by far the most important reason for developing a schedule of your own.

In many cases you will find that schedules provided by the customer list due dates or performance times as some number of "days after award." The problem with this designation is that it fails to specify whether those are *calendar* days or *working* days. For example, 10 working days is 2 weeks, and it requires 14 calendar days to equal that, of course. If you agree to deliver a program in 300 days after award, having assumed that this means 60 weeks, you may get an unpleasant jolt when you discover that the customer means calendar days and requires you to deliver the product in 43 weeks! If the customer has failed to specify whether those are working days or calendar days, you had better make the specification according to your own best judgment. (Of course, you can ask the customer to clarify the meaning of "days," but that may give your competitors more comfort than it does you.)

An even more serious problem arises when the customer has named specific dates for targets on the assumption that the contract will be awarded and work initiated by some presumed date. Unfortunately the estimated start date somehow is almost always wrong. This means some additional negotiation of dates and is usually straightened out in contract negotiations. But why ask for trouble? Those newly negotiated dates may not be favorable. Why not cover the matter in your own proposal, while you've the time to think out what is proper?

And still another problem is that the government indicates in its schedules the various review periods during which the contractor will probably be unable to proceed with further work until the review is completed. For example, the schedule offered in the RFP may state that at two or three milestone points the government will review your progress, product, or report, and render comments and/or approval in 2 weeks, after which the contractor will proceed to meet the next date. Don't count on it! More often than not, the government will take 6 weeks and even more, while you twiddle your thumbs waiting. And an unreasonable government project manager may expect you to still meet all the dates originally listed. How to avoid this? Make your dates x number of days following *completion* of the government review.

Résumés of Key Staff

While you may present résumés of your general staff professionals in the next section, it is advisable in this section to offer the résumés of the key personnel you have proposed as the principal performers on the proposed project—this section should contain *all* the specifics of the proposed program. It is not necessary to offer résumés of general support personnel—typists, technicians, illustrators, and others—but only of the principals—the project director, other project managers or supervisors, and key professional specialists.

The common mistake made here by many is to use boiler-plate résumés—standard résumés drawn from the files. The problem is that anyone who has worked for several years has probably developed a variety of capabilities or subspecialties. An engineer in electronics, for example, may be experienced in radar, digital systems, computer programming, and communications equipment. A psychologist may have worked in both experimental and clinical psychology. An urban affairs specialist may have been in community action projects at an earlier time. That is, each individual may be able to lay claim to various other specialties than the one required for the proposed project. And while the individual's qualifications for the proposed project may be excellent, they must be *featured* in the résumé.

The whole world today believes in specialization, and the customer almost surely wants specialists, rather than generalists, for the program. Therefore, the résumé should be rewritten for each proposal, to feature the specialty experience relevant to the project. It is a great mistake to compromise the ultimate appeal of the proposal by saving those few pennies involved in preparing a set of résumés specifically for the presentation.

Résumé Formats

As in the case of overall proposal formats, on occasion an RFP mandates some specific résumé format. Of course, if the format is dictated, follow it faithfully.

On other occasions the RFP simply specifies what information is required in the résumés. In such cases, the customer's wishes should be respected, and the information provided. (This should have been included in the original checklists as required responses.)

In the absence of such mandates, the format illustrated in Figure 10.4 is recommended. (If possible, use this format, while including every item of data the customer has asked for where such request or requirement is listed in the RFP.) This format is efficient, immediately listing the individual's regular position in the company and proposed position for the project. An individual who is not with your company may be listed as a consultant, or the space may simply be left blank.

A narrative introduction is almost indispensable to your purpose of highlighting that experience most relevant to the proposed project and the proposed position; using a chronological sequence of prior employment forces

R_____ W_____

Data Systems Manager

PROPOSED POSITION: PROJECT DIRECTOR

M_____ has had increasingly responsible positions in the design and development of data systems for over 20 years. While employed as Senior Project Manager with_____Computer Systems, Inc., he directed the development of the LOG-LOGNET system for the Department of Defense, and personally wrote the programs for the FLYBY Missile System control computers.

Since joining_____Data Systems Corporation, M_____has been responsible for all contract projects, including demographic studies for the Department of Energy, pesticide profile programming for the EPA, and design of the Honest Abe logistics network for the US Air Force.

FIGURE 10.4
Suggested introductory text format for résumés.

you to list experience as it occurred or in reverse of its occurrence, which is not your purpose at all. Therefore, use the narrative introduction, in which you may characterize the individual's experience and qualifications as you see fit.

Specific experience—achievements, projects, and prior employers or professional affiliations—may be described in the text or listed in some sequence following the text, as best suits your own situation. But unless the RFP has mandated otherwise, it is probably best to stick to the narrative format, offering the strongest case possible.

Even so, it is not advisable to establish a rigid format for all proposals. In one case the individual's formal educational qualifications may be of supreme importance—the customer may wish to see several Ph.D.s on the project. In another, experience may be far more important to the customer. Therefore you should retain flexibility of format and tailor the résumés to whatever is most important to and will be most influential with the customer in making an award decision. (In one case you will want educational specifics up front; in another they may be left until last or not even mentioned.)

Miscellaneous Other Considerations

Other details bearing directly—not indirectly—on the project and its successful accomplishment belong in this section. If the project requires or your plan depends on some special facilities or resources, such as an electron microscope or in-house computer, details of those resources and how they will be brought to bear belong in this section. If you plan subcontracts or consultants, specify these here. Cover everything in this section which you want to be provided for specifically in the contract—what *you* propose to do and what you expect *the customer* to do.

At some point the customer will correlate this section with the costs you propose in your cost proposal. It is that correlation which will influence the customer's judgment as to whether your proposal is "in the best interests of the government, costs and other factors considered."

One thing you want to try to get across here is some basis on which the customer may evaluate how much *result per dollar* you propose. If the other proposer comes in at 10 percent fewer dollars with 20 percent fewer results, you have a good argument for the real economy of your own proposal. But the argument holds up only if you have been specific and covered everything so that you can demonstrate how much "bang for a buck" you propose.

Section IV: Qualifications and Experience

Unless you have created a special section or chapter for special requirements, such as a management plan, this will be the final section of your proposal. The main purpose of this section is to demonstrate the general and special qualifications of your organization to carry out the proposed program. You have "sold" the program, presumably, and you have also sold your proposed key personnel (with their excellent résumés), but now you must sell your organization. In a large sense, this section is a résumé of your organization. Its purpose is to demonstrate that your organization is the best choice to carry out the proposed program. There are two things to demonstrate here:

1. That your organization is *technically* and *professionally* best suited—has all the proper technical and professional experience and capability with all the physical and financial resources needed to make the plan work well
2. That you are a highly dependable organization with a good track record behind you—that you can be relied upon to carry out the proposed program conscientiously

The Elements of Section IV

In many cases the RFP requires that you present a list of current and past contracts with all pertinent details: a brief description of the work, dollar value, identification of the customer, specific names of project manager and contracting official, history of cost overruns or underruns, and other details which give evidence of the quality and dependability of your performance and furnish references with which to verify your claims. However, even when the RFP does not call for such a listing, it is highly advisable to furnish one.

Here again the tendency of many is to develop a standard list and furnish it in all proposals as boiler-plate material. And again it is a mistake to do so unless your work is so highly specialized that it happens to fit every project for which you bid. In most cases the list should be organized to place the most relevant past and current projects first.

An easy way to do this is to develop a tabular format to standardize the way in which each project is presented, but cut and paste the lists so that you can tailor the order of presentation to the proposal. The format should accommodate the following items:

- Number, name of contract, name of agency, dollar amount, type (fixed-price, cost-reimbursement)
- Brief description of work required, result required
- Names of references (project manager and contracting official), with their mailing address and telephone numbers
- "Remarks" or "Results" column in which to describe history or accomplishments under the contract, such as cost underruns or overruns, late delivery, or early delivery (Obviously, to report favorable results!)

In some cases, where you have been fortunate enough or expert enough to produce exceptionally good results, it may be advisable to use this table twice: once in its normal place (fourth section) and once as an attention-getter in the first section of your proposal.

In this section, as in the case of individual résumés, you should have a bit of introductory text where you can highlight and make a case for your technical and professional qualifications and dependability. In this introduction, of course, point out any exceptional accomplishments (which you have probably made some reference to in your first section). That is, use this section to continue *selling*.

Other elements that belong here are a description of the parent organization to which your own department or division belongs (if such is the case) and where and how the project reports to the organization hierarchy. A brief history of your organization and its founding may also be in order here, and top-level organization charts should be included to illustrate what you say.

Overall physical facilities and resources should be described here, too, to support what has been said before in your proposal. And if the RFP has called for some statement of financial resources or "financial responsibility," this may be included here. (For example, an annual report may be attached.)

Here you may also include additional résumés of qualified staff, who could be called upon, if necessary, to support the program.

One thing relatively few proposers do but which they should is include here any testimonial letters, honors, or awards to the organization. If you do not have testimonial letters, it is probably because you have never asked for them. Few customers think to send you such letters, but a satisfied customer usually will if you ask for it!

Appendixes

Appendixes are most properly used for detailed information which is deemed to be of interest to some, but not all, readers. The purpose is to provide the details to anyone interested in them, but not to slow down the reading progress of anyone not especially interested in finite detail. You might, for example, include as an appendix some drawings or samples of previous work or something referred to in your main text. Or an appendix might be made of some report or paper alluded to briefly in the proposal. Or an appendix might be used simply for extended discussion which you think might be tedious to many of your readers but would be welcomed—perhaps needed—by some of them.

For convenience, you might put all such matter in a single appendix, or you may choose to have several appendixes, depending on whether you think the appended materials belong together or are complete separate subjects.

The judicious use of appendixes is the way to have your cake and eat it too—you can have a terse and dynamic proposal, yet have a mountain of persuasive detail at one and the same time!

Front Matter

There is certain front matter which should precede Section I. A table of contents is mandated by custom and standard publications practice. It is usual practice to have a title page, which is virtually a replica of the cover, except that it carries the date of submittal and, if necessary, a statement that certain data in the proposal is proprietary and not to be released for use other than in the contract. There are, however, several other kinds of front matter which are helpful to your purposes in selling your offer.

Executive Summary

The Executive Summary, which is quite often used by those who write proposals regularly, is nominally an abstract of the proposal for the benefit of higher-level managers who wish only to get a brief overview of each proposal. (In fact, some RFPs may call for such an abstract.) However, the Executive Summary may (and in our view should be) pressed into service to aid in selling. That is, while the Executive Summary should offer an abstract of the proposal, it should be so constructed as to present the chief appeals—reasons for acceptance, using the most persuasive language and presentation possible. One recommended way of doing this is to organize it as a series of points, each a brief paragraph with a number, bullet, or other device to dramatize it. It should, however, be kept as brief as possible—probably not more than ten items, unless the proposal is an exceptionally large one.

Response Matrix

Less commonly used but of equal importance is some sort of response matrix, in which are listed all the must-respond-to items of the original checklists, along with an indicator of where in the proposal those responses are to be found, along the lines of the example in Figure 10.5.

The response matrix all but ensures a high technical score by making it convenient for the reviewers to find each point in your proposal that they wish to evaluate and score, and by providing a ready reference for comparing your proposal with others. The evidence of responsiveness is obvious, of course, and the customer cannot help being impressed with your thoroughness.

Letter of Transmittal

The Letter of Transmittal, not usually required by the RFP, yet obligatory in custom, is addressed to the contracting official as a separate document accompanying the proposals (technical and cost). It is not a part of the proposal proper; yet, most experienced proposers find it helpful to include a copy of the transmittal letter in the proposal, usually bound directly inside the cover, before the title page.

This suggests that the Letter of Transmittal should be something more than a formal message saying "Here is our proposal in response to your Request for Proposals." But the actual recommended content of the Letter of Transmittal and its importance appear to be the subject of much difference of opinion: some proposal writers believe that it's little more than a courtesy while others believe it to be of great importance.

In fact there is this to be said: The Letter of Transmittal is addressed to the contracting official, and it may well be the only part of your proposal the contracting official reads (other than the cost proposal). Contracting officers are usually more interested in the cost proposal than in the technical proposal and are legally responsible for ensuring that the price is within the bounds of good reason. Ergo, it is a means for communicating directly with the contracting officer and trying to enlist support for your proposal. And in many cases that support can be most helpful and perhaps even decisive; at least some contracting officials will fight hard for a proposer with a bottom price if the proposer's offer and proposal are technically acceptable.

It appears wise, therefore, to explain in the Letter of Transmittal those

PROPOSAL RESPONSE MATRIX

ITEM	RFP REFERENCE	PROPOSAL REFERENCE	REMARKS
UNDERSTANDING OF RE-QUIREMENT	Part 1, page 7	Section 1, pp 1-2 Section 2, pp 1-5	EVALUATION CRITERION ITEM
COMPANY EXPERIENCE	Part 2, page 11	Section 4, pp 3-9	EVALUATION CRITERIA
PHYSICAL FACILITIES REQUIRED	Part 5, pp 9-10	Section 3, pp 12-15 Section 4, pp 4-7	

FIGURE 10.5
Suggested format for response matrix.

aspects of your proposal which you believe to be of greatest interest to contracting officials—low costs, cost consciousness, special features which reduce the risks of failure, and other such considerations.

There are several other items which should be in every Letter of Transmittal:

- A statement that the offer made is firm for some specified period of time, such as 120 days. (The RFP generally states the minimum acceptable period.)
- A statement that the signer is authorized or empowered to make the offer on behalf of the organization and that the offer is firm and binding.
- An invitation to communicate with the signer should more information or formal presentation be desired.
- A pledge of full company or corporate support for the project.

The Special Problem of the Mandated Format

Figure 10.6, following, lists these general considerations and formats in the order usually considered proper. Some variation may be made to meet the special requirements and circumstances of different RFPs, such as in the case of the mandated format, where the customer has done more than merely *suggest* a given format—that is, where the customer has made some given format a specific requirement. (But even the suggestion of a preferred format should be

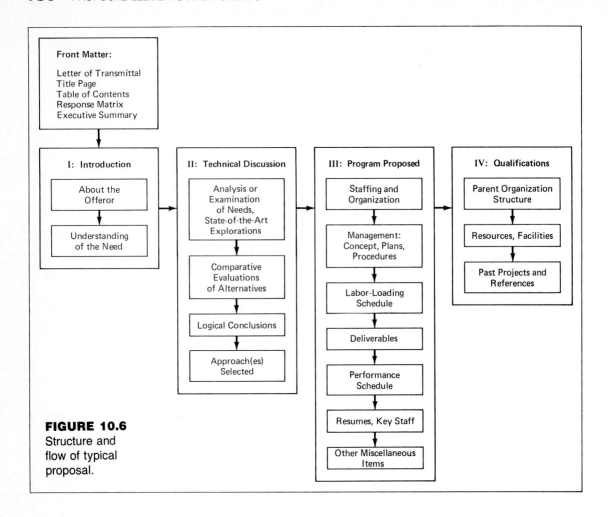

FIGURE 10.6
Structure and flow of typical proposal.

taken into account when designing your proposal.) There are, however, usually at least some problems associated with mandated formats, and it may take a bit of resourcefulness to overcome these so that the proposal format does not hinder your presentation strategy or nullify its impact.

The principal disadvantage of the mandated format is that it limits your freedom strategically. Following the mandated format may be inimical to your own ideas as to how to build up a persuasive presentation. In fact, it may even be difficult to organize a logical and orderly presentation when following a mandated format. Here is a verbatim copy of the proposal format and content specified in an RFP dealing with an energy-related requirement:

1. *Table of Contents*
2. *List of Tables and Drawings*

3. *Short Introduction and Summary*

    This section should contain an outline of the work to be done, difficulties anticipated in doing the work, and the proposed general approach toward solving the identified problems and accomplishing the work.

4. *Technical Discussion of Approaches*

    This section should contain the major portion of the technical proposal. It should be presented in sufficient detail to permit a comprehensive evaluation and should contain as a minimum the following:

4.1 Statement of Work. Major difficulties, if any, anticipated by the offeror in performing the Statement of Work.

4.2 Principles and techniques which may be applied in performing the work and solving identified difficulties, and an evaluation of the various methods considered with substantiation of those selected. Indicate degree of success expected.

4.3 Complete, detailed statement of anticipated solution, including, as applicable, preliminary design layout, sketches, and other information indicating configuration and functions of components.

4.4 Specific statement of any interpretations, deviations, and exceptions to the Statement of Work described in Enclosure IV of this RFP. The Offeror, however, should be aware that major deviations, and exceptions to the Statement of Work may impair the evaluation of the Offeror's proposal. Thus, explicit explanation of deviations and exceptions should be part of this technical proposal.

5. *Program Plan*

    This section should contain the Offeror's proposed Program Plan which divides the entire program into work packages of finite tasks or segments of work. Each task should be identified for: personnel accountability, task product identification/application, start/complete schedule, travel, proposed subcontracts, labor hours by labor type, and material description and quantities. Included in the Program Plan should be a summary of (1) labor hours for each labor type, (2) lower tier subcontracts, and (3) material description and quantities, planned for each month during the proposed period of performance of the contract. Cost estimates should not be included in this Plan.

6. *Program Schedule*

    This section should include the period of performance, proposed duration of project in months by phase or task, and a milestone chart. Include time required for preparation and submission of required reports.

7. *Project Organization*

    This section should show the project team or organization proposed for this contract, the relationship of this program to the overall company organization and the function and responsibilities of the major lower tier subcontractors. As a minimum, it should contain the following:

7.1 Organization chart and a summary of the labor hours or percentage of time key personnel will devote to each major task of this project.

7.2 An estimate of the extent of lower tier subcontracting anticipated together with a list of items or effort to be subcontracted. Cost estimates should not be included in this section.

8. *Personnel Qualifications*
   This section should contain the names of key management and technical or supervisory personnel, down to the third level of proposed project organization structure, to be assigned for direct work on this contract along with pertinent background information on each.

9. *Site/Facilities/Equipment Data*
   This section should contain a statement of available site, plant, laboratory equipment, and test facilities which are proposed for use on this project, if any.
   A specific statement of additional plant, equipment, and test facilities, if any, proposed for this project is required. Indicate their applicability to the project and substantiate their need. Indicate to what extent the project can be accomplished without them. Consider alternate sources, substitutions, etc.

10. *Supportive Data*
    This section should contain the following:

10.1 A listing of current or recent (within the last 2 years) Government contracts or other activity performed by the offeror in this or related fields. Include the name of the sponsoring agency, contract number, amount of contract, subject area of contract, name and phone number of Contracting Officer for any government contracts cited. If necessary for evaluation, the Contracting Officer may solicit from available sources, experience data concerning proposer's past experience.

10.2 Any other pertinent technical information which will aid in evaluation of the proposal.

Aside from the fact that the above leaves something to be desired in grammar and punctuation, a number of redundancies may be noted. Too, the physical format used may cause a bit of confusion. In a proper outline form, with proper subordination, it should appear like this (using captions and omitting most of the text of the original):

1 Table of Contents
2 List of Tables and Drawings
3 Short Introduction and Summary
4 Technical Discussion of Approaches
    4.1 Statement of Work, highlighting anticipated difficulties
    4.2 Principles and techniques to be employed, evaluation of alternatives
    4.3 Anticipated solution, preliminary design (approach)
    4.4 Interpretations, deviations, exceptions
5 Program Plan
6 Program Schedule
7 Project Organization
    7.1 Organization chart, labor-loading chart
    7.2 Subcontracting, if any
8 Personnel Qualifications (Résumés)
9 Site/Facilities/Equipment Data

10 Supportive Data
    10.1 Current and recent contracts, amounts, names, telephone numbers
    10.2 Other technical information

This calls, then, for a proposal of ten sections. However, in this case the customer's demands may be met without deviating greatly from the general format recommended by the authors. In fact, here is the correlation:

Mandated Sections 1 and 2 are part of the front matter and would normally be included in any case, along with an Executive Summary and the other front matter recommended.

Section 3 corresponds to recommended Section I, Introduction.

Section 4 corresponds roughly with recommended Section II, Discussion.

Sections 5, 6, 7, and 8—and possibly part of Section 9—correspond with the recommended Section III, Proposed Program. And the remaining data would normally be in recommended Section IV, Qualifications and Experience. So the major strategy of the recommended standard format and organization may be followed rather closely, in this case, although what would otherwise be Section IV will, instead, be divided into four separate sections.

In one sense, this can be turned to your advantage: by following the recommended or required format exactly and using the same headlines and identifying numbers the customer has listed in the RFP, you make the customer's job of evaluating your proposal, point by point, much easier. This can only work to your advantage.

In the RFP cited here, this is how the customer listed and described the evaluation criteria (the criteria are listed in descending order of importance):

2.0 *Evaluation Criteria*
A comprehensive evaluation of all qualified proposals will be made applying the evaluation criteria set forth below:
2.1 *Quality of Technical Approach*
—Ability to meet statement of work objectives (e.g., complete detailed data specification);
—Ability to demonstrate innovative techniques to develop data in areas where such data are scarce.
    2.2 *Adequacy of experience and qualifications of firm and personnel to perform the scope of activities, including:*
    —Relevant past experience of the organization and key technical and management personnel.
2.3 *Management Plan*
—Overall approach
—Project reporting and cost control
—Commitment of dedicated team and availability
—Interface with other company divisions/groups

This makes it abundantly clear where in the proposal the major stresses should be—i.e., where to show the greatest strength and provide an abundance of detail. It also provides a prominent clue to capture strategy by revealing the customer's major "worry item"; getting data in certain areas where the desired data are expected to be scarce. At least part of the strategic plan should address this need.

Some Main Points to Remember

1. It's to your advantage to make reading and evaluating your proposal easy for the customer. Unless the RFP has mandated some specific format, the proposal format here will prove useful, as a logical presentation that conforms to sound principles of selling.
2. The recommended format is analogous to making a personal sales call. Introduce yourself and say why you are there, discuss the customer's needs to demonstrate full understanding and desire to help, then make your specific proposal and describe your credentials.
3. To accomplish this, a four-section format is offered, which will fit the majority of proposal requirements. The four sections are Introduction, Discussion, Proposed Program, and Our Qualifications as an Organization.
4. Sections II and III of the recommended format are of greatest importance, with Section II devoted to extended discussion of the customer's needs and analysis of possible solutions, and Section III devoted to the specific proposal.
5. Section III, the proposed program, should be quantified to the maximum extent possible and must be as detailed and specific as possible. This is for the dual purpose of fully demonstrating capability and commitment, and of protecting yourself contractually, since it is this section that becomes the contractual obligation.
6. Failure to so quantify can lead to serious trouble later should disputes with the customer arise: the lack of quantification leaves you no defense against unreasonable demands.
7. The format recommended lends itself to implementation of whatever strategies you have formulated. It provides the vehicle for developing all the logical arguments and then translating them into a plan of action, with all details specified and followed by a presentation of your own technical and professional capabilities and resources to do the job.
8. The format includes front matter, wherein is provided several other vehicles to focus the sales attack: a Letter of Transmittal presenting the main argument which is most likely to appeal to the contracting officer; a Response Matrix to make the evaluator's job easier and increase the probability of the proposal getting a high technical score; and an Executive Summary, wherein you can list the several main arguments to support your efforts.

11

Program Planning and Design

Now comes the hard part: making the decisions and committing yourself.

A Time for Action

Section II (Discussion) of the recommended proposal format discussed in Chapter 10 is a time for talk. Section III is a time for action, a time to lay it on the line and make those firm commitments of who, how, when, and how much. Now you must decide who will do what, when it will be done, how much will be done, and what you will deliver.

Here again the use of graphics and tables has a wonderfully sobering and clarifying effect. To sit around a conference table and talk over plans is one thing; to see the commitments laid out in figures on charts and in tables is another. It is like a plunge into cold water. In one recent case, a rather large and well-known corporation arranged to have a small company subcontract to them in submitting a proposal for a $200,000 project. When the proposal manager translated the conference-table speculations into charts and tables and the principals saw the figures, the anomaly was plain. The two companies promptly reversed roles, the large corporation pledging to support the smaller one, the smaller one bidding as the prime contractor. Why? Because the organization chart, the labor-loading chart, and the other documents drafted by the proposal manager showed clearly that the small company would be performing all the key management roles. Obviously the anomaly would not have been lost on the customer.

A great deal of time would have been saved had the principals of the two companies drawn up such "cold water" charts and tables earlier and been able to perceive that their joint venture plan was badly conceived. Somehow, the uncompromising and stark figures staring from the typed page make one face the realities of the commitment. For that reason, it is almost invariably a great time saver to begin designing the specific program proposed in Section III by drawing up at least the following:

1. A list of all tasks and subtasks which must be carried out, together with time budgeted for each task or subtask for every key member of the project staff. (In short, a labor-loading chart.)
2. A project organization chart showing all key functions, the reporting order, and the principal staff members.
3. A schedule of all events, preferably as some sort of milestone chart.
4. A list of deliverable items, clearly identified and quantified.

In some cases, particularly for large projects, a number of other graphics and tables would be useful as starting items, but the above serve well to take the commitment out of the realm of speculation and facilitate decision making. This set of items represents the commitment and the possible exposure (risk) the company faces. The writing must address itself to the cold facts presented by these graphics and tables, for they are the basic design factors.

Staffing and Organization

Logically the section begins with a presentation of the staff and organization plan—the chart of the proposed organization and the text explanation which accompanies it. Figure 11.1 shows a typical organization chart. The shortcoming in this example is that it does not give a clear idea of the project functions to be assigned to each member shown.

Figure 11.2 is a considerable improvement. Here there are project-related functions identified for each staff member, and discussion can proceed from this presentation of the proposed staff.

The customer is almost invariably greatly interested in the staff and their individual qualifications, particularly in a technical project being performed on a custom basis. The functions assigned the various individuals must be realistic, in regard to each individual's personal qualifications and without regard to the normal position in the company. That is, an individual who is a senior-level person in the company is not necessarily a senior-level person in a given project by virtue of that normal company position. The organization chart should reflect a functional organization specifically for that project.

It is wise to advise the customer in your proposal that the project and staff are dedicated—that is, that either they are assigned full-time to the project, if that is the case, or the project is their first-priority responsibility, if full-time

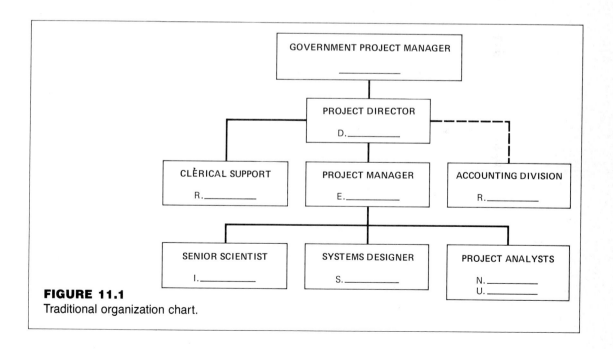

FIGURE 11.1
Traditional organization chart.

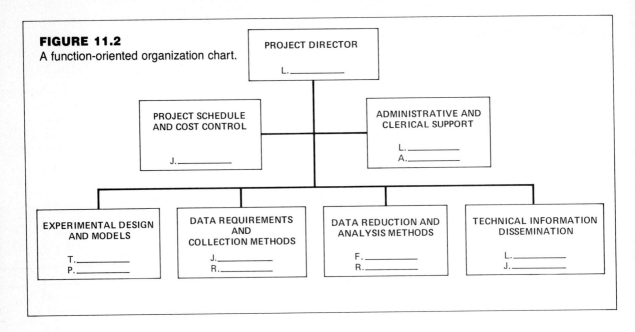

FIGURE 11.2
A function-oriented organization chart.

assignment is not practical. No customer wishes to learn that your organization will not give that customer's project priority. A suggestion that it will not be given priority is an invitation to put your proposal aside and go on to the next one, seeking a contractor to whom the project will have enough importance to give it that priority.

It is also wise to make the authority of the project manager clear to the customer. These are characteristics that should be made plain, both in the graphic representation and in accompanying text:

1. There is a single project manager or director with full authority who can make decisions without delay.
2. The project manager interfaces directly with the government's project manager (who may be called the contracting officer's representative or some other title).
3. The project manager is not in a position of authority in the company but either has been granted full authority for the project or reports directly to someone in the company who can authorize any necessary actions promptly.
4. The project staff have been selected most carefully—it is a hand-picked team—for their qualifications. Each has the proper education and experience for the job.

Management

Logically the next subject to be discussed should be management. In some cases, where the customer has made it clear that management is a major concern or where the nature of the project is such that management is clearly a major concern, there should be extensive discussion—or even a separate section—on management. For that reason, we refer you to Chapter 11 on the design of management systems for projects. Management is important in every project, however large or small, and should be covered immediately after the presentation of your organization and staff.

Résumés

The customer will want to see résumés of your key staff members, and they should appear in this section. A good practice is to introduce each of the several senior project staff here, with just a few sentences about each, advising the reader that a full résumé will be found at the end of the section.

Although the subject of résumés has been covered earlier, it does no harm to repeat here: don't use boiler-plate résumés. Rewrite each résumé to suit the specific requirements of this project. "Strong" résumés often carry an otherwise lackluster proposal. Conversely, "weak" résumés can undo all the good the rest of your proposal has done. Although the use of contractor personnel is legally on a "non-personal services basis"—it is against the law for them to direct Civil Service personnel or be directed by Civil Service personnel—government contract managers tend to regard contractor staffs as extensions of their own in-house staffs. Consequently, they are often as discriminating about the qualifications of contractor personnel as though they were considering them for direct employment.

"Paperhanging"

There is a practice of many companies, especially small companies with small staffs, to insert many résumés of well-qualified people who are not employees of the company, without stipulating that they are not employees. The practice is known as "hanging paper." In some cases, the RFP stipulates clearly that the proposer must specify whether the résumés supplied are of people presently "on board," and often RFPs specify that key members of the proposed project staff must be on board at the time the proposal is submitted. But whether the RFP says anything on the subject or not, hanging the paper of people who are not going to work on the project even if you win is a risky matter as well as a dishonest practice. You will rarely be penalized for using the résumés of well-qualified consultants or people who have agreed to become employees in the event you win the contract, as long as your lead people are on board and you are honest about the rest of the résumés.

Another practice, sometimes employed by relatively large companies, is another version of paperhanging. Some companies have a few employees with exceptionally strong résumés, who are continuously bid as the key staff of every project proposed but who are never assigned to a project. Junior-level people are assigned to the projects actually won. A few of the agencies have become conscious of this practice and take steps to bar it. (They stipulate that you may not substitute others for proposed key staff without approval. If you ask for such approval, you will be required to produce substitutes with equal qualifications.)

Tasks, Subtasks, and Labor Loading

Many RFPs call for some sort of chart or table presenting a complete and detailed listing of phases, tasks, subtasks, and functions necessary to carry out the project, along with a listing of how the labors required to perform these various tasks and subtasks will be allocated among the staff. This is not a call for cost information (although any experienced project manager in the government can make a pretty fair ball park estimate of your costs, after seeing your labor load), and the RFP will usually point this out and even caution you against putting cost information in the technical proposal. But it does afford the government evaluators the opportunity to judge how well you can plan and who, exactly, will be charged with performing the various tasks and functions. Moreover, it gives the government a view of the extent to which your senior people are to be committed. (Sometimes an RFP asks you to list that portion of each senior person's time that will be dedicated to the project.)

Whether the RFP requests such data or not, it is an excellent idea to prepare and include it anyway, for these reasons:

1. Whether the customer has thought to ask for this or not, it does make your understanding of the requirement and your ability to plan and design a program quite clear.
2. You must do this anyway to plan and design the program at all. You should not attempt to cost the job without this kind of data.
3. At some point your technical proposal will be compared with your cost proposal for compatability. This helps greatly to support your cost proposal.
4. It provides an excellent basis for negotiations. It is very much in your interests to have this before you when and if you must negotiate a final price and final set of contract terms.
5. Where the contract is primarily a service, with a tangible end product that is nothing more than a printed final report or program tape, the labor is, essentially, the deliverable. It should be quantified, as every deliverable should be, for the reasons already enumerated.

By the time you have reached the stage of actually designing the program, you will have developed that early flowchart or set of flowcharts into final flowcharts to include in this section. That flowchart—the final version, that is—is the basis for the labor-loading chart; the several functions and tasks on the chart are developed into the various tasks, subtasks, and functions which are included. An example of a labor-loading chart is shown in Figure 11.3.

The chart shown is, of course, for a simple project and would be far more extensive for a larger and more complex project. However, the principle is the same. The result is a matrix which reveals how much time each principal is expected to devote, on which tasks, and what each task or subtask is expected to require.

Obviously, too, you have to be judicious in making the assignments here. For a writing task, such as this is, obviously the writer is going to devote the greatest number of hours; it would be unrealistic to expect otherwise, as it would be unrealistic to assign editing hours to the project manager.

This chart, in fact, together with the functional flowchart is the heart of your project design. Everything should stem from this and from your estimates of how many pages your final product will be, with how many and what kind of illustrations, and all other such details. This, together with the list of specific deliverables and your estimates of such support labor as typing, proofreading,

LABOR-LOADING ESTIMATES				
Task or Subtask	**STAFFING AND HOURS**			
	Project Manager	**Senior Writer**	**Editor**	**Totals**
1 Meeting w/COR	8	8		16
2 Prepare book plan	4	24	4	32
3 Submit for government review				
4 Research, data gathering				
(a) Library	4	20		24
(b) Interviews	12	40		52
(c) Physical inspections	8	30		38
5 Prepare detailed outline	8	40		48
6 Submit for government review				
7 Draft manuscript	16	180		196
8 Edit and internal review	16		40	56
9 Revisions		40		40
10 Final review in house	16			16
11 Submit for government review				
12 Final revisions		40		40
13 Edit and in-house review	16		16	32
14 Deliver to government				
TOTALS	108	422	60	590

FIGURE 11.3
Typical labor-loading chart.

illustrating, and duplicating, is the basis for your cost estimates. Without such planning as this, your cost estimate is likely to be little more than a wild guess. Should your own management, in reviewing your proposal, ask you how you've arrived at your cost estimates, this is your rationale.

Bear in mind, as you design the program, that you are creating the costs by your design. Whether you have anything to do with preparing the cost proposal or not—and it is likely that you will not if you are on the proposal staff of a large organization—the cost proposal will—must—reflect what you have designed. Any hours you add as a safety margin elevates cost. Of course, you can create a wide safety margin and virtually eliminate risks from the project, but at the same time you are reducing your prospects for winning. Designing a project is a trade-off between risk and probability of winning.

If you wish to reduce the risk further, without simply building wide safety margins of extra hours into the design, the way to do this is to expand the labor-loading workup. That is, break the tasks and subtasks down further to enable yourself to estimate the work required more closely. Take each task and subdivide it. Let's take item 4a, for example, Library Research, and break it down further to see what it really entails:

Library research:
    Lab reports and logs
    Similar equipment manuals
    Related system manuals

Each of these might be broken down, in turn, by determining how many such reports, logs, and manuals are likely to be available for inspection.

The effect of this is to enable you to evaluate the 20 hours of writer time you have guesstimated for library research. Upon closer examination and more thought, you may very well discover that there really isn't that much library data available and that 10 hours ought to be more than enough. The simple fact is that when most of us estimate on the basis of very little information except what we call "gut feeling," we tend to estimate on the high side, an instinctive and almost unconscious reaction. The more we detail the item we are trying to estimate, the better we are able to estimate rather than guesstimate. It's more work, of course, but winning is almost always the result of working harder than your competitors did!

The Schedule

The RFP probably has a schedule in it, or at least a list of key dates when certain things are due or when certain milestones are to be reached. Do not handle the schedule problem by the easy expedient of simply stating that you will comply with the listed schedule. It's wrong for several reasons, most of which we have already touched on earlier. Nor should you simply repeat the customer's own words in your proposal. Rather, generate a milestone chart on which are listed all major tasks and milestones. Why? Because the very act of developing such a chart is itself part of the design effort; it will show you when and how each task is phased into the project and enable you to plan your effort more efficiently. Have a look at Figure 11.4 for an example and explanation of this.

The advantage of doing this type of chart rather than a tabular list of schedule or milestone dates is this: In this chart you can see how each task relates to other tasks in regard to start and finish times—for example, some tasks may start before the prior task is finished. This must track with your labor-loading chart, of course, and there is something wrong in your planning if it does not. (If you have allocated 10 weeks for some individual to do a certain

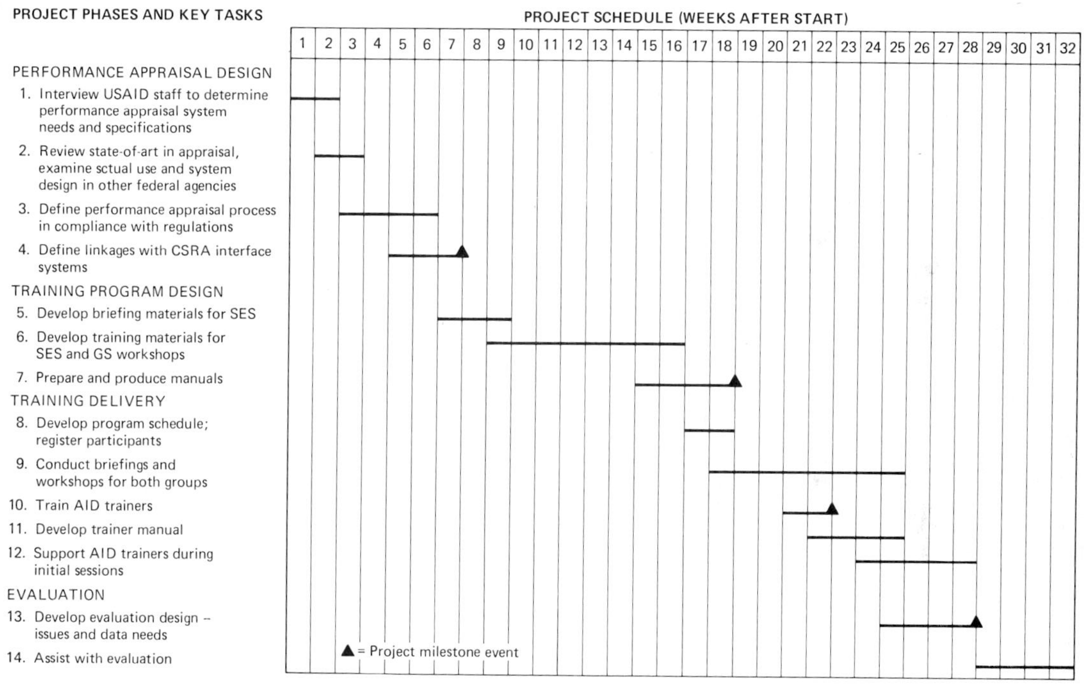

FIGURE 11.4
Time-phased milestone chart.

task and your milestone chart shows that task completed in 6 weeks, there is certainly something amiss, and the customer will surely pick it up. This makes such a chart more than a planning and design tool; it is also a checking device, to verify other aspects of your project design and—not the least of the considerations, certainly—to check your cost estimates also.

Deliverable Items

At the risk of being repetitious, but because it is such a common oversight and such a costly one in many cases, do be sure that your list of deliverable items is specified, quantified, and complete. Every final deliverable should have been listed in that checklist you made so long ago when you started the proposal, and that checklist ought to be brought into play here to be sure that you have neither overlooked any item nor failed to describe it in the most specific terms possible, both qualitative and quantitative. Let there be not the slightest doubt in either your mind or the customer's mind about what you agree to do for the dollars your cost proposal lists.

You should now have a complete design, with every labor hour and other expense accounted for. It is not necessary here, in the technical proposal, to specify all the support functions and miscellaneous expenses, such as postage, telephone, travel, and the like, but be sure to estimate them, nevertheless, to be included in your cost proposal, no matter who prepares it.

The two items which have not been covered here in detail are flowchart development and management planning. That is because each will be covered in chapters yet to come. However, functionally they do belong in program planning and design.

Some Main Points to Remember

1. In Section III you must face the harsh realities of making final decisions and commitments. This is where you must plan and design the program you are proposing and pledging the customer you will accomplish.
2. Designing a program is a matter of discipline, and a great aid to that discipline is our old friend, the graphic representation. Using the graphic tool before you begin to write will save you time and may even make you change your mind about certain earlier ideas you had. Use these graphic representations as part of your proposal presentation—they are excellent methods for explaining your plans—but use them also to help you plan wisely.

3. The items which are of great importance here and must be clearly specified in the design you propose are these: your planned organization and key staff members; your list of tasks and subtasks that make up the whole effort; the estimates of who should perform each of these tasks and the amount of time each should devote; the specific qualifications of each key staff member (be sure to present well-written résumés); the schedule, which is best represented by a time-scaled milestone chart showing start and finish time for each task; and a clearly defined and complete set of deliverable items. Management information and a functional flowchart also belong here.

4. Remember that you, the program designer, are the major cost center in the project. The project will be priced to the customer according to what you have designed into it.

12

Management Plans

Technical and professional competence is one thing. Managerial competence is another matter, equally important to most customers.

What Are Typical Government Concerns about Management Plans?

There is never a time in pursuing a contract for a project when management is unimportant. But there are times when it is more important than at other times—that is, Section III of your proposal (or its equivalent, if you use a different format from that recommended in Chapter 10) should always address proposed management plans and procedures, but many proposals justify (and RFPs often demand) a special section or chapter devoted to management. So what is said in this chapter has application in all cases.

Here, for example, is a paragraph from a Department of Energy RFP, to indicate how they expect the proposer to respond:

> The offeror's Project Management Plan must show the corporate structure and lines of authority to the project manager for this effort and must show the detailed structure of the project organization established to meet the terms of this proposal. The lines of communications within each unit shown on organization charts and responsibility for requesting and assuring support between units of the proposed project structure and from other elements of the corporation must be shown in relation to the requirements of this RFP. The offeror's Project Management Plan must define the project management staff's duties and the project management office location. In addition, the offeror must demonstrate his ability to respond in a *timely* fashion to contract requirements.
>
> The offeror is to discuss the methods and procedures to be used for planning the work scheduled for accomplishing contract requirements. Indicate how targets are to be established and how task requirements are to be defined. Point out the controls to be used in adhering to schedules, inspecting and distributing reports and findings, and in detecting and minimizing human errors.
>
> The offeror is to state how the work is to be monitored, including the frequency and positions involved. Describe the means of reacting to the following problems:
>
>   *a*) Widely fluctuating work loads.
>   *b*) Supporting activity failures.
>
> The offeror will describe the ability to provide backup resources necessary for successful accomplishment of tasks assigned which require quick turnaround time. In particular the offeror should discuss the kinds of graphics facilities, types of reproduction equipment, the extent of computer access and other business equipment available to the project team.

Obviously this RFP required that the proposer prepare and submit in the proposal a Project Management Plan, which would be evaluated and probably bear heavily on the final award decision. Reading the lines of the requirement—and also reading *between* the lines—these authors interpret the customer's wants as including the following:

1. A project organization should be structured especially to meet the needs of this requirement; revealing a *functional* organization is a must.
2. A project manager must be given enough authority (or have inherent authority as a result of the position held in the company) to make decisions and command the proposer's resources to support the project as necessary. The "lines of communication" referred to are a euphemism for lines of *authority.*
3. The location of the project office must be stated. The customer would probably look with favor on a project office location in proximity to the customer's location.
4. The customer expects to require quick reaction to at least some requirements as they arise and wants to be assured and shown evidence of the proposer's ability to react swiftly.
5. The customer wants to be shown that the offeror has clear and practical plans and procedures for identifying the proper milestones and objectives of each task, as tasks are requested.
6. The customer wants detailed explanations, including responsibilities and duties, of how each member of the staff will function.
7. The offeror must demonstrate controls and procedures for handling contingencies, ensuring schedule adherence, and maintaining high quality.
8. The project must have the ability to add staff and reduce staff rapidly, as required. The customer obviously anticipates peaks and valleys of activity.
9. The offeror must show clear plans to meet contingencies—alternative resources available and plans to use them in the event a planned support activity fails to produce or materialize, especially when the task is of the quick-turnaround variety.

The provision for "supporting activity failures" is somewhat cryptic, but apparently is another statement of the need for contingency planning—the alternative plan for the instance when a planned activity fails to function as scheduled.

These are typical of customer concerns about the ability of the proposer to handle the project functions. Except for the requirement for quick-reaction capability, they might well be inferred to be customer concerns in any request for proposals, whether stated by the customer or not. The customer invariably wants a responsive project, a project manager with adequate authority to be responsive almost automatically, a project with adequate resources to meet almost any need, and a project with clear-cut plans and procedures to handle all conceivable problems without milling about in confusion.

There are two special needs here, which do not occur in every project. This customer expects a wide variation in work loads—many peaks and valleys among the flow of requirements—and many quick-reaction needs.

Developing your own management plan for a proposal, then, you should have some standard boiler-plate management plans and procedures which can readily be adapted to each proposal (again, it is risky to use boiler-plate material bodily, without fitting it to the project). You must, however, remain alert for special requirements for which you must draw up special plans and procedures.

One thing the customer has not specified here is evidence of cost consciousness and procedures for cost control. This was probably an oversight, since this appears to be the type of project in which such a factor should be considered. This is especially to be anticipated as a consideration in a cost-reimbursement type of contract since it will affect the final cost of the contract to the government.

Let's consider each of these areas, one by one. But before we do so, let's think a moment about why requirements for management plans vary so widely among the various projects, and what we ought to include in our proposals when the customer has not specified concerns about management. That is, let's look at different *types* of projects and contracts, and what each type implies or what we ought to infer from the type of project. The types include, for purposes of this discussion, the following:

1. Firm fixed-price project
2. Cost-reimbursement development project
3. Task-order support services
4. General support services ("hands and feet")

Firm Fixed-Price Project

The firm fixed-price job is the simplest type of contract. Typically it is a requirement to provide services or products, defined at the outset, at some price agreed upon as a firm fixed price. The customer may or may not have special concerns about management in such a project. Cost consciousness is reflected generally in the project plan and cost proposal, but once agreed upon is naturally no longer of concern. According to the nature of what is to be done, there may or may not be special concerns about management—staffing, organization, quality control, and other matters.

Cost-Reimbursement Development Project

In any cost-reimbursement contracting—any version of the well-known cost-plus type of contract, that is—the government has agreed to pay certain *rates* for labor and other cost units but has not set a final price, except for some maximum. That's the nature of cost-reimbursement contracting and the reason for it is that it is a type of contract used where it is impossible to predict the final cost, either because the government doesn't know at the outset exactly what it will need as the year progresses or because there are a number of imponderable costs which cannot be predicted in advance.

In such a situation, you may expect the government to be concerned that the contractor is cost-conscious and has adequate cost-control methods and procedures. That is, the government wants to be assured that the contractor has the desire and the capability to keep the costs as low as possible.

The general efficiency of the contractor, both technically and administratively, has an effect on both final costs and the quality of the results. The customer is well aware that if it issues a contract to have some research and development performed, under a cost-reimbursement contract, the contractor may prove to be one of the following:

1. A high-cost producer, with good final results
2. A high-cost producer, with poor final results
3. A low-cost producer, with good final results
4. A low-cost producer, with poor final results

Obviously, the customer would prefer that the contractor turn out to be as described by number 3 above, a low-cost producer of good final results. The probability is that the contractor will turn out to be somewhere between the extremes—a mid- to high-cost producer of fair-to-good results. But the customer is going to try to select that proposer who shows the greatest promise of matching the number 3 description above! Therefore, the customer will be scanning the proposals for all evidence that the proposer is well managed—efficient and cost-conscious, with well-thought-out plans and procedures for efficiency and cost control.

Task-Order Support Services

There are numerous contracts which call for support services on a task-order basis—to write manuals, program computers, maintain equipment, prepare drawings, and do a variety of other such chores. The customer does not know in advance exactly what the tasks will be or when they will arise. The agency has customarily used some dollar-volume amount every year, and the customer can tell you approximately what will be spent on this, approximately what typical tasks will cost, and what resources you must provide. But beyond that, the specific requirements are to be ready, willing, and able when the need arises.

Usually for such services the contractor must provide an estimate for each task, as the government issues the request for task estimate. Therefore, the customer is likely to ask you for an accounting of how you estimate tasks, perhaps even for detailed procedural descriptions. If the nature of all or some of the tasks is that the customer needs immediate response and fast service, you'll be asked to provide evidence of quick-reaction capability. And since even if you do the work at the customer's facility—on site—the law provides that the federal employee cannot manage or direct the contractor employee, you'll have to manage your own people, and this may or may not be a major consideration, depending on how complex the work is and whether the individual tasks are ordinarily performed by individuals or small teams or whether the tasks usually require relatively large teams working together. (In the latter case, there is much greater need for management controls, of course.)

General Support Services

General support services—or what we have chosen to so designate—are usually on a somewhat routine basis, without peaks and valleys and without quick-reaction needs. An example of what is referred to is the staffing and operating of a government computer facility or the provision of a number of drafters or engineers to work on site. In these situations, although costs are always a consideration, the various rates are set for the duration of the contract and contractor cost consciousness or cost control will not affect the government's final costs materially. Probably the main management concern, in these contract awards, is with regard to the contractor's ability to maintain a qualified staff—recruiting and replacing losses, that is. Most of the "management" performed by the contractor in these contracts is to serve as a conduit for the "technical direction" given by the government's project manager, converting that technical direction into working orders to the staff.

So you can see that customer concerns about the proposer's management capabilities vary considerably, according to the anticipated needs of the project contemplated. When the customer fails to stipulate the management concerns, it is wise to consider the project from the viewpoint of the customer: what is the project all about, what will the contractor be required to provide, and what are the everyday problems to be anticipated? That is, what can go wrong and how can the contractor plan to react and set things right again (or prevent them from going wrong in the first place)? When you develop sensible answers to these and related questions, you will begin to perceive for yourself what the customer *needs* from you in the way of management plans and management capabilities.

The importance of making an effort to view the project from the customer's viewpoint is this: The customer may be concerned about the management capabilities of the proposers yet not have covered those concerns in the RFP for any of several possible reasons. But that does not relieve you of the necessity of covering those concerns in your proposal. The customer wants you to include in your proposal everything you think important, whether the RFP has requested it or not. Therefore, let's get down to specific cases now and have a look at what sort of things are important.

Résumés and Individual Qualifications

We've said a great deal about résumés already, but there is one specific point we did not cover: information in the résumé of any individual proposed as a manager regarding the individual's management experience. There is a strong tendency in this technological-professional age to stress the technical and professional qualifications of key project staff and to neglect managerial qualifications. In all cases the résumés of those proposed for managerial responsibilities should present some evidence of managerial capability. The manager of an engineering project must be a competent engineer, of course. But the reverse is not necessarily true—the top-notch engineer is not ipso facto an excellent manager. In fact, many excellent engineers are poor managers of engineering projects. The talents required for the two responsibilities have little in common.

One other point about résumés: Experience is not the same thing as accomplishment. It's quite possible for an individual to have many years experience in some given field or even with some given organization yet not be very good at the job. That is, the résumé may be reporting professional survival, rather than professional experience and accomplishment. The way to present true credentials is to list the individual's accomplishments, such as patents issued, programs written, projects managed successfully, and other such items.

Functional Staffing and Functional Organization

It's one thing to claim that you have created a "functional staff," as do many proposal writers, but the customer does not want to read your claims; the customer wants the evidence, and the evidence lies in reporting what you actually propose. If you assign Mary Smith to be a data manager, Mary Smith's résumé must reflect some credentials for that responsibility.

There is also the matter of credibility. If you see fit to assign the chief executive of your organization to be the project manager, the project manager's responsibility had better be something less than a full-time job: the customer is not likely to believe that your chief executive officer has the time to run a full-time project as well as carry out other necessary duties. Far better, if your chief executive officer has some special credentials for the project, to assign the executive some duties such as special consultant to the project or advisor to the project manager. Guard against making assignments that do not make good business or good management sense.

Résumés do not usually carry on them the age of the individual. Yet anyone reading the résumé may be able to judge the approximate age of the individual by dates of education or other obvious clues. If you see fit to assign some young person—someone with only a year to two of working experience—to a senior level of responsibility, it is likely the customer will question your good judgment.

"Functional" organization refers to not only the duties assigned, but to the qualifications of the individuals to carry out those duties.

Design your project organization for one thing only: results achieved efficiently. Not to suit some textbook plan and not to suit the prejudices of your own company about what constitutes good management or good organization, but what makes good sense and gets good results at minimum costs and in minimum time. And make it clear to the customer that this is the main yardstick by which you measure management and organization plans.

Let's hypothesize a large study project which involves a great deal of library research—the building up of a great many books, reports, papers, and files of various kinds. This is a resource to be used by a dozen senior staff members to conduct research by studying the literature. How should this be handled? Should a room be set aside with free access to all who work on the project?

Only a small amount of experience with such projects will be enough to tell you immediately that that would be a bad plan. Within days the room will inevitably be a shambles of scattered reports and books, with a great many already missing, having disappeared into the briefcases and desk drawers of the project staff never to surface again—at least not until the project has become history.

In such a case, it is absolutely necessary to assign a project librarian to control the traffic and keep records of all items withdrawn from the stacks. Moreover, it is more efficient to have a $15,000 librarian searching the files for a document than to have a $35,000 scientist doing so. It takes little explanation to justify the function and the assignee. And if it's not a full-time requirement, the librarian may "wear another hat" and do some other things between stints of helping the staff find what they want.

Contingency Planning

In the example we read from the Department of Energy RFP we found the customer concerned about what the proposer expected to do about contingencies—when some plan went awry and threatened the schedule on a quick-reaction task. This is a common enough problem; you have no way of knowing *what* will go wrong, but you can be sure that something will. This notion was formalized in the famous Murphy's law ("Anything that can go wrong will"), but the phenomenon had been observed long before that, of course. But whether the customer has reminded you of the possibility and asked what you plan to do about it or not, it is always wise to prepare contingency plans. It's especially wise to prepare contingency plans for anything not under your direct control—for example, a support service to be provided by another division of your company or by an outside vendor.

One manager handles this by what he calls the "Chinese menu" method. For every function or task not under his own direct control, or otherwise susceptible to sudden and unexpected failure at the worst possible moment, he has a "Column A" and "Column B" choice, "Column B" acting as his option.

For example, suppose he is depending on his internal graphic arts shop, which does not report to him, to produce a drawing by some deadline date. To protect himself against a possible failure of internal support, he will have already lined up an outside art shop that can produce work swiftly, when needed. Frequently, he has found, just the threat of "going outside" to get the job done has caused the graphic arts manager to decide suddenly that the deadline can be met after all!

So one method of contingency planning is have another source of support in reserve. But there are other kinds of failure than that of a "source," whether it is in house or out of house. And another kind of contingency planning is having an alternative *method* for getting something done. In one case, where the contractor was unable to get a replacement part for a piece of equipment without waiting 6 weeks for a shipment from the factory, he went to a local machine shop and had the part—which was a rather simple one—machined from bar stock.

When our Chinese-menu manager had a temporary overload of work in his typing pool, he contracted with local homemakers to do some typing in their own homes, lending them the typewriters, and met his schedule deadlines.

There were also few jobs in his organization which he could not do himself. When the absence of a suddenly ill key person threatened the schedule, he took off his coat and began to work personally on the project.

He also maintained a roster of part-time people, some who would work at home, some who could come to the office, but all of whom could handle certain tasks. His rosters saved many threatened schedules.

Contingency planning is not something you improvise at the onset of the emergency, although the ability to do that is valuable. It should be a set of resources planned in advance against the probability that at least some things will go wrong.

Careful scheduling is itself a contingency plan. In one case two employees were almost going to physically assault each other over access to a copy camera. One had a short-fuse task and had to use the camera immediately to meet her deadline. The other had a volume of work to be done that day and had claimed the camera continuously. The manager sat the two down and cross-examined them. It soon developed that the first employee needed about 15 minutes work done, whereas the other employee was using the camera continually, but not continuously. That is, there were gaps in his camera work, some of them one-half hour long. It was rather easy to accommodate the first employee's needs in one of the "windows."

The capability for handling all such problems so that contingencies do not—are not permitted to—override deadlines is something the customer prizes. If firm delivery dates are especially important to the customer, it is quite worthwhile to describe your contingency capabilities.

Cost Control

Cost control is a broad subject, pervading almost every aspect of project operation, from staffing and functional flow to subcontracting and purchasing. The wisdom you employ in considering costs generally for every decision and the standard policies and practices you employ to minimize costs are the evidence of cost consciousness. However, the customer interested in how you control and minimize costs wants to know more than just the *preventive* things you do about costs; the customer wants to know the *positive* or corrective things as well.

Cost control implies some set of policies and procedures. *Cost reduction* implies some activity or procedures to seek less expensive sources and less expensive ways of doing things. *Cost avoidance* implies some policies or procedures which inhibit buying at all until it can be proved to be absolutely necessary. If you find a cheaper source of paper for your office copier, that is cost reduction. If you have the old machine repaired and put off buying a new one, that is cost avoidance. And if you require three sign-off signatures to approve a purchase order, that is cost control. All are part of cost consciousness, but each is philosophically oriented a bit differently than the others.

A part of cost control is your purchasing procedure. In many RFPs the customer requires you to include a copy of your purchasing procedures on the assumption that you have a formalized, standard document. Many small companies do not have such a document. For proposal purposes, therefore, they prepare one, thus making it available for future proposals. That is, they invent policies and procedures on the spur of the moment.

The wisest thing to do in preparing such a procedure is to emulate government procurement practices. Prescribe the issuance of bid packages for subcontracts and other purchases with a minimum of three bids or proposals, and then select the most favorable bid or proposal.

Cost control does not stop here, however. It has numerous other applications and influences. One way in which many companies waste money is through the misuse of people—such errors as $25,000 professionals doing their own office copying, and salaried engineers being reduced to little more than drafters in their routine duties.

To prepare a good cost control document, study everything in your operation with a view to waste and policies and procedures to eliminate, or at least minimize, that waste.

Personnel Policies

In many major cost-reimbursement contracts, the customer feels that it is important to know all your personnel policies—salary ranges, fringe benefits, salary reviews, relocation policies, and a myriad of other details about your practices regarding staff. The reason for this is usually that the government is picking up the tab. That is, in many cost-reimbursement contracts you are authorized to charge for the employee's time on an annualized basis, including paid time off (sick leave, holidays, vacations, etc.). The customer therefore wants the policy made a matter of record at the time of the contract signing, so that (1) the government knows what they are obligated to pay for and (2) they can judge whether your conditions are unnecessarily generous—and expensive!

Even when the contract does not specifically authorize you to bill the government for holidays and sick leave, the government is still paying for these costs in the overhead, for they are in overhead. The government wants to know about it. On the other hand, if the government is paying directly for your employees' holidays, as it agrees to do in some contracts, it wants to be sure that these costs have been taken out of your overhead so that the government is not paying twice for the same thing!

If you have a personnel policy manual that explains all these things, you need simply enclose it with your proposal. Otherwise, you will have to either explain it in the text or create a personnel policy manual and enclose it.

Quick-Reaction Capability

There are firms that specialize in quick-reaction services. And there are firms that are so structured that quick reaction is almost an impossibility for them. If quick reaction is a condition of the project, the customer will want to see your technical and management capability for providing such service. You may safely assume that any customer who specifies a requirement for quick-reaction support not only has a need for such support, but will be in deep trouble if the contractor fails to provide it. Therefore, your capability—your *credibility*—for satisfying the need assumes great importance. Ordinarily, your mere assurance that you will provide fast turnaround for tasks is not enough; you must provide *evidence* that you can do so.

The evidence can take several forms. One is the evidence of logic, introduced by showing your specific procedures—and even the forms you use—to turn tasks around rapidly. You might demonstrate, for example, that each quick-turnaround requirement is directed to a "fast track" mode you regularly employ. In showing this you might demonstrate how a typical task is handled from the time you receive the work order until you deliver the job.

But suppose you have never specialized in such work; yet you believe that you can turn a job out as fast as anyone else can, and you wish to submit a proposal. How can you handle this?

The answer is to handle this in the same manner as you handle a requirement to supply your standard purchasing procedures or personnel policies. If you have never prepared formal documentation for these, you develop the systems and documentation on the spot and include them in your proposal. (You need not mention that you have just invented or designed them; the fact that you believe you can handle the project and deliver the desired results is all that matters.)

Consider your normal operating procedures for any current task. Think out where the bottlenecks ordinarily occur and how you can streamline the operation for fast-reaction tasks. Then draw up any forms you need to do such a job and include them in your proposal as your proposed (or established) mode of operation for handling such requirements.

In this, it may well be especially important to show contingency planning provisions—how you handle the unexpected events that threaten delivery dates, the fallback positions you can take to overcome such problems. (The "Chinese menu" method is a good one.)

If, on the other hand, you have handled such requirements successfully, you can describe a few of these—select those that most closely match the types of tasks called for by the RFP—and document accordingly if you have not already documented your methods for such tasks. Descriptions of past tasks accomplished successfully are exceptionally good evidence of your ability, of course, and it will probably be helpful to your cause to specify for whom the tasks were performed and include names, addresses, and telephone numbers of individuals the customer may call to verify your claims.

Estimating Procedures

Most work-order or task-type contracts require you to prepare an estimate each time the customer has a task for you. Basically, the contract works along these lines:

1. You have agreed in your contract to provide certain services on demand and on a task basis at some unit rates as required by the work statement. (The units may be billing rates for different classes of labor, rates for pages of copy, rates for functions, such as proofreading, either by the hour or by the page, and other such rates. Usually in a task-type contract there is a "laundry list" of many such rates.) These are the rates you will use for estimating and billing.
2. The customer issues you a request for an estimate, in a paper which describes the task. You decide what units are applicable, and you return the paper, usually within a few days, with your estimate. (If there is a special rush on, or if you have developed a good working relationship with the customer, you may be able to supply a verbal estimate by telephone and get a go-ahead, with the formal paperwork following later.)
3. If the customer is happy with your estimate, you get the signal to proceed with the customer's formal authorization—in effect a purchase order under the terms of the general contract between you.
4. If the customer balks at your estimate, you sit down and try to negotiate. (Again, depending on the working relationship established, you may be able to handle even this by telephone.)
5. If you can't reach agreement, the contract authorizes the customer to order you to do the job anyway (you've agreed to this when you signed the contract), and the price will be settled later in negotiation or adjudication.

In some cases, your estimate is a ceiling price—a "not to exceed" price—and you will, when the task is finished, bill actual hours and other units of work and cost. In other cases the estimate, when accepted, becomes a fixed price, and you bill that price regardless of your actual hours and units worked.

It is understandable, in light of this, that the customer wants you to describe your estimating practices in your proposal. The customer does not want to ever have to resort to contingency 5, and would prefer not to ever have to resort to the one before it (contingency 4), either. So it is not at all unusual to be required to explain how you estimate tasks.

Here again, as in other cases, the customer wants detailed descriptions— your specific procedures, along with any forms you use. And again, if you don't have such forms and procedures, it is wise to invent or design them on the spot and include them in your proposal.

Planning and Job Control

For task-type contracts—or for any other kind of project, for that matter—the customer may wish you to describe your planning procedures. How do you go about analyzing a requirement and developing a working plan? Who (functionally, that is) in your organization does the analysis? Who does the workload estimating? Who does the costing?

There are some other questions that you should answer even if not specifically asked, when a customer wishes to know how you plan projects or when you believe that you should supply such details. What are your provisions for job control—that is, monitoring to ensure that you don't overrun, slip the delivery dates, or otherwise fail to maintain a firm grip on the job? How about time charges: what is your timekeeping system?

Quality Control

Quality control is logically part of monitoring and general job control, but it is far too important to the customer to allow it to be buried under such general headings. It helps your proposal to make a special paragraph and sidehead of the subject of quality control. But you should understand the basic realities of quality control and explain them to the customer—not because the customer necessarily needs the education (although it is possible that the customer is not schooled in the technicalities of quality control), but because you need to show off your knowledge and sophistication in the matter. Quality control is a difficult matter to prove competence in by any other means than recommendations from other customers; therefore, educational discussion tends to lend at least some credibility to your claims.

For assembly line manufactured products, quality control occurs at several points, primarily as a sampling function. The parts room subjects randomly selected samples of incoming parts to quality control testing, accepting or rejecting each batch accordingly. If the manufacturing process involves subassemblies, subassemblies are inspected (certain key points, such as connections, are routinely examined) and samples are pulled off the line for more extensive testing, such as drop tests and endurance testing. And the same inspection and sampling or testing is applied to the finished assemblies.

Custom work is a different proposition because there is normally no assembly line operation and usually only one or two custom-made end products. Therefore, quality control is usually a 100 percent testing and "sampling" procedure. In fact, quality control is a built-in function (or should be), with suitable reviews and approvals at each stage. If the project you are proposing involves a custom development of some sort, you will usually do well to point this out and supply a detailed description of how the work is checked and reviewed continuously, and of how the next stage of operations is never begun before there is a formal sign-off (written approval) of the current stage.

To illustrate this, the case of a technical-publications project is enlightening. The organization was rather loosely run at first. Quality control should normally be almost automatic in such work because editing and proofreading are inherently quality control functions, as is management review, a customary step in developing technical manuals. In the case described here, the manager was shocked to get a series of complaints from the customer pointing our numerous deficiencies in the products being delivered.

Investigating, the manager discovered that there was no control form of any kind; it was impossible to determine whether an editor had reviewed a manuscript, for example. Moreover, there was not even a sign-off for final review.

The cure was simple: The manager designed a sign-off sheet and issued instructions that no step would be performed without a signature certifying that the previous step had been performed and pronounced satisfactory. Moreover, no product could be delivered to the customer without a formal release by the manager's own signature, ensuring that the manager would at least have the opportunity to see that the normal quality control functions had been certified as complete.

That is positive quality control on a 100 percent basis. Something analogous should be adopted as a required procedure and set forth in your proposal to assure the customer that you may be relied upon to control the quality of your work and end products.

The Management of Staffing

Many customer requirements are such that sudden peaks and valleys of activity are expected, creating many peaks and valleys of project staff requirements. Staffing up rapidly for a peak requirement, especially when the requirement is also on a quick-reaction basis, is difficult at best. A secondary problem is what to do with the now-idle staff when the task is over and another does not come along for some time. The customer is well aware that this constitutes a severe problem for a contractor, but solving such a problem successfully is of critical importance to the success of the project. Therefore, the customer would like to be assured that you can handle such problems successfully. But mere oral assurance is not enough; as in the other cases enumerated here you must provide some evidence, such as a practical plan. (The customer has visions of your failure to do the job because you can't produce the necessary staff on short notice, or of your failing in general because you don't know what to do with excess staff when the task is over. Therefore, there is worry about your plan for handling the problem, and skepticism over mere oral assurances that you can do so.)

The problem here is one of "staffing down," as well as of "staffing up," which makes it more than a recruiting problem. (We'll take about the recruiting problem shortly.) If the project is one of sudden and steep peaks and valleys, recruiting is not the answer; you can't recruit permanent employees for short-term assignments. You can, however, recruit many specialists who make a practice of accepting temporary or short-term assignments, usually at better-than-average rates for such work. They are referred to often as "job shoppers," and they are an excellent answer to the problem, if you can manage to use such temporary employees and stay within the competitive price range.

There are other ways to solve the problem. If you are willing to operate your establishment on an after-hours and weekend schedule, you can almost always find moonlighters who will work at standard rates and give you many evening and weekend hours. If you are a division of a sizable company, you may be able to work out a practical plan for borrowing workers from other divisions, as needs arise. Or you may be able to work out other solutions.

Frequently, for such requirements, the best answer is a combination of several expedients: a minimum cadre of permanent staff of your own, the use of a few consultants or moonlighters, and borrowing workers from another division. The use of a combination of expedients, such as this, has the great advantage of containing within itself the seeds of planning for contingencies; because you have recourse to a variety of staff resources, you can almost always meet the needs unfailingly.

The evidence of such a plan, aside from your explanation of what is obviously a practical idea because it is in common use, is a roster of available part-time and temporary people and letters of agreement from consultants and/or the managers of other divisions of your company, or a letter from the head of your company authorizing you to borrow personnel from other divisions. That is, the customer wants to be assured that you not only *have* a practical plan, but have the means to put it to work.

Recruiting Plans and Capabilities

In many cases, where the project is obviously going to require a sizable expansion of staff—and especially when the staff required are technical or professional specialists known to be in short supply, a rather common condition in our technological society—the customer wishes to know about your recruiting capability. (Unless you can convince the customer that you already have the large number of required specialists on board, ready to be freed from their current assignments and reassigned to the new project immediately, the customer is likely to be quite skeptical of your claim to be able and ready to do that.) The assumption is that you will have to recruit the people rapidly, and you are expected to reveal the workings of your personnel office and recruiting system to show that you can produce the staff reliably.

The thing to do is, of course, to recount similar requirements if you have faced these in the past, and show that you have been successful at producing new staff rapidly. If you have the fortunate circumstance that you have a project winding up and can transfer some of those people, be sure to explain this. But do explain that your personnel office advertises for help regularly so as to maintain a file of résumés at all times; that you have already, in preparing to write your proposal, been on the telephone with many of the people whose résumés populate your personnel filing cabinets; that you also have a number of consultant specialists available to fill in swiftly, at least on a temporary basis, until you can bring permanent people aboard; and also explain any other plan you have or can devise to handle such problems successfully.

A good convincer is to produce a matrix, listing the specialists represented by the résumés, with check marks to identify the people who have already been called by your personnel department and who have agreed to be available on short notice for the proposed project. Be sure, however, that you can identify top management for the project from current staff. Proposing to put a newly hired individual in as project director may not sit well with the customer.

Technical Management versus General Management

So far, we have discussed the development and presentation of management plans primarily with reference to general management problems—recruiting, quality control, estimating, and other such general management and administrative problems. But there is a difference between the problems of general management and those of what we might refer to as technical management. That is, there are, for many projects, two sets of management responsibilities, often requiring two kinds of managers and management staff.

In the sense used here, *technical management* includes the technical direction of the staff, and such technical direction often calls for fairly rare creative skills. It is possible that the customer recognizes and appreciates this distinction and the need for such technical and creative skills in some projects. But whether the customer recognizes it or not, you should recognize it when it is a reasonable assumption, and make a point of it in your proposal.

This may very well call for an unusual individual—an individual with an unusual combination of skills, that is—to serve as the project manager. There is one individual serving in a government office, for example, who brings to his job an unusual combination: he is both an industrial engineer and a lawyer, and his position is with a federal agency concerned with industrial safety and the enforcement or compliance with an array of federal regulations on the subject. The combination is obviously exceptionally well suited to the position, and would be almost ideal skills for the manager of a project for this office.

Today we have a great many multidisciplinary projects—projects in which a variety of technical and professional skills must be combined. The team designing a new missile, for example, is faced with problems in aerodynamics (the air frame), electronics (signal, communication, and control systems), chemistry (the rocket engines with their propellants), mechanical engineering (the missile structure, internal and external), and, frequently, computers (more of the control and communication or guidance systems). Moreover, a great deal of testing is required, creating a need for still other specialists, such as stress analysts.

The problem in such a project is this: Which technical or professional specialist ought to head the team? Which is best suited to function as the technical director, managing the combined efforts of all the other specialists and coordinating the efforts into an integrated whole?

Whatever your decision, if you are faced with such a problem, be aware that such decisions are almost always compromises. It is most unlikely that you will find a genius who is equally experienced, educated, and proficient in all these fields. Yet, in presenting your project manager and proposed project-management plans, you must explain and justify your decisions.

In such situations as these, it is often advisable to select as the project manager whichever of the specialists has had the best experience and track record as the manager of similar technical projects—if you have such an individual available—but indicate that the manager will be supported by a staff whose members will not only each head up the task force handling their own problems—i.e., an engine development team, a control development team, etc.—but will also serve the project manager as a true staff, advising the manager on their own specialties in general technical meetings. Projects such as these are truly problems in technical management. There are no easy answers, of course, but it is important that as a proposal writer offering to undertake such a task you at least reveal an understanding of the problem and an approach to its solution.

Contract Administration

It is not uncommon for an RFP to require you to identify the individual who will be your contract administrator and to discuss contract administration. This would not be a matter of concern to the customer for the typical fixed-price or small project, but it can be a serious matter when a large, cost-reimbursement contract is at stake. The customer considers it an important management matter. That is, the contracting officer is probably concerned about it, for contract administration is primarily the responsibility of the contracting official, while technical and program matters are the concern of the government's project officer. And just as the government places two individuals in positions of different responsibilities for each contract, the contractor is expected to establish corresponding "opposite numbers"—a project manager to act opposite to and interface with the government's project manager (also known by a variety of other titles, depending on the agency) and a contract administrator to act opposite to and interface with the government's contracting official. That is, the contractor's project manager is not expected to be the contract administrator, and should not be. Contract administration has little to do with the conduct of the project.

In many contractor organizations it is the practice to make the comptroller or chief administrative officer of the company the contract administrator for all contracts. Perhaps this makes good sense. However, there are many companies in which this is not a good practice for the simple reason that in these companies the comptroller or other administrative executive is totally unfamiliar with government contracts and therefore not well equipped to cope with problems related to the contract (as distinct from problems related to the project contracted for). It would be difficult in such case to demonstrate the individual's suitability for the position, of course.

This is rarely a crucial matter—seldom does success or failure in a proposal effort hinge on the acceptability of a proposed contract administrator. Yet it is a matter in which a proposal can win or lose a few technical points, which may well become important in a close contest for a contract. So it is worthwhile to try to satisfy the customer, if there is concern about the qualifications of your contract administrator.

Briefly, the duties of a contract administrator are to see to the conformance to all contract terms and conditions on the part of the contractor, and to be responsive to the contracting officer in discussing any administrative matters concerning the contract. Here are some of the kinds of matters which may arise:

1. A cost-reimbursement contract will probably require that your invoices be submitted on federal Form 1034, a public voucher. This form calls for certain entries, usually specified in such contracts, including advising the customer how much money is remaining in the budget for any and all tasks (if the project is by tasks, each task must be so accounted), supplying back-up documentation for all "outside" costs, and sundry other administrative matters, many of them peculiar to the contract.

2. Costs billed to the government may or may not be allowable under the terms of the contract. The contracting official wants access to someone in

your organization who is familiar enough with the contract to answer promptly.

3. There may be other questions as to what is billable—per diem rates, for example—under the terms of the contract. The contracting officer attempting to discuss these with the comptroller or accountant in your company may well have difficulty getting answers because those individuals are not familiar with the contract and its terms.

There may be a dispute in audit which can only be resolved by interpretation of what the contract says. Here are a couple of examples of the kinds of disputes and difficulties that may arise when the contractor does not have a knowledgeable administrator to guide the contractor's project manager and comptroller in what is required by and permissible under the contract.

The Job Corps authorized the contractor operating a large Job Corps Center to supply some quantity of the contractor's own training materials to his own Job Corps Center, specifying, in fact, up to $75,000 worth of training manuals. The contractor proceeded to develop a number of training manuals for the Center, billing the Job Corps (Office of Economic Opportunity then) each month for the work done that month in developing the manuals. And each month the government refused to pay that amount of the bill, declaring that it was not authorized by the contract.

Discussions with the officials proved fruitless. Apparently neither party communicated well with the other. Long after the Center was in operation the matter was still unresolved.

At this point the company held a mass meeting headed by the staff attorney who was nominally the contract administrator, but who was not at all familiar with government contracts. And at this point they dragooned the manager who was responsible for writing the manuals, asking for his opinion, since he appeared to have had a reasonable amount of experience with government contracts—at least, as a project manager.

The project manager asked to see the contract, and read the authorizing clause aloud. The clause specifically authorized the contractor to sell itself (at the Center) up to $75,000 worth of its *own proprietary manuals* at a price "not to exceed that charged the most favored customer." This, the project manager explained, was almost boiler-plate government language in contracts and explained why the government had refused to pay the bill.

The others stared at the project manager, puzzled. He explained that the contractor had been billing the government for research and development—for developing custom-made manuals. The clause did not authorize this. It authorized selling the Center $75,000 worth of *off-the-shelf* manuals published by the contractor, at maximum discount offered anyone else. He suggested that the company print the manuals, with a list price, discount the price, and sell itself $75,000 worth!

They did so, and the government paid the $75,000 bill without a murmur.

In another case, where a task-order contract was in force, the contractor overran a task with authorization from the customer to do so. But when the contractor billed the customer for the overrun amount, it was not paid. The contractor thereupon called on the contracting officer with a complaint about the matter.

The contracting officer was sympathetic, but spread his hands, explaining that the project team that had authorized the overrun was out of funds. They didn't deny the justice of the contractor's claim, but they simply did not have the money left in their budget.

Next, the contract administrator called on the contracting officer. "Is this or is this not a cost-plus contract?" he demanded.

The contracting officer was forced to admit that it was.

"Then *we* have no problem," said the contract administrator. "*You* may have a problem, but we do not. We can appeal this to the General Accounting Office or to a federal court, but you'll have to pay."

That ended the dispute, and the government agency was forced to find the funds to pay the bill.

There are numerous other instances that reveal why a contracting officer prefers that the contractor have an opposite number to deal with, communicate with, and settle matters with promptly. The contract administrator need not be a lawyer or even an accountant, but should understand government contracts and be thoroughly familiar with the contract at hand.

Summary and Recapitulation

The term *management* means many things when applied to projects that have been contracted for. It refers to technical management, general management, and administration. It refers to control and monitoring systems. It refers to personnel systems. It refers to project design and functional planning, to estimating, and to contract matters. And it refers, generally, to a prospective contractor's capability for conducting a satisfactory project.

There are many situations in which the customer wishes the proposer to discuss management matters in great detail. But it is always appropriate, whether the proposal requestor has asked for it or not, to discuss management and present your plans for managing the proposed project.

Here, as in all matters pertaining to your proposal, your oral assurances that you will provide good management are on a plane with a professed dedication to motherhood, apple pie, and the American flag; they're nice to hear, but they are only claims, and the customer wants proof—or, at least, good evidence.

The evidence is apparent when you can provide any or all of the following:

1. Specific plans, policies, procedures, forms, and documentation
2. References to specific examples from your own past projects, furnishing names of individuals from whom verification may be sought
3. In-depth discussions to reveal a complete understanding of what the management requirement ought to be and how you propose to satisfy it

In short, not only *what* you plan to accomplish, but *how* you will accomplish it.

Some Main Points to Remember

1. Those management plans which are almost always appropriate—fit into almost all proposals—include cost control, quality control, functional flow, project organization and staffing, schedule control, and contingency planning.
2. Those management plans which are often called for, whether stated in the RFP or not, include estimating, quick-reaction planning, and recruiting. But be alert for any other requirements of management, whether explicit or implicit in the RFP and work statement.
3. Be careful to discriminate in your planning and proposed provisions for management among general management, technical management, and administration. They are not the same things, and are not necessarily the responsibilities of the same individual (although they may be).
4. Task-type and cost-reimbursement projects usually call for "more management" than do firm fixed-price projects, especially the larger projects. (However, relatively few small projects are cost-reimbursement types.)
5. Don't expect the customer to accept your general assurances that you will provide "good management." The customer hears that often, but he wants some solid evidence that you not only understand what you ought to do to provide good management, but have all the tools for it—policies, plans, procedures, forms, and documentation.

13

Writing Persuasively

All writing must be persuasive, if it is to be successful; the writer must always sell something.

What Do *Communication* and *Clear Writing* Really Mean?

There's more truth than humor in the wry observation that when someone refers to a disagreement as "a breakdown in communications," what is really meant is that the other party "won't do it (or see it) my way." The simple fact is that *communication* really means reaching agreement—what is often referred to as "a meeting of the minds."

Almost countless books, reports, memos, lectures, and training courses have been devoted to the art of *writing clearly*, or communicating. They tend to center on such matters as these: how to express yourself in short, direct sentences; grammatical constructions; vocabulary; and a host of other, largely mechanical measures. Note, however, that all of these measures are directed at the writer, not the reader. Presumably, if the *writer* uses short, direct sentences, employs everyday nouns and adjectives, and organizes the writing by simple and correct grammatical constructions the *reader* will automatically understand what the writer intends the reader to understand. The concept assumes that all readers are objective and cannot mistake the writer's meaning if the writer follows the "rules," is totally unambiguous, and is not obscure in style.

What Does *Understand* Mean?

The objective of writing clearly and communicating is, then, to bring about *understanding* by the reader. If the next few paragraphs were devoted to an explanation of how extreme temperatures strip electrons from atoms, would you "understand" this? Even if pages were devoted to a basic explanation of atomic structures and energy levels—or if you were already well schooled in the nature of matter—would you "understand"?

The answer is, of course, yes, you would "understand" in the classic sense of the term—that is, you would perceive the concept and the logic of the explanation. But still that so-called understanding would be based in faith—belief. You cannot verify the accepted theory of atomic structure by your physical senses, but must accept that theory because it appears logical (but so did earlier theories of the atom, now obsolete and discarded!) and has behind it the *authority* of a great many modern physicists.

In short, a good case can be made to "prove" that understanding really means *belief*, that a reader only *understands* that which he or she *believes*, and that the two terms are almost synonymous. So it is moot whether we understand what we believe or believe what we understand—that is, which follows which. But it is not a moot point that, whichever is the case, if a reader rejects what is written as unbelievable or too difficult to grasp, the writing is in vain. The writer has failed as a writer. Whether belief, understanding, or their lack is involved, it is necessary for the reader to *accept* what the writer has said if the goals of writing are to be realized.

The simple fact is—and this has been pointed out earlier—that we humans strongly tend to believe what we want to believe. It is extremely difficult to overcome a strong bias that is already present. If you doubt this, try to persuade or convince a Harvard graduate that Yale is superior to Harvard in any way—or vice versa. If there is little or no bias, the art of persuasion is largely the art of creating a bias—appealing to a want, even if the want is an unconscious one which must first be aroused and brought to the level of consciousness.

Logic cannot overcome bias. You can produce all the figures, facts, and authoritative opinions you want, to convince the Harvard graduate that Yale is a better law school, but the Harvard graduate will reject them all. The words you and your cited authorities use may be understood, but your logic will not, because the Harvard graduate will refuse to believe it.

What is *Logic*?

Without getting into the formalities and philosophy of logic and logical argument, let's take a very brief look at the basis of logical argument. The classic syllogism consists of two or more premises and a conclusion that stems from those premises. For example:

All Americans are free.
You and I are Americans.
Therefore, you and I are free.

This is a legitimate syllogism, correct in structure, with a correct conclusion drawn from the two premises—if the premises are true. But in this, as in many other cases, "truth" means only what we will both *accept*. If you do not agree that "all Americans are free," the conclusion must be wrong—for *you*, at least. The argument will not convince you.

In short, the validity of any argument depends on the acceptance of the premises. If the reader does not accept the premises, the arguments will fail to be convincing—or persuasive.

But there are other logical faults. For example, here is another syllogism:

All Americans are free.
You and I are free.
Therefore, you and I are Americans.

This syllogism fails for another reason, even if you accept the premises. The conclusion does not follow logically from the premises. It is, in fact, a common logical fault, found all too often in writing, known as *non sequitur*, which means, "It does not follow." The premise was not that *only* Americans are free; therefore, the conclusion is false.

The two basic *logical* faults in argument, then, are invalid premises (or unacceptable premises, which is the same thing, subjectively) and false conclusions. To be valid logically, a conclusion must be the *inescapable consequence* of the premises (assuming that the premises are accepted as truth).

Why Are Premises Rejected?

There are two reasons for the rejection of premises by a reader:

1. The reader *knows* the premises to be false.
2. The reader is so biased as to *refuse* to accept the premises as true.

Words are, at best, uncertain instruments of communication, partly because so many words are loaded with emotion and partly because so many words have multiple meanings or, at least, multiple shades of meaning. For example, I am determined (desirable trait) but you are obstinate (undesirable trait). You might accept a premise that you are determined, persevering, or even persistent, but you are likely to reject a premise that calls you obstinate, mulish, stubborn, or otherwise intractable. Therefore, the words used to present a premise often have a great effect on whether the premise will be accepted. Words must be weighed for their emotional impact and probable interpretation. Exceedingly few of our everyday words are completely free of emotional nuances.

A premise may be badly stated, and so meet with a reader's objections. For example, a premise which is a general but not invariable truth may be rejected because it is so stated as to fail to make provision for exceptions. Republicans are generally considered to be more conservative than Democrats, but not all Republicans are more conservative than all Democrats. Even where the exceptions to the rule are relatively few, many readers may seize upon what the writer may consider to be mere technicality and reject the premise. Perhaps they (the readers) are nit-picking, but nevertheless the result is that the arguments fall flat and carry no weight.

Some writers tend to either make up premises or simply fail to verify those they believe to be acceptable. The reader who knows better will, of course, reject the argument. If you read that a heavy isotope is chemically different from the element of which it is an isotope, you may accept that simply because you have not been schooled in the subject and have no reason to reject it. But if you are thoroughly schooled in the subject, you will reject the premise as something you know to be untrue.

The Effect of Failed Arguments

Presenting what are purported to be facts but which are rejected by the reader as being not true is disastrous to any writing. The reader has lost faith in the writer, and anything the writer says is now suspect—greeted with skepticism. And it does not matter whether the writer is, in truth, mistaken; the mere fact that the reader believes the writer to be totally wrong is enough to destroy any faith the reader might have had in the writer.

Present a thousand valid points—unquestionable facts—and you get no praise. Present a thousand valid points and one invalid one, and you draw down a storm of criticism, often destroying the structure built up by those thousand valid points. As a writer you may be controversial, but you must not be mistaken if you wish to have even part of what you have written accepted by your readers.

The conclusions to be drawn from the various premises offered here are plain enough, then. If you are to be even acceptable in what you write, much less persuasive, you must do at least the following:

1. Understand your readers' probable biases.
2. Fathom your readers' probable wants, conscious or unconscious.
3. Be sure of your facts, when you offer facts.
4. Avoid those emotion-laden words which are likely to butt into reader biases.
5. Keep readers' wants in mind and appeal to them.
6. Be sure your arguments are logically sound.

This is not to suggest that logic sells anyone anything. Quite the contrary, it's emotional appeal that does the selling in that it creates the desire to believe and to buy. But desire is not enough. The reader must be permitted to rationalize the decision to believe or to buy. We need logical proof that our decision is the right one in order to justify decisions to ourselves. But we especially need it when we act for others—such as for the United States government—and may have to defend and justify our decisions to a superior official. But experience instills a certain wisdom; we are not going to believe anything unless some evidence is furnished. And evidence, while it need not be absolute proof, must at least have some basis which enables us to find it credible, convincing.

What we refer to as persuasive writing is primarily the use of language and presentation techniques in order to convince the reader that the arguments and the written representations are highly credible.

There are a number of aspects to this. Pure logic—valid syllogistic development—is one. The use of language—selecting the right words and organizing them into ideas that are easy to follow and believe—is another. The organization of ideas into a persuasive chain of reasoning is still another. And there are a few other areas worth discussing, each in turn.

The Coherent Organization

A disorderly, rambling presentation instills something less than confidence in the proposal. And unless well organized and thoroughly planned, a proposal may even come across to a reader as incoherent, with all that that implies about the proposer. That is, it has an emotional impact on the reader, as well as a rational one.

To ensure coherence and order, a proposal must be constructed with a definite pattern and a definite theme. These are, in fact, guidelines for the reader, providing direct assistance in following the logic of the presentation and grasping the main points of the various arguments. Philosophically, it's akin to advice of the fabled rustic lecturer who advised others to "tell 'em what you're going to tell 'em, tell 'em, then tell 'em what you told 'em." That is, telegraph your main message, deliver it, and then summarize or recapitulate it. Or, more simply, give the reader a road map.

What Is *Theme*?

Theme is even harder to define than is strategy. Yet it has almost equally great importance, although for different reasons. A dictionary definition—that theme is a subject, topic, or the like—is not of much help for our purposes here. Perhaps an example will help a great deal more than a dictionary definition.

In a previous chapter you read a brief history of the TFX-111 airplane procurement. You read that the winner was the proposer who focused all attention on how the objective of having a common-use airplane would be met. And you read also of the second-place proposal, which laid all stress on the claimed superiority of its design. In one case the proposer was trying to demonstrate better understanding of the need and greater technical competence. In the other case the proposer was trying to demonstrate the art of keeping one's eye on the ball.

If the capture strategy is, as we represent it here, to be the furnishing of a *reason to buy*, it seems fairly obvious that the customer must be made *acutely aware* of that reason. But mentioning it occasionally is not enough; it must be stated frequently, implied frequently, and reinforced frequently. That reason ought to show up in every technical argument, as a premise or as a conclusion, as a reason or as a result. To put it briefly, that reason must become the *theme* of the proposal.

If you watch a television show on a regular basis, you soon become aware of its musical theme. After a short while you can recognize the beginning of the show without watching the set, simply by recognizing that musical theme; it's an identification.

Musical themes are selected for appropriateness: the theme music for a situation comedy is quite different from that for a dramatic series or a suspense series. The music is selected to suggest the nature of the show, as well as to give it a permanent identification.

But "theme" doesn't have to be music. The old radio series "The Inner Sanctum" was characterized by the eerie creaking of a door, suggestive of an old house and mysterious goings-on. Other horror shows have been characterized by loud screams, such as might be expected in torture chambers, and by loud knocks, such as are associated with séances and astral spirits. Again, these themes were selected for their appropriateness.

So in the case of the TFX-111, one offeror used the theme "commonality," while the other used the theme "an aerodynamic solution to an aerodynamic problem." Each theme reflected the focus and strategy of the proposal. One said, "Buy my design because it will meet your need for a common-use airplane." The other said, "Buy my design because it is technically the best design for the purpose." And while the latter may well have been true, it wasn't good salesmanship. It was most difficult, if not impossible, to prove beyond doubt that the delta-wing design was truly superior to the swing-wing design. But there was no doubt that, as far as the customer was concerned, that commonality was the objective of the effort.

In the case of a proposal, theme is more than an identifying characteristic, although it is also that. It is a repeated sales message driving home the main strategy, reminding the customer again and again of the reason for buying the offer made in the proposal.

But the theme in a proposal is even more than that. It is as much a reminder to the proposal writers of where they are going and what they are trying to prove as it is to the customer. It helps to unify the proposal, to prevent it from rambling aimlessly along every byway. It guides the writers in every aspect of the proposed program and the various strategies arrived at. It is the subject of all major discussions in the proposal, the objective of all design efforts, the premise or conclusion of all major technical arguments. That is, to pursue the TFX-111 example further, "commonality" was the objective of every aspect of designs proposed, and the result of all design effort, as argued. The proposer, with an eye on the ball at all times, never permitted the customer to lose sight of the ball either! Long before finishing reading the proposal, the customer was entirely satisfied that the proposer understood the problem thoroughly, was conscientiously addressing proper design objectives, and was thoroughly "on board" with the customer at all times. The customer could not have helped but get a comfortable feeling and a growing sense of satisfaction and confidence in the proposer. If there were any questions of design superiority or inferiority, the customer invariably resolved them in favor of the proposer who so well understood the goal of the project!

When Is the Theme Established?

Logically, it is not possible to settle upon an effective theme before settling on a capture strategy, just as it is not possible to formulate capture strategy before identifying customer needs and concerns. Therefore, since it must stem from customer needs and concerns, via the strategy formulation, its establishment should be the next order of business after the capture strategy is decided upon.

The theme is a word or phrase and may actually, although not necessarily, be used as such. That is, if you have a short, catchy word or phrase such as "commonality" for a theme, you might go to the extreme of actually using the word or phrase as a running foot or head—that is, it might actually appear at the top or bottom of each page as a slogan. In some cases, that might be appropriate; in others, it might well be overkill and actually have an adverse effect, rather than a beneficial one. Each case is a matter of judgment, and must be considered on its own merits.

But whether the theme is expressed as a recurring slogan or not, the thematic message, as a reflection of the capture strategy, must be expressed continuously. And as important as it is to do this so that the customer is not permitted to lose sight of the suggested reason to buy, it is equally important that the proposal staff be totally aware of the theme their writing must support and reflect.

Take that case cited earlier, wherein a proposer offered the U.S. Navy a "what's wrong with this picture?" concept for training junior officers in naval security regulations. Let's review how the proposer arrived at the successful capture strategy.

The proposer analyzed the requirement and came to the conclusion that the most effective strategy would be one focusing on the most effective way to teach the subject—impart the skills—via the printed page. That is, the strategy was to be technical or program strategy—the best way to get the job done, or functional effectiveness.

Designing the program to be proposed, the proposer reasoned thus in the following manner. There is no especial difficulty in teaching the language of the regulations themselves via the printed page. But that could be done with the original Navy manual of security regulations; such an objective did not really require a special training manual. Therefore, it must be the objective of the training manual to achieve something more than learning of the words and sentences which constituted the regulations. And that objective, the proposer reasoned, must be the *skills* required to *apply* the regulations. These would include the ability to (1) establish specific procedures for any given installation or facility and (2) the ability to inspect any given office or facility and detect weaknesses, faults, or violations of security regulations.

Such skills call for visual scanning of physical facilities—both are really physical inspections—to translate regulations into practice and procedures.

Moreover, to be effective in the real-life application, such skills and abilities must become almost reflex—the student must be able to react to and detect a security violation or weakness without prolonged study.

The program, the reasoning went on, therefore called for a great deal of *visual* presentation and a great deal of instructional *drill:* visual presentations to enable the student to acquire *relevant* skills, drills to condition reflexes. And to combat the tedium of such drills in what is at best a subject of little intrinsic interest, the visual drill was to be based on a "what's wrong with this picture?" methodology. Many line drawings would be used, each with at least one security violation or weakness shown as it would appear in an actual inspection. The student is expected to identify what's wrong.

Several relevant themes are possible for such a proposal and strategy. Here are some of the possible themes which might have been used:

Design geared to most-relevant skills (or behaviors).
Visuals are the key to success.
Drill is the key to success.
The "what's wrong with this picture?" technique simulates *relevant* behaviors.

The first theme suggested is too general to be of great value. Besides, it reflects a well-accepted truth and therefore has nothing special to say.

The second suggested theme is somewhat better, but still does not focus well enough on some *special reason* for the customer to buy. Nor is it likely that the proposer would be the only one to say this; the thought would almost surely occur to competitors.

Virtually everything said above applies equally to the third suggested theme.

The fourth suggestion has the virtue of being probably a unique idea among those offered in the various proposals submitted, and it is a convenient springboard for all the other arguments: It's visual, it provides ample drill, and it does indeed aim at the development of the most relevant skills or behaviors, satisfying all requirements of the strategic concept used for the program design.

The theme may be a reflection of a broad concept or approach, but ideally it should reflect as closely as possible one or more *specific reasons* for accepting the proposal as the winner. It should be a constant reminder to the customer of what the proposal offers that is *different* from and *better* than other proposals.

Of course, that means that the theme must reflect *strength*. All the best thematic expression in the world is of no value if your proposal cannot back up the promise implied in the theme. General Dynamics' "commonality" theme in proposing for the TFX-111 could not have won the day if the proposal did not present a credible approach to achieving that promised commonality. The "what's wrong with this picture?" theme could not have won favor unless the proposal showed how it would work and persuaded the customer that it was a viable and practical idea. No theme can work if it comes off as an empty promise.

In most situations proposers find that they are working from a set of strengths and a set of weaknesses in relation to the proposal. One proposer is strong in regard to well-qualified staff, but perhaps weak in directly related experience, while another is weak in that it is a new and untried organization while being strong in regard to financial capability. It is important in selecting a theme that the theme does not point to some inherent weakness and bring it to special attention. Rather, if you are strong in an area you consider to be critical in importance—and particularly if you believe your competitors to be far less strong than you in that area—a theme might be selected to focus precisely on that (assuming, of course, that the theme also reflects your basic strategy).

One clever and effective use of theme is to highlight and dramatize some feature of your proposal which is truly unique and attractive. The ideal is to be able to claim, as did insurance salesman Frank Bettger, some exclusive capability you can offer your customer—if you are sure that what you offer is, indeed, a capability your competitors cannot offer, and if it is important enough. What you must not do is defeat yourself by using the wrong theme—offering something of limited value and importance or something everybody else can offer. Yet even that last point is not necessarily a bar; in some circumstances offering something everyone else *could* offer, but has not thought to offer, is a valid strategy. It was so in the case of a beer-advertising campaign of some years ago, when the advertiser dramatically announced that his bottles were sterilized by live steam before being filled. The sterilization process was in common use in the brewing industry, but of course the public did not know that. It *appeared* to be a new or different way of safeguarding the public's health through sterilization of the bottles because no one had ever advertised it before. And once one advertiser had publicized the method, no one else dared say "me, too"! So it became an effective theme.

Theme As a Test of Strategy

A theme is a reflection of the strategy, of course. It must therefore be given the same prominence as the strategy. In a print advertisement the headline would reflect the theme directly; in a proposal other means must be found. And the best possible place is as soon as possible.

One place a theme might be presented early in the proposal is on the cover itself. That is, if the theme is a slogan or brief phrase, it might be printed somewhere on the cover. ("Commonality" would work well for that.) And if it can be supported by an illustration, that could be used in conjunction with the theme on the cover. Again there is serious danger of overdoing it if you try to make it a force-fit; not every theme lends itself to simple illustration. However, it ought to be possible, in most cases, to summarize a theme (that is, really, to summarize your basic strategy) in a brief phrase. In fact, if you are unable to do so, consider the possibility that you have not really boiled your basic idea down to its essentials. In fact, difficulty in expressing the essence of your strategy in a brief phrase may be the test of whether you truly have a well-defined strategy or are merely pursuing some rather vague and general concept.

Take the TFX-111 case again. One problem with "an aerodynamic solution to an aerodynamic problem" is that it is not necessarily specific to the project being discussed—it might be offered as a theme for *any* aeronautical design effort. On the other hand, "commonality" was highly specific to the problem under discussion and was a strategy for *that* proposal, rather than a general strategy which might have been applied to a large number of proposals.

That is not to say that you must necessarily create some slogan and use it verbatim. It is to say that you must be able to express your basic strategic concept as an understood theme in a brief phrase or, at most, a simple sentence. That *concept* (not necessarily those words) must shine through the pages of your proposal and be reinforced as frequently as possible so that the customer understands it clearly. In this light, let's look back at one or two of the cases cited earlier.

One is the case in which the successful proposer persuaded the Postal Service that to have a permanent staff of experts in just about everything in EDP would be impractical. You'll remember that the strategy was to persuade the customer that it would be far more practical to retain a contractor who had the capability for swift—almost instantaneous—recruiting of any specialists needed. Having established that as a strategy, the proposer then adopted the theme that all the customer's needs would be satisfied by recruiting the right specialists almost literally overnight for every need. The proposal then concentrated on the theme—focused at every point possible on the proposer's methods and ability to accomplish the promised recruiting, building the customer's confidence steadily. The strategy was to address the *essence* of the customer's need, and the theme addressed the essence of the strategy.

Another is the case in which the successful proposer offered a new idea—failure-probability analysis. He started with an attention-getting, bold discussion along these lines: Usually, in designing any kind of maintenance-training program, we go to the engineers and technicians and ask them what a maintenance technician ought to know. That is how we decide what information to incorporate in the program. This is wrong because it's second- and third-hand information. Let's go to the source, the equipment to be maintained. Let's "ask" that equipment what it needs in the way of maintenance. And the mechanism by which we shall do that asking is by a failure-probability analysis.

Now, having gotten attention through that rather startling introduction, the proposer proceeded to play on the theme of his plan to ask the equipment by explaining failure-probability analysis and using the term as a theme throughout the proposal.

There were subthemes developed also, although they were carefully kept subordinate to the major theme. One was derived as follows. There are only two kinds of electrical or electronic failure: short circuits and open circuits. Every electrical or electronic failure is a degree of one of these—a 50-ohm resistor which has increased in value to 5,000 ohms is, essentially, an open circuit, just as a leaking capacitor is a short circuit. This was justified— anticipating growls of disapproval and disagreement by engineers—by stating that this was a convention for maintenance purposes, for diagnosing failures (rather than for design use) on a simple go/no-go basis. And to demonstrate the validity of it, the example was used of a badly frayed conveyer belt which, although still doing its job, would be unhesitatingly replaced by a maintenance man as being in imminent danger of failing. That is, for maintenance purposes the belt is either "good" or "no good."

The subtheme was, then, go/no-go maintenance is effective maintenance, and some effort was expended to demonstrate its desirability as a maintenance concept.

If you cannot capture the essence of your strategy in a simple phrase or sentence, how can you be sure that your customer grasps it? You can't, of course, which is why it is essential that you make this test. Your strategy cannot work if it eludes the customer.

Technical Argument

Technical argument refers to the formal organized presentation of your case to make or prove whatever point you are making. The subject of the argument or the point addressed need not be "technical" at all—that is, an argument written to prove that Jonathan apples are as tasty as Delicious apples is a technical argument, just as any syllogism is a technical argument. A proposal usually contains a number of technical arguments and is itself, overall, a technical argument intended to prove that your organization and your plan are the ones best suited to the customer's needs.

To be at all effective, the argument(s) must be structured in one of several possible patterns or organizations. Among the several possible organizations are these:

From the general to the specific
From the specific to the general
Historical or chronological
Order of importance (usually ascending)
Order of complexity (from the simple to the complex)

Each organization has its own uses. Chronological order is usually well suited to formal reports and general texts, for example, whereas from the general to the specific is usually more useful for proposals, especially when trying to prove a specific point, as in discussing the customer's problem and presenting the analysis which led up to the approach you propose. But all have their uses, even in a proposal. The typical proposal must present a number of arguments, and some of those require different approaches to organization than do others. For example, if you are explaining a truly complex matter, you will most likely find it best to begin with simple concepts and analogies and progress to the more complex ones, as you would in a training program.

The greatest hazard, which entraps so many proposal writers, is that of mixing methods, being inconsistent in the organization selected, or misleading the reader as to how the argument is organized. The confusion this produces in the reader has a disastrous effect on the credibility of the proposal: It does not help you to be the best-qualified organization or have the best possible plan for the project if the customer is unable to understand your plan and follow your reasoning.

This does not mean that you must preface every argument or discussion with a specific message saying "We will go from the general to the specific" or "This is the history." You must, however, somehow let the reader know where you are going. All that is required are simple clues. A paragraph may open with, "In its simplest form" or, "The development goes back to beginnings in 1963." This is especially important when you switch to another organization. The reader needs some kind of transition to bridge the gap if confusion is to be avoided. Here is an example of two paragraphs, where such a change is made *without the proper transition:*

> The total history of solid-state electronics is not as recent as one might think. In fact, the ability of a solid-state device to function usefully in electrical equipment has beginnings over 100 years ago, when it was discovered in the laboratory that electrical current would flow in one direction only through metals with oxide outer skins. And in the years following, the early days of radio, bulky copper oxide rectifiers were employed commonly, later giving way to the smaller and more efficient selenium rectifiers, and ultimately to today's tiny silicon rectifiers.

> Modern transistors amplify through the control of current flow in a semi-conductor material. The current flow is actually the number of electrons flowing through the material, at any given instant, in some linear ratio to the amplitude of the input signal. That is, it is the *number* of electrons flowing through the device which is significant to the function of amplifying, in the conventional transistor. XYZ Electronics Corporation, however, now has a radically new and different solid-state amplifier, known as an MIA or Metal Interface Amplifier, which amplifies on the principal of electron *velocity*, rather than electron volume.

As you can see, this argument would then go on to present details of how the new MIA functions, with a presentation of electrical characteristics and advantages, and other evidence to sell it to the reader. However, there is no transition between the two paragraphs; the reader has not been prepared for the transition from a brief history of solid-state development to a simple-to-complex presentation of the MIA device. That is, there is no transition from rectifiers to transistors, nor from historical-technical reporting and explanation to purely technical explanation. Such a transition could have been effected rather smoothly by something such as the following (to introduce the second paragraph of the example):

> Rectifiers are strictly go/no-go devices: the current flows at full volume or it does not flow at all. That is, the rectifier is strictly an on-off switch. The transistor to which it led, however, more closely resembles a common light dimmer than an on-off switch: it can turn the current *partially* on or off, controlling the amount of current flowing, at any given instant. This is, in fact, how it amplifies—by controlling the current flow in direct ratio to the signal supplied. Or, since current itself refers to the volume of electrons moving along a conductor, to the number of electrons flowing at a given instant.

A transition is thus supplied, bridging the explanation of rectifier operation to the more sophisticated function of the transistor, leading to the even more sophisticated explanation of the MIA.

Writing Transitions

A transition, sometimes called a "bridge" by writers and editors, is simply that, a bridge. It begins with the thought just expressed and extends it or links it to the new subject being introduced. Every sentence should bridge to the next sentence and every paragraph to the next paragraph. The failure to provide transitions is one of the principal faults found in writing generally. The lack of transitions results in jagged edges in the writing; the use of them produces what may be thought of as smooth writing, writing that marches in regular cadence to logical climaxes and conclusions. It signifies organized, orderly thinking, which is certainly one of the effects we want to achieve in a proposal.

The Principal Causes of "Bad Writing"

Poor writing is only rarely the result of the writer's inability to use the language effectively. Most of the writers of poorly written papers have had at least a high school education and are perfectly capable of expressing their thoughts in words. What really militates against effective writing—what *causes* individuals to write badly—is one or the other, sometimes both, of the following:

1. The writer may be exceedingly self-conscious about the writing—conscious, that is, of the image of the author—and may therefore be driven to extremes to present a favorable image.
2. The writer may not have really thought the subject out or may not have completed research and planning—really may have no clear idea of what he or she wants to say. The failure to say it is, therefore, inevitable.

The first case causes such sentences as the following (from a United States government publication):

> Firms that undertake subcontractors should be fully aware that privity of contracts will not exist between the subcontractor and the United States Government.

The language following goes on to explain, generally, what that first sentence means—that the United States government has no responsibility for subcontracts let by its own contractors; subcontractors are on their own in negotiating and performing on subcontracts. That could have been said in the first sentence! (If it had been, the second sentence would have been unnecessary.) And aside from that, there are other faults. The message is intended for the subcontractors, not for the prime contractors. Therefore, it should have said "Firms that undertake subcontracts," rather than "Firms that undertake subcontractors." The writer is therefore guilty of the second cause of bad writing, as well as the first: the thought expressed is not logical, whether because the writer failed to reason the matter out or because of simple carelessness in expressing the idea. In this case the real intention is apparent; in other cases utter confusion might arise.

By far the most serious fault is that of "bad thinking," which inevitably must display itself as "bad writing." What appears on the page is what the writer has mentally formulated, of course. (What else can you write, except what you have in your mind?) It's quite easy to deceive ourselves into thinking that we really understand something and are prepared to explain it to a reader, when in fact we do not understand the matter at all. And to cover this up—to deceive ourselves, as well as our readers—we ramble on glibly with an assortment of generalities and meaningless nouns and adjectives. Here is a case, taken from a government training manual dealing with value engineering, purporting to explain the analytical method for solving problems:

> The strictly analytical approach is substantially singular in purpose. The problem is stated exact. A direct approach to the solution is taken, proceeding through a step-by-step progression of experiments, evaluations and mathematical manipulations to arrive at a single answer. An analytical problem is one that frequently has only one solution that will work.

This paragraph has little but jagged edges; there are no noticeable transitions between the sentences, for one thing. For another, the argument does not appear to be headed in any particular direction or to any logical conclusion. But even more serious is the fact that the reader can't tell what the writer is trying to say! If the "strictly analytical approach" has only one purpose (which is what the writer presumably means by that first sentence), what *is* that purpose? And what does "The problem is stated exact" mean?

It seems fair to judge that the writer of these words had not really thought out the proposition at all, did not know what to try to prove or what point to make. So it is hardly surprising that the point was never made!

The fact is that analysis is not a problem-solving method per se. Analysis, when used in connection with problem solving, is used to find the *cause* of the problem, not to solve it. Despite the fact that the solution may well become obvious when the cause is identified, that is not always the case.

The writer of this passage should have made that point plain. But it would have been entirely proper to point out what analysis is, too. Analysis is the process of separating something into its constituent parts or elements, so that each may be examined and the structure reviewed. The passage should have read something like this:

> Analysis is the process of separating the object of study into its individual components, so that each component and the structure may be studied. Applying this method to problem solving, analysis reveals the cause of the problem, which is usually a faulty component or some fault in the structure. This is a direct attack on the problem, carried on in an orderly, disciplined progression of evaluations and, often, experiments and mathematical analyses. Frequently, in using this method, it will be found that the problem has a single cause, and correcting or removing that cause is the only satisfactory solution to the problem.

Even this may not be a correct presentation, since it is by no means clear what final point the writer wished to make. (But it does seem clear that the writer failed to demonstrate that "the analytical approach" is a problem-solving technique or method!)

But even this is a mild case. For classic bureaucratic prose, witness the following, taken from the Federal Procurement Regulations:

> A direct cost is any cost which can be identified specifically with a particular final cost objective. No final cost objective shall have allocated to it as a direct cost any cost, if other costs incurred for the same purpose, in like circumstances, have been included in any indirect cost pool to be allocated to that or any other final cost objective. Costs identified specifically with the contract are direct costs of the contract and are to be charged directly thereto. Costs identified specifically with other final cost objectives of the contractor are direct costs of those cost objectives and are not to be charged to the contract directly or indirectly.

Translation: The contractor is not to charge the same costs to a contract twice by including them in both the direct charges and the indirect charges. Nor may the contractor charge to a contract any costs incurred for another project or contract. And even then the writer of this clause is not satisfied, but goes on to add confusion by using equally horrendous constructions to add the totally unnecessary observation that if a direct cost is incurred for another contract it should be charged to that other contract!

The final irony is that a new set of regulations has been drafted, with the dual purpose of making the procurement regulations uniform and easier to comprehend. But this clause appears in the new regulations, without significant change!

This is a case where the writer knew exactly what to say, but insisted on making it as difficult to comprehend as possible. The writer was no doubt aided and abetted in this by government legal minds.

The Cures for Bad Writing

Fortunately bad writing is a curable disease since we know the principal causes. In fact, bad writing may be cured by following rather simple rules:

1. Do as much research as necessary before you begin to write, to be sure that you have accumulated all the data and have an entirely clear and complete understanding of what you wish to present to the reader.
2. Plan your writing in advance by outlining in great detail. *Do not* list in your outline the things you plan to talk *about*. *Do* list in your outline the things you plan to *say*—the main points, that is.
3. As you prepare your first draft, forget about you, the writer, and any ideas you may have about your "professional image." The reader cares nothing for your image, but only for the information you are offering. Instead, think about your reader and what you want the reader to *understand*. One professional man who writes well claims that he imagines himself explaining the matter to a grade school student.
4. Do not expect to produce a final manuscript with your first draft. It's a writers' cliché that all good writing is *re*writing. Even the most experienced professional writers do not expect to produce a final manuscript without at least one rewrite.

Each sentence you write must have a point; each paragraph must have an objective. Each sentence making up the paragraph must contribute to the point of the paragraph. Once you have made your point, begin the next paragraph and begin to build up the information and argument to make the next point.

The logic of a paragraph may be somewhat difficult to see in narrative form. If you wish to check yourself, take a paragraph you have written and synopsize it by putting it into outline form, where you must organize and group the information, properly subordinated. If you have trouble doing this, there is an excellent probability that your paragraph is faulty. Do this exercise a few times and you will soon be able to do a certain amount of self-editing, with immediate improvement in your writing.

How to Tell Whether You Know What You Are Talking About

Many writers fall into the trap of mistaking familiarity with technical or professional jargon for understanding of the subject. Knowing the terms and platitudes in common vogue in their fields, they learn how to utter this jargon as explanation, and they deceive even themselves!

For example, take the case of "behavior," used commonly in the education and training field. Everyone in that field knows that the development of instructional materials must not begin until "behavioral objectives" are prepared, if accepted methodology is to be followed faithfully. Professionals in that field use the word "behavior" freely. Yet, a shocking number of such people cannot explain the term or the concept in lay language. Asked to explain what "behavior" means in instructional processes, they tend to fall back on the platitudes and the jargon itself as explanation.

A test for true understanding is the ability to translate that jargon into lay language, language that a grade school student can follow. Unless you can do so, there is reason to doubt that you are ready to write on the subject. Repeating technical terms and technical idioms is not evidence of understanding. If you want to test your own understanding of any subject, try explaining it to someone who is completely a lay person in that field! You'll soon learn whether you have a true understanding or have merely committed some terms to memory, along with a knowledge of when and where to employ them.

Being that lay person is one of the important responsibilities of an editor. The editor must try to stand in the stead of a typical reader and arrest the writer with a query when something is unclear or ambiguous.

Beware of Technical Idiom

An idiom is an expression—sometimes a word, sometimes a whole phrase—which has special meaning and which does not mean what a literal translation would imply. For example, a German idiom which means "he was at his wit's end," would translate literally as "then was advice expensive." And when you greet someone with "How are you?" you do not really want an accounting of the other's state of health, but are simply being courteous!

A common technical idiom among those dealing in anthropology and other subjects where Darwin's theories of evolution are useful refers to genetic changes brought about by external conditions—adaptation. And those who do not specialize in this field and are not especially familiar with Darwin's work tend to accept that idiom literally: they believe that when the climate became colder, creatures began to grow fur coats to cope with the cold! Of course, this is not a literal truth. The theory explains that when the climate became cold, those mutants who happened to grow fur survived, while those without fur perished. So, in the long term of evolutionary process, the species, as such, appeared to adapt. In retrospect the net effect is that of adaptation, but this is an illusion used as a kind of code among those working in the field. The specialists understand that "adaptation" really means survival of the fittest.

Such idioms as this and other such codes or cues are dangerous to use if you do not truly understand what they mean, *in detail.* Many of them are even more subtle. In electronics we talk about radio energy (waves) being reflected from certain objects, and for many years we thought that the word was an accurate explanation. Today, we know that so-called reflection is actually a phenomenon more accurately called "re-radiation."

The Hazards of Not Being Entirely Accurate

There are actually two hazards involved in misusing such terms or in using such terms—idioms and code expressions—in place of true explanation. One is the obvious hazard of failing to bring understanding to the reader who is not familiar with the terms and concepts. But the other is an even greater hazard to your credibility–of misusing the terms with a reader who *does* fully understand the terms and concepts!

Once a reader finds you in some gross error your general credibility is severely damaged, and everything you write is likely to be read with a degree of skepticism and with a corresponding reduction of your ability to persuade. Persuasion depends heavily on credibility, on developing in the reader a large degree of confidence in what you write. It becomes important therefore that you not only avoid being trapped in careless errors of important fact but also keep your explanations crystal clear and easy to grasp.

Aids to Communication

Perhaps you noted the observation earlier that words are, at their best, less than perfect instruments of communication. General semantics would explain this by speaking of "referents," those words or images which your own words invoke. For many things, each of us has a personal referent. If you speak or write the word "chair," each listener or reader has an image of a chair. But while one refers that word to a straight-backed, wooden chair, another images an overstuffed easy chair, and still another thinks of an office chair.

We try to shape this image by adjectives, hoping that we shall be able to guide the reader into the referent we intend. Still, the net effect is not entirely what we wish for. That is, if our intent is simply to present the *idea* "chair," we shall succeed. But if it is important to our purpose that the reader "see" the exact kind of chair we have in mind, words alone cannot accomplish that. We need an aid, something which communicates more efficiently and accurately: an illustration, which may be a drawing or a photograph.

Writers must learn that they are not restricted to words alone, and that the organization of words is not the entire task of writing. The writer is responsible for communicating with the reader by any means possible to perfect that communication. The writer must think in terms of what the reader is to "see." And the writer who fails to utilize *all* means for accomplishing this is failing in the duties of a writer.

For everything you wish to present to your reader, consider which is the most effective and most efficient way to do so. The cliché about a picture being worth a thousand words is not necessarily true. There are some ideas and concepts which are exceedingly difficult to illustrate directly; words must be the principal conveyors of information to explain the emotion of love, for example. But in a great many cases, a single illustration can express more than an entire page of densely packed word symbols. A photograph of the chair you refer to will present all your readers with the same image.

But even where you must depend on words alone, there are devices which help. Analogies are useful. Instead of the abstract and little-known word "oblate," the shape of the earth is easily explained by comparing it to a common orange. Caution: to use an analogy effectively your must analogize the idea to something the reader is familiar with. There are some people in this world who have never seen an orange; the analogy would not be very helpful in such a case. Unless you can use an object with which you are sure the reader is familiar, a drawing is a necessity. (Try to explain a rhomboid or a parallelogram in lay terms to even a well-educated person who has forgotten high-school geometry!)

The Singular Advantage of Familiar Referents

The human strongly tends to resist new and different ideas. The need to learn something new represents a degree of insecurity; the old, familiar ideas are comfortable. When you are compelled to offer something new, especially when you are trying to persuade a reader to actually buy and try something new and different, the battle is somewhat uphill. But there is a way to make the new and different more palatable: present it in such a way as to make it appear less strange and new by linking it to the old and familiar. One vendor of lemon juice packages it in a plastic container that resembles a lemon. Selling the concept of failure-probability analysis was made easier by comparing it with the well-known reliability analysis. A new product is shown to be an improvement over an old one, rather than something entirely different. And, of course, the more familiar the referent, the easier it is for a reader to accept it and accommodate the concept. (Persuasion to *accept* represents "understand.")

Implications and Inferences

If words have various nuances or shades of meaning—connotations, that is, as distinct from their denotations—sentences and phrases are similarly open to connotative meanings. Just as idioms are not to be interpreted or translated literally, so do words and phrases have nonliteral meanings implied by the writer, whether deliberately or unconsciously.

Such subtle implications (and some which are not so subtle) can result from the structure in which the words or phrases are offered, the context in which they are used, or the general environment in which they are used. As an example of the latter case, there was a time, prior to World War II, in which the Japanese had gained a reputation for cheap and shoddy merchandise. If you wanted to praise a camera made in Japan, you might have to say, "It's a Japanese camera, but it's a good one." Consider, however, even today, when Japanese cameras are recognized as being fine instruments, the effect of saying, "It's a good camera, but it's Japanese." The first sentence implies that a good Japanese camera is an exception to the rule, that you expect the reader to be skeptical about Japanese cameras. The second construction—and note that the words are exactly the same; only the construction has been changed—suggests that you are not recommending it, which is the opposite net effect of the first sentence!

These are implications made by the writer as a result of the construction. If you say, "It's a Japanese camera," you've no way to estimate how the reader might interpret your meaning—what the reader might *infer*. A reader who remembers keenly the days of shoddy Japanese merchandise might infer that you are warning him off. But a younger person, who is aware that the Japanese produce many fine cameras, might infer that you are recommending the camera.

Are you responsible for what a reader infers? Certainly you are. As a writer, it is part of your responsibility to consider *all* the ways in which a reader might interpret what you have written—all the inferences that might be drawn. And should you perceive that you might reasonably expect a reader to misinterpret your meaning, it is incumbent upon you to take some step to guard against unintended meanings.

Connotations change with time. Once, to refer to someone as a "rascal" was to pass the judgment that the individual was unscrupulous, dishonest, unethical, or perhaps all three. The term is rarely used in that sense today, having been replaced by "scoundrel" or some more specific word. "Rascal" now has an almost idiomatic meaning, being used fondly to refer to a mischievous young child or animal.

Once it was perfectly honorable to be a janitor. Today, the term would be offensive to those who prefer to be known as "stationary engineers" or "custodians." We call these words euphemisms, but they are simply terms that others find more acceptable because the original term is considered somewhat derogatory or unflattering. (Undertakers now prefer to be referred to as "morticians.") This is not a small matter. An injudicious choice of words can antagonize a reader, which is hardly to be recommended when you are trying to sell the reader something.

The True Art of the Professional Writer

Much of what has been said in this chapter has been what not to do—don'ts, rather than dos. But the most important "do" and "don't" is yet to come. It has been said, truly, that the greatest offense a writer can commit is to bore the reader. Of course, the reader retaliates by not reading further. And at that point the writer has failed completely. The true art of the writer lies in somehow inducing the reader to turn the page—and continue turning pages until the end.

To accomplish this, it is necessary on every page to give the reader some reason to want to know what is on the next page. Fiction writers accomplish this by suspense, of course, something not available to proposal writers. Or is it? Actually it is, to at least some degree. In fact, it is inherent in the format and organization recommended for proposals.

The opening of the proposal offers at least two opportunities to so pique the reader's interest as to ensure that pages will be turned. For one thing, the first page is a place where you can and should say something attention-getting as you introduce yourself and summarize, most briefly, what you can offer: an outstanding expert, an unusual facility, an innovative idea, or whatever you have been able to come up with.

But you have a second opportunity in the introductory section to plant a bit of suspense: in presenting the brief understanding of the requirement or problem, a bit of creative imagination can help you produce some provocative point, with the promise of detailed exploration in the pages to come.

This tactic should be extended throughout the proposal by continuously planting seeds of expectation—telegraph to the reader a hint of what is yet to come. For example, if you utilize the discussion section properly, you will have exposed at least one or two problems. This is a place to dramatize those problems, and stress the difficulties. But be sure to advise the reader that solutions will be forthcoming in later sections of your proposal. Build suspense by stressing the difficulties to be overcome, while expressing confidence in the solutions you will soon offer the reader, in the third section! And here, when you are finally compelled to end the suspense and reveal your solutions, you can carry the tactic a bit further by discussing the qualifications necessary to carry out the project successfully and promise to reveal the qualifications in the last section! Always save something for the next page, but always indicate to the reader, somehow, that more is yet to come.

The reader may be compelled to read your proposal, but is not compelled to pay attention and remain alert. It's your job to persuade the reader that the time spent reading your proposal is time well spent.

This chapter has covered a variety of subjects related to writing well, although in necessarily abbreviated fashion. You do not have to be Ernest

Hemingway to write a good proposal, a proposal worth reading. But you do have to produce a proposal that is at least not stultifyingly dull.

Some Main Points to Remember

1. Do recognize that "understanding" and "believing," or "accepting," mean pretty much the same thing. You can't *compel* a reader to accept anything you say; you must *persuade* that acceptance.
2. Logic is not persuasion, although you do need logic as a backup. You must provide the reader a reason to *want* to believe.
3. Confusing the reader is a good way to lose your chances for persuasion. Establishing and maintaining a distinct theme is a good beginning to guiding the reader away from possible confusion.
4. Theme is not enough. Your text must be orderly and organized, along some specific lines. The ideas must flow smoothly into one another, the connection between them obvious, the progression continuous.
5. Use our version of Murphy's law: Anything that can be misunderstood will be. Write so that you cannot be misunderstood.
6. Be sure that you yourself know what you are talking about, that you truly understand your subject and have thought the matter out completely, before you attempt to present it to anyone else.
7. Use language carefully. Avoid misleading idioms, remembering that your reader may not understand them, and be careful about the *connotations* of the words and phrases you employ.
8. If at all possible, have a good editor review your manuscript and help you accomplish all the above.

14

Presentation
Strategies

All selling begins with getting attention. But then
you have to hold the reader's attention, too.

The Proposal as a Presentation

Most RFPs today include a notice somewhere that "unnecessarily elaborate proposals are neither necessary nor desired," and that such unnecessary elaboration may be construed by the government as a lack of cost consciousness on the part of the proposer. This leads to speculation on the part of the proposers—especially those who have not had a great deal of experience in proposal writing—as to what the government considers "unnecessarily elaborate proposals." Does this mean that the proposal should not be typeset or printed? That illustrations should be little more than rough sketches? That cheap paper stock is to be used for covers?

The RFP does not specify beyond the general injunction against unnecessary expense in preparing the proposal, nor can it. However, it is safe to assume that such notices refer to earlier days, especially in proposing for major defense and space contracts, when some large corporations actually bound proposals in morocco leather, in multivolume sets, each with its own custom-made case for storing the set of volumes! It is safe to assume that the government does not wish you to go to these extremes.

On the other hand, the government does not intend to restrict you from making up a *thoroughly professional-looking* proposal. Typesetting and printing, especially if the RFP calls for a large number of copies, is not an offense to the customer's cost-avoidance aims, and certainly the proposal may be suitably bound by any acceptable method, such as side-stitching (stapling), binding posts, or plastic spiral spines.

In one case a firm opened a branch office in the Washington, D.C. area, assigning a manager to begin a pursuit of contracts there and arming him with nothing more than a subscription to the *Commerce Business Daily*, a battered portable typewriter, and access to an office copier. And for 3 months, that manager spent his full time pursuing contracts, writing eleven proposals. The time constraints prevented him from utilizing the typesetting and printing equipment of the home office and stopped him from having such work done locally, so he typed his proposals on the portable, made copies on the office copier, used company letterheads as covers, and corner staples as binders.

At the end of the 3 months he had won five contracts, despite the complaints of the home office that his proposals were a bit shoddy-looking compared with the beautifully typeset and professionally printed and bound proposals produced by the home office. And during that 3-month period, unfortunately, the home office had had no luck at all with their physically handsome proposals, which further irritated the home office staff at the success of the new branch office!

All of this is not to say that you should work under such handicaps, or that they are an aid to winning. Quite the contrary, they are a handicap to winning, a liability. But it does demonstrate that it is the *content* of the proposal that carries the day, if at all, not the cosmetics. Yet it does help, most definitely, if the proposal has a pleasingly professional appearance. As one reviewer was overheard to say when he saw the attention-getting gold covers on one set of proposals, "Now there's a contractor who *cares!*" Obviously this is not a bad impression to make on a customer.

The proposal is a presentation, of course, a point we have made frequently in these pages. It represents you and your organization. A neat, professional appearance in a proposal is of the same necessity as a neat haircut, a clean shave, a shined pair of shoes, and a well-pressed suit are to a salesman. So at least part of the consideration in formulating a presentation strategy is the general physical appearance of the proposal and its general impact on the customer. But presentation strategy does not stop there. There are at least three other things to consider:

1. Clarity, effectiveness, and efficiency in communication
2. Means for dramatizing and accentuating your capture strategy
3. Special, attention-getting ideas to capture customer interest

Let's consider these one at a time, for each merits its own discussion.

The Objective Is Clear and Swift Communication

Too many writers concentrate so intensely on the words they will use that they neglect more effective means for communicating their messages clearly and unmistakably. It is a rare proposal that would not be vastly improved by greater and more effective use of graphic devices of several sorts—charts, plots, diagrams, line pictorials, and even photographs. And in far too many cases, the graphic illustrations which are used have been improvised either as an afterthought, to parallel the verbal presentations, or to simply comply nominally with an RFP requirement for a few charts and diagrams.

In fact, for many sections of most proposals, such graphic presentations ought properly to be the *primary* means of communicating the information, with language serving as a supplement. That is, the proposal writer should pose the questions before writing—while planning the presentation, that is—along these lines:

1. Exactly what idea or information am I trying to get across here? (What is the main point I wish to make?)
2. Will words alone transmit this message and make this point? (Or will words do it as effectively and efficiently as some graphic presentation would?)
3. Will this require a great deal of text (e.g., several pages or several thousand words) to get across in language alone?
4. Is there some graphic method to present the concept in a single page?
5. Is there some graphic method to present the *main point* in a single page?

The writer's job is not to write words, but to communicate information. It should not be left to the illustrator to develop the illustrations, but only to execute them professionally. It is the writer who must *conceive* what is to be presented graphically, and how it is to be presented.

One ground rule for successful salesmanship, which applies well to successful presentation, is this: Make it as easy as possible for the customer to place the order. Or, in the case of a proposal, as easy as possible to grasp the information and appreciate the main point.

Another consideration is to make important points with as much impact as possible—dramatize them, that is. Consider, for example, that you wish to show some order-of-magnitude difference in cost. Compare the impact of describing that difference in words with the impact of *showing* it in a graph or bar chart.

Graphics, then, may be used to dramatize, as well as to communicate more effectively.

Graphics should not "support" text. Graphics should be an independent means of presentation, which are *supported* by such text as necessary. And the less text required to do this, the better the presentation.

Bear in mind that in most proposal competitions, the proposal reviewers—the customer, in effect—are faced with a number of proposals to read. Some of the reviewers have the habit of taking an initial look at each technical proposal by scanning the headlines and studying the visuals briefly, gaining a first impression. The less actual reading they have to do to understand what you are offering, the better they will like you and your proposal! Anything you do to accelerate their reading and grasp of your offer is appreciated.

If you have been in on the initial analysis and planning sessions, you should have been able to make a few notes then and there on what visuals you will be likely to be able to use effectively. Of course, you do have the original rough flowchart to begin with, but many other types of visuals are needed. If you have a professional illustrator available, you need only give the illustrator some rough "writer's sketches" to work from. But with today's availability of templates and many other "prefab" artist's aids, even the lay person can usually do an adequate job of making up most of the visuals needed.

There are many models to choose from—flowcharts, system models, networks, matrices, graphs, and various hybrids. Each has its own advantages and drawbacks. Choosing the best type for a given need depends primarily on what you are trying to show or what main point you wish to make. Let's look at a few of these and discuss their pros and cons. You'll find that while some of the graphics available are pure discipline—simply translating a concept or plan into a graphic version which enables you to get it all on to a single page—others call for creative imagination, offering you a variety of alternatives for how *best* to represent it. For some of the examples we're going to look at now, we can offer you a few basic principles or rules; for others, we offer only some examples of what can be done with a bit of imagination and an illustrator's skills.

In that connection, however, consider this point: As the writer of a proposal, it is up to you to determine where, for what reason, and how to resort to graphics. The illustrator is, in many cases, your "mechanic" or technician, who executes your ideas. However, many illustrators can contribute more than artistic skills. In some cases, your illustrator may know of certain graphic techniques and methods unknown to you, and be able to suggest better ways. In many cases, your illustrator is more than an illustrator—is an *artist*, in fact—and can offer many creative ideas. Therefore, it is wise to sit down with your illustrator and discuss your ideas, seeking any guidance or ideas the illustrator can provide. That is, in some cases you may be telling the illustrator exactly what you want done, but in others you may get a great deal more help and add substantially to the impact of your proposal if you discuss what net effects you are trying to accomplish, and solicit ideas.

Flow Charting

Flow charting is a method of describing or documenting a series of actions—including a full program or project—graphically, so as to see the entire program in overview, almost at a glance. Flowcharts illuminate several aspects which are not readily discernible from textual descriptions alone:

- Each separate function or phase
- The sequence of functions, phases, and events
- Relationships between and among various functions, phases, and events

Engineers and others who work with drawings as a matter of course in their disciplines usually have no trouble with the concept, since flowcharts are a logical extension of engineering drawings and they are trained to think in terms of logical flow.

The problem newcomers have with flow charting is also its greatest strength: flow charting is a discipline, primarily, rather than an art, and it *forces* decision making. One can be somewhat vague in writing about a subject (and many writers are), and generalize. But it is nearly impossible to do this in a flowchart: the specific little blocks and lines with arrows are highly specific and represent decisions—decisions about what the SOW says (as you interpret it), and decisions about what you propose to do and how you propose to do it.

Decision making is seldom easy, and most of us resist it, at least unconsciously. Yet, decision making is a must for proposal writing. Most customers will not accept vague generalizations: they want to know exactly what you propose to do, exactly how you propose to spend the large sum of money you are asking for.

In the discussion of analytic techniques, we described flow charting as a highly valuable tool for developing overall approaches and strategies. Its initial value lies in its focus as the objective of the initial brainstorming session, as a way to translate initial reading of the RFP and SOW into a working plan for a proposal.

But they are equally useful as presentation tools. The major organizing logic of a flowchart (or any other visual) should be discernible in not more than 5 seconds of review—generally accomplished with brief words and headings outlining the major dimensions and format. Several illustrative flowcharts follow (Figures 14.1 and 14.2).

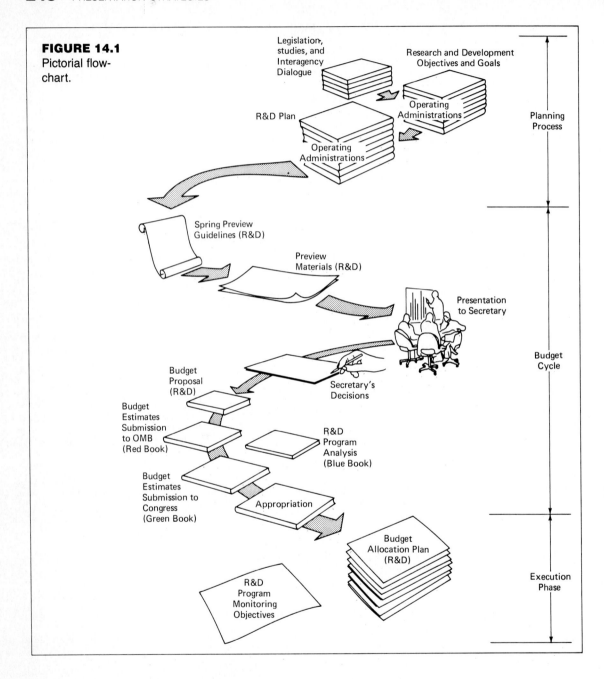

FIGURE 14.1
Pictorial flow-chart.

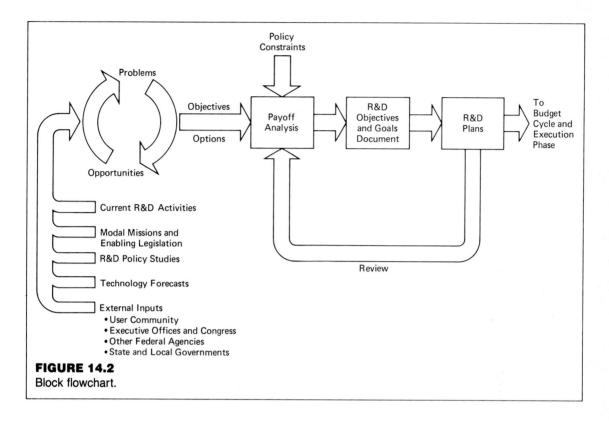

FIGURE 14.2
Block flowchart.

System Models

A close cousin to the flowchart is the system model, a conceptual way to portray your view of critical elements in the project and client environment.

One reviewer of analytic and evaluative proposals said: "I want models—they're the first thing I look for. To me, the proposers' understanding is best displayed by how they characterize the environment in which I deal on a daily basis. There is no single best way to construct a model—I have seen a dozen different and all equally valid descriptions of a project environment. I am excited by those which show me new ways to view the problem. For me, the important thing is that the model be internally consistent, and identify the 'boundary conditions' that define the domain of the consultant's intended endeavor."

The keys to a system model are logic, simplicity, and a delineation of how your project fits into the environment of the problem and organization. There are an infinite number of ways to characterize any situation, so don't get hung up on the specifics of the model. Figures 14.3 and 14.4 show a typical systems model submitted as part of a winning proposal. This two-step model first snapped a broad picture of macroscopic factors, then adjusted the focus to the more immediate problem environment addressed in the proposal.

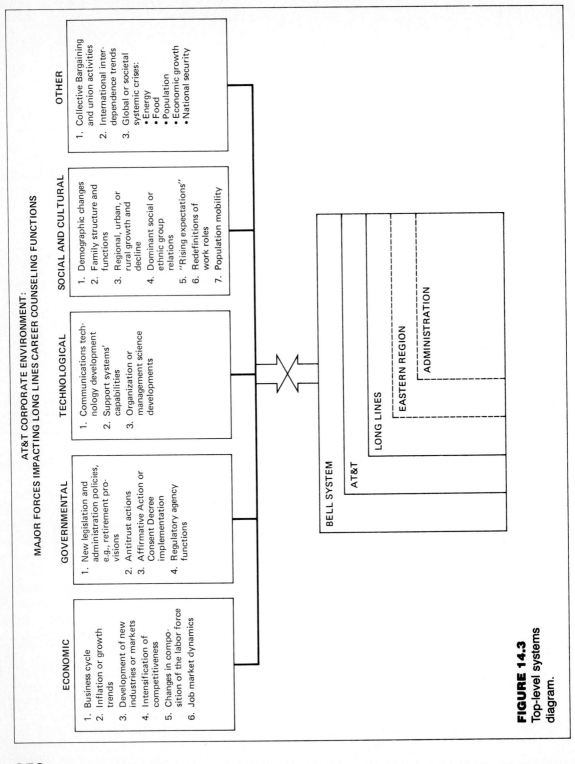

FIGURE 14.3
Top-level systems diagram.

AT&T CORPORATE ENVIRONMENT:
MAJOR FORCES IMPACTING LONG LINES CAREER COUNSELING FUNCTIONS

ECONOMIC

1. Business cycle
2. Inflation or growth trends
3. Development of new industries or markets
4. Intensification of competitiveness
5. Changes in composition of the labor force
6. Job market dynamics

GOVERNMENTAL

1. New legislation and administration policies, e.g., retirement provisions
2. Antitrust actions
3. Affirmative Action or Consent Decree implementation
4. Regulatory agency functions

TECHNOLOGICAL

1. Communications technology development
2. Support systems' capabilities
3. Organization or management science developments

SOCIAL AND CULTURAL

1. Demographic changes
2. Family structure and functions
3. Regional, urban, or rural growth and decline
4. Dominant social or ethnic group relations
5. "Rising expectations"
6. Redefinitions of work roles
7. Population mobility

OTHER

1. Collective Bargaining and union activities
2. International inter-dependence trends
3. Global or societal systemic crises:
   • Energy
   • Food
   • Population
   • Economic growth
   • National security

BELL SYSTEM

AT&T

LONG LINES

EASTERN REGION

ADMINISTRATION

FIGURE 14.4
Detailed systems diagram.

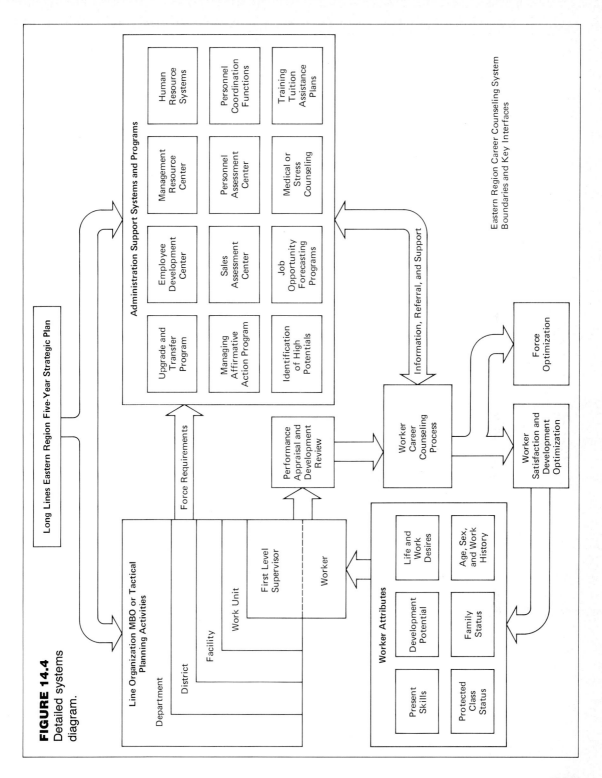

1. WHAT ACTIVITIES MUST OCCUR FIRST: Activity *b* can occur only after activity *a* is completed.

2. WHAT ACTIVITIES CAN FOLLOW: Activities *d* and *e* can begin after completion of activity *c*.

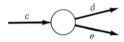

3. WHAT ACTIVITIES CAN OCCUR SIMULTANEOUSLY: Activities *l* and *m* can be undertaken at the same time.

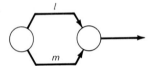

FIGURE 14.5
Basic logic rules
of networks.

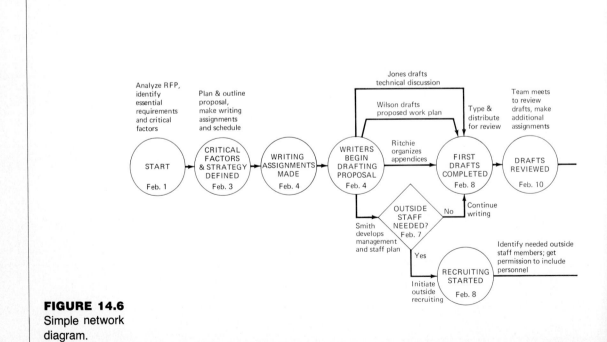

FIGURE 14.6
Simple network
diagram.

Networking

Networking is a graphic technique used to display project implementation logic and timing. There are 150 or so variants of networking techniques, all descendants of two primary types—CPM (used for decades in the construction and engineering fields), and PERT (born of the Polaris program).

Networks are constructed according to some basic logic rules for sequencing activities and events. Feedback loops, decision points, and other fancy bells and whistles aren't allowed in networks, unlike the looser guidelines for flowcharts and system models.

Simple, straightforward projects don't require networks. Bar charts are usually sufficient to show overall logic, timing, sequence and duration of project tasks. But a weakness of bar charts is that dependencies between activities are not clearly highlighted.

Networks overcome this limitation by showing the sequence, interrelationship, and duration of major activities in relationship to each other and to time. To understand how to use networks, you must realize they are simply a logical series of activities and events: where activities (arrows) are defined as things which consume resources and time; events (circles) are defined as points in time. In sequencing your activities, you must pay attention to the three questions in Figure 14.5.

Figure 14.6 shows an example of how the networking technique may be used to clarify proposal writing responsibilities and lay out an overall plan and schedule for producing the proposal. Its initial value is as an analytic tool and

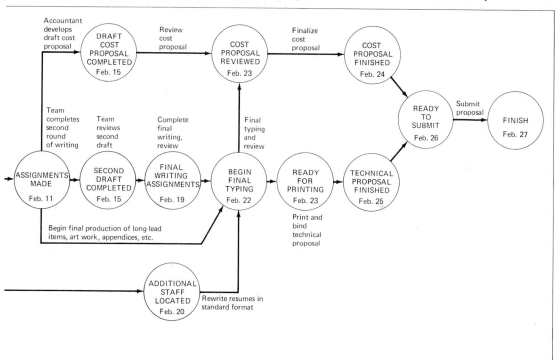

monitoring device for implementation. You need not worry about the total accuracy of the logic.

In using both a bar chart and a network, it is important that the activity logic of each display "calibrate" with the other. The reader should be able to see the relationship between the network display and the bar chart display and track activities in each.

Performance Networks

The power of the networking technique may be improved by building in the concept of performance measures. The performance network is based on the logic of conventional networks, but adds qualitative and quantitative measures at project milestone points. This concept is particularly effective in communicating the achievement expected at interim project points. (See Figure 14.7.)

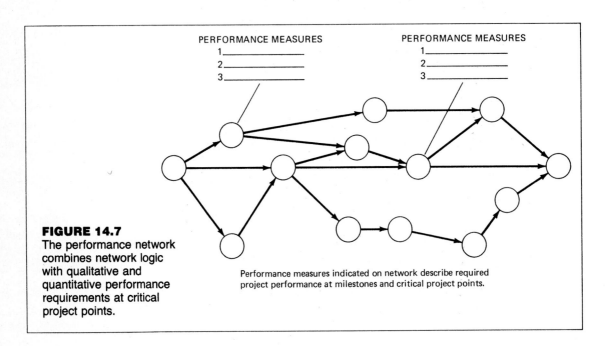

PERFORMANCE MEASURES
1_____
2_____
3_____

PERFORMANCE MEASURES
1_____
2_____
3_____

FIGURE 14.7
The performance network combines network logic with qualitative and quantitative performance requirements at critical project points.

Performance measures indicated on network describe required project performance at milestones and critical project points.

Matrices

Matrices are simple and powerful display devices. The strength of the matrix method lies in its ability to display orthogonally any two variables or dimensions the writer wishes to highlight.

Figure 14.8 shows how one proposer used a matrix to overcome limited corporate experience. The RFP called for demonstrated capability in a certain type of project and client environment. While the proposer did not have this specific experience, aspects of other projects closely paralleled the requirement. The proposer demonstrated capabilities by inferring the key content

SPECIALTY AREAS REQUIRED BY PROJECT

CLIENT	International Development	Program Planning	Management Systems Design	Tri-Square or Logical Framework	Organization Analysis and Development	Computers and Data Processing	Budgeting and Accounting	Implementation Planning	Training Program Design	Training Program Delivery
Agency for International Development, State Department	X	X	X	X	X			X	X	X
American National Red Cross		X		X	X			X	X	X
American Public Health Association	X	X			X					
Canadian Corrections Service		X		X	X			X		
Commerce Department		X		X			X		X	X
Environmental Protection Agency		X	X		X		X			
Forest Service, Agriculture Department		X	X	X		X	X	X	X	X
National Center for the Study of Professions		X	X	X	X	X	X	X	X	X
Nigerian Government, Office of Civil Service	X	X		X	X	X	X	X		
Save the Children Foundation	X			X					X	X
Treasury Department		X	X		X	X	X	X		

FIGURE 14.8
Corporate experience matrix.

PROPOSED COURSES AND

EXECUTIVE DEVELOPMENT OBJECTIVES		CATEGORY	INTERPERSONAL/ PSYCHOLOGICAL		
REQUIRED EXECUTIVE SKILLS (FROM 1976 OFFICE OF PERSONNEL MANAGEMENT STUDY)	DEVELOPABILITY OF SKILLS	TITLE OF PROGRAM	Models for Management	Managing Achievement Motivation	Program Management Systems
		LENGTH	3 Days	3 Days	5 Days
1. ORAL COMMUNICATION SKILL. Effectiveness of expression in individual or group situations.	High				O
2. WRITTEN COMMUNICATION SKILL: Ability to express ideas clearly in writing and in grammatical form.	High				
3. LEADERSHIP: Effectiveness in getting ideas accepted and in guiding a group or an individual to accomplish a task.	Moderate		△	△	△
4. INTERPERSONAL INSIGHT: Skill in perceiving and reacting senstitively to the needs of others; objectivity in perceiving impact of self on others.	Very Low		△	△	
5. PLANNING AND ORGANIZING: Ability to efficiently establish an appropriate course of action to accomplish a specific goal, and to make appropriate use of human and fiscal resources.	Moderate		O		△
6. PROBLEM ANALYSIS: Skill in identifying problems, securing relevant information, identifying possible causes of problems, and proposing alternative courses of action.	Moderate		O		△
7. STRESS TOLERANCE: Ability to perform under pressure and opposition.	Low			O	
8. FLEXIBILITY/ADAPTABILITY: Ability to modify behavioral style and management approach to each goal, or to adapt to changing organizational needs and situations.	Low		△	O	
9. DECISION-MAKING/DECISIVENESS: Ability to make decisions through the appropriate use of logic or reason, render judgments, and take action or make commitments.	Moderate				△

FIGURE 14.9
Another type of matrix—summary of proposed executive development program.

areas required by the project and listing these horizontally along the matrix. Vertically, the proposer listed all past client projects, and with check marks in the relevant cells, conveyed overall depth and capability in each of the dimensions required by the proposal. The narrative reinforced the visual by choosing particular cell entries and describing how particular aspects of each project equipped the proposer for this job.

Think of the matrix as a vise clamping your specimen to the workbench and leaving your hands free to work. It provides versatility throughout the proposal—technical discussion, program planning, management planning, and so forth. Matrices organize the relationships you wish to highlight and are particularly useful to structure alternative approaches: the matrix summarizes

SEMINARS TO BUILD EXECUTIVE SKILLS

PROPOSED SEMINARS AND COURSES										
PRACTICAL ANALYTIC METHODOLOGIES			COMMUNICATIONS			SUPERVISORY		SELF-MANAGEMENT & GOAL ORIENTATION		
Problem-Solving-Decision-Making	Developing Sound Work Plans	Research & Evaluation Technqiues	The Craft of Clear Writing	Effective Briefing Techniques	Writing a Work Statement	Setting Performance Standards	Career Counseling Techniques	Time Management	Career Planning	Self-Development Strategies
3 Days	2 Days	3 Days	3 Days	2 Days	1 Day	2 or 3 Days	2 Days	1 or 2 Days	3 Days	1 Day
○			○	△		○	○	○		
	△		△	○	△	△				
△	○			△			○	○		△
						○	○	○	△	△
△	△	○	○	○	○	○			○	
△	△	△	○		△	○			○	
				○				△		○
○				○						△
△	○	○			○			△		○

△ = Major impact on executive skill
○ = Secondary impact on executive skill

major dimensions of each alternative. Figures 14.8 and 14.9 are matrix examples which succinctly organize and convey information.

Simple Graphs and Charts

The grandparent of all the visual techniques, the simple chart or graph, provides the ultimate flexibility in displaying numerical data and analysis.

Charts visually highlight selected relationships among data elements and portray comparisons, trends, and relationships. The data displayed may be your analysis of more voluminous data included as RFP appendixes, or an original compilation from your own or other sources.

FIGURE 14.10
Simple charts and
graphs displaying
numerical data.

NUMERIC DATA
Budget Outlays for Administration of Justice by Subfunction (in billions of $)

FISCAL YEAR	1970	1971	1972	1973	1974	1975	1976
Administration of justice:							
Federal law enforcement activities	.6	.7	.8	1.0	1.1	1.3	1.5
Federal litigative and judicial activities	.2	.3	.3	.4	.4	.5	.7
Federal correctional activities	.1	.1	.1	.1	.2	.2	.2
Criminal justice assistance	.1	.2	.4	.6	.8	.9	.9
Total administration of justice	1.0	1.3	1.6	2.1	2.5	2.9	3.3

(Source: *The United States Budget in Brief,* Fiscal Year 1980)

MULTIPLE CURVES CHART

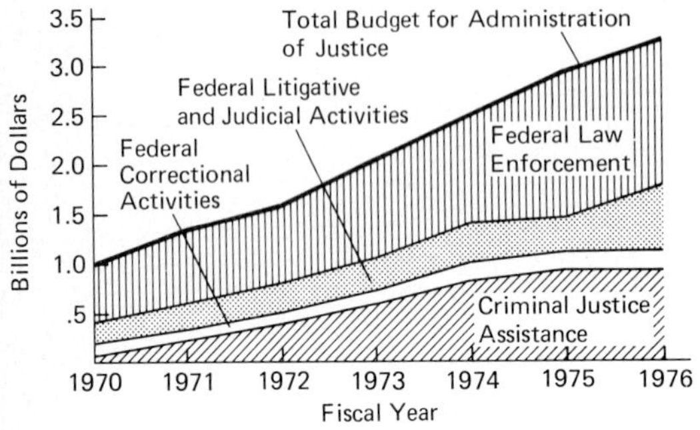

THE INDEX CHART

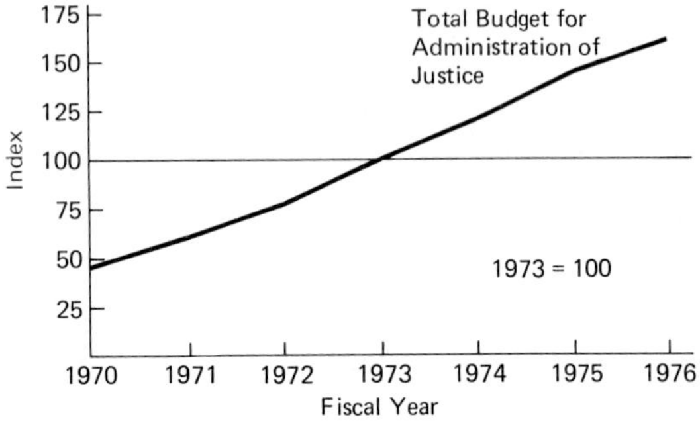

CUMULATIVE CHART

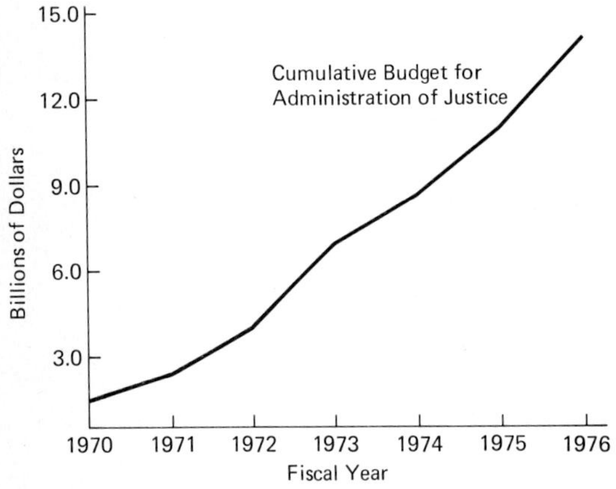

SUBDIVIDED COLUMN CHART

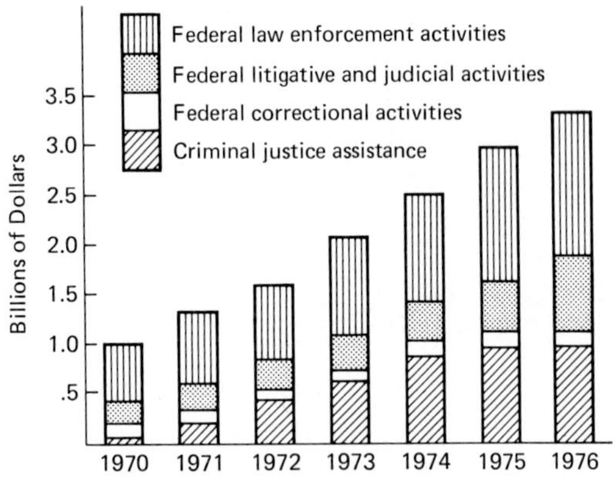

Figure 14.10 shows a simple table of quantitative data and a few of the many ways in which this data can be interpreted and displayed. The best way, of course, will be a format which highlights the point or conclusion you wish to emphasize.

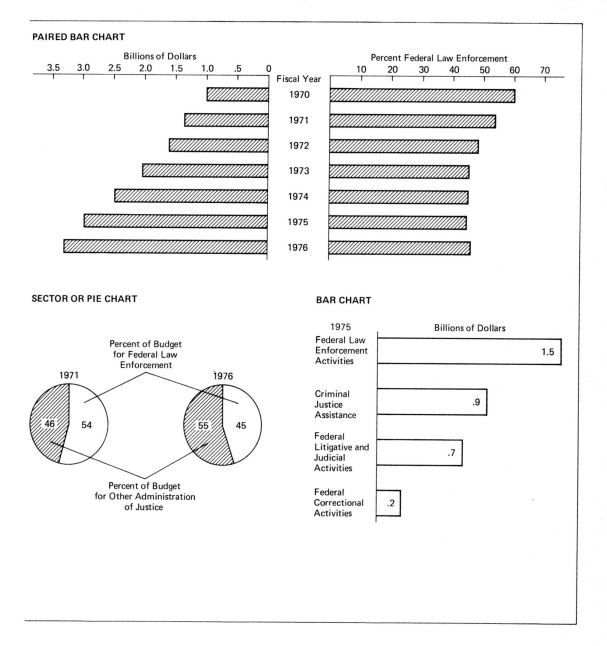

Hybrid Visual Formats

You can combine and piggyback individual presentation methods to produce special visual formats for displaying complex programs.

Figures 14.11 and 14.12 are from a proposal to upgrade the planning and budgeting capability of a developing country. Several presentation techniques were interrelated to describe a complex program in a simple fashion.

OUTPUTS: SPECIFIC PROJECT RESULTS

1. Appropriate organization structure, staffing profiles, and responsibilities of units defined for improved planning and budgeting systems.

2. Implementation plan developed which shows changes required to legally implement revised responsibilities.

3. Revised budget accounting system to accommodate needed changes and provide controls developed.

4. Budget forms and instructions reviewed and revised to correct identified weaknesses.

5. Training program developed for the revised system.

INPUTS: KEY ACTIVITIES AND RESOURCES REQUIRED

KEY PROJECT ACTIVITIES	RESOURCES (WORKER-MONTHS)
1. Team begins work	–
2. Interview key BOB, NESDB, other staff	1
3. Develop model of current system	4
4. Define and analyze alternative models	6
5. Revise budget accounting system	8
6. Review and revise budget forms	6
7. Develop FY 82 BOB instructions	4
8. Develop and test training program	1
9. Prepare training materials	1
10. Train agency & BOB staff	4
11. Assist in use of new system	9
12. Evaluate first year results	2
13. Finalize required org. structure, staff profiles, units responsibilities	6
14. Modify and improve system as needed	4
15. Develop implementation plan	4
16. Conduct intensive project reviews	6
17. Project completes hand-over to Thais	–

FIGURE 14-11
A hybrid of the matrix idea—overall project objectives and activity plan.

DESCRIPTION OF PROJECT RESULTS:

1a. Overall system and organization structure defined; includes resp. of BOB & agencies down to section & program level.

1b. Staff profiles defined by number of persons, skills, and education, and experience required. Includes job descriptions.

2a. Plan shows specific changes to Bud. Procedures Act and other legislation.

2b. Includes time-phased schedule showing sequence for change.

3a. System includes chart of accounts, coding structures, control procedures to achieve required benefits.

3b. Designed for compatibility with current and future EDP systems.

4a. BOB forms and instructions developed in clear, precise form, including examples of how to use. Ready by Dec. 1981 to be included in FY 82 materials sent to agencies.

5a. Training program developed, pilot tested, refined, and finalized. Materials translated into Thai.

5b. Thirty persons in BOB and thirty persons in agencies trained in operation of revised budget system.

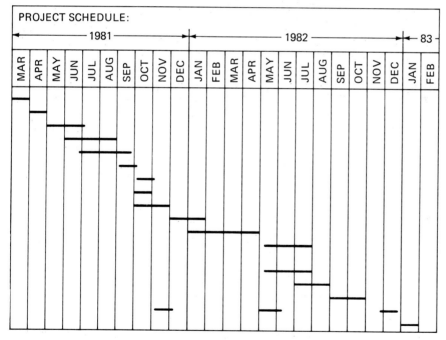

Figure 14.11 summarizes the overall project objectives and deliverables, using a bar chart format to describe the timing and resource requirements of seventeen key project activities.

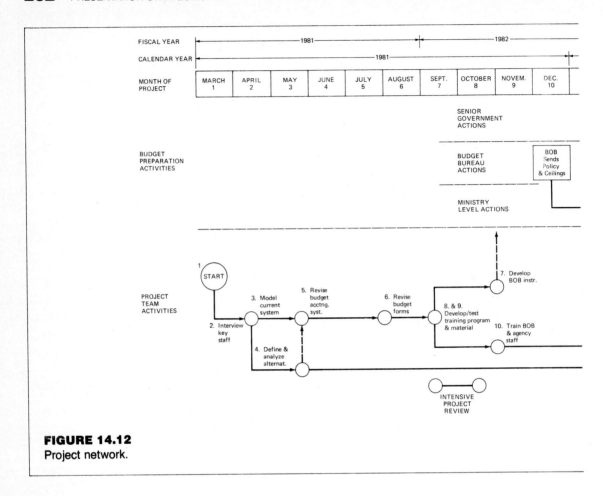

FIGURE 14.12
Project network.

Figure 14.12 displays these key project activities using a network to illustrate the sequence of tasks. Figure 14.12 includes a flowchart of budget preparation processes in the government and highlights the relationship between proposed project activities and the ongoing budget cycle.

Keep Them Simple

Figure 14.13 is perhaps the ultimate in simplicity, and is really nothing more than an expanded sentence summarizing major activity in successive weeks of a 5-week project training and guided application program. But it provides a good visual break, and the vertical dimensions can be expanded or contracted to meet aesthetic layout considerations—such as filling the remainder of a page under a short finishing paragraph at the top of the page when a new topic is to begin on the overleaf.

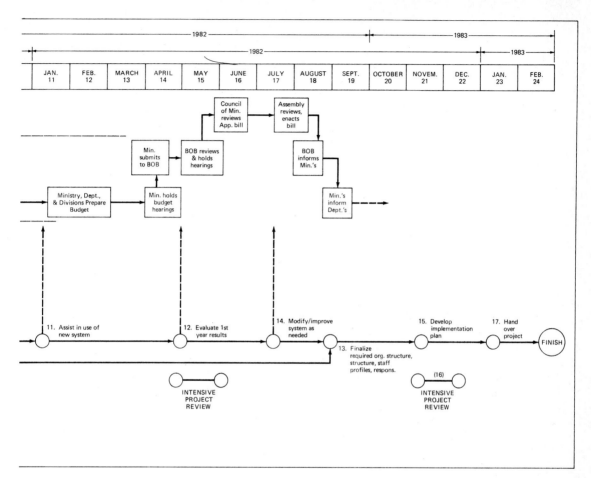

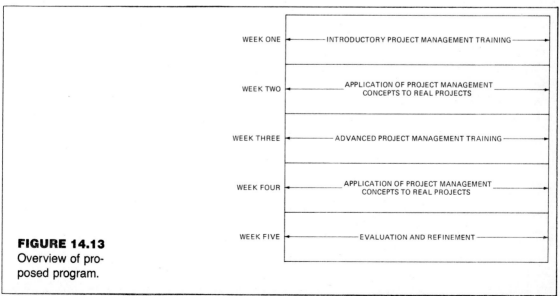

FIGURE 14.13
Overview of proposed program.

TRAINING SCHEDULE FOR WEEK ONE		
	MORNING	**AFTERNOON**
DAY ONE	PLANNING AND MANAGING SOCIAL AND ECONOMIC DEVELOPMENT PROJECTS • Why development efforts fail • Requirements for success • Relationship of projects and programs • The development project cycle	PROJECT MANAGEMENT SYSTEMS—BASIC CONCEPTS • Fundamental principles • Potential benefits • Role of project management in national development • Setting performance specifications
DAY TWO	ESTABLISHING PROJECT OR PROGRAM OBJECTIVES • Problem definition or analysis • "Top-down" and "bottom-up" planning approaches • Hierarchy of objectives • Defining project purpose and goal	WORKSHOP: Sample case in establishing project or program objectives
DAY THREE	DEVELOPING THE PROJECT PLAN • The Tri-Square management matrix • Work breakdown structures • Clarifying assumptions and constraints • Identifying activity steps to achieve objectives	WORKSHOP: Sample case in developing the project plan
DAY FOUR	BUDGETING THE RESOURCES REQUIRED • Identifying financial, human, and material resource needs • Alternative budgeting techniques • Cost-benefit and cost-effectiveness	WORKSHOP: Sample case in budgeting the resources required for projects and programs
DAY FIVE	ASSIGNING RESPONSIBILITIES • Coordinating different agencies and ministries • Identifying who should be involved at each step • Organizing the project team • Project management roles	WORKSHOP: Sample case in assigning responsibilities and coordinating multiple agencies

FIGURE 14.14
Training schedule for week one.

Again, in the name of simplicity, Figure 14.14 shows a day-by-day summary training agenda for the first week displayed in the 5-week schedule.

Work Breakdown Structures

The Work Breakdown Structure (WBS) is an efficient technique for systematically analyzing large, complex projects. Use of this technique defines the total project in a way that ensures all elements are included in proper relationship to each other.

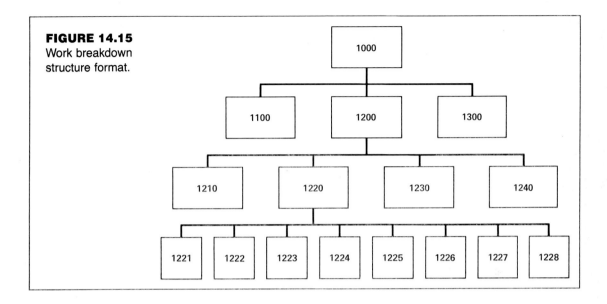

FIGURE 14.15
Work breakdown
structure format.

WBS diagrams portray the project graphically, expanding it in a level-by-level fashion down to the degree of detail needed for effective planning and control. The WBS charts break the overall project into a series of subprojects, and continue the top-down splitting of subprojects into more specific elements, each of which is a manageable task or work control package.

WBSs evolved from the management approaches used by NASA and system contractors to plan complex efforts successfully. It can be used for much simpler projects as well.

The technology is in common use today for large and technologically complex projects. Among its features is that the project financial accounts can be assigned to individual tasks to permit overall financial control.

Figure 14.15 shows the overall WBS format; Figure 14.16 is an example of the top-down analysis approach.

These figures are simple examples of a graphic presentation known as a "tree," because it has a trunk, which has branches, each of which branches again, in progression. Such trees may be used to show all possibilities, as in "logic trees," or to show a branching structure as such.

Figure 14.17 is such a logic tree, sometimes also referred to as an "algorithm" to signify that it is a graphic equivalent of a formula or equation. The example shown is the beginning of troubleshooting logic or diagnosis of typical TV problems. In fact, it is an exercise in Aristotelian logic, whereby you must inevitably arrive at a final correct answer if you pose the right questions and get an accurate series of "yes" or "no" answers.

In practice, such logic trees are generally far more complex and extensive than the simple example shown, and indeed this one would grow rapidly in size and complexity were it to be extended to final conclusions—i.e., to the right questions. Such trees are commonly used by computer professionals, although

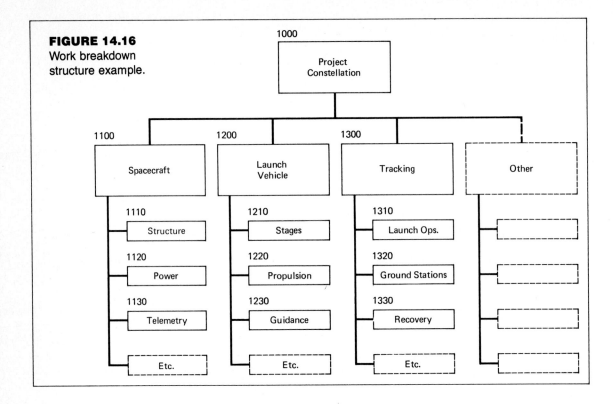

FIGURE 14.16
Work breakdown
structure example.

they do not resemble the example physically, to think out and represent to others the logic of a computer software package. Between computer specialists such diagrams are good communication devices. When using the concept to communicate with lay people, use such everyday terms as those in the example.

Some general guidelines or "rules" for developing such trees follow:

1 Generate an Initial List of Objectives Define the general problem or program area. Identify as many project objectives as possible without attempting to structure or organize the objectives. Brainstorm to develop a long list, using your careful reading of the RFP and the RFP checklist to create possible objectives.

2 Identify an Overall Objective Identify an overall project or program objective, that is, an objective to which all others on the list will relate. Write this objective on the top of a chart; all other objectives will be listed below it.

3 Define Objectives One Level Down Ask, "What subobjectives are necessary to accomplish this overall objective?" Write those objectives and add lines which connect with the higher project objective to which they contribute. These objectives are candidates for individual projects.

Test the adequacy of the objectives listed. Is the *full* set represented? Is it plausible that if these objectives are accomplished, the program goal will be achieved? A second test question is "are all the objectives necessary?" If any does not logically contribute to the higher objective, prune it from the tree.

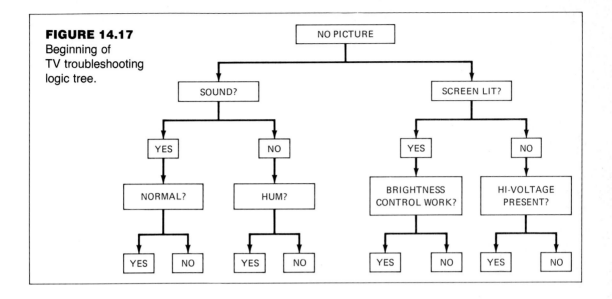

FIGURE 14.17
Beginning of
TV troubleshooting
logic tree.

4 Extend the Tree Down One More Level Identify objectives for the next lower level by using the same logic. Identify and list all subobjectives which contribute to the higher objective. Test for necessity and sufficiency: dropping those not necessary, adding others which are.

5 Check the Nature of the Lowest Level Objectives Review the objectives at the lowest level of the tree. Ask the question, "Is this the basis of a project task, end product, or deliverable? If not, continue the top-down process by going to the next lower level. Continue until you reach objective statements of manageable size of such scope that you can realistically estimate the resources needed to achieve the objectives.

6 Review the Logic of the Tree In reviewing the tree, some objectives may be missing. If so, add them. An intermediate level of objectives may be needed to create a more logical linkage. Check your original list of objectives against the tree. Which are not represented? Should they be included?

Look at the linkage between a set of objectives at one level, and the next higher level. Test for necessity and sufficiency. Are all the objectives necessary, and does each one contribute logically? Are they sufficient—if they are all achieved, is it likely that the next level objective will be reached? If they are not sufficient, you must either define additional objectives, or make certain assumptions. Keep a running list of the assumptions you are making in your vertical logic.

Compare the objectives at each level. They should be roughly of the same magnitude, and degree of abstractness or specificity. Objectives at each level should be discrete, nonoverlapping objectives, not the same objective stated in slightly different ways. Your completed tree provides a solid basis for subsequent development of the program plan.

Special Cases

The next two figures, 14.18 and 14.19, are examples of creative graphics used to illustrate rather complex management relationships, drawn from proposal efforts. Such presentations may be a great aid to your proposal in showing your

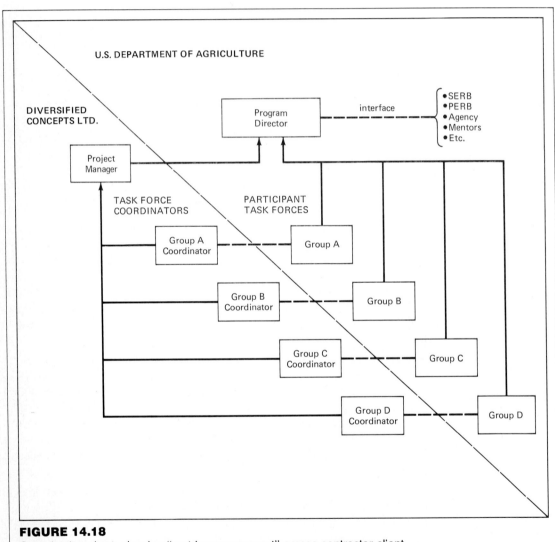

FIGURE 14.18
Organization chart, showing "matrix management" across contractor-client organization lines. (Used with permission of Diversified Concepts Ltd.)

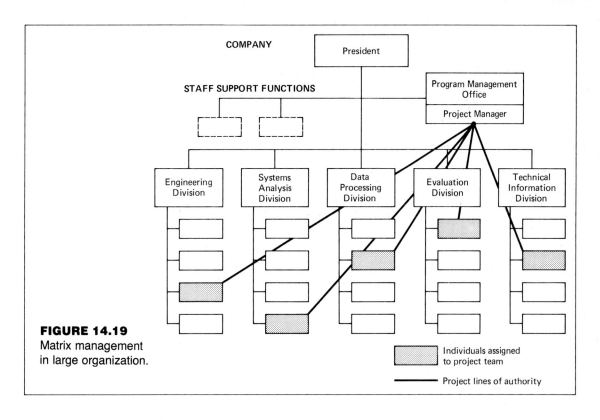

COMPANY

President

STAFF SUPPORT FUNCTIONS

Program Management Office

Project Manager

Engineering Division

Systems Analysis Division

Data Processing Division

Evaluation Division

Technical Information Division

Individuals assigned to project team

Project lines of authority

FIGURE 14.19
Matrix management
in large organization.

ability to develop sophisticated management plans and present them effectively. But they can be double-edged, too: they can be confusing to the reader, and great care is required to explain them (after making them as self-explanatory as possible, of course!).

For some of the problems discussed earlier, when the customer shows special concern about your management capabilities, matrices are a great help in getting your information across compactly, often in a single page. Figures 14.20, 14.21, and 14.22 are examples of such matrices. One is used to enable the reader to take in, almost at a glance, the technical and professional capabilities of the entire staff proposed. Another summarizes the positions proposed and functions to be assigned to the various staff members proposed. And a third one breaks down the various tasks and shows which functional staff people will have specific responsibility for each of the tasks enumerated.

PROJECT CANDIDATE	EDUCATION		CAPABILITIES AND EXPERTISE								
	Highest Degree and Field	College of Highest Degree	Government Budgeting	Audit & Budget Control	Data Processing	Capital Invest. Budget	Accounting	Evaluation	Training in Government Budgeting	Management Systems Development	Organizational Analysis and Development
Dr. S———	PhD, International Economics	Indiana University	X	X	X	X	X	X	X	X	X
R———	MS, Industrial Engineering	Cornell University	X		X	X	X	X	X	X	X
J———	MBA, Business Administration	Harvard University	X	X	X	X	X	X	X		X
L———	BA, Accounting	University of Illinois	X	X	X	X	X	X	X	X	X
Dr. W———	PhD, International Economics	University of California Berkeley	X	X		X	X	X	X		X
D———	MS, Development Economics	Wayne State University	X	X	X	X	X	X	X	X	X
F———	BA, Business Administration	University of Washington	X	X		X	X		X		
Dr. G———	PhD, Education Administration	Syracuse University	X	X	X	X	X	X	X	X	X
Dr. P———	PhD, Psychology	University of North Carolina	X	X	X	X		X		X	X
M———	MBA, Business Administration	Stanford University	X		X	X	X	X	X	X	X
S———	BS, Business Administration	Bangkok Technical Institute		X			X	X			

FIGURE 14.20
Team qualifications and experience summary.

POSITIONS FOR WHICH INDIVIDUALS ARE QUALIFIED AND AVAILABLE

PROJECT CANDIDATE	Project Manager	Budget Specialist	Audit Advisor	Evaluation Coordinator	Training Specialist
Dr. S_____	X		X		
R_____				X	
J_____		X			
L_____			X		
Dr. W_____	X				X
D_____		X		X	
F_____			X		
Dr. G_____	X				X
Dr. P_____				X	X
M_____		X	X		
S_____					X

FIGURE 14.21
Candidate and position options.

TASKS AND SUBTASKS	RESPONSIBILITIES			
	Project Manager	Senior Consultant	Research Analyst	Tech. Writer
TASK 1: DEVELOP PROJECT MANAGEMENT SYSTEM (PMS)				
1.1 Interview director and key staff	△	▲		
1.2 Review agency documentation		△	▲	
1.3 Develop overall system design (draft)	O	△		▲
1.4 Review draft design with FS staff	△	▲		
1.5 Develop individual system components	O	△	▲	
1.6 Write system procedures manual (draft)		O	▲	▲
1.7 Submit products for FS staff review	△			
1.8 Synthesize FS staff comments, refine as needed	O	△		▲
1.9 Submit final design and manual	O	△		
TASK 2: APPLY PMS CONCEPTS TO 4 PRIORITY PROJECTS				
2.1 Select 4 projects for analysis	△			
2.2 Review project documentation	O	△	▲	
2.3 Develop draft plans for 4 projects		O	△	▲
2.4 Submit draft plans for FS staff review	△			
2.5 Synthesize comments, refine as needed		O	▲	△
2.6 Submit final project plans	△			
TASK 3: TRAINING PROGRAM				
3.1 Develop training materials	O	△	▲	▲
3.2 Schedule training		△		
3.3 Deliver 5-day formal training		△	▲	
3.4 Write and submit final report	O	△	▲	▲

FIGURE 14.22
Task and responsibility matrix.

Responsibility code:

△ = Primary responsibility for doing work
▲ = Support responsibility for doing work
O = Direct supervision of work

Selling with Captions and Titles

Headlines and figure captions are intended to guide the reader in following presentations and main points presented. The headline announcing your first proposal section, for example, is often "Introduction," and the opening discussion used to introduce yourself is headlined by many proposal writers as "General." Perhaps these headlines help the reader grasp the fact that this is the beginning of the presentation, and only rather general, introductory information will be presented here. At the same time, such headlines say essentially nothing.

Similarly, the caption for a proposed organization chart is likely to say just that: "Proposed Organization" or something equally obvious. Again, it offers little information to the reader.

Each headline and each figure caption offers the proposer an opportunity to do some selling—make an important point, and make it somewhat more dramatically than is possible with body copy alone. That first section, for example, might be titled, "An Insight into the Need," to give the reader a *reason* to be interested in reading that section, in the hope that that a fresh and perhaps important viewpoint is to be made available. But if only to avoid the trite, worn-out clichés "Introduction" and "General," a new and fresh section or chapter title helps command attention. Use titles and sideheads to do more than tell the reader what you are about to discuss or present. Use them to give the reader a reason to read. Use them to dramatize important points. Use them to highlight advantages of your offer. Use them to reinforce messages of importance. Use them to *sell*.

To illustrate this further and, possibly, to stimulate your own thinking, here are some typical headlines and captions you might encounter, and along with them are some suggested other versions.

Typical Caption or Headline	Alternative
Chart of Proposed Organization	A Dedicated Team, Organized for Results
General Background	Profile of Offeror and Qualifications
Weight Considerations	Design to Meet Weight Requirements
Cost Considerations	A New Way to Cut Costs
Milestone Chart	Milestone Objectives That Will Be Met
Proposed Staff	A Staff Selected for Qualifications
Company Resources	The Proposer Has the Resources to Do the Job
Understanding of the Problem	Hazards to Be Expected and Overcome
Functional Flow chart	A Bird's Eye View of the Project
Contractor Qualifications	What It Takes to Do the Job

When and How to Develop Headlines and Captions

The process of developing the headlines and captions should begin when the project begins: with initial analysis and planning of the proposal. Any topic or illustration that merits its own headline, subhead, or caption should have been surfaced and considered during the planning stages, and should have found its way into the proposal outline. Headline and caption planning should begin at this point, with the full intention of devoting some portion of text to each. In the actual planning process, the outline should be made the subject of a brainstorming session, with all proposal writers assembled to discuss the proposal and suggest ideas for the various headlines and captions.

Headlining As a Planning Tool

In its net effect, this session is actually a planning tool in itself. The session revolves around the proposal outline, at the onset. Hence, it does not take place until an at least first-draft or tentative outline has been prepared. At this point, "working titles" have probably been assigned as temporary headlines and captions, drawn from the outline. The objective of the session is not merely to decide on what headline or caption wording will be most effective, but to actually select a set of selling points to implement the general (capture) strategy formulated earlier—that is, to present the customer with a set of reasons for buying your offer.

Such a session is necessarily a hard-headed, practical approach to the selling problem. The leader must require the group to address the main issues, to suggest wording for the headlines and captions that will, indeed, provide the reader those reasons for accepting the proposal. In fact, the leader must play devil's advocate, probing each suggestion and playing the customer's role by asking "Why? What's in it for me?"

One reason it is important to do this as early as possible—certainly not later than following a rough, first-draft proposal and even earlier, if at all possible—is that selection of the headlines and captions dictates the focus of the portion of text headlined or the illustration captioned. The headline or caption spells out the main selling point or main argument presented. The text that is headlined or illustration that is captioned should then be focused on presenting that point or presenting that argument effectively. If a rough draft has been developed prior to this session, the draft must be reviewed in light of the selling points agreed upon (and represented by the headlines) and rewritten, if necessary, to focus on the points made.

This in itself helps greatly to bring focus, theme, and consistency or uniformity to the final proposal draft. It also serves as a reference against which to evaluate how effectively the strategy has been employed. A final review of the proposal is greatly facilitated.

A Few Basic Ideas for Presentation Strategies

The surrounding circumstances of custom projects—and proposals are almost invariably written to propose custom projects—are almost infinitely variable in their differences. Therefore, it is inevitable that presentation strategies must be developed individually for each individual case. In the chapters preceding this one you've read of several presentation strategies that have worked well. Some of them will fit a great many cases; others were suitable for only one, unique application. Actually, that's fortunate, for if everyone used the same tactics and techniques for presentations, they would no longer be strategies at all, and would lose their effectiveness, as far as outshining your competitors is concerned. But here are a few basic ideas which may be used in almost all cases.

General Format Strategies

"Format" is another of those words which has been used and misused so much that it has lost its original meaning, which was to identify the special characteristics in which a given book or series of books was physically designed and organized. People now talk about the format of a meeting, or the format of almost anything susceptible to having an original or distinctive design. In the sense we use it here it refers to the manner in which the copy of your proposal is arranged and organized.

We have talked, in this chapter, about a variety of methods available to you to get attention, dramatize your points, highlight messages, sharpen communication, add to impact, and press home sales arguments. The judicious design of formats can also accomplish many of these things. Here is one format (Exhibit A) which has been used successfully and is, in fact, almost a standard format in at least one highly successful contracting firm:

Management Systems Plan

What———Corporation proposes to do for the Forest Service: apply advanced Systems Engineering and Systems Management to the development of training programs.

The———Corporation has studied the expressed needs of the Forest Service for a series of engineer-training programs. We have noted the several fields of specialization—construction, photogrammetry, cartography, and others—but we have studied the requirement from the viewpoint of the overall mission of the Forest Service and the entire forestry system. It is our belief that rather than develop a series of engineer-training programs to cover these many areas, we would better serve the needs of the Forest Service by . . .

EXHIBIT A

In Exhibit A each major topic is introduced by a headline, which is followed by a "blurb"—a phrase or two following, presenting the main point (usually the *selling* point) of what is to follow immediately. Note that this example, taken from a successful proposal to the U.S. Forest Service, does include a blurb that addresses the customer's interests directly: what the proposer proposes to *do for* the customer.

In using this format, each major topic—that is, each major point the proposer wishes to make—is expressed or telegraphed in a centered headline, followed by the brief blurb, which is a sales message, followed by the body copy or full textual explanation and argument. It's virtually a print advertisement!

To further exploit this idea, each major point, with its centered headline, begins on a new right-hand page. This whole idea gives the points greater impact and all but forces the reader to take note of each major point. Further, the blurb following the headline telegraphs what the body copy is all about because it focuses directly on the promised benefit. Thus, a reader could skim through the proposal, reading only the major headlines and the blurbs, and get an appreciation or abstract of the entire proposal in a few minutes.

If the proposal is typeset, rather than typed, the headlines are set in some large, bold type, and the blurb is set in smaller type, but in boldface or italics to separate it from the body copy and guide the reader's eyes to it.

This approach has proved to be quite effective and has been used, sometimes with slight variations, to win some large contracts.

Exhibit B varies this idea, using a device known as a "gloss," once quite

---

Management Systems Plan

The————Corporation proposes to conduct a complete systems analysis of Forest Service engineer training needs.

The————Corporation has studied the expressed needs of the Forest Service for a series of engineer-training programs. We have noted the several fields of specialization—construction, photogrammetry, cartography, and others—but we have studied the requirement from the viewpoint of the overall mission of the Forest Service and the entire forestry system. It is our belief that rather than develop a series of engineer-training programs to cover these many areas, we would better serve the needs of the Forest Service by performing a complete systems analysis and designing a complete system of training programs for Forest Service engineers.

The————Corporation has performed a trial-run systems analysis already, showing that many training needs are redundant.

In preparing this proposal, we have already conducted a brief systems analysis, to test our theory that this is in the best interests of the Forest Service and the needs described in the RFP. The results of this admittedly abbreviated effort are shown in Table 2-2. They show clearly that the training needs of many Forest Service engineers overlap those of other Forest Service engineers. To produce an unrelated series of training programs, then, would be to introduce many redundancies both in the training-development effort and in the administration and conduct of the actual courses. The proposed systems analysis would eliminate these redundancies and result in a far more efficient and less costly system of training, without a doubt, as the table shows clearly.

A full systems analysis would bring about many economies.

EXHIBIT B

common in technical books and textbooks. The physical format is a bit different from the example just shown, but the general idea is the same in that the gloss, appearing in the margin rather than under the headline, serves the same purpose as the blurb. With the gloss, however, you need not restrict yourself to one message per headline, but may write a gloss every paragraph or two. In Exhibit B the same copy appears, using glosses instead of a blurb.

Here again, the glosses constitute sales messages and would enable a reader to glance swiftly through a proposal and pick up the general approach and plan proposed. And again, for maximum impact you can start each new topic or major point on a new right-hand page.

Several variations of this basic idea are possible, of course. One might be to put all running text on right-hand pages only, with abstracts on left-hand pages. Or you might increase the visual impact by boxing the blurb as shown in Exhibit C:

Management Systems Plan

> What———Corporation proposes to do for the Forest Service: apply advanced Systems Engineering and Systems Management to the development of training programs.

The———Corporation has studied the expressed needs of the Forest Service for a series of engineer-training programs. We have noted the several fields of specialization—construction, photogrammetry, cartography, and others—but we have studied the requirement from the viewpoint of the overall . . .

EXHIBIT C

This device directs the reader's eye to the blurb, of course, further dramatizing the message and indicating to the reader that you believe it to be an important enough message to especially draw it to attention.

Some organizations use special paper for their proposals, paper which has a running head or foot (that is, a line of copy appearing at the head or foot of each page) with the name of the company or some general slogan, or even the company logo. This also serves a more subtle purpose: If the company is a well-known one—an IBM, GE, or RCA, for example—the name or logo is a constant reminder to the reader that a large, prominent corporation is the proposer. This has a salutary effect on *some* customers, but not on all. It would probably be more useful to have some slogan which reflects the theme or general strategy of the proposal. In the case we have been discussing here, a suitable running head or foot might be something such as "Efficiency Through a Systems Approach" or "A Systems Design for Greater Economy," if that is the general theme of the proposal. Or one could combine two ideas by using a running head of something such as "———Corporation Offers Greater Economy Through a Systems Design."

Another Way to Exploit the Graphics Method

One use of graphics that we have not touched on, but which occurs widely and quite successfully, is the "6-foot diagram." This is the use of a functional flowchart which encompasses the entire project, no matter how large and complex, in a single drawing which often does run, literally, to 6 feet in length! And if the idea is a bit breathtaking to you in contemplating it, consider the impact such a drawing has on the customer.

This is another method which has enjoyed wide success in that it does at least two things for you:

1. It does demand attention when the customer unfolds a large drawing that presents the entire project in all its ramifications. It's rather difficult to overlook the proposer who has done this.
2. It leaves little question—if your diagram is accurate and complete—about your understanding and your ability to plan a large and complex project. It's an excellent indication that the proposer knows what he or she is about and has done all the homework necessary in preparing the proposal.

In addition to these two effects, such a chart or flow diagram quite often gives the customer far better insights into the requirement and the project than the RFP and work statement conveyed. Remember that the customer often does not have a really clear understanding of the project; the proposer who studies the requirement carefully and develops a complete, detailed functional flowchart often develops a far better understanding of the project than the customer ever had. In such case, your proposal and diagram has already performed a great service to the customer and likely has greatly impressed the customer with regard to your capabilities. In our own experience, we have found such diagrams to be most helpful in selling the proposal.

As an additional twist—one which heightens the effect of the diagram—we have often mounted a copy of that endless diagram on art board, hinging it in one or two places so that it can be transported and handled, and delivered it with the proposal. The customer may then set the diagram up or mount it on a wall while studying your proposal and discussing your approach with others.

The one factor which makes some proposers reluctant to prepare such a diagram is the presumed cost of duplicating it. Obviously it cannot be reproduced on ordinary office copiers except by sections, with the resulting laborious and usually unsatisfactory expedient of piecing together several copies of it. And to have a printer produce ten or twenty copies is rather costly because it has to be done on a large press. But there is a simple and inexpensive way to make copies rapidly. There are few localities today which do not boast a blueprint shop in the area, and these shops utilize machines which make copies on special paper by an ammonia process or other chemical means. The machines they use for this must have a transparent or at least translucent original, so it is wise to draw your original on translucent drafting paper or on mylar plastic. However, a great many of these shops have a large copy camera and can make a transparent film positive from your original, even if it is drawn on opaque paper or is a paste-up of smaller sections. You need only check with your nearest blueprint shop ahead of time to determine what their needs are to serve you in this.

One word of caution: Use these ideas about presentation and presentation strategies properly—*for what they are worth*. That is, do not expect any of these devices to win a contract because they are clever, dramatic, or impressive. They do help, of course, or they would not be recommended to you, but they help you make your points dramatically, they help you achieve credibility, and they help you get attention. That is, they can help you in selling a *good plan* and a *good* proposal. They will not help you at all if you do not have a good proposal—an attractive offer, soundly based on a good strategy. That is the first requirement.

Some Main Points to Remember

1. You should not go to extremes in dressing up your proposal—no ribbons and bows—but it should be professional in appearance—neat, orderly, clean, reflecting pride in your work. Neatness counts, but content is more important.
2. Use graphics freely, but be sure that you use them wisely: Use graphic representations to communicate more effectively, to dramatize important points, to strengthen your arguments. Use graphics always with a specific purpose, never because you think it's time for an illustration.
3. There is a wide variety of graphics you can use, many of them not especially difficult to develop. Each has its own advantages and disadvantages. Think carefully about *why* you are using an illustration at all and what you are trying to accomplish with it when you decide what type to use.
4. Don't use your illustrator as a mere technician. Many illustrators can be helpful in suggesting graphic ideas. Use your illustrator as a consultant, to help you conceive the best graphic presentations.
5. Become familiar with at least some of the basic types of graphics—bar charts, pie charts, milestone charts, logic trees, functional flowcharts, matrices, pictorials, and networks.
6. Don't use illustrations to support text. Quite the reverse, use illustrations to convey information, and use whatever text is necessary to support the illustration—but not to *explain* the illustration. If you have to explain the illustration, it is probably a poorly conceived illustration. Good illustrations require little explanation.
7. Beware of illustrations which are too complex or too "busy" to get the main message across swiftly. Perhaps you are trying to do too much or show too much in a single illustration. An illustration that confuses or frustrates the reader may do you (your proposal) more harm than good.

8. Use your captions and titles wisely, for their selling impact. Make every headline and figure title or caption do some selling for you. Make them highlight the importance of what the paragraph explains or the illustration shows.

9. Formats—the typography and physical layout of the pages—can be used effectively with a little imagination. Again, the main idea is to highlight, dramatize, point to the important sales messages—what your proposal will *do for the customer,* the benefits your plan will bring.

10. Do not expect presentation strategies and techniques to do the whole job, to substitute for a good plan. Develop a good plan, then use presentation strategies to help sell it.

15

Unsolicited Proposals

For some companies the unsolicited proposal is a shortcut to a contract, without competition. But it's not as easy as some people think it is.

What Is an Unsolicited Proposal?

Those not too familiar with the proposal process and with government procurement in general ask many questions about unsolicited proposals. The possibility of winning government contracts by offering unsolicited proposals is obviously an attractive one. And if one reads the A and H sections of the *Commerce Business Daily*, one can find frequent notices of sole-source procurements issued to contractors as a result of unsolicited proposals.

Here, for example, is the wording of such a notice, published in the *Commerce Business Daily* on April 11, 1980:

> *A—ECONOMIC EVALUATION OF MUNITION WASTEWATER TREATMENT. Negotiations will be conducted with V. J. Ciccone and Associates, Inc., Woodbridge, VA, pursuant to their unsolicited proposal.

This was issued by the U.S. Army Mobility Equipment Research and Development Command, Fort Belvoir, Virginia. How did it come about? Was the contractor simply struck one day by a good idea and then began sending it out to every agency that might be interested? Or did the contractor have some special reason for believing that the Fort Belvoir MERDC (Mobility Equipment Research and Development Command) would have a special interest in this idea?

Novices in government procurement like to believe—naively—that one need merely come up with a good idea and then find a customer among the myriad federal agencies. Would that it were so! The facts are somewhat different.

In theory, anyone having a good idea may seek any federal agency likely to be interested and submit an unsolicited proposal. Since the proposal is unsolicited, developed and submitted solely at the initiative of the proposer and presenting an original, possibly unique, idea, the idea is assumed to be a proprietary one. Therefore, if the agency is in fact interested and wishes to accept the proposer's offer, the resulting procurement is noncompetitive. The agency does not have the moral or legal right to invite others to bid competitively to use the idea submitted in an unsolicited proposal. To safeguard the government's interest—to prevent the proposer from having a license to steal as a result of being awarded a contract without competition—the contract is negotiated. The negotiation serves as a substitute for competition, to keep the price within some reasonable range.

In theory, the proposer and the contracting official, supported by the technical or program staff, meet, negotiate, and come to mutually acceptable terms, with the government having the right to reject the proposal if suitable contract terms are not reached.

All this is theory. The practice is somewhat different.

What Is an Unsolicited Proposal—*Really?*

It is unlikely that there has ever been a case such as that just described—that is, where a proposer with a good idea has simply submitted it on an entirely unsolicited basis to one or more potential buyers and found a customer. It is all but impossible to win government contracts that way—without personal calls, discussions, and other advance preparation for an unsolicited proposal. This does not change the nature of the proposal; it is still, legally and morally, an unsolicited proposal offering an original idea. But the proposer does not go to the expense and trouble of preparing a proposal without some firm indications that it will be favorably received, seriously studied, and probably accepted.

It is more likely that this is the scenario:

1. The proposer knows the way around the agency—probably has already done some work there, is thoroughly familiar with the agency and its missions, along with all the problems.
2. In the course of this prior work, either the proposer becomes very familiar with a specific problem in the agency, does some study of it and develops an idea for a solution, or someone in the agency suggests that a certain problem exists and that the agency would regard favorably a contract to solve the problem. Whereupon the proposer either studies the problem and develops a potential solution or decides that a prior experience or something on the shelf in the office will be appropriate.
3. The proposer therefore does some checking around with the right people in the agency to verify that (1) there are funds available for such a project or service and (2) the agency would welcome an unsolicited proposal.
4. The proposer enters into some extended discussion before preparing the proposal, to ascertain just what the agency will be likely to accept. The proposer may even produce a "white paper" or rough draft of some sort and submit it, off the record, for informal review prior to preparation of a formal proposal.

All of this is perfectly legitimate and perfectly good marketing practice. However, even this is not without its problems. The problems stem from the fact that to make a procurement in the normal manner—by issuing an RFP and work statement, reviewing proposals, selecting one, and making an award—is both time-consuming and laborious. It's a great deal of work and takes a number of months—rarely fewer than six months, and often a year or longer, from the time the requirement is recognized until the time a contractor is at work. For many government executives this becomes onerous, a burden to be shouldered in addition to the normal workload and an impediment to the speedy carrying out of their missions. Ergo, government executives are pleased to find—or make—shortcuts which relieve them of much of that burden and speed up the procurement process. An award made without competition—a sole-source award of any kind, that is—can be completed in a few weeks and without writing work statements and much other documentation. Therefore, some government agencies may succumb to the temptation to make some awards in this manner: utilizing unsolicited proposals and other justifications for noncompetitive awards; that is, arranging with a contractor known to them to offer an unsolicited proposal which is not truly unsolicited. It has been solicited from a single source, based on an off-the-record, oral work statement. This is illegal, no matter how worthy the motives of the agency or how great the needs which caused the agency to adopt the subterfuge.

There is no way to know how often this is done, compared with awards made for truly unsolicited proposals. There is no doubt, however, that it is sometimes the case. And because of that, many contracting officials are properly suspicious of any proposal that purports to be unsolicited. In many cases, the burden of proof that the proposal is unsolicited is on the offeror.

Proving That the Proposal Is Unsolicited

Proving that a given proposal is truly unsolicited may be difficult. A proposal that offers to provide some methodology or resource which is clearly proprietary with the offeror is sufficient in itself to justify a sole-source award in many cases, and will probably be accepted as prima facie evidence of the proposal's proper standing as unsolicited. However, it is an excellent idea to bring the contracting official "aboard" at some early date in the process, perhaps by including the official in distribution of any "white papers" or "position papers" and other correspondence originated in connection with the unsolicited proposal. Certainly, a complete file should be maintained against the possibility that a skeptical contracting officer will demand proof about the origins of the proposal.

Pros and Cons of Unsolicited Proposals

The obvious advantages of using unsolicited proposals to win contracts are that there is no competition for the award, and the award is all but certain before you undertake to write the actual proposal. It is also usually easier to negotiate a fair price with an assured profit when there is no competition. But there are also disadvantages: It may take a great deal of marketing effort to line up a good opportunity for an unsolicited proposal, and it is most difficult to win such an opportunity in an agency where you are not known and don't know anyone in authority. Still, there are many small companies that get most of their government business in this manner, and there are many large companies that win a significant portion of their business by this route.

The Proposal Itself

Physically and functionally, an unsolicited proposal is not materially different from one submitted competitively. The chief differences are these:

1. You need not worry about getting attention or standing out from the crowd because there are no others.
2. You need not worry about what competitors are likely to offer because there are no competitors.
3. You need not worry too much about cosmetic appearances, but need merely prepare and submit a clean, legible proposal.
4. You need not make that strenuous front-end effort to analyze the customer's problems, intentions, and worry items. You have already been over all of that with the customer, and you know what you are going to offer and why the customer needs it.

However, this is not a license to write a careless or pro forma proposal. Far from it, you must still prepare a careful presentation, providing all the reasons why the customer needs and will benefit from your offer. In most cases the executive who has agreed to regard your proposal with some favor must, at the least, get the concurrence of others, perhaps a superior. And the executive is keenly aware that the files must contain a proposal that *justifies* the contract award, should the GAO (General Accounting Office) or the inspector general of the agency wish to check into the background of the contract at some later date. Therefore, you must still do your very best to prepare a thorough proposal with thorough arguments to persuade the customer. Anything less raises the risk that your proposal may be rejected after all, advance discussions notwithstanding.

Some Main Points to Remember

1. An unsolicited proposal is one for which no announcement or request (solicitation package) has been issued and which originates, presumably, at the proposer's own initiative. Theoretically, at least, it offers an idea which has not occurred to the customer or it offers to supply some proprietary capability.
2. Truly unsolicited proposals—those submitted without talking to the customer first and getting at least an expression of distinct interest and assurance that money is available—are a waste of your time and money. It is essential that you have discussed your ideas with the customer first and gotten agreement—interest in reading your proposal.
3. The authorization for noncompetitive procurement via unsolicited proposals

has led to some improper procurement practices, making many contracting officials somewhat suspicious of all proposals professing to be unsolicited. Be sure, before you spend your time and money, that there are no such obstacles in your way.

4. Work closely with your customer in developing and submitting an unsolicited proposal. You can waste a great deal of time and money if you do not heed this.

5. There are many bureaucrats who have little to do, and are happy to talk to you, leading to the false assumption that the customer is interested and has the authority and money to buy from you. Beware. "Qualify" your customer as you would any customer in a commercial situation, before you spend time and money. Find out whether that interested individual has the authority and budget to buy, or has enough influence to get the procurement approved and funded.

16

Concentration

Incubation

Illumination

Some Important Miscellaneous Matters

Some trivia, afterthoughts, and random ideas that appear to have no other proper home than a chapter called "miscellaneous." (And perhaps to repeat and reinforce some especially important points.)

There are many miscellaneous details, some of them bearing directly on the subject of proposal writing, some of them related only indirectly to proposals, but still of interest to anyone who plans and writes proposals. Some of these matters, in fact, have a direct bearing on strategies you may employ. So, despite their designation as "miscellaneous," they are not unimportant, but should be studied with the same care as you have devoted to the earlier chapters.

Protests and Appeals

It is well beyond the scope of this book and the intent (not to mention the qualifications) of the authors to offer legal counsel here. For that, you should consult an attorney who specializes in, or is at least familiar with, federal procurement practices and procurement regulations. However, there are many broad provisions of the regulations which are useful to know when writing a proposal. One of these areas is that of your possible recourses when and if you believe that you have been unfairly treated in connection with a federal procurement.

The most basic step you can take in contesting a procurement action of any kind is that known as a "protest." This is the name applied to an administrative appeal, as distinct from an actual lawsuit. The regulations provide this mechanism as at least the first step in contesting a procurement action.

The agency responsible for handling protests is the General Accounting Office, an agency that reports to Congress and is the watchdog of Congress over the other agencies, most of which are in the executive branch, reporting to the President. The GAO, as it is more familiarly known, is staffed with a number of lawyers who devote their full time to processing protests. There are enough such complaints filed to make the job a full-time one for a large number of GAO employees.

To file a protest with GAO, you need merely write a letter to the Comptroller General, who is the head of GAO. In the letter you simply set forth the particulars of your complaint or protest. You may utilize the services of an attorney at this point, but it is not required; there is no specific legal format mandated to file a protest.

It is not even necessary to file your protest with GAO. You may make your protest to the contracting officer of the agency in question. The procedure following a protest to the contracting officer is slightly different from that following a protest lodged with GAO, but the net effect is not much different. In either case the contracting officer will respond either directly to you or through GAO, and you will have the opportunity to respond to that response. In some cases there may be several such cycles before a decision is rendered.

Moreover, if you have made your protest to the contracting officer and are unsatisfied with the outcome, you are still privileged to take the matter up with GAO. Tactically this may offer some advantages.

It's a fact of life that few protests result in a reversal of an award decision, although it has been known to happen. One reason for this is that it is so easy to make a protest that many totally unjustified protests are filed, and the agency in question can justify its action and decisions readily.

You do not have to wait for an award to be made to lodge your protest. You may protest *any* procurement action, if you see fit to do so. Recently, a client of one of the authors received an RFP with an impracticably short response time specified. This led him to suspect the agency had "wired" the contract for some favored contractor by making it virtually impossible for anyone else to respond and write a proposal. When he called the contracting official to complain informally, he was advised that the RFP had not been synopsized (not published in the *Commerce Business Daily*); therefore, an extension of time was legally impossible! Not fathoming either the logic or the legal basis for such a declaration, the client filed a protest, calling the RFP "defective," a term signifying that the document is not in conformance with procurement regulations, either in letter or intent. The result? The response time was formally extended by issuing a revised RFP.

You may contest any procurement action or document you believe to be defective in any way. If verbal explanations do not satisfy you, you may compel an official position to be taken and decision issued by making a written protest.

Considering Protest Possibilities in Writing Proposals

The lawyer who suspects that a trial may go against a client is likely to be alert for any trial incident that will constitute grounds for appeal, and even to attempt to provoke such an incident. In some cases a parallel strategy may be employed in a proposal. Where the RFP or SOW is believed to be flawed— legally defective—in any way, and it does not appear to be desirable strategy to protest at once, seeds may be planted in the proposal for a later protest, after the award decision has been made. In one such case, where the proposer was almost certain that he could not come close to the price of a competitor, he found the procurement documents had idealized the qualifications of the contractor. That is, the evaluation criteria and other statements made in the RFP called for such qualifications on the part of the contractor that it was certain that only this proposer could meet them fully. The proposer was sure that the competitor who would win with a low bid could not measure up to these ideal qualifications. The proposer therefore went on to write a proposal for a contract he was rather sure he would not be awarded. But in writing his proposal, he went to lengths to stress his match with the idealized qualifications and evaluation criteria, fully anticipating the lodging of a protest. As it turned out, he was entirely right: The competitor who did not actually meet what the RFP specified as required qualifications but whose price was low enough won the award, and the proposer referred to here filed his protest. The result? The customer admitted that the protester was technically justified in his protest, but the agency simply did not have the budget to utilize his services. Presumably, had he persisted in his protest, the end result would have been to force the cancellation of the procurement, whereupon the agency would have reissued the RFP, amended to overcome its earlier defects. But that would have meant a lengthy delay. To settle the matter, the agency awarded the protester a smaller contract, and the protester, satisfied, withdrew his protest.

Should you lose your protest, but still feel that you have been victimized by improper procurement actions or defective documents, you still have the right to bring formal legal action—to sue in federal court. At this point, of course, a suitably qualified lawyer is a necessity.

A Common Myth about Protests

Many small contractors are fearful of lodging protests, believing that the action will land them on some kind of blacklist, barring them from ever winning contracts. That this is sheer nonsense has been demonstrated again and again. Still the fear persists. The truth is that a protest is an entirely businesslike procedure, raising no more hackles on the part of federal executives than do demands for formerly "privileged" information, under the Freedom of Information Act. In fact, having lodged a protest, you are likely to command a great deal of respect from the agency in future contacts and be treated with the greatest of consideration. Protesting is far more likely to be helpful rather than harmful to you in future contract pursuits, whether or not you win your point in the specific protest action. Many of those who protest, do so routinely as a matter of course, not expecting to win anything as a direct result of the protest, but knowing that it is likely to pave the way for future proposals to that agency!

Freedom of Information

Although there have been some complaints about the Freedom of Information Act interfering with the work of certain agencies, such as the FBI, by and large FOI has been implemented rather smoothly, and has been a boon to alert contractors.

Under FOI you have the right to ask for a copy of any current or past contract, which will usually include the technical proposal and the bottom-line costs to the government. (The agency will probably delete the cost analysis, as being largely proprietary.) If there are portions of the proposal which the proposer has declared to be proprietary or confidential, these will be deleted from the copy you are given.

In many cases the agencies are somewhat reluctant to part with the information, or perhaps they simply do not like being put to the trouble of getting it for you. Going strictly by the letter of the law, they can respond to your simple and direct request with a flat "no" or by simply ignoring it for a long time. However, they cannot ignore or refuse your request if you specifically invoke the Freedom of Information Act. That is, cite the Act specifically by stating in your request that you request the information under authority of the Freedom of Information Act. They cannot then refuse your request, unless the information is classified or otherwise legally exempted from FOI.

Occasionally you may encounter a junior-level government employee who is not fully aware of what you are legally entitled to demand under FOI. In such case, stand your ground and insist on seeing someone in higher authority. This invariably does the trick and results in your getting the information you have requested.

Should You Ask Questions?

Almost invariably, reading an RFP results in questions occurring to you. Few RFPs are as complete or as specific as they ought to be. Unfortunately, asking for clarifications is almost certain to bring about a modification to the RFP, which will be sent to everyone who has asked for and received a copy of the RFP. You may very well be doing more for your competitors' benefit than for your own! It is therefore wise to avoid asking questions directly, as much as possible; there are other ways:

1. There are firms in Washington—consultants of one type or another—who can often get you the information you want without revealing that the request is connected with the RFP, hence avoiding the modification going out. (This works if the agency is in Washington, unless you are willing to have the consultant incur the travel expense in your behalf.)
2. Searching in the agency's own library may produce materials that provide the answers you want, without alerting the people connected with the procurement. Librarians are very helpful people.
3. You can often handle the problem by offering options in your proposal, sometimes even gaining a great strategic advantage by so doing.
4. If you are reasonably sure that there will be a "best and final" stage in the procurement, you can wait until then to ask your questions, and handle the

problem in the supplemental submittal you are invariably invited to make, following a best and final negotiation.

5. If you happen to know your way around the agency, in many cases you can approach the problem obliquely.

There is one exception to this rule about asking questions: If you attend a preproposal conference, you will almost surely find a number of attendees who have virtually no qualifications for the project and are not really familiar with the field of interest at all. This is especially true when business generally is slow and firms are seeking new business almost desperately. You can easily tell when this is the case by the "dumb questions" being asked by such attendees, questions which make it obvious that the questioner is totally unfamiliar with the work or the environment. There are also present at such conferences a firm or two that are marginally qualified: they're not totally unfamiliar with the work nor totally unqualified, but neither are they well-qualified.

Despite these problems, such firms occasionally win a contract over better-qualified competitors, either because they have hired an expert to write a competent proposal for them or because in their ignorance they have bid the job too low and won the contracting officer's heart!

In such situations it is occasionally wise to ask questions to which you know the answers, but these kinds of competitors probably do not. The answers will either alert them to the true magnitude of the job and what it must cost or will scare them out of the competition entirely.

Two-Step Procurement

There is a species of procurement known as two-step, usually considered to be an IFB—Information for Bid and Award—which is the solicitation form utilized for advertised procurement, in which the award goes to the low bidder. Being a two-step procurement, however, the process involves the preparation of a technical proposal as step one, with cost proposals being step two.

As the first step, the proposer writes a conventional technical proposal, following all the procedures for any proposal. The objective here is to qualify for the second step: only those whose proposals are deemed to be technically acceptable are invited to participate in step two. Therefore, the strategy for the technical proposal is not to sell the proposal per se, because you can't do that, but strictly to qualify for step two. In short, step one is a prequalification exercise to overcome the hazard of being compelled to accept a low bid from someone who is not technically qualified to do the job properly, a common problem in advertised procurements.

Step two is, then, simply a price quotation for the project you proposed in the first step, and the award will go to the lowest bidder.

Advance or Draft RFPs

In some cases, particularly when a long-range, major procurement is anticipated, an RFP will be issued in draft form many months, even a year or more, before proposals are wanted. The draft RFP does not solicit proposals. It is issued to give prospective proposers ample advance notice for their preparatory research. Some time later, the final RFP is issued, usually with at least some changes. Now proposals are solicited.

This is fairly rare, but it does take place.

"Research and Development Sources Sought"

Near the back page of the *Commerce Business Daily* is a column which appears quite often, entitled "Research and Development Sources Sought." In this column are listed descriptions of future projects for which proposals will be sought later. The purpose of the notice is to prepare a list of qualified proposers, and the notice invites all interested parties to submit a "capabilities statement." If the capabilities statement is acceptable to the customer, the respondent will be placed on a list of those who will be invited to propose when the RFP seeking a contractor is issued later.

Your standard company brochures are rarely satisfactory to use for this purpose. For one thing, they are usually too general. For another, the customer is seeking a specific, tailored response.

At the same time, it is usually not very difficult to prepare a capabilities statement that will qualify you and get you on the list to receive the RFP. Read the notice carefully and prepare a special statement that does respond specifically to the notice. List your company's experience, past contracts relevant to the anticipated need, a few key résumés, and your physical facilities and resources, if they are relevant.

The column in the April 10, 1980 issue, for example, has three such notices. The first is from the Jet Propulsion Laboratory in Pasadena, announcing that it will seek a contractor to make a manufacturing cost analysis of a parabolic dish concentrator, and providing some additional details. The second is from the Naval Research Laboratory in Washington, D.C., which will later seek a contractor to develop, design, and test gallium arsenide field effect transistor amplifiers to operate at 18 GHz and above. And the third is from the Air Force Office of Scientific Research, at Bolling Field in Washington, which will want a contractor to serve as an Air Force Manufacturing Studies Board to perform case studies of defense production industries as explained in a little more detail in the announcement.

These requirements tend to be rather technical, although not necessarily in "high technology." They may and do range over a rather wide variety of needs and fields of interest.

Safeguarding Your Own Proprietary Data

One hazard of unsolicited proposals is the possibility that the agency to which you submit your original, proprietary idea may reject your unsolicited proposal, but take your basic idea and make it the subject of an RFP, inviting everyone to bid on the basis of your idea.

Even in the case of solicited proposals, submitted in response to an RFP, there is the potential hazard that while your proposal is rejected, the customer may pass on your idea or your approach to the successful proposer as a directed line of attack on the project.

And even if neither of these eventualities come to pass, there is always the possibility that someone else may request a copy of your proposal or a contract which embodies your successful proposal, and thereby gain access to information you consider to be proprietary or otherwise confidential.

The proper safeguard against these hazards is to make it known that certain data in your proposal is proprietary and is not to be released to anyone outside of the group of reviewers and others connected with the contract, while not restricting the government's right to use the information in connection with the procurement should you be awarded the contract or should the government gain the information in some other manner—that is, from some other source. Today, most RFPs include instructions for safeguarding information you consider to be proprietary or otherwise confidential. The instructions include a statement—you are given suggested wording—to be reproduced on the title page of your proposal, along with language or indicators of what else you must do. The precise wording is not that important, as long as your notice complies with certain basic principles, per the following:

1. Place a paragraph on the title page of your proposal, advising the reader that the proposal contains certain data deemed to be proprietary or confidential. In that paragraph, identify the pages on which such confidential and proprietary data occur.
2. Be sure that your notice does not restrict the government from use of or access to that data, in event you are awarded the contract. (Presumably, it was part of your proposal to offer this to the government.) Say this specifically. Say, also, that this restriction does not apply (restriction, that is, against unauthorized disclosure of the data referred to, outside of those who have need to read your proposal) to any information the government has gotten through any other source, even if the other source provides the same

information. That is, you are restricting the government from using you as the source, unless you are awarded the contract!

3. You must specify which data is restricted, or at least which pages or paragraphs are affected by the restriction. This must be in the general paragraph.

4. You must mark the data as restricted or confidential where it appears in the proposal. You may do so by a simple notice on the page, which says: "This page contains proprietary and restricted data."

5. You cannot impose a blanket restriction on the entire proposal, but must specify the proprietary and confidential data. Obviously, not *everything* in your proposal is proprietary information. Read the RFP carefully. It probably includes instructions and a suggested paragraph to place on your title page.

On Creativity

Most really good proposals and certainly all great proposals are written with imagination by creative people. And most creative people don't really know how they got that way. Yet there is no great mystery about the nature of creativity—at least, there have been studies of the subject, which appear to have revealed a great deal about the matter of how some individuals come up with new ideas. But perhaps we ought to qualify that word "new" a bit:

There are some who insist that there is really nothing new (under the sun or elsewhere)! Every "new" idea or development, these people insist, is an adaptation of an older idea or a recombination of things already known. Take TV, for example. In one sense, it represents combining the radios of older times (circa the 1920s) with the oscilloscope, a laboratory instrument in common use since about 1937. (Crude TV was broadcast experimentally about 1910 but was on an entirely different principle and not really related to today's TV.) The U.S. Navy experimented with radar in 1923 but not much happened until about 1941, when Great Britain, under the pressures of standing alone in World War II, began to develop it further. Rocket ships carry intercontinental missiles and have carried men to the Moon, but the Chinese invented rockets many centuries ago. In each case, the new invention was an adaptation to a new need. Creativity, according to this theory, is the art of adapting an old idea to a new need or combining two or more older ideas to produce something "new," represented by the combination; that is, it is the combination that is new.

Whether or not that is always the case—and the argument has merit, for how can the mind conceive something for which it has no referent?—it is certainly the case frequently. And in that case, a good memory is certainly a great help, for it enables you to have a large store of information on which to draw for ideas. It is probably safe to say that creative people usually have unusually good memory circuits.

One thing does appear to be certain about creativity—the creative process, that is—and it is this: the creative inspiration appears to surge forward most frequently from the subconscious mind when the conscious mind is relaxed. The process has been described by a great many people of acknowledged great powers of creativity.

The creative process takes place in three stages: concentration, incubation, and inspiration (some call this "illumination"). First comes the intense concentration of the everyday, garden-variety conscious mind, thinking about a problem and trying to think up one or more solutions. Then, when the conscious mind has tired of the effort, having dredged up a great many "solutions" of doubtful value, comes the incubation stage. In this stage the conscious mind lets go and goes on to more prosaic pursuits. And finally, sooner or later, when the conscious mind is quite relaxed, thinking of nothing more dramatic than boating a fish struggling at the end of a nylon line, comes—suddenly and unexpectedly—the inspiration, the answer. All in a sudden flash of brilliant genius!

The accepted explanation for this is that it is the *sub*conscious or *un*conscious mind that solves problems. The subconscious allegedly never forgets anything, and hypnotists have provided a great deal of evidence to support this belief. Therefore, the subconscious is far better equipped to search its store of remembered ideas and match one up with the problem at hand than is the more fallible and forgetful conscious mind. (So even people with poor memories have a fighting chance to be creative!) The problem is in passing the matter on to the subconscious with orders to work on it, because there appears to be no direct way for the conscious mind to communicate with the subconscious mind.

That's the role of concentration. Evidently, if the conscious mind concentrates hard enough and long enough, it will finally get a message through to the subconscious. The message is this: Here's a problem for you to work on; let me know when you come up with something.

Communication between the two minds appears to be easiest when the conscious mind is relaxed. (That's why the hypnotist relaxes you, so that the way to reach the subconscious is opened.) Thus it is in those relaxed moments that the inspiration comes, your subconscious telling you what it has come up with.

That explains why many people awake in the middle of the night with a bright idea. (It's the subconscious, apparently, that does the dreaming, too.) It also explains why, when you have tried to remember someone's name and can't, a few minutes later, when you are no longer thinking about it, the name suddenly flashes into your mind: Your subconscious has been trying to get through to you, but all your circuits were busy, until you stopped your conscious efforts to remember and relaxed. As soon as your subconscious stopped getting a busy signal, the connection was made and the message transmitted.

One gentleman who makes a business of publishing newsletters and reports for small businesses recounts his early days, when he managed to turn a dollar now and then, by stumbling over a few ideas that had not occurred to anyone else as having a profit potential. (In fact, he admits, it was really his wife who saw the profit potential in the things he came across.) After several such adventures, some of which actually paid him rather handsomely, he began to try to reason out just what it was that he was doing, so that he could continue to do it on purpose, and not by chance. He searched consciously for a long time, for the key, he relates. And then he woke one morning with the hot flash: His business was *selling information!* And from that day on, his fortunes began to improve steadily, as he now knew what to pursue.

Does this mean that you have to go into a trance or visit a swami to get good ideas? Certainly not: Many people have good, "new" ideas consciously, spontaneously, and frequently. Some people are simply gifted with good memories, driving curiosity, and lively imagination. Others are dogged pursuers, who get there just the same. And some have discovered certain "tools" or methods which help them to be creative on schedule. Let's look at a few of these.

Some reference has been made in this book to value engineering, or value analysis, and its methods. Value analysis is a method for being creative. Primarily, it is directed toward simplifying, rather than creating new ideas, by eliminating the unnecessary, and searching out new and better ways to do the same old thing. And that, in turn, is based on the idea of *function*, or what something is supposed to *do*, rather than what it *is*. And the "something" referred to need not necessarily be a machine or device of some sort; it could as easily be a system, a job, or a method. And while value analysis is supposed to be a discipline performed by a team of people, the methods are readily adaptable to the imaginative individual. Anyone who has ever found a simpler way to do a job has practiced value analysis, although without knowing it.

The system depends on asking questions about whatever you're studying:

1. What is it?
2. What does it do?
3. What does it cost?
4. What else would do that?
5. What would *that* cost?

The key questions are 2 through 5, but especially 2—What does it *do?* That is, what is it *supposed* to do? What's the reason for its existence?

Take the office machine known commonly as a "check writer," for example. What does that do? If you say "writes checks," your *form* will be right, for the rules of the discipline are that you must strip all the adjectives and adverbs away and answer in just two words: a verb and a noun. But your answer will be wrong: machines do not write checks; people write checks. And why would you spend $100 or more to buy a machine that does what you can already do very easily?

No, "writes checks" is not the purpose for the machine nor the reason you buy one. You buy such a machine to *protect* checks, to prevent others from altering checks you have written and stealing money from you. The machine perforates the check as it engraves the right numbers, making it difficult indeed to alter that check in any way that would not be easily detectable by the bank teller.

So the right answer is "protects checks," because that answers the question of what it is *supposed* to do. Now, with that correct answer, you know what you are searching for as a lower-cost alternative: something else that will protect checks and will cost less, not something else to write checks.

Value analysis is not the only methodology used to promote creativity. There are other methods, most of which also depend on asking questions and seeking helpful answers. In one system you imagine yourself to be the object and ask yourself the questions, to wit: If I were a diesel engine, what would I feel the greatest need for? Charles Kettering, the famed inventor of the automobile self-starter, the electric cash register, and a number of other useful devices, revolutionized the diesel engine by using just such a method! He was probably responsible for improving it to the point where it began to come into common use, whereas it had previously suffered from too many drawbacks to be popular.

There is also the "what if" method. What if I put the engine in the rear of the car? What would happen? What if I made the ice-making machine small enough to go into people's homes? What if I added a radio control to a powered garage-door opener? What if I reversed the usual procedures?

That latter method, trying the procedures in reverse, is not used nearly often enough. It's quite amazing how often systems are designed backward. It's like driving your car in reverse: It moves, but you don't have full control and you don't get the same power.

"What if I eliminated that step?" is often a good question to get the creative juices flowing. A great many systems and sets of procedures have too many steps, unimportant steps. Quite often, examining a system step-by-step and asking yourself "What does that do?" for each step, will lead you to improved systems. Here's a case in point.

A printing plant did a great deal of government printing, but the poor accountant was getting into deeper and deeper trouble every month, as the Government Printing Office kept returning the monthly bills for one contract, refusing to pay them because the various items were not accurately detailed. That is, the printer was to bill for each item—plates, negatives, collating, staples, padding, cutting, or whatever the job called for. And the shop, turning in its accounting every month, thoroughly confused the poor accountant, who knew nothing about printing and binding. The manager, however, made aware of the situation, found a simple solution: he simply *eliminated* the step of transferring the detailed information from the shop work ticket to the monthly invoice! Instead, he made a copy of the shop ticket and attached it to the invoice, with the invoice listing only the final price and the contract number!

These are the kinds of thinking to apply to proposals. Find better ways, simpler ways to get the job done for the customer. Find simpler ways, also, to present and explain your ideas in your proposals. Find better ways to help the customer note and remember your proposal, too. Here, for example, is a proposal idea you can have free. For some reason, hardly anyone ever uses photographs in a proposal. How about photographs of your staff, along with their résumés? It doesn't make your plan any better, but the customer is almost certain to take note and remember your proposal! You can also use photos when describing your location, facilities, and physical resources. Photographs of your staff engaged in a research project, holding staff meetings, conducting interviews, making tests, or whatever action shots are appropriate.

Here's another idea that has been used with great success in the private sector but apparently has not been picked up by contractors seeking government business. A complimentary newsletter, sent to those with whom you'd like to do business. It's a thinly disguised sales promotion, of course, but you can make it palatable and worth reading by burying the commercial pill in a sugar coating of useful information every month, such as describing your current projects and what information or ideas they uncover every month. It doesn't have to be a fancy, typeset thing: a 4-page, typed letter will do nicely to keep your name in front of those who ought to know your name (for your good). It might produce some spontaneous, noncompetitive business, perhaps even an unsolicited proposal or two, but certainly will help you get more consideration when you bid to these customers under regular RFPs.

The Proposal Library

Several times in these pages you have been sternly counseled against the use of boiler plate. That doesn't mean that you shouldn't have a file of boiler-plate material—merely that you should rarely, if ever, use it without change. Quite the contrary, if you are going to write more than an occasional proposal, having a proposal "library" or set of proposal central files is a must. Here are a few of the items that should be in that set of files:

1. Copies of all your past proposals, both winners and nonwinners, but especially the winners.
2. Master (fully detailed) résumés of your entire staff.
3. Résumés of all available consultants, part-time people available, and potential new hires.

4. Copies of any of your competitors' proposals that you have succeeded in acquiring.
5. Copies of all procurement regulations you have managed to acquire.
6. Any books, reports, pamphlets, memoranda, and other documents dealing with how to write proposals, make bids, or sell to the government.
7. Master (detailed) descriptions of all current and past projects and contracts your organization has to report on.
8. Any agency personnel directories which have come your way.
9. Information about your own company, with organization charts, facilities, other resources, and history.
10. Any government publications bearing on federal procurement, such as GAO reports and agency publications explaining the procurement practices and policies of the agency. (Almost all federal agencies have such publications.)

Depending on what your organization does and what kinds of contracts you usually pursue, you'll also want as complete a library as possible of books, papers, and other information on your own technical or professional field. But don't overlook the need to have the same kinds of items on *related* fields. For example, although you may be in a high-technology field, an RFP may require the proposer to include a safety program or an environmental-control plan. A request for an R&D program may include a training requirement. A research job may require the development of a survey plan. Especially if the task is something corollary and not directly related to your main field of interest, you will need to have some information on the subject readily at hand.

Also useful in your proposal files are descriptive brochures of other organizations that might be good prospects to serve you as subcontractors or even as co-bidders in a joint venture, or as suppliers of some needed materials or services.

Bitter-Experience Department

This is a good chapter in which to pass on a few words of what we hope is wisdom gained from unfortunate experience. One of these areas concerns the fear some contractors have of "leaving money on the table." That is, the fear of settling for less money than the customer was prepared and ready to spend.

Several stories have appeared in the Washington-area press and in national news magazines about a member of Congress who shared a cab with strangers a few months ago and overheard their injudicious conversation. Apparently the two were with a consulting firm and were negotiating or proposing a contract to a Washington federal agency for a consulting job of some sort. They were speculating as to how much the agency would pay, and they agreed that the agency would likely be willing to pay $25,000 for a job which they could do profitably for $15,000. They evidently agreed, then, to charge $25,000 for the job.

The member of Congress was outraged and is today pressing for legislation and holding hearings to investigate such abuses.

What is involved in this fear of leaving money on the table is plain greed. And greed can easily cost you a contract, as in this example.

A firm submitted a proposal to NASA for a long-term project. The RFP explained that it was to be a cost-reimbursement contract, and that NASA had $500,000 budgeted for the project. The firm bid the project for approximately that amount.

In a best and final session, of which the firm was a finalist, NASA invited them to amend their cost proposal, if they chose to. But after lengthy debate the firm decided that their proposal was easily so superior to all others that they need not do anything about their cost estimates.

They lost the contract to a firm that bid $465,000. Ironically, too, they might well have actually billed the entire $500,000, had they won the contract, because it was a cost-reimbursement type of contract. In any case there would have been little risk in reducing their estimate. But greed overcame them and they lost, as they deserved to.

A good principle is this: Don't worry about leaving money on the table. If you believe that you can turn a fair profit at the price you bid, bid at that price. Far better to have a good chance of winning at a fair price than a marginal chance at an exorbitant price. Your competitors are not stupid, and it would be dangerous to assume that they are less competent or less efficient than you. If you can do the job for x dollars, probably your competitors can too.

Another mistake many proposers make out of greed is trying to win contracts they are only partially qualified for—trying to stretch their capabilities and credibility too far. That is, instead of arranging for a joint-venture cobid with another firm that has the qualifications they are weak in (or arranging a subcontract agreement), they try to get the entire contract for themselves and wind up with nothing. Again, better a 75 percent chance of winning one-half the job than a 10 percent chance of winning it all. Here's a case in point.

It had become rather common knowledge in the industry that NASA was unhappy with a certain contractor who operated a NASA facility, billing about $5.5 million a year. Competition for the contract was quite intensive, understandably. But despite big-league competition from some major corporations, the contract was won by a new, small firm. But that firm was actually a joint-venture cobid by two established small firms, neither of which was large enough to be credible for the contract alone, but which were successful when they pooled their resources and capabilities for this project. The contract comes up every 3 years, and at this writing the firms have kept the contract for over 10 years. Their decision to cobid was a wise one.

Cobidding involves a problem: There must be a legal entity to contract with, and the government is not going to write escrow checks nor assign contract responsibilities in escrow. Some legal entity must execute the contract and be the responsible, single contractor. Therefore, for a cobid or joint venture, you must do either of two things: Arrange for one of the parties to be the prime contractor and the other the subcontractor, or create a new legal entity, as a partnership or new corporation.

Forming another legal entity, owned by both companies, is probably a bit "stronger" an appeal than a prime contractor and subcontractor combination, but it involves other problems, of course, including the fact that as a new organization the organization itself has no track record. But even aside from that drawback, the contract would have to be large enough to make such an arrangement worth making; it would not do for smaller or short-term contracts, unless the principals plan to pursue much other business as a new entity. On the other hand, the chief drawback of the prime contractor and subcontractor arrangement is that the prime contractor appears to lack some critical skills or capabilities. Therefore, wisdom must be exercised in determining which firm is to appear as the prime contractor and which as the subcontractor. These are the factors to consider in making that decision:

1. What is the *main* capability required?
2. What are the evaluation criteria?
3. Which firm is in the strongest financial position?
4. Which firm has the bigger "name" (if either does)?
5. Which firm looks better on paper generally?

The consideration here is, of course, that the customer is going to attach more importance to the credentials of the prime contractor than to those of the subcontractor. If, for example, the job calls for delivering a series of training programs, but the contractor must first develop the programs, the firm most attractive as the developer should be the prime contractor. Development is the main capability required, with delivery being a support function. However, all aspects must be considered to try to select as the prime contractor that firm which appears to have the greatest assets and the fewest liabilities as a contender for the contract. At the same time, emphasis should be given to both firms in the proposal, explaining that the *legal* relationship is that of prime contractor and subcontractor, but the *working* relationship will be that of equal partners in a joint venture, with total commitment by both firms.

Psychological Factors in Proposals

A proposal should never *look* cheap and dirty. That is, it must never appear to have been assembled hastily and carelessly, but ought to strive for the opposite effect—that it has been the subject of a great deal of tender loving care and that great effort has gone into thinking out the problems and designing a detailed program. And perhaps the most effective way of conveying that impression is by presenting a wealth of detail, which presumably could not have happened without a great deal of work. But in many cases it does not really require a great deal of work to supply a wide array of minute detail!

To give that detail to a proposal for a Job Corps Center, the successful proposer for the Fort Custer, Michigan, center created an entire lengthy appendix, listing films, slides, books, and other learning aids, while spending relatively little effort to collect this data. A list of 6,000 films and audiovisual programs was purchased from the Government Printing Office for $3. An armload of manufacturers' and publishers' catalogs was obtained by sending out requests. From this mountain of data, the proposer quickly assembled an impressive compilation as an appendix.

Don't Reinvent the Wheel

Contractors who do custom work often forget that a great many things already exist on the shelf which can be bought far more cheaply than new ones can be created. The proposer who bid successfully for the Job Corps Center used the public library to design vocational training programs. The proposer's staff brought back an armload of borrowed how-to books on the pertinent subjects—handyman repairs, auto repairs, and other such subjects. The books were examined and the ones thought most suitable for each vocational program were selected. The remaining books were then returned. Someone was assigned to prepare an outline of the content of each book that was selected. These outlines were soon converted into outlines of training programs, from which were then derived sets of training objectives, and to which were matched some of the learning aids from the compiled lists.

For $12,000 a 3-volume, 1,000-page proposal was developed which, the customer guessed, must have cost $50,000 or more. The customer was duly impressed and expressed the opinion that the fact the company had done so much work to prepare a proposal indicated that it would be a most diligent contractor!

Some proposal writers do their finest writing with scissors and paste!

The Right Mental Set

Some people program themselves to lose, while others program themselves to win. That mental set comes through between the lines of a proposal. No one who does not believe that the proposer is going to win ought to write any part of the proposal. A person who programs to lose will, of course, lose. (It's a self-fulfilling prophecy.) If some member of your proposal team can react only with objections to writing the proposal—negative vibrations and forecasts of doom and hopelessness—you are well advised to excuse that individual from working on the proposal; no good can come of that individual's contribution. He or she will write defensively, almost apologetically, and the customer will sense it. What you want to strive for are positive approaches, confident addresses to the problems, aggressive plans for success. The customer wants to be assured that you are confident in your knowledge of your own plans and program. You must identify and acknowledge the problems you anticipate, of course, but you must then offer solutions, with expressed confidence that the solutions will solve the problems. No one ever won a contract by writing a proposal in the expectation of losing.

Staffing the Proposal Team

Most proposal-writing efforts are team efforts, of course, and most companies do not have permanent proposal departments, but form ad hoc teams for each proposal. This is one of the major problems. For one thing, a group of people working together for the first time is not a team, and there is rarely enough time in developing a proposal for waste motion and getting to know each other. For another thing, not only must the team have leadership, but the leader must know exactly what functions are required to carry out the job. Far too often, because of these problems, the proposal which finally issues is something far less in quality than the organization should be able to produce—the proposal does not, in fact, do the organization justice. Let's put this another way and make it stand alone, so that you can digest and appreciate its full meaning:

> Contracts are awarded to the proposer who has offered the best proposal, not necessarily—and often not—to the proposer who is actually best qualified for the project. That is, proposal-writing skills are often more important in winning contracts than are capabilities to perform on the contract.

To maximize the probability that your organization does turn out a proposal that truly represents your organization and its full capability, it is important that your ad hoc proposal team always be organized so as to include adequate provision for several key functions. These are the functions that are often neglected in assembling a proposal team:

1. *Leadership*—Someone must lead who understands the proposal process with its many problems and needs, especially under the conditions of an improvised effort.

2. *Coordination*—Proposal writing is a dispersed and often multidisciplinary project, with a short fuse and no time to do things over, except at a great sacrifice of quality.
3. *Editing and rewriting*—Some professional editing and writing skills should be made available to the team since the professionals are not necessarily skilled writers and need the help.
4. *Procedures*—At least some general standardized procedures and practices must be followed to avoid wasted time resulting from misunderstandings or people running off in different directions—tools for the coordinator to work with.

This does not mean that you need to have a heavy overburden of people to perform the functions listed; in many cases, a single person can perform all these functions—wear several hats, that is. But the functions must be performed, and unless you are fortunate enough to have an exceptional leader or coordinator, it is essential that you have also these at least, as well as some generalized procedures that everyone understands:

1. Specific clearly understood writing assignments.
2. A detailed outline, with the writing assignments keyed to the outline.
3. A comprehensive schedule listing all milestone dates—for first draft, for reviews, for final draft, for illustrations, and for all production needs.
4. Management alerted to handle the review promptly, without using up valuable time which may well be needed for some final changes after management review.

Someone in your organization—whomever you deem best suited to the job—should be permanently assigned to head up or coordinate proposals, as a part-time duty or second hat to wear, if proposal writing is not a continuous function in your organization. That is, that individual need not necessarily be the decision maker for proposals, but ought to be the individual who organizes the people and the work; monitors the work as it progresses, to ensure that nothing "falls between the cracks"; arranges for all support and production; and generally sees that problems are solved and that everything moves along.

Setting up a schedule for a proposal is not something you can do arbitrarily: schedule constraints are imposed on you by the proposal due date. The schedule must be constructed in reverse, working back from the due date, to schedule whatever time is needed for each function. For example, a first cut at a schedule might begin to take shape somewhat as follows:

Delivery: Close of business 7/25/82
In mail: Not later than 7/21/82
Final production (copying and binding 6 sets): 7/20/82
Final revisions, modifications: 7/17/82
Final review: 7/14 to 7/15/82
Typing and proofing: 7/12–13/82

Eventually, having plugged in dates and time allowances for each function, you have a schedule which dictates to you what is necessary to meet the final delivery date. It is, of course, wise to build some "air" into the schedule, to provide for contingencies. For example, the above allows 3 days for mail delivery. If circumstances make it absolutely necessary, you can clip a couple of days from that by either using an express service that guarantees 24-hour service, or by sending someone from your organization to hand-carry the proposal, a resort often used.

It often happens that the professionals who are charged with designing the program and writing the bulk of the technical content are totally innocent of any knowledge of what is needed to transform their scrawls on yellow legal pads into a finished proposal ready for delivery. Unless you make them keenly aware—usually by imposing strict deadlines—they are likely to assume that they can hand their copy to you on the 15th, for a proposal to be delivered on the 17th!

Debriefing

Not everyone is aware that as a proposer, you have the right to request a debriefing, once you have learned that your effort was unsuccessful. Relatively few proposers request debriefings, for some reason, but it is often a wise thing to do.

Simply put, a debriefing is a meeting with the customer's staff, technical and procurement specialists, to explain to you in what ways your proposal was deficient or, at least, not as good as the one that won the contract. Presumably, you will gain important information for future proposals to the agency.

There are cases where debriefing serves you little purpose. Any case which has such circumstances surrounding it that you do not believe there will be a parallel situation at a future time is one in which debriefing is likely to be of little value to you. In general, there are two such situations:

1. A proposal to an agency that rarely requests proposals—does little contracting, or, at least, little in the fields of your interest. Since you are not likely to be proposing to that agency again, the information you will receive is probably of little use.
2. A proposal for something highly unusual or foreign to your normal activities. Again, a case wherein the information will be of limited value because you will not, in all probability, bid such a project again.

The immediate benefits to be derived from debriefing are, of course, general information on what you did poorly in your proposal, what the agency considers to be especially important, and what they generally like and dislike—that is, their own biases.

But there are some other benefits. For one, the fact that you are interested enough to request debriefing makes a good impression, which is likely to be helpful in future bids to the agency. For another, it gives you the opportunity to get better acquainted with the people in the agency, and also gives you a chance to make a good general impression on them through personal contact.

Debriefing is almost sure to pave the way for the future, to at least some degree. In addition to being given a critical review of your proposal and, probably, justifications for selecting the proposal which was the winner, you have the opportunity to ask specific questions, for your future guidance.

Best and Final Sessions: What Are They—*Really?*

Those events known generally as "best and final" sessions may be regarded as either of two things: preliminary negotiations or final screening to select a winner. In a sense, they are both. The customer asks questions, which may or may not be sincere efforts to get answers or clarifications of items mentioned in your proposal. They may be screening questions, to help make the final selection from a field of neck-and-neck finalists.

They may also be simply an effort to get the lowest possible prices, with the questions and invitation to submit a technical supplement merely a smokescreen, to hide the real intent.

When you attend a best and final, you should have present at least two people, representing both the technical or program side and the marketing or business side of your company. You will have to make a judgment at the session as to whether you should come back with a price reduction or not and whether it is necessary to modify the program you offer. At this point, you are close to a contract, presumably, but it's as easy to lose it here as at any other point in the process.

Characteristically, the purpose of the government in this activity is to get information, not to give it, and you will usually find the government people rather guarded in what they will tell you. Still, skillful or adroit questioning may help you determine how many others are also invited to best and final sessions, how important a price reduction is likely to be, and whether you are a front runner or just one of a group in a final wring-out. Therefore, it is wise to bring with you the shrewdest people on your staff at reading between the lines and leading customers on in negotiations. It's a game calling for skills and experience, and is likely to make the difference between winning and losing.

Evaluation Criteria

The criteria most commonly cited for evaluating proposals include these:

1. Understanding of the problem, requirement, or need
2. Practicality of approach
3. Quality of staff proposed (résumés)
4. Experience of the proposer organization
5. Cost (usually least important, rarely weighted)

Of these, there is a strong tendency to place greatest weight—that is, to be most influenced by, even if weighting does not suggest this—on the résumés. Customers in the bureaucracy have a tendency to regard contractor staff as an extension of their own (despite the law forbidding using contractor staff as extensions of government staff). Consequently, there is a tendency to scrutinize résumés as closely as though the contractor staff were being considered for civil service positions. It is usually most worthwhile to give great care to the preparation of the résumés.

When Size of Proposal Is Limited

Occasionally an RFP limits proposers to some page length. In most cases, it is possible to stay within the specified page length without difficulty by single spacing the typing and using narrow margins. In other cases, it develops into a hardship, offering the proposers some difficulties in presenting their full plans and credentials.

The customer's objective is to prevent the submittal of extraordinarily long proposals, such as a few proposers are fond of submitting. This assists the customer in the review and evaluation process, of course. The customer has an idea of how much information is appropriate and necessary, but sometimes ignores the fact that some proposers may, in fact, have a great deal more information to offer than do other proposers.

When you are faced with this limitation and you believe that the limitation is a serious disadvantage for you, there are some possible ways to skirt the limitation, while not violating the letter of the mandate to keep your proposal to a maximum of x number of pages. Recognize, however, that unless you are most careful, you do risk having your entire proposal disqualified as nonresponsive. Therefore, the first requirement is to read the exact wording of the limitation clause most carefully, for there are variations among such clauses.

Such clauses often exclude résumés from the page-count limitation, for one thing, placing no limitation on pages devoted to staff résumés. The limitation might also exclude pages devoted to general information about the proposing organization—that is, the company's "résumé." In general, the limitation applies to the body of the proposal, which may ordinarily be interpreted to exclude front matter—letter of transmittal, table of contents, executive summary, and other such material appearing before the proposal proper. In all cases, read the clause most carefully and, if necessary, call the contracting official to clarify any questions about what is and what is not covered under the page limitation. However, be most careful here, too, in how you phrase your question. Some questions may bring answers you do not want to hear, by suggesting expedients to get around the page limitation. For example, suppose you wish to provide one or more appendixes, under the theory that appendixes are not included in the page limitation. Asking the direct question "Does this page limitation include appendixes?" may very well bring an instantaneous "Yes" in response. Rather, if you wish to ask this question, approach it indirectly: "This limitation applies to the body of the proposal, does it not?" Getting a "Yes" to that carries the broad implication that it does not include appended materials.

Another escape hatch is the use of "exhibits." These might be such items as a copy of some report cited, photos or other illustrations, sound tapes, or any other information which would not normally be a part of the proposal proper, but can be logically and justifiably offered as a supplemental item. Usually, you supply only a single copy of anything designated an exhibit, but let all readers of the proposal know that there are exhibits.

These evasions of the limitation, however, should be undertaken only after thorough editing is put to work to boil your final draft proposal down to the essentials. If, in spite of effective editing—and editing almost invariably reduces the bulk of a draft, since writers tend to overwrite—you still have difficulty presenting your proposal within the stipulated page limit, you should resort to other measures.

Appendix

1 Specimen Proposal

2 Brainstorming and Value Engineering or Analysis

3 Cost Presentation

4 Samples from a Recent RFP
Proprietary-information notice.   Mandated format.   Evaluation criteria.

5 Glossary of Terms

1 Specimen Proposal

The proposal presented here is a "for instance." It was presented to the U.S. Forest Service (part of the Department of Agriculture) and was successful, winning a contract for over $80,000.

Certain portions of the original proposal have been deleted in the interests of presenting the proposal proper within the space limitations. For that reason, information about the organization and staff résumés is not included here. Further, names of the proposer and staff have been deleted. Except for those omissions and some minor editing, the proposal is exactly as it was presented successfully.

The proposal does not follow all the "rules" recommended by the authors—it did not fully exploit all the possible opportunities to sell. At the same time, you will find that it has many assets as a proposal:

- The requirement is painstakingly and intelligently analyzed.
- The reader is "educated" to appreciate the technical arguments.
- A distinct strategy of benefits offered the customer is employed.
- Graphics have been used selectively, but effectively.
- A most detailed plan is presented; little is left to imagination.
- Deliverables are clearly enumerated and described.

I: HOW _____ CORPORATION VIEWS THE REQUIREMENT

The Educational Systems Division of _____ Corporation is pleased to offer its professional services to the Forest Service of the U. S. Department of Agriculture in response to RFP_____ :Orientation Training System for Engineers. We believe that our experience and capabilities closely match the most critical requirements set forth in the RFP. (See Section IV for details of experience and resources available.)

AN OVERVIEW OF THE FOREST SERVICE NEED

We recognize that the basic goals envisioned by the Forest Service in the RFP are orientation in the Forest Service organization, familiarization with the Forest Service mission, and applications of the various engineering disciplines to Forest Service needs. Conversely, there is no thought or intention of teaching the disciplines to the students, who are graduate engineers, already fully trained in their basic disciplines. It is our understanding, also, that the Forest Service engineering staff will lend us technical support in the substantive matter aspect of the project. At the same time, if the experience and knowledge of the Forest Service engineering staff are to be translated effectively in the training materials that will be parts of the training system, we must have technical competence on our staff so that we can properly interpret the information supplied us.

Further, an initial task analysis is envisioned by the Forest Service, and during this analysis, the preliminary designs and objectives identified as Appendix C of the RFP will be examined closely, evaluated, and, if necessary, modified.

We believe, however, that our task will not be one of modifying this work as much as it will be one of expanding, detailing, and translating this work into a physical reality of materials and procedures. This we expect to be a relatively complex task, since it involves the following considerations and needs:

(1.) Subjects: A great diversity of subjects to be covered is readily apparent. This will involve not only many skills, but will require close matching and integration to ensure proper component interfaces.

(2.) Media: At least some specialized services will be required, especially in development and production of 3 D, slides, tapes, 8-mm loops, etc.

(3.) System Design: Overall educational strategies must be developed, such that the total training system accomplishes its purpose, all components are designed to meet specific needs, and all are structured for proper interfacing and evaluation.

(4.) Motivation: Motivating the student is always an important consideration, but is of special importance here. The student must be made to feel that his work in the Forest Service is important and that a Forest Service career is a worthy one. The training strategy must address this goal effectively and consistently.

Even this brief overview of the basic problem parameters points dramatically to the need for system management. The services of many skilled individuals are required, but these services must be carefully coordinated, and the products resulting from these services must be coherently integrated. Standards and specifications must be developed. Procedures must be written. And the management plan must be articulated and made operative by a well-chosen staff of vigilant, alert people who are expert at their respective specialties.

In summation, then, we believe that no single organization includes all necessary capabilities, at least not at equally high levels of excellence. To provide the best staff, services, and products to the Forest Service, we anticipate the need to survey the field and arrange for the services of the best organizations and personnel. We also anticipate the need to make expert recommendations to the Forest Service, and to review these recommendations with Forest Service at each critical point. We expect, in fact, to maintain with Forest Service a virtually continuous dialogue for all parameters of the project. We will, in fact, recommend that the Forest Service organize a small project-management staff in such a manner that Forest Service is in complete command of the project, yet is not burdened with administrative chores.

SOME GENERAL PROBLEMS AND NEEDS

In general, we are in complete accord with the plan described in the RFP. We firmly believe, for example, in an objective analysis of the total problem as the first phase of any undertaking. Our goals, in such an analysis, are as follows:

(1.) Define the problem. We believe that a problem is not truly defined until we are satisfied that we have clearly discriminated between causes and effects and have identified first causes. This resolution ensures that we are attacking the problem--not the symptoms.

(2.) Define the student. In the present case, the Forest Service has given us an apparently clear definition of the student. We would wish here to expand the definition slightly to examine the various disciplines in which the students have been trained.

(3.) Define terminal skills. Here again the RFP is clear, and we would probably not go beyond verification of the definitions already provided.

(4.) Define goals and objectives. Normally, we perform a relatively exhaustive study here, developing detailed outlines of proposed content, including text, graphics, and, frequently, media.

(5.) Implementation. In the case of a complete system, such as that under discussion here, implementation plans are most critical. There must be coherence, coordination of functions, and integration of components in a multi-media system, such as that envisioned here. And--most important--there must be a highly specific plan of action to get the system installed and working smoothly. In any complex system, we may safely assume that problems will arise in the first stages of developing and installing the prototype. There should be established plans and procedures for troubleshooting and correcting these problems.

(6.) Special considerations. There are two special considerations that require our attention in this project: motivating the student to pursue a permanent career in the Forest Service and sustaining his interest in the orientation-training program under discussion. To some extent, these problems are related, but to solve them effectively, we propose distinct strategies and tactics.

To motivate the student in a Forest Service career, we believe, he must have a favorable image of himself in the role of Forest Service engineer. We must convince him that the Forest Service engineer is a dignified professional person doing significant work and pursuing a worthwhile career. This image must be conveyed to him and continuously reinforced throughout the orientation period and even beyond that.

Sustaining his interest in the orientation program requires careful design of the system to achieve variety, pacing, multi-sense appeal, and student involvement. Moreover, the entire program should be structured that (1) a central coordinating or recurring theme is apparent, and (2) the entire program is on a steadily rising note, reaching a climax of appeal of involvement at the end.

The following graph illustrates this concept. The early surge of interest (A) should be developed by a dramatic or other attention-getting device--a movie or an entertaining introduction of some sort, for example. Interest should then build steadily throughout the program by proper structuring and by increasing pace and variety. Subsystem 12, the 40-hour field problem, should be the highest point of interest--the climax (B).

_____ Educational Systems Division has carefully studied all these aspects of the problem and has developed a set of strategies for their solution. Each will be described in detail in this proposal.

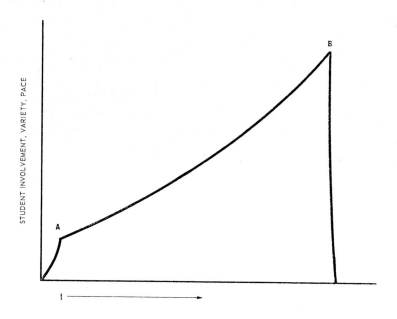

FIGURE 1-1
STUDENT-INTEREST CURVE

II: PRELIMINARY ANALYSIS AND DISCUSSION

THE NEED FOR SPECIFIC OBJECTIVES

"Teaching to the examination" is sometimes regarded as a shallow and superficial method of loading the scales in favor of the instructor. On the other hand, it can be a perfectly sound and valid approach to training--if the examination covers all the desired behaviors.* Then, mastery of the examination is mastery of the subject.

In a sense, this describes much of modern educational principles. Learning is defined in terms of the behaviors that will demonstrate achievement of the learning; causing the student to display these behaviors is then the goal of the training program. This concept is formalized in such educational principles as operant conditioning, reinforcement, mathetics, etc.

Operant conditioning is a principle that describes the process of training the student to respond to a stimulus. Properly trained, the student always makes the correct response to the stimulus.

Other related principles are pursued. Reinforcement, for example, is "rewarding" the student for correct responses, possibly by a simple approval of the response. On the other hand, incorrect responses are discouraged. And mathetics is a behaviorally based method of organizing presentation.

We subscribe to these and many other pertinent educational principles. In general, we believe that each principle has appropriateness to certain situations, and

---

*"Behavior," in the educational sense, is the means of describing learning in terms of what the student will do to demonstrate learning--"solve $ax = 1/a+x$," "tie three square knots," "differentiate a non-linear function," etc. are behaviors.

we employ numerous methods for identifying appropriate principles and for employing techniques to apply each principle where it is suitable.

We approach each training problem with a searching analysis and definition of the root problem Before any serious effort is made to formulate a solution, we must be convinced that we fully understand and have accurately identified the problem.

In analyzing the present need of the Forest Service, we will consider, in turn:

The Target Population - Who is to be trained.

The educational background and/or skills of those in a

training program will determine, to a great extent, the level

and content of the curriculum to be designed. However, since

it is usually not possible to describe an archetype or "typical"

student, we must define the spectrum--the extremes of the population--

and do so in a manner that enables us to gauge where the population

tends to group or, if possible, describe several "typical" students,

all of whom will be t rained.

Terminal Skills and Behaviors - We must determine, concurrently,

what they are to be trained to do.

Job skills and knowledge must be broken down into their component

parts and segregated into manual skills and conceptual skills until

specific behaviors and specific subject areas are defined with enough

precision to enable a training design to be synthesized.

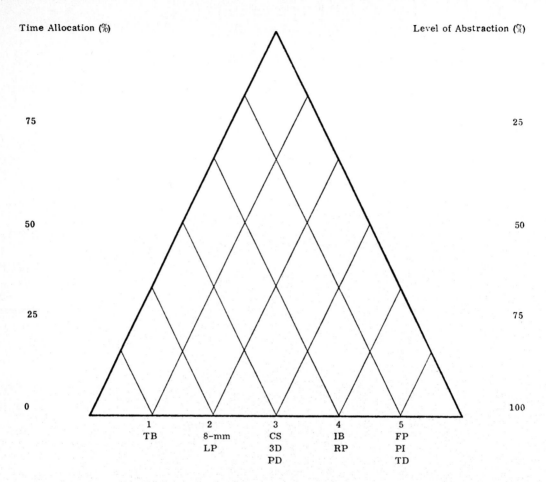

Time Allocation (%)   Level of Abstraction (%)

Training Involvement/Technique

Legend:

Case Study	CS
Field Problems	FP
In-Basket Problem	IB
Lecture-Conference Lesson Plan	LP
Panel Discussions	PD
Programed Instruction	PI
Slide Tape Programs	ST
Team Decision Activities	TD
Three Dimensional Simulation	3D
8MM Continuous Loop Films	8MM

FIGURE 2–1
TRAINING-PARAMETER RELATIONSHIPS

Training Design - How they are to be trained.

The task analysis will also result, finally, in a recommended

design which will include the various subjects to be taught,

the tests and other ancillary materials, the length of the program,

and the scope of non-programmed training, such as lab or

workshop sessions. Strategies will be developed at this point

for teaching, for testing, and for motivating.

In the succeeding project phase, consideration will be given to training techniques and

materials, which will include the following:

Conventional texts -- manuals, etc.

Programmed texts, workbooks

Slides, charts, posters, and other graphics

Audio-visual -- tapes, movies, transparencies, etc.

Lectures, seminars, workshops

Simulations, role playing, demonstrations, exercises

Any or all of these may be used in conjunction with available physical facilities and

equipment. In addition, actual operational problems may be used as training exercises

by preparing suitable materials to create an on-job-training environment.

We also recognize that a relationship exists among such parameters as the

length of time allotted each program sub-section, the type of material involved in the

learning process, and the level of abstraction of this material. Some of these relation-

ships are indicated on Figure 2-1.

There is little question, based on our past experience, that the scientific study of the training problem through strictly disciplined task analysis and the

systematic synthesis of a training program developed along logical, objective lines

is mandatory.

UNITY AND THEME

A properly designed system is something more than an integrated collection

of components. Correctly conceived and developed, a system has a clearly defined goal

and a set of strategies for achieving that goal. The design begins with a need. An

abstract solution is formulated. The required functions and relationships are then

designed ("black-box" design). Only then are components designed, and each component

must be so designed that it supports the central theme or philosophy of the system and

directly contributes to achievement of the goal. Only when these things have been

accomplished can we have any confidence that our design is coherent and efficient.

It is important in training, educational, or information systems design that

the user--the student, in this case--be fully aware of the system's theme and goals.

And if this can be achieved by subtle means, the effect is greater than if the theme is

directly dinned into him.

We have developed a strategy for making the student constantly aware of the

theme through symbolization of the Forest Service engineer as a clean-cut, vigorous

outdoorsman who is, at the same time, a serious and dignified professional man. This

and other details of our plan will be revealed in the next section.

THE CRITICAL ROLE OF MANAGEMENT

We expect management of the whole project to be of critical importance.

In management, as in the technical aspects of the work, we propose to employ a systems engineering approach. This approach requires a broad-gauge analysis of specific items related to the Master Orientation Training System across the life-cycle of Research & Development, Investment, and Operation. The exhibit on the following page illustrates the two-dimensional matrix, in a preliminary form.

Inherent in the systems engineering approach are three important factors that influence all elements--time, cost, and control. The first two, time and cost, are governed by the constraints of the Forest Service budget. The latter, control, is the subject of the Systems Management portion of the A____ proposal.

The systems engineer takes an overview of the total program. This overview examines the progress of a program through its life-cycle of research and development, investment, and operation. In the case of the Forest Service Orientation Training, five elements are examined and related, as shown in the exhibit following this page, across three phases of the life-cycle. (The fourth phase, Disposal, is not considered to be significant in this program.) This overview permits A____, and the Service, to relate the specific task of preparing training materials to the other relevant elements. Further, it makes it possible to apply a rational system-management approach to the implementation of the program, particularly by identifying the significant interfaces.

All of these considerations underlie both design and management, and are considered during the systems analysis.

WHAT IS "SYSTEMS ANALYSIS"?

Systems Analysis is a general procedure or methodology that utilizes a mix of disciplines to solve a specific problem. Engineering problems in particular are the best example, and most common application of system analysis. Two points must be made at the outset: (1) The engineer must ask himself "Am I asking the right question?":

Table 2-1 SYSTEMS ENGINEERING APPROACH TO FOREST SERVICE
Training Requirements

Phase / Element	R & D Phase	Investment Phase	Operational Phase
I. Forest Service			
A. Institutional Environment	Develop statement of long term objectives.	Translate objectives into specific programs.	
B. Personnel	Define functional tasks	Establish position descriptions	Enhance professional capabilities
C. Requirements	Derive procedure for measuring needs.	Measure present and projected manpower needs	Reduce attrition
II. Engineering Courses			
A. Subject Matter	Define engineering disciplines to be taught.		
B. Instructional Material	Determine Methodology	Prepare instructional materials	Utilize training material
C. Teachers	Determine professionals needed	Indoctrination of teachers	Teach courses
III. Engineering Trainee	Establish kinds of engineers to be recruited and number	Recruit and train engineers	Integrate into Forest Service operations.
IV. Physical Environment	Define career environment	Re-examine in light of changing conditions.	Estimate future environment that FS will be responsible for.
	Define training environment.	Prepare class room facilities	Utilize facilities
V. Interfaces	With universities and colleges	Analyze changing concepts of land use and land values; study impact of new technologies.	Optimize utilization of natural resources.

and (2) the engineer must then look at the problem in its broadest context. As an
illustration, assume that the engineer has asked the correct question; e.g., how can the
Forest Service provide access to point "A" from point "B." Simply a transportation
problem; therefore, cut a road from point "B" to point "A." The systematic analysis
will look to a number of alternate solutions, however, such as air drop or navigable
waterway. Assuming, further, that a road is the optimum choice, the engineer then
applies system analysis to a finer level of detail. He will examine the necessary combination of route and vehicles. From these basic needs, he will derive the requirements
for structures; the maintenance facilities for the road and vehicles; the fuel needed; the
personnel, and their maintenance during construction and operation of the road. The
engineer will consider trade-offs between high investment to obtain a low annual
maintenance, and vice versa. He will tie all elements together with a plan for system
integration that includes the necessary control for effective management of the road
building project. As a system analyst, the Forest Service Engineer will consider the
project in terms of its impact on the environment, possible multiple uses, and the
optimum exploitation of natural resources.

In summary, system analysis tackles a problem in terms of a function to
be performed--in this example, access to a specific location. It considers alternative
techniques that satisfy the functional requirement, then applies the same procedure to
lower levels of detail. The end-product will be a project plan that has the highest
estimated cost-benefit ratio, considering all implications.

OTHER CONSIDERATIONS

There are three other considerations to be borne in mind in such a program
as that proposed here: practicality of the design, instructor guidance, and new-
knowledge "fallout."

Practicality of Design

There is always the danger in developing a complex system of so over-complicating the design that the system falls of its own weight. In the present case, such diverse elements as straight texts, programmed texts, slide and movie projectors, demonstrations, and lectures are to be used. If the system is unwieldy by requiring split-second synchronization of various presentations, the system will become an intolerable burden. It is of importance, therefore, to design a system that will, on the one hand, take advantage of all available techniques and methods, yet flow smoothly and easily from one to the next. For example, an instructor should not be required to go directly from a movie presentation to a slide presentation. Rather, he should be able to keep the students busy with useful study that provides him time to set up the slide projection without interrupting class work.

This problem of sequencing will be carefully considered in the design development.

Instructor Guidance

A system of diverse elements and multi-faceted presentations, no matter how well planned, must be accompanied by clear instructions for its use. We consider it vital to prepare an Instructor's Guide. (In practice, this may become several guides.)

<u>Fallout</u>

It is highly likely that new training knowledge may be derived from such a program as this. Throughout program development, field testing, and revision, it will be one of our goals to observe, study, and document for the Forest Service any such findings. The Final Report will discuss this aspect of the program thoroughly.

III: A PROGRAM TAILORED FOR SUCCESS

THREE IMPORTANT POINTS REQUIRING FURTHER DISCUSSION

The specific proposal of the_____Educational Systems Division is to implement the philosophies and ideas discussed earlier. Generally, these are in accord with the overall plan set forth in the Request for Proposal. There are several points, however, that we believe should be raised now. We will not attempt to reach decisions here, since those should be logically arrived at after the analysis, study, and review contemplated as Phase 1 of the project. Those points that we wish to discuss specifically here are as follows:

- Preliminary Analysis
- Conceptual Design and Strategies
- Management

PRELIMINARY ANALYSIS

The tentative conclusions drawn from our preliminary analysis of the Forest Service's needs are represented by Table 3-1. Here we have suggested means of meeting objectives envisioned by the Forest Service. Obviously, as we have stated before, these are preliminary analyses and conclusions, but they will serve to illustrate the strategies we envision at this time.

CONCEPTUAL DESIGN AND STRATEGIES

We mentioned earlier the need to arouse the student's interest rapidly at the onset of the program and to sustain that interest in a steadily rising curve through various techniques and methods to get the student involved and to arouse his enthusiasm.

The concept of involvement means, first, the amount of active work the student must invest in the learning effort. Reading a textbook, listening to a lecture, or observing a film are inherently passive and represent a low order of involvement. Working through programmed courses, workshops, group discussions, and role playing, represent various higher orders of involvement.

Ideally, the student must also become "intellectually" involved: he must not be doing work mechanically and unthinkingly, if he is to be really involved; he must be truly interested and earnestly trying to perform. This kind of involvement requires much more subtle and imaginative techniques than those that merely make him work for his learning. There are many writing techniques that offer us direct assistance in arousing and sustaining student interest.

For example, it is well known that the most important word in the language to a reader is YOU. That is to say, any written material is inherently more interesting to a

Table 3-1 PRELIMINARY CHART OF TRAINING PROGRAM

ITEM	Time Allotments (Hrs.)	MEDIA	TECHNIQUES	REMARKS
SS-1 TECHNICAL ORIENTATION	10.0			
1. History of Engineering in the Forest Service	1.5	Text	Descriptive narrative, intrinsic and linear programming.	Text produced will include test or history of engineering.
2. Mission of Forest Service Engineering	5.5	Text	Selected reading assignments, descriptive narrative, reading assignments, intrinsic programming.	Narrative statement required by student outlined in text.
3. The Engineering Organization	1.5	Text	Student assignment--Regional Engineering Organizational Chart.	Text developed for student guidance.
4. The Engineer as an Individual; Duties, Responsibilities, Opportunities for Training and Development, Career Potentials, Challenges	6.0	Text	Adjunctive-intrinsic program.	Adjunctive technique used jointly with Forest Service publications.
5. Basic Forest Service Programs; Forest Service Appropriations	1.5	Text	An intrinsic program.	Intrinsic program will present (1) basic FS programs, (2) major appropriations, (3) resource or functional activity to which appropriations apply. (Will be geared specifically to the FS engineer.)
SS-2 FOREST SERVICE TRANSPORTATION SYSTEM PLANNING	32.0			
1. Transportation system defined and transportation system objectives	4	Text	Adjunctive-intrinsic program with post-test evaluation.	
2. System planning, management and maintenance procedures	10.0	Text	Actual systems in FS critiqued.	A progressive combination of reading assignments and contractor generated text showing how to plan, manage, and maintain FS transportation systems.
3. Transportation system records: a. Classification b. Standards c. As management tools	3	Text	Adjunctive-intrinsic programmed instruction.	

330

Table 3-1   PRELIMINARY CHART OF TRAINING PROGRAM

ITEM	Time Allotments (hrs.)	MEDIA	TECHNIQUES	REMARKS

4. Relationship of Transportation System Planning to the Multiple-Use Management Concept:
a. Reconnaissance
b. Surveys
c. Design
d. Construction
  1. Methods of accomplishment
  2. Contracting officer - engineer relationship
	7	Text	Selected reading assignments and descriptive narrative.	Ratio of generated narrative to reading assignments 1:10.

5. Private, Local, State and other transportation systems	4	Text	Selected reading assignments and descriptive narrative.	Ratio of generated narrative to reading assignments 1:10.
6. Planning and management, associated student study time.	4			
SS-3 REVIEW OF SUB SYSTEMS 1 and 2	8			
1. A written examination and a review designed to re-establish a common pre-determined level of transportation system planning knowledge.	1.5	Text	Summary of SS-2 followed by a multiple-choice test.	
2. A comprehensive examination of the principles underlying basic multiple-use management in the Service.	1.5	Text	Problem presentation and analysis by student.	Multiple-use guides and plans.
3. A simulated transportation system planning exercise designed to make the trainee apply transportation system planning principles to management decisions involving transportation system considerations.	3.0	Wall charts, overlays supporting instructor guidance	Panel simulation of transportation planning. Each panel presents its findings.	Separate problems for each panel of five.

Table 3-1 PRELIMINARY CHART OF TRAINING PROGRAM

ITEM	Time Allotments (Hrs.)	MEDIA	TECHNIQUES	REMARKS
4. A series of problem solving exercises designed to explain and clarify the organizational structure of the Forests and Regions.	1.0	Text	Multiple-choice questions and problems on structures of forests and regions.	
5. A re-definition of the relationship of management and technical training.	0.5			
6. The Training Plan for Career Development	0.5			
SS-4 PROGRAM SUPPORT ENGINEERING	16.0			
1. Introduction to Forest Engineering, general applications.	1.5	16-mm sound-color film	Brief introduction, film, then follow-up discussion.	Modify existing film titled "Potential Unlimited" (dub in new sound).

2. Forest Service resource management. Functions served by engineers.
A. Recreation
  1. Ski lifts
  2. Sanitation systems - (Public Health Service Codes)
  3. Water systems - (Types, Water Pollution Control Administration)
  4. Buildings - boat ramps
  5. Planning advice - (Master Planning)
  6. Signs
	2.5	35-mm sound slide	Five separate 10-minute films, 2-to-5 questions after each one. (Quiz shown on final frame.)	

B. Timber
  1. Economics of timber access - haul roads.
  2. Development of preliminary timber sale plans - photogrammetry.
  3. Timber type maps - cartography
  4. Logging systems.
		35-mm sound-slide presentation on text.	10-minute film, shows timber-access haul roads and their management problems.	Instructor guidance in its form of text and large wall charts will present (1) timber sale plans, (2) photogrammetry, (3) timber cartography, (4) logging system management.

Table 3-1   PRELIMINARY CHART OF TRAINING PROGRAM

ITEM	Time Allotments (Hrs.)	MEDIA	TECHNIQUES	REMARKS

C. Lands
1. Rights of Way acquisition.
2. Special use permits.
  a. dam proposals
  b. special use roads
  c. water diversion structures
3. Boundary surveys - property corners.
	1.5	35-mm sound-slide presentation and text	10-minute film, shows boundary surveys.	Lesson plan presented for rights-of-way acquisition and "special-use" permits.

D. Watershed Management
1. Economics of watershed rehabilitation.
  a. Planning - (photogrammetry - cartography)
  b. Contour trench construction - (Plans, inspection maintenance)
2. Water-hydrologic information needs.
  a. Reservoir impacts, analysis
  b. Water quality analysis
3. Channel stabilization
4. Impact of Engineering improvements on watershed management
	1.5	35-mm sound-slide presentation	10-minute filmstrip "Do's and Don'ts" of Watershed engineering.	Workbook assignments used as follow-up after film.

E. Range and Wildlife Management
1. Range Allotment Analysis plans and maps-(photogrammetry, cartography.)
2. Water developments.
3. Range revegetation.
  a. equipment
  b. economics
	1.5	35-mm sound-slide presentation	10-minute film strip.	Workbook assignments.

F. Administration 1. Communications 2. Buildings 3. Planning-staff responsibilities.	1.5	Guidance text for instructor	"In Basket" problem.	Competition between groups solving administrative problems.

333

Table 3-1 PRELIMINARY CHART OF TRAINING PROGRAM

ITEM	Time Allotments (Hrs.)	MEDIA	TECHNIQUES	REMARKS

G. Job Corps
1. Site selection, design, construction
  a. Buildings
  b. Sanitation systems
  c. Water systems
2. Transportation requirements.
  a. Access roads.
  b. Interior roads, ramps, parking
3. Maintenance
	1.5	35-mm sound-slide presentation of actual Job Corps activity	10-minute filmstrip followed by actual Job Corps experiences.	Contractor will supply text of Job Corps experiences also.

H. Fire Control
1. Equipment development
2. Airport construction and maintenance.
3. Heliport-helispot construction and maintenance.
4. Fire lookout-detection systems.
5. Communications.
6. The engineer on a fire may be responsible for and serve as:
  a. Transportation officer
  b. Communications officer
  c. Plans chief
  d. Equipment boss
  e. Other fire fighting positions depending on needs, training, and interest.
	1.5	16-mm color movie, 15 minutes long- "Fire Plow Performance." (Described on page 130, OEO publication No.OE-34006-63)	After film is shown, instructor presents a "Fire review" of detailed fire control.	Rent copies of film from Department of Agriculture.

I. Wilderness areas 1. Mapping 2. Boundary posting 3. Access 4. Signing requirements.	1.5	Use engineering maps of remote Forest Service areas.	Classroom simulation of actual problems in field. (All supporting text developed by contractor.)	The steps of developing the map, how boundaries were posted, and access procedures.

Table 3-1 PRELIMINARY CHART OF TRAINING PROGRAM

ITEM	Time Allotments (Hrs.)	MEDIA	TECHNIQUES	REMARKS
SS-5 PHOTOGRAMMETRY AND MAPPING	8.0			
1. Introduction to aerial Photography-Maps-Photogrammetry in the Forest Service. A. Aerial photography. (1) Origin (2) Uses (3) Coverage and availability (4) Types	1.5	8-minute film: sound, color and black and white	LP (lecture) and class discussion.	Verbal check of students' value judgments.
B. Maps (1) Accuracy standards (2) Types (3) Control requirements (4) Production methods (5) Uses	1.5	Maps and 15-minute film: sound, color and black and white	LP (lecture) and class discussion.	
C. Photogrammetric and Mapping Equipment (1) Types (2) Uses (3) Limitations	2.0	5-minute 8-mm films	Films and display of special equipment.	Students may handle special items suitable for classroom use.
2. Using photogrammetry to meet the needs of the Forest Service.	3.0	P. I. Text	Case study.	Split class into 4 panel groups, each making independent study and recommendations.
SS-6 CADASTRAL ENGINEERING	12.0			
1. Current conditions of property lines and corners in the Regions and in the Forests to which the trainees are assigned.	1.0	P. I. Text	Student essays.	150-word pre-assigned essays to be judged by small student panels to select the four most cogent.
2. Property line survey goals, protection and maintenance.	2.5	Handouts, charts	LP (lecture), class discussion.	
3. Systems of land surveying. a. rectangular b. metes and bounds	3.0	8-minute film: sound, black and white, some animation. Handout.	Instructor questions students verbally; class discussion and self test.	Each of 4 groups to prepare 10-question true-false quiz for another group to answer.

Table 3-1   PRELIMINARY CHART OF TRAINING PROGRAM

ITEM	Time Allotments (Hrs.)	MEDIA	TECHNIQUES	REMARKS
4. Relationship and importance to other Forest Service programs.	2.5	Handout, charts		Brief quiz.
5. Cadastral surveys for Rights of Way acquisition programs	2.0	Handouts	Case study and class discussion	
6. Land line survey monuments and accessories.	1.0	P. I. Text		Multiple-choice quiz.
SS-7 EQUIPMENT MANAGEMENT DEVELOPMENT	6.0			
1. The Forest Service Fleet a. Why is a fleet operated b. How is it funded c. What is the policy on rentals	0.5	P. I. Text		Written quiz on intrinsic program.
2. Equipment management records and reports for equipment used by the Forest Service including: a. Types b. Costs c. Capabilities d. Maintenance standards	2.0	Tape with filmstrip (8 minutes), handouts	Case study.	Test: fill out report forms.
3. Fleet equipment management	2.0	P. I. Text	Case study.	Four class groups, each making independent study and recommendations.
4. Special equipment needs of program divisions	0.5	P. I. Text		Written quiz on intrinsic program.
5. Equipment development centers. a. Functions - development - testing - specifications b. Methods for satisfying project needs c. Use of the centers	1.0	10-minute silent black and white film with instructor narration; charts	LP (lecture).	

Table 3-1 PRELIMINARY CHART OF TRAINING PROGRAM

ITEM	Time Allotments (Hrs.)	MEDIA	TECHNIQUES	REMARKS
SS-8 INTRODUCTION TO MATERIALS ENGINEERING	16.0			
1. Management problems and materials engineering	2.5	P. I. Text, handouts	In-basket cases.	Group discussion.
2. Soil classification systems	1.5	Charts	LP (lecture).	
3. Materials engineering procedures. a. pre-construction investigation -sampling -testing -alternatives -recommendations	5.0	P. I. Text, 4-minute, 8-mm film loop	LP and case studies ("Teaching to Learn").	One-hour orientation; then break class into 4 groups, each making independent study and recommendations. Each group presents its findings in panel form.
4. Forest Service specifications.	2.0	Charts	LP (lecture).	
5. Application of materials engineering: a case study	5.0		Case study.	Teams as in 3 (above) with a committee to coordinate the plans presented.
SS-9 SAFETY IN FOREST ENGINEERING	4			
1. The hazards of Forest engineering	2.5	15-20 minute film: sound, black and white	LP (lecture), case studies.	Lecture and group discussion.
2. The engineer's role in the Safety program	1.5	P. I. Text and short animated film	Case studies, LP (lecture).	Brief intrinsic program, and group discussion, with lecture.
SS-10 INTRODUCTION TO ELECTRONIC DATA PROCESSING	4			
1. Introduction to data processing	1.5	Charts; 5-minute animated film	P. I. Text and LP (lecture).	
2. Applications and programming	2.0	Handouts; three 3-minute film animations		Workbook exercise.
3. Summary	0.5		LP (lecture).	

PRELIMINARY CHART OF TRAINING PROGRAM

ITEM	Time Allotments (Hrs.)	MEDIA	TECHNIQUES	REMARKS
SS-11 INTRODUCTION TO ENGINEERING RESEARCH	6.0			
1. Objectives of the Program and Methods used. the Research organization, locations and financing.	1.0	P. I. Text, handouts	LP (lecture).	Lecture and group discussion; workbook assignment.
2. How research and administration communicate	1.5	Tape, filmstrip		
3. Examples of research findings that have improved administration, review current studies and their impact on Forest Service administration.	2.5		Case studies.	Brief quiz.
4. Future of Engineering research.	1.0	15-20 minute film: sound, color		Motivational session with film following instructor.

reader when it is addressed directly to him, rather than to some completely unidentified or hypothetical third person. It becomes even more attention-getting when it clearly relates the reader's interests--health, prosperity, general welfare--to the content. This and many other similar principles well-known to professional writers, such as those on the Educational Systems Division staff, will be artfully employed to develop material that is interesting, as well as informative.

Another excellent device for creating involvement is to make learning competitive, and we propose to do this in many areas. For example, in case studies we will develop situations where various individuals or teams propose the solutions, with due recognition to the individual or team who reaches the one closest to the "school solution." Still another way of getting a high degree of involvement is by having the student teach. One way in which we could accomplish this is to have individual students or groups of students concentrate on given areas of study and then teach each other. For example, in Item 3 of sub-system 8, we might have a class break into four teams, each of whom would prepare themselves in "sampling," "testing," "alternatives," "recommendations," respectively, and we would then have a panel for each of these subjects to teach the rest of the class.

If we were to plot the interest level from Table 3-1, it would have a series of interest peaks and valleys, or a series of anticlimaxes. Each of these is a point at which we would be in danger of "losing" the student due to his flagging interest. Therefore, in our analysis we will study means of reorganizing the order of presentation so as to most nearly approach the idealized curve of Figure 1-1 and offer these findings to the Forest Service at the conclusion of Phase 1 of the proposed project.

As an example of how we might prepare some of our material, we present

Appendix C, in which we have outlined a computer/programming orientation or familiarization course. The Appendix includes some introductory material, an outline, and some sample materials showing a mix of programming and writing techniques, with the use of graphics.

The computer training program, as we see it, is to be designed for the engineer user. We plan to teach the engineer specific applications of the computer in his work in the Forest Service, rather than the mechanics of the computer itself. For example, we intend to lert him to existing Forest Service programs that will eliminate long and tedious slide rule computations on his part. We plan to tell him how existing programs and existing computers can make his engineering job not only easier, but more effective. We do not, at this point, plan to teach him such things as the differences between analog and digital computers, how computers execute the user's programs, or other purely mechanical information. We do intend to orient him by showing him what the computers can do for him during his engineering and managing tasks.

Still another consideration in involvement is the broad one of causing the student to identify himself with the entire program generally and with Forest Service especially. To accomplish this it is desirable that we cause the student to develop a highly satisfactory self-image by creating in his mind a favorable image of the Forest Service engineer and then persuading him to see himself in that role.

Overt efforts to do this--e.g., indoctrination lectures--may cause him to treat the effort lightly and dismiss it as propaganda. It would be far more effective to implant the image by unobtrusive, yet continual means.

An excellent means for doing this is by the use of a simple symbol that portrays the Forest Service engineer in the semi-heroic role of a clean-cut outdoorsman who is also a professional man.

We propose to develop an omnipresent character a la Smokey the Bear. The character will not be humorous, however, or at least not ludicrous. Any humor attached to it will be light, good-natured, and in no way derogatory so that it will not diminish the professional stature or dignity of the symbol.

We will develop several designs, working closely with Forest Service, and ask Forest Service to review these and assist us in selecting the best one.

Once selected, the symbol will be used freely in the materials.

MANAGEMENT

Management of the proposed project is a critical area. Whenever several people are preparing portions of a coherent system, a need for standardization immediately arises. When separate organizations are working independently or semi-independently on a single project, the need becomes even more acute. And "standardization" includes the preparation of written standards and specifications, coordination directives, uniform procedures, and documents of a similar nature. In addition to this, there is a need for active, overall monitoring, liaison, and control, if we are to avoid extensive revisions later.

This inevitably involves a great deal of staff work, ordinarily performed by a prime contractor. It is in recognition of these and related problems that we propose to become a prime contractor to the Forest Service for the development of the system under discussion. As a prime contractor, we would be assigned a responsibility for handling all these matters of component interface compatibility, coherent system design, and total management.

We envision the probability of vending or sub-contracting much of the work. We have had the assistance, for example, of the _____ Corporation (Appendix B) in developing the technical plans set forth in this proposal, and we would subcontract audio-visual work to them. (We, of course, would be responsible to Forest Service for the work.)

In the same philosophy, we have engaged the services of Mr. _____ as a special consultant. He will aid us throughout the project in developing successful results.

We are entirely receptive to having the Forest Service designate vendors or subcontractors to us for any part of the work proposed. This will enable the Forest Service to exercise preferences, while securing our services in management of the program development.

After the subcontractors have been selected, it is our intention to apply a System Management Plan to the preparation and implementation of the training program. This is a "total concept" approach which considers, as interrelated components, the objectives of the program, the requirements, and the methodology. It is also a systems engineering approach which provides continuing supervision of the specific tasks in preparation of course material.

Mr. _____ will be designated as project manager. He will direct the overall project and participate directly in all phases of activity, especially with regard to physical systems and subject-matter coverage. Dr. _____ will also be employed directly in this project, concentrating on educational technology and evaluation procedures. Mr. _____ will assist Mr. _____ in the systems analysis and production phases.

Regular procedures will be established for close liaison between the project manager and Forest Service staff members. In this way, an orderly flow of work will be accomplished at_____, while periodic reviews and approval of drafts will be provided the Forest Service. There will be a final review before training materials are put into production.

We feel that such a plan will fulfill the requirements of Forest Service management since it will permit control of time, costs, and program content, with simplicity and effectiveness.

In addition, there will be an assured uniformity of end products with regard to such factors as the level of education attained by the Forest Service trainees and standard formats for printed materials, illustrations, audio-visual materials, etc. Duplication of introductory material will also be avoided.

Full control will be maintained by the Forest Service project manager over the total program at all stages of development, from initiation to contract completion.

OUTLINE OF
<u>MANAGEMENT SYSTEM PLAN</u>

PREFACE: What _____ proposes to do for the Forest Service--Apply advanced Systems Engineering and Systems Management approach to the preparation of a training program.

I. Introduction

    A. Objective of the program--"The result is a competent, mature, proven professional engineer able to assume responsible leadership positions in the organization." Longer range (5 years) achieved by incremental steps.

    B. Requirement--The Forest Service Training Program

        1. Integrated training--The five-year program

        2. Orientation training--Introduction to the Forest Service

    C. The Systems Engineering approach

        1. The Total System concept

        2. System Management
            a. Purpose
                (1) To ensure uniformity of end-products. Consider such factors as the level of education of the Forest Service trainees; standard formats for type font, page size, illustration, s film strips, slides, nomenclature; and prevent redundancies or duplications of material.

                (2) To establish regular procedures. Set up channels for liaison with Forest Service staff and technical experts. Provide an orderly flow of work by scheduling review and approval of drafts and proofs of training material.

                (3) Maintain full control over the total program from initiation to contract completion.

II. Scope of Work

    A. Introduction

        Why _____ is bidding "all"--The total system approach.

    B. System Management
        1. What _____ would do for the Forest Service

Provide a total management system for the preparation and implementation of the Orientation Training Program.

2. Three levels of management must be considered.
   a. Overall systems management through all phases of the program.

   b. System management of the specific _____ tasks of preparing course materials.

   c. A self-disciplining management approach applied to the Forest Service engineer trainee.

      (1) Personal career log book designed by _____ (See p. 3)

      Guide to five-year career program, provide permanent record of achievement. Master Achievement Plan (MAP).

3. The requirements of management

   a. Control of time, cost and manpower; with simplicity and effectiveness.

   b. End-product definition; clearly stated achievable objectives.

   c. Ability to reconsider the allocation of resources.

4. Methodology to be employed
   a. Implementation
      (1) Install a Program Management System. Utilize Critical Path Method (CPM), and a regular reporting procedure to provide program overview.

      (2) Install project management at level of each "part" and sub-system element. Use CPM to maintain control at the project level.

   b. Result
      (1) Advanced program control through CPM; known targets and schedules.

      (2) Establish criteria; evaluate students, instructors, content, materials.

   c. Provide feedback, appropriate to each level of management.

   d. Organize; based upon the functions, establish an appropriate structure for the prime and sub-contractors.
3. Report progress.

C. Training Materials

(Suggested Outline)

FOREST SERVICE
ENGINEER'S
CAREER
M. A. P.

I.   Master Achievement Plan for Forest Service Engineers

            A.   Your objectives

            B.   The terrain

            C.   Record of accomplishment

II.   Forest Service Orientation for Engineers

            A.   Objectives

            B.   Course plan

            C.   Engineering subjects

                    1.

                    2.

                    3. etc.

III.   Engineering Management

IV.   Engineering Disciplines

V.   Professional Societies

VI.   Forest Service Engineering Career Bulletins

ORGANIZATION

The project organization will follow the lines of Figure 3-1. The same basic staff will be used in several sub-organizations to preserve continuity. (Some sub-organizations will exist only in the early part of the project--task analysis team, standards-writing team, etc.).

Those shown in the chart are key personnel having highly specialized skills. Additional staff is not shown, although planned.

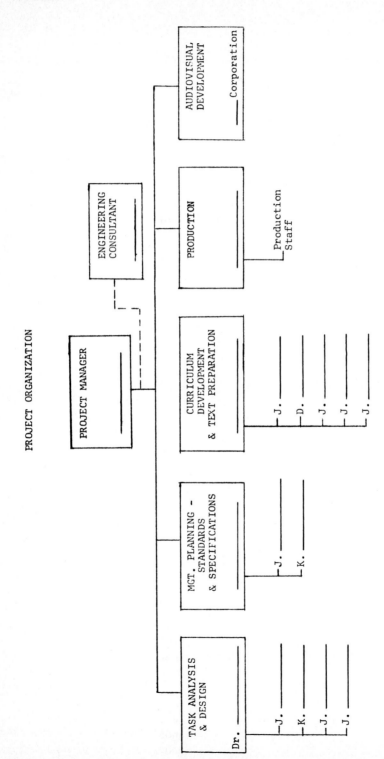

PROJECT ORGANIZATION

Fig. 3-1

PERFORMANCE SCHEDULE

The following list describes the milestone events in the proposal program.

A more detailed presentation is offered by Figure 3-2:

1. Task (Systems) Analysis and Design.

2. Submit Task Analysis and Design for review and approval by Forest Service.

3. Revision of Task Analysis and Design.

4. Final submission of Task Analysis and Design.

5. Preparation of standards, specifications, and management plan.

6. Submission of standards, specifications, and management plan to Forest Service for review and approval.

7. Final revised plan submitted to Forest Service.

8. Drafting of outline of materials for training and approval by the Forest Service.

9. Preparation of all materials for training.

10. Submission of drafts to Forest Service as each component of the system is completed.

11. Revisions following Forest Service reviews.

12. Camera-ready copy prepared of all training materials.

13. Field testing of training program.

14. Final revisions.

15. Camera-ready copy of complete packaged training program submitted to Forest Service.

    Delivery: Part 1.....180 calendar days after award
                           Part 2..... 240 calendar days after award
                           Part 3..... 240 calendar days after award

DELIVERABLE ITEMS

The following describes the physical items to be delivered to Forest Service:

(1) Report of Task Analysis, describing content outlines and

system design.

(2) Program materials:

   (a) Texts--Camera-ready originals plus 1 copy each

   (b) Audio-visuals--Originals plus one print of each.

    Both (a) and (b) in tested and revised (to 90/90) form

(3) Monthly progress reports.

(4) Final report.

Brainstorming and Value Engineering or Analysis

Brainstorming, highly recommended for analytical sessions and strategy formulations, is not a rigidly structured system, but it does have a few basic rules and procedures:

1. The group—which may be of any size—must address one single question, and one only, posed by the leader. The leader must make the group totally aware of what it is being asked to respond to, to offer ideas on. For each individual question asked or point addressed, a separate session should be held.
2. All responses, even those which may sound wild, are accepted seriously and recorded, preferably on a blackboard where everyone can see them. No judgments—no laughter, jeers, or sneers—are permitted during this phase.
3. When the group runs out of ideas, all items on the blackboard are reviewed and examined. Here, the weeding-out takes place, leaving the residue of ideas which appear sound and practicable.

When using brainstorming as part of value engineering or value analysis—highly recommended as a way of getting down swiftly to essence—remember the first question to ask is: "What is the function?" And that has to be answered with just two words: a noun and a verb. That is, the question is phrased: "What does it *do*?" (Or: "What is it *supposed* to do?")

When the task is analyzing the requirement or problem, the question is directed to what the proposed program is supposed to do for the customer.

In the case of the proposal which appears as the first appendix, the proposed program is supposed to *train engineers.* That is, to train *Forest Service* engineers. (It is permissible to compound the noun in this manner, if necessary for the meaning.).

Once the first question is answered—functionally—and everyone is satisfied that you have indeed determined what "it is supposed to do," you can begin to identify secondary or supporting functions. Secondary functions, in this case, are concerned with *what subjects* the Forest Service engineers are to be trained in, what other problems the customer has indicated must be solved, what needs must be satisfied, etc.

The method can be applied to all questions and all elements—the basic need or problem to be solved, the surrounding needs and problems, costs, strategies, approaches, organization, staffing, and all other matters.

If you are unable to summarize each function in a simple verb-noun combination, it is a signal that you have not yet boiled the question down to fundamentals—to functions—and are still distracted by other factors than basic functions.

Charted as simply as possible, you can and should develop the proposal somewhat along these starting lines (working from left to right):

The need or requirement must be summarized as "what is it?" and each function must be "what does it do?". When you examine the various support functions, scrutinize each to see if it is indeed a *support* function—is it *needed*? Or is it one of those "nice to have, but not really necessary" functions? If the latter, it should probably be thrown out as an unnecessary cost. If you are unsure, try excluding the function and see what happens: can you still achieve the basic function and satisfy the need? That is the acid test. (The "what if" method.)

Of course, as you do this, you are in fact defining or beginning to define your approach and even designing the system. And as you examine each proposed method for performing each necessary function, you are developing a technical or program strategy.

Take the case of the Postal Service and its need for computer programming specialists. The need, as presented by the customer, was for a staff of such specialists. The need, as *re*defined by the successful proposer was for the *availability* of such specialists. The basic function was to provide specialists. One way to perform the function was to have all the specialists on staff. But another way was to have them available on short notice, as consultants or temporary employees. The latter was a more practical way of satisfying the need. The support functions were to have rosters, collect résumés, file résumés, and supply other mechanics necessary to perform their basic functions. Each necessary function was identified and defined, and then alternative ways of performing each function were explored to find the best ways. And that leads naturally to approaches, strategies, and designs.

If cost is the question—how to minimize—the same method may be applied. Each function is identified, and all alternative ways of performing the function are explored, but in terms of the cost of each alternative, to find the lowest-cost ways, as well as to eliminate all functions not absolutely necessary to the end goal of the program.

If time is the main concern, to find the optimum each alternative is examined with a view to "how long will *that* take?"

The complete set of questions to be addressed include these:

1. What is it? (Functional definition in most basic terms.)
2. What does it do? (What is it supposed to do?)
3. What does it cost? (How long does it take? How many workers does it require? Etc.)
4. What else would do the same thing? (*How* else can we do the same thing?)
5. What would *that* cost? (How long would that take? How many workers would that require? Etc.)

This can be done on any scale—for individual functions, for individual components, for subsystems, for entire systems, for approaches, for strategies, for almost anything that requires decision or choice. It may be used for basic analysis, for program design, for review. But you must apply discipline, and disciplined thinking is what it's all about—keep your eye on the ball. Remember what you are trying to accomplish—the simplest system, the lowest-cost system, the fastest system, the most spectacular system, the most innovative system, or whatever your end goal is.

Appendix 3 Cost Presentation

Although program designers must deal with costs when preparing a proposal, writing the cost proposal is usually left to the accounting people except in those small companies where several key people wear several hats each. For most proposals, the cost proposal, a separate "volume," is a comparatively simple document unless a great many materials are involved, in which case there is likely to be a long list of items and their costs. But these will appear as supplements to the cost form, which is likely to be a DD 633 if the proposal is to the military or a technological agency, or a Form 60 if to other agencies. The two are quite similar to each other except that the DD 633 is somewhat longer, anticipating "hardware" procurements, with raw materials, components, and subcontracts to be accounted for.

Frightening though such forms may appear to the uninitiated, they are really quite simple in principle. The customer wants to know how you arrive at your bottom line, the price the government has to pay. And what you are asked to provide breaks down into the following items:

- Your estimated direct labor costs
- Your overhead rate
- Your other direct costs
- Your G&A rate
- Your fee or profit margin

Direct labor is that labor you pay on your payroll, which is applied directly to the contract.

Overhead rate is the percentage of direct labor dollars needed to pay such items as are in your overhead pool—rent, heat, light, travel, secretaries, fringe benefits, taxes, insurance, and all those other items necessary to conduct a business, regardless of how much or what kind of business you do.

Other direct costs are any other costs necessary to perform on the contract for which you are bidding. They are usually subdivided on the cost forms, to include accounting for these items:

- Subcontracts
- Materials and purchased parts
- Consultants
- Travel and per diem
- All other direct costs, such as printing, telephones, and other items not already covered in the above

Regardless of which cost form you are asked to supply—and some agencies will supply a home-made form used in the agency—all ask you to supply essentially the same information. (You may, if you prefer, supply the information on your own form, but few do that.)

For large contracts, the government is often not satisfied to have you merely supply the overhead and G&A *rates,* but may ask you either to supply the expense pools, showing how the rates are derived, or to present your estimate of actual overhead and G&A dollars anticipated, detailed on an item-by-item basis. In such cases, it is all but inevitable that you will have to have your accountant prepare this.

Typically, for a small contract, the cost sheet might appear as shown.

Sample Cost Sheet

	Rate	Hours	Extension	
Direct Labor:				
Project manager	$20	400	$8,000	
Second Investigator	15	500	7,500	
Typist	6	200	1,200	$16,700
Overhead:	Rate	Base		
	0.75	$16,700		12,525
			Subtotal:	29,225
Other Direct Costs:				
Printing: 450 pp., 200 copies				2,700
Telephone tolls				300
Consultants:				
10 days @ $300/day				3,000
Travel and per Diem:				
3 round trips to California:	$750			
12 days per diem @ $40/day:	480			1,230
			Subtotal:	36,455
G & A:				
6.8% × $36,455				2,479
			Subtotal:	38,934
Fee:				
15% × $38,934				5,840
			Total Price:	$44,774

Appendix **4** # Samples from a Recent RFP

Following are several sample items copied from an actual RFP issued by the National Library of Medicine, a bureau of the National Institutes of Health, which are in turn part of the Public Health Service, all part of the Department of Health and Human Services, until recently the Department of Health, Education and Welfare, more familiarly known as HEW. These "live" examples illustrate clearly several of the points made in the preceding chapters.

Proprietary-Information Notice

To protect your proprietary data, the RFP instructs, place the following notice on the cover (title) page of your proposal, "specifying the pages of the proposal which are to be restricted in accordance with the conditions of the legend."

> Technical data contained in pages _____ of this proposal shall not be disclosed, except for evaluation purposes; *Provided* that if the contract is awarded to this offeror as a result of or in connection with submission of this proposal, the Government shall have the right to use or disclose this technical data to the extent provided in the contract. This restriction does not limit the Government's right to use or disclose technical data obtained from another source without restriction.

The RFP goes on to state the following also:

> The Government assumes no liability for disclosure or use of unmarked technical data and may use or disclose the data for any purpose and may consider that the proposal was not submitted in confidence and, therefore, is releasable under the Freedom of Information Act (5 USC 552).

What this RFP instruction fails to stipulate and should stipulate is that in addition to filing this notice on the cover or title page of your proposal, you should also mark each page listed in that notice with something along the lines: "This page contains confidential or proprietary data, as stipulated in notice on title page." Even this, however, is somewhat weak in that it restricts the entire page, of which only a single paragraph may be proprietary. It is best to indicate the specific paragraphs that line refers to by marking the paragraph in some manner: by a marginal note or by placing the paragraph in a box.

355

Mandated Format

This RFP has a "recommended" format for proposals which, although it is not clearly mandated, it would be wise to follow. In this case, as in most, the recommended format does not differ a great deal from the general format suggested by the authors of this book, but is entirely compatible with it. Following is a verbatim copy of the format recommended:

1. *Recommended Technical Proposal Format and Content*
   The following format is recommended for the submission of your technical proposal. The aspects treated are associated primarily with research studies and/or service contracts. If the requirement to which you are responding does not fall within those categories, some of the following paragraphs may not apply and therefore need not be addressed in your proposal.

    I. *TABLE OF CONTENTS*
       Provide sufficient detail so that the important elements of your proposal can be located readily.
   II. *INTRODUCTION*
       This should be a one- or two-page summary of your concept of the proposed work, your interest in submitting a proposal, and the importance of this effort in relation to your overall progarm. It should provide the Government's technical reviewers with a perspective in studying the detailed proposal.
  III. *PROPOSAL*
       Prepare the technical proposal in conformance with the Technical Evaluation Criteria (see next section) incorporating in your presentation the following aspects:
       A. *Technical Aspects*
          1. *Objectives*
             State in your own words what appear to you to be the overall objectives of this project and your plan for fulfilling those objectives. Relate published documentation of completed work which is relevant to this project and your proposed approach.
          2. *Approach*
             Describe your technical approach to this requirement. It should be specific, detailed, and complete enough to demonstrate clearly that you fully understand the requirement. Stating that you understand and will comply with the specifications, or paraphrasing the specifications or parts thereof, is considered inadequate. Use as many subparagraphs, appropriately titled, as necessary to outline clearly the general plan of work. Discussing phasing of work, if appropriate. Include experimental design and possible or likely outcome of approaches proposed.

3. *Schedule*

Provide a schedule for completion of the work and delivery of items specified in this RFP. Performance or delivery schedules shall be indicated for phases or segments, as applicable, as well as for the entire project. Schedules shall be shown in terms of calendar months. Unless the request for proposal indicates that the stipulated schedules are mandatory, they shall be treated as desired or recommended schedules. In this event, proposals based upon your best alternative schedule, involving no overtime, extra shift or other premium, will be accepted for consideration.

B. *Offeror's Qualifications*

1. *Corporate*

Give general background, experience, and qualifications. *LIST AS REFERENCES SIMILAR OR RELATED PROGRAMS PER-FORMED FOR THE GOVERNMENT, INCLUDING CONTRACT NUMBERS, COGNIZANT AGENCIES, AND NAMES AND TELE-PHONE NUMBERS OF THE CONTRACTING OFFICER AND THE PROJECT OFFICER.*

2. *Personnel*

Describe the experience and qualifications of personnel who will be assigned for direct work on this program. Information is required which will show the composition of the task or work group, its general qualifications, and recent experience with similar equipment or programs. Special mention shall be made of direct technical supervisors and key technical personnel, the role of each person in the project/task, and the approximate percent-age of the total time each will be available for this project.

a. *Principal Investigator/Project Manager*

List name of Principal Investigator/Project Manager responsi-ble for overall implementation of the contract and key contact for technical aspects of the project. Discuss his/her qualifica-tions, experience, and accomplishments. State the estimated time to be spent on the project and the areas or phases which he/she will supervise directly.

b. *Other Participants*

List all other professionals who will be participating in the project. Discuss their qualifications, experience, and accom-plishments. State the estimated time each will spend on the project and the areas or phases for which each will be responsible.

c. *Additional Personnel*

List names and titles of additional personnel, if any, who will be required for full-time employment or on a subcontract or consultant basis. State why they would be needed, how they were selected, what their qualifications are, what they would do in performance of the contract, and for how long they would serve. A letter of commitment must be provided for each consultant proposed.

      d. *Résumés*

Each résumé should indicate educational background, recent experience, specific technical accomplishments, when the individual joined your organization, and the position he/she currently occupies.

   3. *Facilities*

Describe facilities available for this procurement: location, total space, how much space would be devoted to this project, relevant in-house equipment, etc.

  C. *Other Considerations*

Record and discuss other factors not included elsewhere which support your proposal. Using specifically titled subparagraphs, items may include:

1. Unique arrangements, equipment, etc., which are mandatory for effective implementation of this program.
2. Equipment and unusual operating procedures established to protect personnel from hazards associated with this project.
3. Other factors requested in the Statement of Work.
4. Recommendations for changing reporting requirements if such changes would be more compatible with your proposed schedules.

This format is followed by several paragraphs exhorting the reader to exercise great care in providing the detailed information called for, and elaborating on the listed evaluation criteria, which follow the format instructions.

Evaluation Criteria

The section presenting the evaluation criteria reads as follows:

  3. *Technical Evaluation Criteria*

Your technical proposal should be as specific and complete as possible. The technical merits of each proposal will be carefully evaluated in terms of the requirements and in relation to the criteria, which are listed and weighted in order of their relative importance in the table on the next page.

  4. *Weight of Cost or Price and the Technical Proposal*

In the selection of an offeror(s) for award:

(X) You are advised that primary consideration will be given to technical factors, rather than cost or price. It is pointed out, however, that should technical competence between offerors be considered approximately the same, then cost or price could be paramount.

( ) You are advised that primary consideration will be given to cost or price, rather than technical factors.

( ) You are advised that the technical factors and cost or price are of approximately equal value.

Criterion	Weight (%)
A. *Qualifications and Availability of Personnel* The offeror's personnel who will assigned/available for work under this project will be evaluated upon their qualifications, educational or otherwise, and their relevant experience, particularly that which was obtained within the past two (2) years, with emphasis in such areas as: 1. Experience in installation of cabling and installation of interfaces from terminals to computers. 2. Experience in maintenance and installation of equipment such as modems, terminals, and special interfaces. 3. Experience, both hardware and software, in the design and implementation of Micro-Computer Systems such as Intel 8080 and Z80 microprocessors. 4. Experience in the design and implementation of intelligent terminal systems. 5. Experience in the design and implementation of communications protocols, including packet networks X3 and X.25. 6. Experience in the design and implementation of an LS-11-based system. 7. Experience in systems analysis support for packet networks. 8. Availability of personnel will be evaluated in such areas as (a) size of available labor pool; and (b) the percentage of their time committed to the contract.	60
B. *Related Corporate Experience* Corporate experience will be evaluated based upon the projects and the extent of participation on those projects which dealt with the same types of technical disciplines as listed in A above. The offeror should highlight those projects which were worked on within the past two (2) years. In addition, the offeror shall describe and be evaluated upon: (1) Level of experience and other activities (e.g., development, documentation, maintenance, and upgrading) relevant to the work required by this procurement. (2) The type and extent of experience with program design, implementation, and documentation.	30
C. *Understanding the Requirement, Technical Approach, and Management Plan.* Your proposal will be evaluated upon: (1) Your management approach in terms of the decision-making hierarchy, the method for allocating resources, and the offeror's internal procedures for interfacing with the Government from a technical standpoint. (2) Your operational approach to solving problems—technical, delivery schedule, cost, or other.	10
Total possible score:	100

5. *Best Buy Analysis*
A final best buy analysis will be performed, taking into consideration the result of the technical evaluation, cost/price evaluation, and ability to complete the work within the Government's required schedule. The Government reserves the right to make an award to the best advantage of the Government, cost/price and other factors considered.

These evaluation criteria and the recommended proposal format are part of the boiler plate of the RFP of the agency, used in all its procurements for services of a technical or professional nature. In some ways these are more clearly and distinctly set forth than are those of other agencies, although other agencies often give far more detailed breakdowns of how the individual items are to be weighted in evaluation. Moreover, many other agencies assign an actual weight to price or cost. It is especially because practices vary so widely among the agencies that it is critically important to read the RFP carefully and understand exactly how proposals are to be reviewed and evaluated.

Appendix 5 Glossary of Terms

Abbreviations and acronyms have become a necessity, with the proliferation of lengthy titles and designations, such as the Alcohol, Drug Abuse, and Mental Health Administration (ADAMHA) and U.S. Army Missile Research and Development Command (MIRADCOM). In many cases the acronym becomes more familiar than the original name—NASA is an example. How many people would recognize "National Aeronautics and Space Administration" as swiftly as they recognize "NASA"? Unfortunately, even these acronyms change, as titles change, and both terms become perpetuated. The U.S. Army Mobility Equipment Research and Development Command at Fort Belvoir, Virginia (U.S. Engineer Corps), for example, is today known by both terms, MERADCOM and MERDC, its older acronym.

Therefore, we offer here as many such acronyms, abbreviations, and other jargon as we find to be still in general use, and in some cases we offer more than one such term for the same reference, without apologies.

AAC Alaskan Air Command (USAF)

AASRA Army Aviation Systems Rest Activity

ADAMHA Alcohol, Drug Abuse, and Mental Health Administration (PHS)

ADC Aerospace Defense Command (USAF)

ADP Automated Data Processing

ADTS Automated Data and Telecommunications Service (GSA)

AEC Atomic Energy Commission

AFCS Air Force Communications Service

AFLC Air Force Logistics Command

AFOSR Air Force Office of Scientific Research

AFSC Air Force Systems Command

AGE Aerospace Ground Equipment

AID Agency for International Development (State Dept.)

AMA Air Materiel Area

AMSAA Army Materiel Systems Analysis Agency

ARMCOM Army Armament Command

ARRADCOM Army Armament Research and Development Command

ATC Air Training Command (USAF)

AVRADCOM Army Aviation Research and Development Command

AVSCOM Army Aviation Systems Command

BC Base Command

BIA Bureau of Indian Affairs (DOI)

B/L Bill of Lading

BLM Bureau of Land Management (DOI)

BMD Ballistic Missile Defense (USA)

BMEWS Ballistic Missile Early Warning System (USAF)

BOA Basic Ordering Agreement

BPA Blanket Purchase Agreement (GSA/FSS)

CBD *Commerce Business Daily* (DOC/GPO)

CDC Center for Disease Control (PHS)

CETA Comprehensive Employment and Training Act (DOL)

CFR Code of Federal Regulations

CIA Central Intelligence Agency

CO Contracting Officer

COB Close of Business

CONAD Continental Air Defense Command (USAF)

CONUS Continental United States

COR Contracting Officer's Representative (also COTR and GTR)

CORADCOM Army Communications Research and Development Command

COTR Contracting Officer's Technical Representative (also COR and GTR)

CPAF Cost Plus Award Fee (contract form)

Note: Parenthetical notations identify parent agency or provide cross-references and explanations, where appropriate.

CPFF Cost Plus Fixed Fee (contract form)

CPSC Consumer Product Safety Commission

CSA Community Services Administration (GSA)

DACA Days After Contract Award

DARCOM Army Development and Readiness Command

DARPA Defense Advanced Research Projects Agency (DOD)

DC District of Columbia

DCA Defense Communications Agency (DOD)

DCAA Defense Contract Audit Agency (DOD)

DCAS Defense Contract Administration Services (DOD)

DSASD Defense Contract Administration Services—District (DOD)

DCASR Defense Contract Administration Services—Region (DOD)

DEA Drug Enforcement Agency (DOJ)

DIA Defense Intelligence Agency (DOD)

DIDS Defense Integrated Data System (DOD)

DLA Defense Logistics Agency (DOD)

DNA Defense Nuclear Agency (DOD)

DOC Department of Commerce

DOD Department of Defense

DOE Department of Energy

DOI Department of the Interior

DOJ Department of Justice

DOL Department of Labor

DOT Department of Transportation

DSA Defense Supply Agency (DOD)

EAM Electronic Accounting Machine

ECM Electronic Counter Measures

ECCM Electronic Counter-Counter Measures

ECOM Army Electronics Command

EDA Economic Development Administration (DOC)

EEO Equal Employment Opportunity

EEOC Equal Employment Opportunity Commission

EPA Environmental Protection Agency

ERADCOM Army Electronics Research and Development Command

ESA Employment Standards Administration (DOL)

FAA Federal Aviation Administration (DOT)

FBI Federal Bureau of Investigation (DOJ)

FBM Fleet Ballistic Missile

FCC Federal Communications Commission

FDA Food and Drug Administration (PHS)

FmHA Farmers Home Administration (USDA)

FRA Federal Railroad Administration (DOT)

FOB Free on Board (contract term)

FOI Freedom of Information (Act)

FSC Federal Supply Classification

FSS Federal Supply Service (GSA)

FTC Federal Trade Commission

FTS Federal Telecommunications System

FWS Fish and Wildlife Service (DOI)

GOA General Accounting Office

GEM Ground Effect Machine

GFAE Government-Furnished Aerospace Equipment

GFE Government-Furnished Equipment

GNP Gross National Product

GPO Government Printing Office

GSA General Services Administration

GTR Government Technical Representative (also COR and COTR)

HDS Office of Human Development Services (Dept. of Health and Human Services, formerly HEW)

HHS Health and Human Services (formerly HEW)

HRA Health Resources Administration

HSA Health Services Administration (Dept. of Health and Human Services, formerly HEW)

HUD Department of Housing and Urban Development

ICC Interstate Commerce Commission

IFB Information for Bid (solicitation form 33)

IG Industrial Group (supply classification)

INS Immigration and Naturalization Service (DOJ)

indef qty indefinite quantity (solicitation and contract stipulation)

IRS Internal Revenue Service (Treasury Dept.)

JP-4 Jet Fuel (for USAF aircraft)

JP-5 Jet Fuel (for Navy aircraft)

LEAA Law Enforcement Assistance Administration (DOJ)

MA Maritime Administration (DOC)

MAC Military Airlift Command (USAF)

MAP Military Assistance Program

MEDLARS Medical Literature Analysis and Retrieval System (NLM/PHS)

MERADCOM Army Mobility Equipment Research and Development Command

MERDC Army Mobility Equipment Research and Development Command

MESBIC Minority Enterprise Small Business Investment Companies

MICOM Army Missile Command

MILSATCOM Military Satellite Communications Systems

MIRADCOM Army Missile Research and Development Command

MSHA Mine Safety and Health Administration (SHA/DOL)

MSC Military Sealift Command (USN)

NAB National Alliance of Businessmen

NADC Naval Air Development Center

NARADCOM Army Natick Research and Development Command

NARS National Archives and Records Service (GSA)

NAS National Academy of Sciences

NASA National Aeronautics and Space Administration

NAVAIR Naval Air Systems Command

NAVELEX Naval Electronic Systems Command

NAVFAC Naval Facilities Engineering Command

NAVSUP Naval Supply Systems Command

NBS National Bureau of Standards (DOC)

NHTSA National Highway Traffic Safety Administration (DOT)

NIDA National Institute of Drug Abuse (PHS)

NIE National Institute of Education

NIH National Institutes of Health (PHS)

NIMH National Institutes of Mental Health (PHS)

NIOSH National Institute of Occupational Safety and Health

NLM National Library of Medicine (PHS)

NMC Naval Materiel Command

NOAA National Oceanic and Atmospheric Administration (DOC)

NOL Naval Ordnance Laboratory

NRC Nuclear Regulatory Commission

NRL Naval Research Laboratory

NSA National Security Agency (DOD)

NSF National Science Foundation

NSN National Stock Number (supply classification)

NTIS National Technical Information Service (DOC)

NUSC Naval Underwater Systems Center

OCE Office Chief of Engineers

OCED Office of Comprehensive Employment Development Programs

OCR Office of Coal Research

OEO Office of Economic Opportunity

OFPP Office of Federal Procurement Policy

OIC Officer in Charge

OICC Officer in Charge of Construction

O&M Operations and Maintenance

OMB Office of Management and Budget

ONR Office of Naval Research

OPM Office of Personnel Management (formerly Civil Service Commission)

OSD Office of Secretary of Defense

OSHA Occupational Safety and Health Administration (DOL)

PBGC Pension Benefit Guaranty Corporation

PBS Public Buildings Service (GSA)

PHS Public Health Service (Dept. of Health and Human Services, formerly HEW)

PO Purchase Order

R&D Pesearch and Development

RDTE Research, Development, Test, and Evaluation

RFP Request for Proposals

RFQ Request for Quotations

SAC Strategic Air Command (USAF)

SBA Small Business Administration

SBIC Small Business Investment Companies

SCS Soil Conservation Service (USDA)

SOW Statement of Work

SSA Social Security Administration (Dept. of Health and Human Services, formerly HEW)

TAC Tactical Air Command (USAF)

TACOM Army Tank-Automotive Command

TARADCOM Army Tank-Automotive Research and Development Command

T&M Time and Material (contract type)

TECOM Army Test and Evaluation Command

TROSCOM Army Troop Support Command

UMTA Urban Mass Transportation Administration (DOT)

USA U.S. Army

USAF U.S. Air Force

USC United States Code

USCG U.S. Coast Guard (DOT)

USDA U.S. Department of Agriculture

USMC U.S. Marine Corps (USN)

USN U.S. Navy

USPS U.S. Postal Service

VA Veterans Administration

WSE WWMCS Systems Engineering (DOD)

WWMCCS World-Wide Military Command and Control Systems (DOD)

Index

Index

NOTE: Page numbers in *italics* indicate illustrations.

Proposal Checklist

Strategies

[ ] *Capture strategy:* Is it clear? Does it address *immediate* objectives of RFP and SOW? Does it promise to deliver what customer wants, what customer needs?

[ ] *Technical or program strategy:* Is there one? Is it properly conservative or innovative, per customer wants? Is it practical?

[ ] *Cost strategy:* Is one developed and implemented? Does proposal support it? Can you defend it?

[ ] *Presentation strategy:* Is there one? Is it integrated with other strategies and theme? Is it attention getting, yet professional and business-like?

Theme

[ ] *Theme:* Is it formulated and expressed clearly? Does it reflect capture strategy? Does it recur? Does it characterize entire proposal? Is it easy to grasp, to remember? Does it relate directly to customer wants or needs? Is it dramatized as well as articulated?

Problem or Requirement Definition

[ ] *Definition:* Does it prove understanding? Is it restated in your own terms? Is essence of need expressed, with extraneous trivia stripped away? Does it "track" with your proposed project? Does it agree with customer's own concept? If not, are you prepared to prove your interpretation? Have you truly *analyzed* RFP and SOW?

Technical Discussion

[ ] *Opening statement:* Does it bridge properly from problem definition? Does it lay groundwork for discussion? Conversely, does discussion proceed directly from the opening problem statement (is it germane)?

[ ] *Conservative approach:* Are the "security" and risklessness of this approach stressed? Is it shown to have extremely sound foundations?

[ ] *Innovative approach:* Is it shown to be not radical or risky? Is it demonstrated to be evolutionary not revolutionary?

[ ] *Discussion:* Does it recap entire analysis, show customer all aspects? Are all premises and technical arguments soundly constructed? Does it proceed logically to selected approach? To program proposed?

Proposed Program

[ ] *Project:* Is it delineated in *detail* with specific organization, staffing, procedures, management?

[ ] *Management:* Is everything covered? Procedures? Controls? Quality assurance? Contingency plans?

[ ] *Deliverable items:* Are they specified clearly? Quantified? Is listing complete?

[ ] *Schedule:* Is it specific? If in days, does it stipulate calendar or working days?

[ ] *Labor:* Include labor-loading chart? Is it compatible with costs? With organization and management plans?

[ ] *Résumés:* Are they rewritten to match this RFP and proposal? Is all key staff on board? If not, are suitable explanations made and backed up?